COMMENTARY

UPON

THE ACTS OF THE APOSTLES.

VOL. II.

COMMENTARY

UPON

THE ACTS OF THE APOSTLES.

BY JOHN CALVIN.

EDITED FROM THE ORIGINAL ENGLISH TRANSLATION OF
CHRISTOPHER FETHERSTONE, STUDENT IN DIVINITY,

BY HENRY BEVERIDGE, ESQ.

VOLUME SECOND

WIPF & STOCK · Eugene, Oregon

Wipf and Stock Publishers
199 W 8th Ave, Suite 3
Eugene, OR 97401

Commentary Upon the Acts of the Apostles, Volume Two
By Calvin, John and Beveridge, Henry
Softcover ISBN-13: 978-1-6667-3062-3
Hardcover ISBN-13: 978-1-6667-2236-9
Publication date 5/24/2021
Previously published by Calvin Translation Society, 1844

This edition is a scanned facsimile of the original edition published in 1844.

COMMENTARY

UPON

THE ACTS OF THE APOSTLES.

CHAPTER XIV.

1. *And it came to pass at Iconium, that they went together* [or at the same time] *into the synagogue of the Jews, and spake so, that a great multitude both of Jews and Gentiles believed.*
2. *And the Jews which believed not stirred and with envy infected the minds of the Gentiles against the brethren.*
3. *Therefore, they were long time conversant there, behaving themselves boldly in the Lord, who bare witness of the word of his grace, granting that signs and wonders might be done by their hands.*
4. *And the multitude of the city was divided: and some stood with the Jews, and some with the apostles.*

IN the chapter last going before, Luke declared how Paul and Barnabas took in hand their embassage unto the Gentiles. Furthermore, it might seem to be an unprosperous and unlucky beginning, in that they were not only expelled out of Antioch, but also enforced by the obstinate wickedness of certain to shake off the dust from their feet. But though they had but short entertainment[1] in one place, yet

---

[1] "Verum quamvis duciter accepti," but however harshly they were received.

do they not yield; because they consider that the Lord had called them upon that condition, that they should do their duty though the whole world and Satan did say nay. Therefore, we see that they came not only ready to teach, but also armed to enter conflicts, that they might courageously proceed in publishing the gospel, even through the midst of combats.

And assuredly, that which was once spoken to Jeremiah is common to all the prophets and ministers of God, " They shall fight against thee, but they shall not prevail," (Jer. i. 19.) Now, whithersoever they fly, they carry with them the same courage[1] still ; whereby it appeareth that they were not only furnished for one combat, but even for continual warfare ; which Luke doth now prosecute.[2] He saith first, that they came to Iconium, and therewithal he showeth that they sought not there some haven where they might rest quietly; but they entered the synagogue as if they had suffered no hurt at all.

I refer the word Κατα το αυτο, forasmuch as it signifieth among the Grecians, *together, or at the same time,* rather unto the Jews than unto Paul and Barnabas. Therefore, I interpret it thus, not that they went in both together, but that they followed the multitude at the solemn and appointed time of the meeting, whence we gather that they spake not secretly with a few men, but in a great assembly of people; whereby they declare their boldness and ready desire; they are so far from fearing envy, or avoiding danger.[3]

That a great multitude believed. As Luke did before show the power of the Spirit in Paul and Barnabas, so now he commendeth another grace of God in that prosperous success which they had. For one only sermon which they made was not without fruit, but it brought forth many children of God, as well of the Jews as of the Gentiles. If one, or

---

[1] " Animi præsentiam," presence of mind.
[2] " Quod Lucas nunc prosequitur," as Luke now relates in detail.
[3] " Ut invidiam fugitent, aut periculum formident." from shunning envy, or dreading danger.

two, or a few, had believed, they might have thought that they sped well; but the Lord confirmeth them far better, when as they gather such plentiful fruit of their doctrine even in a short time. For they knew that so many hearts of men were converted to believe, not so much by their voice, as by the power of the Spirit; whereby they might also assure themselves that they themselves were defended by the outstretched hand of God, which did not a little encourage them.

2. *And those Jews which believed not.* Lo, they are persecuted now afresh, and that by the Jews, for they were like firebrands to inflame the minds of the Gentiles; for it is to be thought that the Gentiles could abide to hear the gospel preached, unless they had been incensed to resist by these fans.[1] I interpret κακωσαι in this place for to resist[2] with a malicious affection, or to enforce to do hurt. Under the name brethren, Luke comprehendeth, in my judgment, all the godly; to wit, that they were vexed and troubled whosoever embraced the gospel, as if some pernicious sect had risen to spread discord, to trouble the peace of the city, to shake the public state; yet if any had rather restrain it unto Paul and Barnabas I am not greatly against him.

3. *A long time.* Luke declareth here, that Paul and Barnabas did not depart the city so soon as they saw some set against them, for when he saith that they behaved themselves boldly, he giveth us an inkling[3] that there was cause of fear offered them. Whence we gather that they stood stoutly, and that through rare constancy and courage they counted all dangers as nothing, until they were compelled by violence to depart to another place. This clause, επι κυριω, may be expounded diversely, either that they behaved themselves stoutly in the Lord's cause, or that they trusted to his grace, and were thereby encouraged. I have followed that which was more common, that they behaved themselves

---

[1] " Nisi flabellis illis accensæ fuissent ad resistendum," had not these like fans kindled their resistance. [2] " Inficere," to infect. [3] " Innuit," he intimates.

freely and boldly in the Lord, that is, being holpen not by their own strength, but by his grace. He showeth immediately after, after what sort they were encouraged in the Lord; to wit, because [that] he approveth the doctrine by signs and miracles. For seeing that they knew thereby that the Lord was present with them, and that his hand was nigh to help them, they were worthily pricked forward to behave themselves stoutly. But in noting one kind, he doth not exclude other kinds, for the Lord did lift them up unto boldness, and establish them in constancy by other means. But it seemeth that Luke did speak of miracles expressly, because the Lord showed in them his power openly before all the people. Therefore, Paul and Barnabas were not a little emboldened when the Lord did so deliver their doctrine from contempt.

Furthermore, we must note this phrase, that the Lord gave witness to the gospel in miracles, for it showeth the true use of miracles. This is, indeed, the first end, that they may show to us the power and grace of God; but because we be wrong and perverse interpreters of them, lest they be drawn unto abuse and corruption, God doth never suffer them to be separated from his word. For if miracles were wrought at any time without his word; first, that was very seldom; secondly, there came but small fruit thereof; and God hath wrought miracles, for the most part, whereby the world might know him not simply, or in his bare majesty, but in his word. So Luke saith, in this place, that the gospel was established by miracles, not that some confused religion might possess the minds of men, but that Paul's doctrine going before they might be brought unto the pure worship of God.

Whence we may easily gather how foolishly the Papists deal, when as they endeavour to lead away the world from the reverence of God and the gospel by bare miracles. For we must hold that principle, that those miracles which came from God at any time did never tend to any other end but that the gospel might have his perfect and full authority.

Now must we see whether the gospel command us to call

upon the dead, to burn incense to idols, to translate unto feigned saints the grace of Christ, to take in hand vowed pilgrimages, to invent profane worshippings, whereof there is no mention made in the Word of God; but there is nothing more contrary to the gospel than that these superstitions should take place. Whereupon it followeth that the Papists do wickedly make engines of the shoars[1] of the gospel to oppugn it. To the same end tendeth that which Luke saith, that the Lord granted that by the hands of his servants miracles might be done; in which words he teacheth that those were only ministers who obeyed God, and that he was the author, who used their hand and industry. Wherefore, in speaking properly, we cannot say that they were Paul and Barnabas's miracles, but the miracles of God alone, who doth so work by men, that he will not have his glory darkened by their ministry.

Furthermore, we must note the title of the gospel, which Luke putteth in here, that it may be made to us more amiable; for in calling it the word of grace, it hath a most pleasant taste, because salvation is offered to the world in it through Christ. And we must understand the contrariety with the law, wherein only the curse is set before us. Therefore, let us remember that God speaketh to us in the gospel to this end, that he may reconcile himself to us, and may testify that he is merciful to us. Neither doth this hinder that it is *the savour of death unto death* to the reprobate, (2 Cor. ii. 16,) because they change not the nature thereof by their fault. Read those things which we have spoken in the second chapter touching signs and wonders.

4. *The multitude was divided.* The most troublesome part of the tragedy[2] followeth now, for the city is divided into two parts; and at length Paul and Barnabas (being enforced by the uproar of the people) depart unto another place. If it be demanded what was the original of the discord, assuredly it flowed from the gospel, to which, notwithstanding,

---

[1] 'Fulturis," the props or stays.   [2] " Catastrophe," the catastrophe.

there is nothing more contrary than to cause discord; but the frowardness of men causeth that the gospel, which ought to be the bond of unity, is (so soon as it cometh abroad) the occasion of tumults. Wherefore, so soon as any schism ariseth, before we condemn those who seem to be the authors, it behoveth us wisely to consider who ought to bear the blame. We hear here that one city was divided,[1] whereby some were brought unto Christ. The Spirit of God pronounceth this to the praise, and not the shame, of Paul and Barnabas. The same rule must we observe at this day, lest the gospel be burdened with false envy, if it bring not men together[2] unto God, but the wicked rage against it. It is assuredly a miserable matter to see division among men. But as the unity is accursed which doth separate us all from God, so it were better that a few should depart an hundred times from all the whole world, and, in the mean season, come in favour again with God, than that disagreeing with him continually, they should have peace with the world.[3]

5. *And when there was an assault made of the Gentiles and Jews, together with their rulers, to do them violence, and to stone them,*
6. *When they knew the matter, they fled into cities of Lycaonia, to Lystra and Derbe, and to the country lying nigh there about on every side:*
7. *And there they preached the gospel.*
8. *And there sat a certain man at Lystra, impotent in his feet, who had been lame from his mother's womb, neither had he ever walked.*
9. *This man heard Paul speak: who, beholding him, and seeing that he had faith to be healed,*
10. *Said with a loud voice, Arise upright upon thy feet. And he leapt up and walked.*

5. Mark how far forth the holy champions of Christ did suffer. They give not back when their enemies do only

---

[1] " Schismate," by a schism.   [2] " Omnes pariter," all alike.
[3] " Mundi pac."

set themselves against them; but when the sedition waxeth hot, and they be in danger of stoning, though they have many favourers of their doctrine, they go no further, but remembering the saying of Christ, wherein he warneth the faithful in patience to possess their souls, they avoid the fury of the enemy. And though they fly, lest they[1] throw themselves headlong into death, yet their constancy in preaching the gospel doth sufficiently declare that they feared not danger. For Luke saith that they preached the gospel in other places also. This is the right kind of fear, when the servants of Christ do not run wilfully into the hands of their enemies, of them to be murdered, and yet they do not foreslow [abandon] their duty; neither doth fear hinder them from obeying God when he calleth; and so, consequently, they can afford, if need be, to go even through death itself to do their duty.

8. *A certain man at Lystra.* Luke reciteth one miracle which we may think[2] was one of many; but there was mention made of it alone by reason of the famous event. For we shall see by and by what happened. Luke reckoneth up the circumstances, which do more plainly set forth the power of God, when he saith that the man did never walk, and that he was a cripple even from his mother's womb, and that he was suddenly healed by the voice of Paul alone before the eyes of all men, and that his legs, which were dead, were made nimble, so that he leapt up without making any stop.[3]

9. *He heard Paul speak.* Hearing is set down first, that we may know that the faith which Luke will commend by and by was conceived of Paul's doctrine. Therefore, when he heard Paul, he hoped to be healed. But the question is, whether this was promised to him specially; for God doth not command us to hope for everything by

---

[1] "Temere," rashly, omitted. [2] "Probabile est," it is probable.
[3] "Sine difficultate," without difficulty.

and by,[1] when he offereth unto us eternal salvation in the gospel. I answer, that this was a singular and extraordinary motion of the Spirit of God in the cripple, as it was on the other side in Paul, when he knew his faith by beholding him only. It may be that many may receive the gospel, and yet they shall not be cured of those diseases wherewith they are vexed. But forasmuch as God was determined to show a token of his grace in the cripple, he prepared his mind before, and made him capable of this that should come upon him.[2] Wherefore we must not make this a common rule, because the cripple believed that he should be healed, but it was a peculiar preparation to receive the gift of healing. And this kind of faith is likewise particular which giveth place to[3] miracles, which many of God's children do want, who are, notwithstanding, indued with the Spirit of adoption.

Whom when Paul beheld stedfastly. We know how doubtful and how deceitful a thing the countenance of man is, therefore there could no sure judgment be given thereby of faith, which hath God alone to be witness thereof; but, as I have already said, the cripple's faith was revealed to Paul by the secret inspiration of the Spirit, as he was to the apostles their only guide and master to work miracles.

10. *He said with a loud voice.* Many old books,[4] and those of great credit, add, "I say to thee in the name of Jesus Christ," and surely we see how careful the apostles were to magnify the name of Christ in all miracles; therefore I think that that was expressed by Luke, and yet we cannot find it commonly now in the printed books, [copies.] Whereas Luke saith afterward, that the lame man leapt up, it serveth not only for the commendation of God's power, but also such readiness and willingness to obey did testify that he was rightly prepared by the Lord; so that he did already walk in mind when as his feet were as yet dead.

---

[1] " Protinus," forthwith.
[2] " Hujus accessionis," of this accession.
[3] " Locum," room for.
[4] " Codices," manuscripts or copies.

Although his speed in rising made the power of God more manifest, to which end also Paul exalted his voice, that the sudden change might the more move the multitude.

> 11. *Furthermore, when the multitude had seen what Paul had done, they lifted up their voice, saying, in the speech of Lycaonia, Gods being made like to men are come down to us.*
> 12. *And they called Barnabas, Jupiter, and Paul, Mercurius, because he was the captain of the speech.*[1]
> 13. *And Jupiter's priest, which was before their city, bringing bulls and crowns* [chaplets] *unto the gates, would have done sacrifice with the multitude.*

11. *Furthermore, the multitude.* This history doth abundantly testify how ready and bent men are unto vanity. Paul uttered not that word abruptly, *Arise;* but he added it as it were a conclusion to the sermon made concerning Christ. Yet the people ascribe the praise of the miracle unto their idols, as if they had heard no word of Christ. Indeed, it is no such wonder, that the barbarous men fell unto superstition which they had learned[2] from their childhood, so soon as they saw the miracle. But this vice is too common every where, and it is so bred in us, to be perverse and wrong interpreters of the works of God. Hence come such gross dotings of superstitions in Popery, because catching rashly at miracles, they take no heed to doctrine. For which cause we must take the better heed, and be the more sober, lest we happen with the sense of the flesh to corrupt (whereunto we are so bent) the power of God, which shineth and appeareth to us for our salvation. And no marvel if the Lord would have only a few miracles wrought, and that for a short time, lest through the lust of men they should be drawn unto a far contrary end; because it is unmeet that he should set his name to be mocked of the world, which must needs be, when that

---

[1] " Dux esset sermonis," took the lead in speaking
[2] " Imbiberant," had imbibed.

which is proper to him is translated unto idols, or the unbelievers corrupt his works, to invent corrupt worshipping, while that setting the word aside, they catch at every divine power which they feign.[1]

Gods like to men. This was an opinion drawn from old fables, which, notwithstanding, took the beginning of truth.[2] The books of the poets are full of these toys, that the gods were often seen upon earth in the likeness of men; and yet we may well think that this came not of nothing,[3] but rather that profane men did turn that into fables, which the holy fathers taught in times past concerning angels. And it may be that Satan, when he had men besotted, did with divers jugglings delude them This is of a truth, whatsoever was God's, whensoever it went with the infidels,[4] it was corrupt by their wicked inventions. The same must we likewise think of sacrifices, wherein God did exercise his[5] even from the beginning, that they might have the external signs of godliness and of the worship of God. And after that the unbelievers invented to themselves strange gods, they abused the sacrifices unto their sacrilegious worship. When the men of Lycaonia see unwonted power in the cripple that was healed, they persuade themselves that it is a work of God; this is all well.[6] But it was evil done, in that they forge to themselves false gods in Paul and Barnabas, according to the old [wonted] error. For what is the cause that they prefer Barnabas before Paul, save only because they follow the childish surmise [fiction] concerning Mercury, the interpreter of the gods, in which they had been nourished? By which example we are taught what a mischief it is to be accustomed and acquainted with errors in youth, which can so hardly be rooted out of the mind, that even through the works of God, where-

---

[1] "Numen quodlibet... a se confictum," any kind of deity feigned by themselves. [2] "Originem a veritate duxerant," had derived their origin from truth. [3] "Non fuisse de nihilo confictum," was not feigned without some foundation [4] "Ubi ad infideles transiit," when it was transmitted to unbelievers, the heathen. [5] "Fideles suos," his believing people. [6] "Recte hactenus," so far right.

by they ought to have been redressed, they wax more hard.

13. *Also Jupiter's priest.* Though Luke doth not express with what affection he [this priest] was moved to be so diligent, yet it is to be thought, that, forasmuch as there was great hope of most plentiful gain offered, he was moved with covetousness. For he had great hope of gain in time to come, if it should be noised abroad that Jupiter appeared there. For this opinion would by and by have followed, that Jupiter was more delighted in the temple of Lystra than in any other. And so soon as such superstition hath once filled the minds of men, they spare no cost to offer sacrifice.[1] The world is indeed of itself inclined to this, but then came the sacrificing priests, who are like fans and bellows. And it is not to be doubted, but that the whole multitude was moved with ambition, to be so desirous to offer sacrifice to Paul under the name of Jupiter, that their city might be the more famous and noble. Hence hath Satan so great liberty [license] to deceive, whilst that the sacrificing priests set nets to get gain, and the people are delighted to have errors confirmed.

14. *Furthermore, when the apostles, Barnabas and Saul, had heard, rending their garments, they ran in into the press, crying,*
15. *And saying, Men, why do ye these things? We be also men subject to like miseries as you are, preaching to you that you turn from those vain things unto the living God, who hath made heaven and earth, and the sea, and whatsoever are in them:*
16. *Who in times past suffered all nations to walk in their own ways.*
17. *Though he left not himself without witness, doing good, giving to us from heaven rain and fruitful times, replenishing with food and gladness our hearts.*

[1] "Donaria," gifts.

18. *And when they had thus said, they scarce appeased the multitude, that they should do* [from doing] *sacrifice to them.*

14. *When the apostles had heard.* In that Paul and Barnabas rent their garments, and leapt into the midst of the multitude, it appeareth thereby how zealous they were for the glory of God; [not] being content only to speak to the people,[1] they troubled the preparation of the sacrifice so much as they are able. It cometh to pass sometimes that even hypocrites refuse excessive honour; but they rather provoke the simple to give it them with their feigned modesty. There was no such thing in Paul and Barnabas; for they declared, both by words and also by all gesture of body, that they were so far from taking pleasure in that worship which the men of Lystra gave unto them, that they did utterly detest it. This is holy anger, wherewith the servants of God must be inflamed so often as they see his glory profaned and overthrown by the sacrileges of men. And, assuredly, no man shall be able otherwise to serve God sincerely and faithfully, unless he put on that affection of jealousy, whereof Paul speaketh in the Second Epistle to the Corinthians, (2 Cor. xi. 2,) that those men to whom the Lord hath committed the charge of his Church be no less courageous and stout to defend the glory of their Lord, than a husband is vigilant to defend his wife's chastity.

Therefore, we must take good heed that we suffer not that honour to be given us which may darken the glory of God; but rather so soon as there appeareth any profaning of God's glory, let this heat break out, whereof we have an example in Paul and Barnabas. And though the teachers of the Church ought especially to be indued with zeal, yet there is no one of the godly which ought not to be sore displeased, when he seeth the worship of God polluted or given to some other; because it is written of all,

---

[1] " Verbis non contenti," not contented with words.

"The zeal of thine house hath eaten me up, and the rebukes of them that rebuked thee fell on me," (Psal. lxix. 10.) And if so be it holy men being yet compassed about with the flesh did so greatly detest idolatry, how shall we think them to be affected now, when they are stripped out of all the affections of the flesh? When as the world abuseth their names and persons unto superstition, it thinketh it doth them a great pleasure; but it is greatly deceived. For they will stand up first against their worshippers, and will indeed declare that they never make more account of anything, than that the worship of God might remain whole and sound to him. Moreover, there can be no greater injury done to them, than when the honour which is taken from God is given to them; which must needs be when any divine thing is ascribed and given them.

Whereas Luke saith that Paul and Barnabas did rent their garments, it appeareth by other places of Scripture that this rite and custom was used among the men of the east country, so often as they would by external gesture express either great sorrow or detesting of any thing. When Luke calleth Barnabas an apostle together with Paul, he extendeth the signification of the word farther than unto the chief [primary] order which Christ appointed in his Church; like as Paul maketh Andronicus and Junias excellent among the apostles. But if we should speak properly, they were evangelists and not apostles; unless peradventure because Barnabas was made Paul's fellow in office, we place them both in like degree of office, so may he be truly called an apostle.

15. *Men, why do ye those things?* They begin with a reprehension, as the matter did require; that done, they show to what end they were sent. Afterward they preach concerning the only God, and show that he was unknown to the world. Lastly, that they may more strongly pluck out of their hearts the deceits and sleights of the devil, they teach that this ignorance was without excuse. Therefore the first part of the sermon is a reprehension, wherein the

men of Lystra are condemned for worshipping mortal men preposterously instead of God. Though the reason which they allege seemeth to be cold. For it were an easy matter to gather thence, that it is not unlawful to worship those who are delivered from human miseries by death. By this means all the superstitions of the Gentiles should stand untouched, which were wont to count none gods but those who were dead. With the same colour also have the Papists coloured their idolatry, who worship rather the dead men's bones, stones and wood, than living men in whose nostrils is breath.[1] I answer, that Paul and Barnabas drew this argument from the matter which was now in hand, We be miserable men; therefore you do falsely and filthily imagine us to be gods, and worship us as gods. If idolatry be handled generally, this shall be a perpetual reason to condemn it, and shall alone be sufficient enough, that the perfect and whole worship of godliness is due to God alone, and that therefore it is profaned, so soon as it is in any point given to creatures, whether they be angels, or men, or stars. But occasion shall oftentimes be offered, that many things may be spoken against one kind of idolatry, which do not appertain unto another, (neither are agreeable to the same;) and yet shall they be of no small force for the matter which is in hand, as Paul and Barnabas, by confessing that they be mortal men, subject to divers calamities, had a fit reason to reprove the fury and madness of the people.

We preach to you. An argument drawn from contraries. For here they show that the end of their coming was quite contrary; to wit, that they might remove superstitions, which had hitherto reigned. For it is all one as if they had said, Doth the miracle move you? Then give credence to our words. And the sum of our embassage is, that all feigned godheads wherewith the world hath hitherto been deceived may be done away and perish. And this is a general doctrine, whereby they do not only appease the present madness, but also reprehend all manner [of] super-

---

[1] "Quam vivos et spirantes homines," than living, breathing men.

stitions, and whatsoever was contrary to, or disagreeing with, the rule of godliness. For without doubt they call all that vain which men have invented to themselves of their own brain. And we must mark this definition, that all religion is vain which departeth and degenerateth from the pure and simple Word of God. There is no express mention made indeed of the Word, because they spake to the Gentiles. But because God is no otherwise rightly worshipped than according to his appointment, it followeth out of Paul's words, that so soon as men depart from that worship which God hath commanded and doth allow, [approve,] they are wearied foolishly and vainly with a vain and unprofitable labour. For that religion wherein God hath not the pre-eminence is nothing worth, neither hath it any truth or soundness.

And this was the cause that sincere and perfect godliness was never found, neither did it ever flourish in the more part of the world. For they stood only about the removing of the old idolatry; and the other thing was in the mean season foreslowed, [neglected,] to bring men unto the true God alone, after that they had forsaken idols. They turned, indeed, the name of an idol sometimes into the name of God, but under that colour they did nevertheless cherish the old errors, which they should have endeavoured to redress. So the priests of France begat the single life of great Cybele.[1] Nuns came in place of the vestal virgins. The church of All Saints succeeded Pantheon, (or the church of All Gods;[2]) against ceremonies were set ceremonies not much unlike. At length came in the multitude of gods, who they thought would be lawful and tolerable if they had once decked [masked] them with the titles of saints. Corruptions are not by this means purged, neither are the stables, both profane and full of filth, turned into the temple of God; but the name of God is mixed with profane pollutions, and God himself is brought into a filthy stall. Wherefore, let us

---

[1] " Sic Galli sacrifici magnæ Cybeles cælibatum genuerunt," so the priests of Gaul gave rise to the celibacy of great Cybele.   [2] " Pantheo successit Pantagion," Pantagion (All Saints) succeed Pantheon, (All Gods.)

remember that the apostles did not only employ themselves to overthrow idolatry which had long time reigned in former ages, but did also take great heed that pure religion might reign afterward, having put all corruptions to flight.

Who hath made heaven and earth. We know that the order of teaching doth require that we begin with things which are better known. Seeing that Paul and Barnabas spake to the Gentiles, they should have in vain essayed to bring them[1] unto Christ. Therefore, it was expedient for them to begin with some other point, which was not so far separate from common sense, [perception,] that after that was confessed they might afterward pass over unto Christ. The minds of the men of Lystra were possessed with that error, that there be more gods than one. Paul and Barnabas show, on the contrary, that there is but one Creator of the world. After that that feigned number and multitude of the gods was taken away, there was passage now made unto the second member, that they might teach what that God was who was the Creator of heaven and earth. The case standeth otherwise at this day between us and the Papists; they confess that there is but one God, and they admit the Scripture. Therefore, it remaineth that we prove to them out of the Scripture what God is, and after what sort he will be worshipped of men.

16. *In times past.* Because the men of Lystra might object that that God was unknown hitherto, Paul and Barnabas prevent them, and say, that all men wandered indeed in darkness, and that all mankind was stricken with blindness, but that they deny that any prejudice must be made[2] according to the perverse ignorance of the world. These were two no small lets for the unbelievers, long antiquity of time, and the consent almost of all nations. Paul and Barnabas remove both in this place. If, say they, men have erred many years, [ages,] and if the world have wan-

---

[1] " Statim," forthwith, omitted
[2] " Debere præjudicium fieri," that any thing should be prejudged, (any judgment should be founded on)

dered without reason and judgment, let not, therefore, the truth of God, when it appeareth, be less precious to you. For seeing that it is eternal, and is not changed, it is an unmeet thing that the long prescription of years should be set against it. They prove that there is no more aid or patronage to be found in the number of men. There is no cause (say they) why the conspiracy of all the whole world should keep you from coming to the right way. Blindness hath got the upper hand among all people; but God doth now (appear and) give light to you. Therefore, your eyes must be open, and you must not slumber and sleep in darkness, though all people have been drowned therein hitherto.

Their ways. If he had only said that men were deceived until that time through God's sufferance, we might easily gather thereby that all men can do nothing else but err, so long as they be not governed of God. Yet he speaketh far more plainly when he calleth errors the *ways* of men. For we are plainly taught by this, what the wisdom and understanding of man's mind can do in beholding and keeping the way of salvation. All people [nations] (saith he) have walked in their own ways; that is, they have wandered in darkness and death. It is all one as if he should say, that there is no sparkle of true reason in all the whole world.

Therefore, there is but one rule of true godliness, that is, that the faithful, casting from them all confidence in their own wit, do submit themselves to God. For the ways of men are now as they were in times past; and the examples of all times teach how miserably blind those men be who have not the word of God to give them light, though they think they can pass other men in quickness of sight. Immediately after the beginning of the world, the more part fell away unto divers superstitions and wicked worshippings. Whence came that, save only because it pleased them to follow their own imaginations? When it might have seemed that the world was purged with the flood, it fell again [relapsed] straightway to the same vices. Therefore, there is nothing more deadly than to lean to our own wisdom.

But Paul and Barnabas show no cause here why the Lord

suffered the world to err so long; and assuredly we must count the will of God alone the chiefest law of equity. God hath always a good reason for his works; but because it is oftentimes hid from us, it is our duty reverently to wonder at his secret counsel. We must, indeed, confess that the world was worthy of [deserved] such destruction; but there can no other reason be brought why the Lord had mercy rather on one age than on another, save only because it seemed good to him that it should be so. Therefore, Paul calleth that time which was appointed of God for preaching the gospel, the time of fulness, (Gal. iv. 4,) lest any other opportunity be sought. And we must remember that which we had in the first chapter, that it is not for us to know the times and seasons which the Father hath placed in his own power. So that the cavil of the Papists is refuted, who say that it cannot be that God suffered his Church to err so long. For whence, I pray you, came the Gentiles but from the ark of Noah, when there was a certain singular purity of the Church? (Gen. ix. 9.) Also, the posterity of holy Shem, together with others, did degenerate. Yea, Israel, the peculiar people of the Lord, was also left for a long time. Wherefore, it is no marvel if God did punish the contempt of his word with the same blindness under the reign of his Son as he did in times past.

17. *Notwithstanding, he did not suffer himself to be without witness.* Paul and Barnabas take from the Gentiles in this place the cloak [pretext] of ignorance. For how greatly soever men please themselves in their own inventions, being at length convicted of error, they fly unto this fortress, [asylum,] that they ought to bear no blame;[1] but that God was rather cruel, who did not vouchsafe so much as with one hiss to call those back whom he saw perish, [perishing.] Paul and Barnabas cut off[2] this frivolous objection, when they show that God lay hid in such sort, that he [still] bare

---

[1] " Nullum sibi debere culpam imputari," that no blame ought to be imputed to them.   [2] " Anticipant," anticipate.

witness of himself and his divinity. Notwithstanding, we must see how these two things can hang together; for if God bare witness of himself, he did not suffer (so much as in him lay) the world to err. I answer, that this kind of testimony, whereof mention is made, was such as that it made men without excuse, and yet was it not sufficient to salvation. For that of the apostle is true, that by faith it is understood that the worlds were ordained by the word of God, (Heb. xi. 3.) But faith is not conceived by the bare beholding of the heaven and earth, but by the hearing of the word. Whereupon it followeth, that men are brought by the direction of the word alone unto that knowledge of Almighty God which bringeth salvation. And yet this letteth not but that they may be made without excuse, even without the word, who, though they be naturally deprived of light, are blind notwithstanding, through their own malice, as Paul teacheth in the first chapter to the Romans.

Giving rain and fruitful seasons. God hath, indeed, revealed himself to all mankind by his word since [from] the beginning. But Paul and Barnabas show that there was no age on which God did not bestow benefits, which might testify that the world is governed by his government (and commandment;) and because the light of doctrine had been buried long time, therefore they say only, that God was showed by natural arguments, [evidences.] And it is to be thought that they did, in such sort, set forth the magnificence and greatness of the works of God as became them; but it was sufficient for Luke to touch the (sums and) chief points of matters. Neither do I so understand it, that they intreated subtilely, and after the manner of the philosophers, of the secrets of nature, for they spake unto an unlearned multitude; therefore it behoved them to set that before them plainly which the most ignorant did know. Notwithstanding they take this principle, that in the order of nature there is a certain and evident manifestation of God, in that the earth is watered with rain; in that the heat of the sun doth comfort it;[1] in

---

[1] "Vegetat," causes it to vegetate.

that there cometh such abundance of fruit out of the same yearly, it is thereby gathered for a surety, that there is some God who governeth all things. For even the heaven and earth are not moved or governed by their own motion, and much less by fortune. Therefore it remaineth, that this wonderful workmanship of nature doth manifestly show the providence of God; and those who said that the world was eternal spake not as they thought, but they went about by malicious and barbarous unthankfulness [ingratitude] to suppress the glory of God, wherein they betrayed their impudence.

Filling with meat and gladness. The ungodliness of men is more convict in that, if they knew not God, because he doth not only set before their eyes testimonies of his glory in his works, but doth also appoint all things for their use. For why doth the sun and stars shine in the heavens, save only that they may serve men? Why doth the rain fall from heaven? Why doth the earth bring forth her increase, save only that they may minister food to men? Therefore, God hath not set man upon earth that he may be an idle beholder of his work, as being set upon a theatre, but to exercise himself in praising the liberality of God, whilst that he enjoyeth the riches of heaven and earth. And now, is it not more than filthy frowardness [depravity] not to be moved with so great goodness of God in the manifold abundance of things? To fill the hearts with meat, doth signify nothing else but to give food which may satisfy the desires of men. By this word *gladness*, Paul and Barnabas do mean that God doth give more to men, according to his infinite goodness, than their necessity doth require; as if it had been said, that men have meat given them not only to refresh their strength, but also to make their hearts merry.

If any man do object that it falleth out so oftentimes that men do rather mourn, being hungry, then rejoice, being full; I answer, that that cometh to pass contrary to the order of nature; namely, when the Lord shutteth his hand because of the sins of men. For the liberality of

God should flow unto us abundantly of his [its] own accord, as it is here described by Paul and Barnabas, unless it were kept back by the lets of our vices. And yet there was never so great barrenness wherein the blessing of God in feeding men did quite wither away. It was, indeed, well said of the prophet, Open thy mouth, and I will fill it, (Psalm lxxxi. 10,) that we may know that we be hungry through our own fault, whilst that we do not admit the goodness of God. But how unworthy soever we be and straight,[1] yet the fatherly love of God breaketh through even unto the unworthy. Especially the generality of mankind doth testify that the benefits of God do never cease, wherein he appeareth to be our Father.

18. *When they had said thus.* Luke said before that they did not only use words, but they ran also with violence into the multitude.[2] Now he addeth, that the fury of the people was scarce appeased[3] with that vehemency, whereby appeareth how mad and untamed the heat of the world is toward idolatry. For if they believe the [them] gods, why do they not believe their word, whereby they put from them false honour? But all idolaters are sick of this disease, that they are oftentimes ready to shake off the yoke, unless religion be subject to their will and pleasure. Wherefore, no marvel if the prophets say oftentimes that men are carried into the blind affection of superstitions, even as brute beasts are carried into their lust.

19. *And there came from Antioch and Iconium Jews, by whom the multitudes were persuaded, and when they had stoned Paul, they cast him out without the city, thinking that he was dead.*
20. *And as the disciples stood about him, he arose and entered into the city: and on the morrow he went forth with Barnabas to Derbe.*

---

[1] " Sed quam libet simus restricti," but however we may be restrained (in ourselves.)   [2] " Sed etiam cum impetu irruisse in turbam," but also rushed impetuously among the multitude   [3] " Repressum," repressed.

21. *And when they had preached the gospel to this city, and had framed many disciples, they returned to Lystra, and to Iconium, and Antioch,*

22. *Strengthening the souls of the disciples, and exhorting them to continue in the faith, and that through many afflictions we must enter into the kingdom of heaven.*

19. *There came.* Paul and Barnabas can hardly stay the people from doing sacrifice; but a company of knaves do, with small ado, persuade them to stone Paul, whom of late they made a god. Whereby appeareth how much more men be bent unto superstition than unto the true worship of God, and how arrogant superstition is, which will always bear the chief sway in appointing the worship of God. The servants of God seek no other thing but to bring men under obedience of him, which is salvation and felicity alone. They challenge to themselves no lordship, they hunt after no gain; and yet the world cannot abide them. For almost all men murmur; and now and then there rise tumults. Those who are thus stubborn against God, they be too too ready to believe seducers, and willingly submit themselves to their tyranny. So the Pope had liberty to deceive at his pleasure, and not only to oppress miserable souls with slavery, but also cruelly to torment them. Whatsoever he commanded it was obediently received, and even at this day, though he make impossible laws, yet dare no man once mutter against them. Nevertheless, the yoke of Christ is sweet, (Matth. xi. 30,) and yet few there be who will suffer it.

Therefore, in this history is most lively painted out unto us the frowardness of the world. Paul might have reigned under the title of Mercury, with the commendation of all men; he will not be a god. Because he serveth Christ faithfully, he is stoned. His constancy is commended, to the end we may follow it. He was indeed wonderfully delivered by the Lord; but as touching himself he suffered a most cruel kind of death. Therefore, we must make like account of this testimony, which he doth also recite in the Second Epistle to the Corinthians, (2 Cor. xi. 25,) as if he had been slain. Furthermore, we need not doubt but that the common sort made insurrection against him outrageously.[1] So that, what violence soever the wicked do to the servants of Christ, it is never called in question; the laws are whist, [silent;] judgments cease; the magistrate is asleep; there is no patron to be found.

20. *As the disciples.* Though no man defended Paul, yet Luke showeth that the godly were desirous of his life;[2] yet they did so moderate themselves, lest they should attempt anything with great danger to no end, seeing they could not help him unless it were done privily. And surely we must always mark what the Lord hath brought to our hand. If I, standing upon the bank, shall see a man in the midst of the water, and cannot reach him my hand when he is like to be drowned,[3] what is remaining for me to do but to commend him to the Lord? And [but] if there be any hope to help him, then must I endanger myself.[4] Therefore, we will not say that Saint Paul was left alone by the disciples through sloth, seeing they could not help him; and they declare their love and care when they stand about him after he is cast out.

They went to Derbe. It appeareth plainly by this that Paul was miraculously saved, seeing that, on the morrow, after he was cast out for dead, he taketh his journey, being fresh and sound; whence it is also gathered what an invincible heart he bare against all evils and afflictions. For he creepeth not into a corner, where, like an overworn soldier, he may live idly; but he goeth to the same places where he was uncourteously and cruelly handled but a little before. Notwithstanding Luke showeth that the church was first planted among the men of Derbe, he addeth afterward, that Paul and Barnabas returned unto the churches which they had ordained, that they might confirm the disciples; where-

---

[1] "Quin tumultuose in eum insurrexeret vulgus," that the mob rose tumultuously against him.   [2] "De ejus vita sollicitos," were anxious for his life.   [3] "Naufrago," when shipwrecked.   [4] "Periculum subire," run the risk.

by he giveth us to understand that the use of the Word consisteth not in instruction only, whereby the hearer is only taught, but that it is also available for confirmation of faith, in admonishing, exhorting, and reproving. And Christ doth not only command his ministers to teach, but also to exhort; and Paul saith that the Scripture is profitable not only to teach, but also to exhort, (2 Tim. iii. 16.) Wherefore, let not pastors think that they have done their duty as they ought, when they have well trained up their people in true knowledge, unless they employ themselves to this part also. Again, let not the faithful neglect the Word of God, as if the reading and preaching thereof were unnecessary; because there is no man who hath not need of continual confirmation.

22. *And exhorting them.* This was the principal way to confirm, in that they provoke the disciples who had before embraced the Gospel and did profess it, to go forward by exhorting them; for we are far from being so ready and stout[1] as we ought. Therefore our laziness needeth pricks, and our coldness must be warmed. But because God will have his exercised with divers combats, Paul and Barnabas admonish the disciples to be ready to suffer tribulation. A very necessary admonition, that we must go on warfare in this world, that we may live well and godlily. If the flesh should not molest us, if Satan should attempt nothing, if the wicked should not trouble us with some stumblingblocks, it were no such troublesome thing to persevere; because that were a sweet walk through a soft and pleasant way; but because there arise on every side, and every minute of an hour, [moment,] infinite assaults, which provoke us to fall away, there ariseth the hardness,[2] and therefore is it that the virtue of constancy is so rare. Therefore, to the end we may persist even unto the end, we must be prepared for war.

But Luke speaketh not in this place only of the persecu-

[1] "Prompti et strenui," prompt and strenuous. [2] "Difficultas," difficulty.

tions which the adversaries raise against us with drawn swords and flaming fires; but he comprehendeth under the word *tribulations,* all sorrows and miseries whereunto the life of the godly is subject; not because the faithful alone are miserable; because this is the common state both of the good and bad. Whence also cometh that famous proverb, It is the best not to be born; and the next to die very quickly.[1] But when as God doth oftentimes spare the wicked, and doth fat them with prosperity, he is more sharp and hard[2] toward his children. For besides common molestations, they are oppressed peculiarly with many discommodities, and the Lord doth humble them with such exercises, keeping their flesh under correction lest it wax wanton; he awaketh them, lest they lie sleeping upon earth. Unto these are added the reproaches and slanders of the wicked; for they must be, as it were, the offscourings of the world. Their simpleness is laughed at; but they use[3] wicked mocks and scoffs, principally against God. Last of all, the lust of the wicked breaketh out into open violence; so that they have need to strive[4] with many tribulations, and it cannot be but that all their life shall be envied and unquiet amidst so many enemies. But this is the best comfort, and which is sufficient enough to confirm their minds, that this way (though it be hard and sharp) leadeth unto the kingdom of heaven. For we gather by this that the miseries of the godly are more happy than be all the doting dainties and delights of the world.

Therefore, let us remember, first, that this condition is set down for us, that we suffer many tribulations; yet let us also remember to add this, to mitigate the bitterness thereof, that by them we be brought unto the kingdom of God. Furthermore, their babbling is frivolous,[5] who gather hereby that patience is a work which deserveth eternal salvation,

---

[1] "Optimum est non nasci, proximum vero, quam citissime mori," the best thing is not to be born; the next best to die as soon as possible.
[2] "Austerior est ac durior," he is more harsh and austere [3] "Maxime uruntur," they are most of all stung by. The translator appears to have read "utuntur" [4] "Valde infesta," exceedingly troubled. [5] "Futilis et stulta," futile and foolish.

seeing that the cause of salvation is not in this place handled, but after what sort God useth to handle his in this world; and the comfort is added, not to extol the dignity and merit of works, but only to encourage the godly, that they faint not under the burden of the cross. All mankind, as we have said before, as well one as other, is subject to many miseries; but the afflictions of the reprobate are nothing else to them but the very entry of hell; but these turn to the saints to an happy and joyful end, and for them they fall out well; and so, consequently, they be helps for salvation, because they take part with Christ.[1] We must note that Paul and Barnabas being not content with the plural number, do plainly set down many tribulations, lest any man, after he hath suffered one or two, or[2] a few, do at length sink down.[3] Therefore, let the faithful think that they must pass through continual miseries; that done, let them prepare themselves not for one kind of persecution only, but for divers kinds. For though God handle some men more courteously and gently, yet doth he pamper none of his so daintily that he is free from all tribulations.

23. *And when by voices* [suffrages] *they had ordained them elders through all churches, having prayed with fasting, they commended them to the Lord, in whom they had believed.*
24. *And passing over through Pisidia, they came to Pamphylia.*
25. *And when they had spoken the word at Perga, they went down to Attalia:*
26. *And thence they sailed to Antioch, from whence they were commended to the grace of God unto the work which they had fulfilled.*
27. *And when they were come, when the Church was gathered together, they showed what great things God had done by them, and that he had opened to the Gentiles the door of faith.*
28. *And they were there no small time with the disciples.*

---

[1] "Communicant cum Christo," make them to be partakers with Christ.
[2] "Aut saltem paucis," or at least a few.
[3] "Tandem succumbunt, at length succumb."

23. *When they had ordained elders.* By this it appeareth sufficiently, that it is not enough if men have been once taught the doctrine of godliness, and to have [hold] the sum of faith, unless they go forward continually; therefore, Christ did not only send his apostles to preach the gospel, but he commanded also that there should be pastors appointed, that the preaching of the gospel might be perpetual and in daily use. Paul and Barnabas do mark that this order was set down by Christ, when they assigned pastors to every church, lest, after their departure, doctrine should cease and be whisht, (silent.) Furthermore, this place teacheth, that the Church cannot want an ordinary ministry, neither can any be counted Christians before God but those who, during their whole life, are willing to learn. I take it that those are called elders, in this place, who had the office of teaching enjoined them; for it appeareth by Paul that some were only censors of manners, and such as had authority to punish enormities, (1 Tim. v. 17.) Now, forasmuch as Luke saith, that they were set over every church, the difference between their office and the office of the apostles is gathered hence. For the apostles had no certain place of abode, but they went to and fro to found new churches; but pastors were set and appointed, every man to his own church, and were, as it were, placed to watch[1] over their congregations.

Had ordained by election. The Greek word χειροτονειν doth signify to decree, or ordain a thing, by lifting up the hands, as they used to do in the assemblies of the people. Notwithstanding, the ecclesiastical writers do often use the word χειροτονεια in another sense; to wit, for their [the] solemn rite of ordaining, which is called in Scripture, *Laying on of hands.* Furthermore, by this manner of speech is very excellently expressed the right way to ordain pastors. Paul and Barnabas are said to choose[2] elders. Do they this alone by their private office?[3] Nay, rather they suffer the matter

---

[1] " Ad præsidium,' as a guard   [2] " Eligere," to elect.   [3] " An soli hoc privato officio faciunt," do they alone do this by their peculiar office?

to be decided by the consent of them all.[1] Therefore, in ordaining pastors the people had their free election, but lest there should any tumult arise, Paul and Barnabas sit as chief moderators. Thus must the decree of the council of Laodicea be understood, which forbiddeth that the people have liberty granted them to elect.[2]

They having prayed with fasting. They had a double end and reason of their prayer; the first, that God would direct them with the spirit of wisdom and discretion to choose the best and most meet men, for they knew that they were not furnished with so great wisdom but they might be deceived; neither did they so much trust to their diligence, but that they knew that the principal point did consist in the blessing of God, as we see men's judgments err daily where the heavenly government is not, and that all their labour is nothing worth where the hand of God is not. These be the true signs and tokens[3] of the godly to call upon the Spirit of God, that he may govern their counsels. And if so be it this rule be to be observed in all businesses, so often as the government of the Church is in hand, which dependeth wholly upon his will and pleasure, we must[4] beware that we attempt nothing unless we have him for our guide and governor. And the second end of their prayer was, that God would furnish with necessary gifts those pastors which were chosen. For it is a harder matter to fulfil such a function faithfully as a man ought, than that man's strength is sufficient for it. Therefore, they crave God's help even in this part also, having Paul and Barnabas for their authors.

They fast likewise, that even that may be a help[5] to stir up the ferventness of their prayers; for we know how great our coldness is otherwise. Not because it is always necessary that we should pray fasting, seeing that God doth invite even those who are full to give thanks; but when we are urged by any necessity to pray more fervently than we

---

[1] " Omnium suffragiis," by the suffrages of all. [2] " Plebi electionem permitti," election to be given (left) to the people. [3] " Auspicia," auspices. [4] " Sollicite," anxiously. [5] " Adduntur jejunia, tamquam adminicula," fastings are added as helps.

used commonly to do, this is a very profitable provokement. And now we have already declared what a weighty matter the choosing of pastors is, wherein the soundness of the Church is handled. Wherefore, no marvel if Luke write that they used extraordinary prayers. And it is profitable for us to mark this use, and other [uses] of fasting, lest we imagine with the Papists that it is a meritorious work, or lest we place the worship of God in it, seeing it is of itself nothing, neither is it of any importance with God, save only inasmuch as it is referred unto another end.[1]

They committed themselves to the Lord. We gather hereby, first, what great care Paul and Barnabas had for the salvation of those who, by their industry,[2] were turned unto the Lord; for they testify, that in this infirmity of the flesh men be subject to more dangers, than that their faith can continue stedfast through his [its] own strength. Therefore, this is the only refuge and aid, if the Lord keep them continually whom he hath once received. And when Luke saith, that they were commended to God in whom they believed, there cometh no small confidence hence unto us; because he assigneth this office to God as proper to him, to save and defend all those who by true faith have embraced his word.

24. *Passing through Pisidia.* We have already said that Paul and Barnabas came to Antioch of Pisidia. Being now about to return to Antioch of Syria, whence they were sent away, they go through Pamphylia, which is the middle region toward the mount Taurus. And Perga and Attalia are cities lying near together. And whereas Luke saith, that they preach the Word in the one only, we may thereby guess that they had not opportunity offered them everywhere to teach, which they were wont to neglect or let pass nowhere.

26. *When they had been commended.* Luke might have said that they were ordained there to be the apostles of the

---

[1] " Nisi quatenus alio refertur," except in so far as it has reference to something else.   [2] " Cura et labore," by their care and labour.

Gentiles; but by a circuit of words[1] he doth more plainly express that they were neither sent away of men, neither did they attempt any thing trusting to their own strength, but that their whole journey, together with the success, was committed to God, the author thereof. Therefore, their preaching was no man's work, but a work of the grace of God. And the word *grace* is referred as well unto the power and efficacy of the Spirit, as also unto all the rest of the signs of favour; because all those gifts be free which God bestoweth upon his servants. And the sentence may be thus resolved, that they prayed God that he would show forth his grace to further the labours of his servants.

27. *After they had called the Church together.* As those who return from an embassage used to give an account of their acts, so Paul and Barnabas declared to the Church all the sum of their voyage, that it may thereby appear what good success they had, and how faithfully they behaved themselves in their office; and also that they may exhort the faithful to give thanks to God, as the thing itself gave them large matter;[2] therefore Luke saith, Not that they did extol the things which they themselves had done, but whatsoever things the Lord had done by them. It is word for word *with them;* but according to the phrase of the Hebrew tongue, it is all one as if it had been said, *in them,* or *by them,* or *towards them,* or simply *to them,* in the dative case. Therefore Luke doth not say συν αυτοις, but μετα αυτων; which I say for this cause, lest any unskilful man ascribe some part of the praise to Paul and Barnabas, as if they had been partners with God in the work; whereas he doth rather make him the only author of all those famous facts which they had done.

Luke addeth immediately after, that the Lord had opened the door of faith to the Gentiles; for though they were sent unto the Gentiles, yet the strangeness [novelty] of the matter causeth them to wonder not a little; and not only

---

[1] " Verborum circuitu," by a circumlocution.   [2] " Amplum materiam," ample materials.

the sudden change did make the Jews astonished, but also because it was to them as it were a monster, that unclean men, and such as were strangers[1] from the kingdom of God, should be mixed with the holy seed of Abraham, that they might both together make one and the same Church of God. They are now taught by the event itself, that it was not for nothing that there were apostles sent to them. Moreover, it is said that the door of faith was set open to the Gentiles, not only because the gospel was preached to them with the external voice, but because, being illuminated by the Spirit of God, they were called effectually unto the faith. The kingdom of heaven is indeed set open to us by the external preaching of the gospel; but no man entereth in save he to whom God reacheth out his hand; no man draweth near unless he be drawn inwardly by the Spirit. Therefore, Paul and Barnabas show and prove by the effect that their calling was approved and ratified by God, because the faith of the Gentiles was, as it were, a seal engraven by the hand of God to establish the same, as Paul saith, (Rom. xvi. 25; 2 Cor. iii. 7.)

CHAPTER XV.

1. *And certain which came down from Judea did teach the brethren, that unless they should be circumcised according to the manner of Moses, they could not be saved.*
2. *And when there arose sedition, and disputing not a little to Paul and Barnabas against them, they appointed that Paul and Barnabas, and certain other of them, should go up to the apostles and elders to Jerusalem about this question.*
3. *And when they were sent by the Church, they passed through Phenice and Samaria, declaring the conversion of the Gentiles, and they brought great joy to all the brethren.*

---

[1] " Impuros et alienos," impure men, aliens.

4. *And when they were come to Jerusalem, they were received of the Church, and of the apostles and elders, and they showed what things soever God had done with them.*
5. *And there arose certain of the sect of the Pharisees which believed, saying, That it was needful that they should be circumcised, and to declare that the law of Moses must be kept.*

1. When Paul and Barnabas had endured many combats against the professed enemies of the gospel, Luke doth now begin to declare that they were tried by domestic war; so that it was meet that their doctrine and ministry should be proved by all means, to the end it might the better appear that they were furnished by God, and armed against all the assaults of the world and Satan. For that was no small confirmation for their doctrine, in that being shaken and battered with so many engines, it stood nevertheless, neither could the course thereof be broken off by so many hinderances. Therefore, to this end doth Paul boast that he suffered fights without and terrors within, (2 Cor. vii. 5.) This history is most worthy the noting; for though we do naturally abhor the cross and all manner [of] persecution, yet civil and domestic discord is more dangerous, lest haply they discourage us.[1] When tyrants bend their force and run violently upon men, flesh indeed is afraid; and all those who are not endued with the spirit of fortitude do tremble with all their heart; but then their consciences are not properly touched with any temptation. For this is known to be as it were the fatal estate of the Church. But when it falleth out so that the brethren go together by the ears, and that the Church is on an uproar within itself, it cannot be but that weak minds shall be troubled and also faint; and especially when the controversy is about doctrine, which alone is the holy bond of brotherly unity. Finally, there is nothing which doth more indamage the gospel than civil discord, because it doth not only pierce and wound weak con-

---

[1] " Plus tamen et intestinis dissidiis est periculi ne animos nostros frangant vel debilitent," yet there is more danger in intestine dissensions, lest they weaken or dispirit us.

sciences, but also minister occasion to the wicked to backbite.

Wherefore, we must diligently note this history, that we may know that it is no new example, if among those who profess the same gospel there arise some wranglings and strife about doctrine, when proud men can get them a name, (whereof they are so furiously desirous,) by no other means but by bringing in their own inventions. It is certain, that as there is but one God, so there is but one truth of this God.[1] Therefore, when Paul goeth about to exhort the faithful unto mutual consent, he useth this argument, " One God, one faith, one baptism," &c., (Ephes. iv. 6.) But when we see wicked men arise, who go about to divide [rend] the Church by their factions, and also either to corrupt the gospel with their false and filthy [spurious] inventions, or else to bring the same in suspicion, we ought to know the subtilty [artifice] of Satan. Therefore, Paul saith elsewhere that heresies come abroad, that those who are tried may be made manifest, (1 Cor. xi. 19.) And, assuredly, the Lord doth wonderfully make void the subtilty of Satan, in that he trieth the faith of his by such trials, and doth beautify his word with worthy and excellent victory; and causeth the truth to shine more clearly which the wicked went about to darken. But it is very convenient to weigh all the circumstances of the history which Luke noteth.

Which came down from Judea. This cloak and colour was very forcible to deceive even good men then. Jerusalem was honoured not without cause among all churches, because they reverenced it even as their mother. For the gospel was deducted, as it were, by pipes and conduits[2] from that fountain. These seducers come thence; they pretend the apostles; they boast that they bring nothing but that which they learned of them. They blind and blear the eyes of the unskilful with this smoke; and those who are light and wicked do greedily snatch at the colour which is offered

---

[1] " Certum quidem est, sicuti unus est Deus, ita unam esse ejus veritatem," it is certain, indeed, that as God is one, so also his truth is one   [2] " Per rivos," by streams.

them. The perturbation of the Church doth, like a tempest, shake those who were otherwise good and moderate, so that they are enforced to stumble. Therefore, we must note this subtilty of Satan, that he abuseth the names of holy men that he may deceive the simple, who, being won with the reverence of the men, dare not inquire after the thing itself. Luke doth not express, indeed, with what affection these knaves were moved; yet it is likely that perverse zeal was the cause which moved them to set themselves against Paul and Barnabas; for there be certain churlish natures which nothing can please but that which is their own. They had seen that circumcision and other rites of the law were observed at Jerusalem; wheresoever they become, they can abide nothing which is not agreeable thereto, as if the example of one church did bind all the rest of the churches with a certain law. And though such be carried with a preposterous zeal to procure tumults, yet are they pricked inwardly with their ambition, and with a certain kind of stubbornness. Nevertheless, Satan hath that he would; for the minds of the godly have such a mist cast before them, that they can scarce know black from white.

Therefore, we must beware first of this plague, that some prescribe not a law to other some after their manner, that the example of one church be not a prejudice[1] of a common rule. Also, we must use another caution, that the persons of men do not hinder or darken the examination of the matter or cause. For if Satan transfigure himself into an angel of light, (2 Cor. xi. 14,) and if, by sacrilegious boldness, he usurp the holy name of God, what marvel is it if he do like wickedly deceive men under the names of holy men? The end shall at length declare that the apostles meant nothing less than[2] to lay the yoke of the law upon the neck of the Gentiles; and yet Satan meant under this shift to get in. So it falleth out oftentimes that those who contrary [oppose] the doctrine of Christ, creep in under the title of his

---

[1] "Communis regulæ præjudicium," be not prejudged as a common rule
[2] "Apostolis nihil minus esse in animo," that the very last thing the apostles meant was.

servants. Therefore, there is one only remedy, to come to search out the matter[1] with sound judgments; also it behoveth us to prevent an offence, lest we think that the faithful servants of God do therefore strive among themselves, because Satan doth falsely abuse their names, that he may set certain shadows by the ears together to terrify the simple.

2. *When there was sedition arisen.* This was no small trial, in that Paul and Barnabas are haled into a troublesome tumult. There was mischief enough already in the matter [dissension] itself; but it is a more cruel mischief when the contention waxeth so hot, that they are enforced to fight with their brethren as with enemies. Add, moreover, the infamy wherewith they saw themselves burdened among the simple and unskilful, as if they would trouble the peace of the Church with their stubbornness. For it falleth out oftentimes so, that the faithful servants of Christ are envied alone, and bear all the blame, after that they have been unjustly troubled, and have faithfully employed themselves in defence of a good cause. Therefore, they must be endued with invincible courage to despise all false reports which are carried about concerning them. Therefore, Paul boasteth in another place that he went through the midst of seditions, (2 Cor. vi. 5.) But the servants of God must observe such moderation, that they abhor so much as they can all discord; if at any time Satan raise tumults and contentions, let them endeavour to appease them, and, finally, let them do all that they can to foster and cherish unity. But again, on the other side, when the truth of God is assailed, let them refuse no combat for defence thereof; nor let them fear to oppose themselves valiantly, though heaven and earth go together.

And let us, being admonished by this example, learn, so often as there ariseth any tumult in the Church, wisely to weigh through whose fault it came, lest we rashly condemn the faithful ministers of Christ, whose gravity is rather to

---

[1] " Ad rem ipsam quærendam accedere," to enter upon the investigation.

be praised, because they can abide so valiantly such violent assaults of Satan. Secondly, let us call to mind that Satan was bridled by the wonderful providence of God, that he might not put the doctrine of Paul to the foil. For if he had been suffered to do hurt at his pleasure, so soon as the faith of the Gentiles had been pulled down and overthrown, the gospel preached by Paul should have fallen to the ground, and the gate should have [been] shut against the calling of the Gentiles. Thirdly, let us learn that we must in time prevent dissension, of what sort soever it be, lest it break out into the flame of contention; because Satan seeketh nothing else by the fans of dissension but to kindle so many fires. But again, seeing we see the primitive Church on an uproar, and the best servants of Christ exercised with sedition, if the same thing befal us now, let us not fear as in some new and unwonted matter; but, craving at the Lord's hands such an end as he now made, let us pass through tumults with the same tenor of faith.

Unless ye be circumcised. Luke setteth [defineth] down briefly in these words the state of the question, to wit, that these seducers went about to bind men's consciences with necessity of keeping the law. Circumcision is indeed mentioned alone in this place; but it appeareth by the text that they moved the question about the keeping of the whole law. And, because circumcision was, as it were, a solemn entrance and admission into other rites of the law, therefore, by *synecdoche*, the whole law is comprehended under one part. These enemies of Paul did not deny that Christ was the Messiah; but though they gave him their names, they retained therewithal the old ceremonies of the law.

The error might have seemed tolerable at the first glimpse. Why doth not Paul then dissemble, at least, for some short time, lest he shake the Church with conflict? for the disputation was concerning external matters, concerning which Paul himself forbiddeth elsewhere to stand and strive too much. But there were three weighty causes

which enforced him to gainstand. For, if the keeping of
the law be necessary, man's salvation is tied to works,
which must be grounded in the grace of Christ alone, that
the faith may be settled and quiet. Therefore, when Paul
saw the worship of the law set against the free righteousness of faith, it was unlawful for him to hold his peace,
unless he would betray Christ. For, seeing the adversaries
did deny that any should be saved, save he which did observe the law of Moses, by this means they did translate
unto works the glory of salvation, which they took from
Christ, and having shaken assurance, they did vex miserable
souls with unquietness. Again, it was no small thing, neither
of any small importance, to spoil and rob faithful souls of
the liberty gotten by Christ's blood. Though the inward
liberty of the Spirit were common to the fathers as well as
to us, yet we know what Paul saith, that they were shut up
under the childish ward and custody of the law, so that
they did not much differ from servants; but we are loose
from the schoolmastership of the law after that Christ was
revealed, (Gal. iii. 24,) and we have more liberty, the time
of our nonage being, as it were, ended. The third vice
of this doctrine was, because it darkened the light of the
Church,[1] or at least did put in, as it were, certain clouds,
that Christ the Sun of righteousness might not give perfect light. In sum, Christianity should shortly have come
to nothing if Paul should have yielded to such beginnings.
Therefore, he entereth the combat, not for the external uncircumcision of the flesh, but for the free salvation of men.
Secondly, that he may acquit and set free godly consciences
from the curse of the law, and the guilt of eternal death.
Last of all, that after all hinderances are driven away, the
brightness of the grace of Christ may shine as in a pleasant and clear heaven. Moreover, these knaves did great
injury to the law when they did wickedly corrupt the right
use thereof. This was the natural and right office of the
law, to lead men by the hand, like a schoolmaster, unto

---

[1] " Evangelii," gospel

Christ; therefore, it could not be worse corrupt than when, under colour of it, the power and grace of Christ were diminished.

After this sort must we look into the fountains of all questions, lest by our silence we betray the truth of God, so often as we see Satan, by his subtilty, aim right at it; neither let our minds be changed and wax faint through any perils, or reproaches and slanders, because we must constantly defend pure religion, though heaven and earth must [should] go together. The servants of Christ must be no fighters, (2 Tim. ii. 24;) therefore, if there be any contention risen, they must rather study to appease and pacify the same by their moderation, than by and by to blow to the assault.[1] Secondly, they must take good heed of superfluous and vain conflicts; neither shall they handle controversies of any small weight; but when they see Satan wax so proud, that religion cannot any longer continue safe and sound unless he be prevented, they must needs take a good heart to them, and rise to resist; neither let them fear to enter even most hateful combats. The name of peace is indeed plausible and sweet, but cursed is that peace which is purchased with so great loss, that we suffer the doctrine of Christ to perish, by which alone we grow together into godly and holy unity.

The Papists cause us at this day to be sore hated, as if we had been the causers of deadly tumults, wherewith the world is shaken; but we can well defend ourselves, because the blasphemies which we endeavoured to reprove were more cruel[2] than that it was lawful for us to hold our peace; there we are not to be blamed, because we have taken upon us to enter combats in defence of that cause, for which we were to fight even with the very angels. Let them cry till their throats be sore; Paul's example is sufficient for us, that we must not be either cold or slack in defending the doctrine of godliness when the ministers of Satan

---

[1] "Quam ut classicum protinus caniant," than forthwith to blow the trumpet.   [2] "Atrociores," more atrocious.

seek to overthrow it with might and main; for their brain-sick distemperature ought not to pass[1] the constancy of the servants of God. When Paul did zealously set himself against the false apostles, sedition began at length[2] by reason of the conflict; and yet the Spirit of God doth not therefore reprove him; but doth rather with due praises commend that fortitude which he had given that holy man.

They determined, &c. The Spirit of God put them in mind of this remedy to appease the tumult, which might otherwise have gone farther with doing much hurt, whereby we be also taught, that we must always seek such means as be fit[3] for ending discord; because God doth so highly commend peace, let the faithful show[4] that they do what they can to nourish the peace of the Church. The truth must always be first in order with them, in defence whereof they must be afraid of no tumults; yet they must so temper their heat that they refuse no means of godly agreement; yea, let them of their own accord invent what ways soever they can, and let them be witty in seeking them out. Therefore, we must observe this mean, lest being carried away through immoderate vehemency of zeal we be carried beyond the just bounds; for we must be courageous in defence of true doctrine, not stubborn, nor rash; therefore, let us learn to join together these two virtues which the Spirit of God commendeth in Paul. When he is drawn into the field by the wicked, he is not afraid boldly to offer himself; but when he doth meekly admit the remedy which was offered, he declareth plainly what small desire he had to fight, for otherwise he might have boasted that he did not pass for the apostles,[5] and so have stood stoutly in that; but the desire of peace did not suffer him to refuse their judgment. Moreover, ignorant and weak men should have conceived a sinister opinion, if they should have seen two men only separated from all the servants of Christ; and godly teachers

---

[1] " Superare," overcome [2] " Exarsit," blazed forth [3] " Aptas et commodas," fit and convenient [4] " Re ipsa," in reality.
[5] " Nihil se morari apostolos," that he cared not for the apostles.

must in no case neglect this way to cherish faith, that they may show that they agree with the Church.

Paul, indeed, did not depend upon the beck of the apostles, that he would change his opinion if he should have found them contrary to him, who would not have given place even to the very angels, as he boasteth in first chapter to the Galatians, (Gal. i. 8;) but lest the wicked should slanderously report that he was a man that stood too much in his own conceit, and which was too proud, and which did please himself with an unseemly contempt of all men, he offered to give an account of his doctrine, as it became him, and as it was profitable for the Church; secondly, he presented himself before the apostles with sure hope of victory, because he knew full well what would be their judgment, seeing they were guided by the same Spirit wherewith he was governed. Notwithstanding, it may be demanded for what purpose the men of Antioch sent Paul and Barnabas unto the rest of the apostles; for if they did so greatly reverence them, that they stood in doubt until they had given judgment on this side or that, their faith was hitherto vain and altogether none? But the answer is easy, seeing they knew that all the apostles were sent[1] by Christ alone with the same commandments, and that they had the same Spirit given them, they were fully persuaded of the end and success, and, undoubtedly, this counsel proceeded from honest and stout men, who were not ignorant that the knaves did falsely pretend the names of James and Peter. Wherefore, they sought nothing else but that the apostles might further a good matter with their consent.[2]

To the same end were all holy synods assembled since the beginning, that grave men, and such as were well exercised in the word of God, might decide controversies, not after their own pleasure, but according to the authority of God. This is worth the noting, lest the Papists pierce any man with their loud outcries,[3] who, to the end they may overthrow

---

[1] "Pariter," in like manner [2] "Suffragio," suffrage. [3] "Ventosis suis clamoribus," with their vain clamour

Christ and his gospel, and put out all the light of godliness, thrust upon us Councils, as if every definition and determination of men were to be counted an heavenly oracle; but if the holy Fathers had their sitting at this day, they would cry with one mouth, that there was nothing more unlawful for them, neither did they mean any thing less than to set down or deliver any thing without having the word of Christ for their guide, who was their only teacher, [master,] even as he is ours. I omit this, that the Papists lean only unto untimely[1] Councils, which breathe out nothing but gross ignorance and barbarism; but even the best and most choice must be reckoned in that number, that they may be subject to the word of God. There is a grievous complaint of Gregory Nazianzene extant, that there was never any Council which had a good end. What excellency soever did flourish and was in force in the Church, it cannot be denied but that it began to decay an hundred years after; therefore, if that holy man were now living, how stoutly would he reject the toys of the Papists, who, without all shame, most impudently bring in the jugglings of visors instead of lawful Councils, and that to that end, that the Word of God may pack,[2] so soon as a few bald and foolish men have set down whatsoever pleased them?

3. *Being brought on the way by the Church.* Whereas, by the common consent of the Church, there were joined to Paul and Barnabas companions, who might, for duty's sake, conduct them, we may thereby gather, that all the godly were on their side; and that they did never otherwise think but that the cause was theirs as well as the apostles. Wherefore they determined the journey of Paul and Barnabas with like minds as they took it in hand; to wit, that they might tame and put to silence those troublesome spirits who did falsely make boast of the apostles. Whereas he saith shortly after, that they certified the brethren in their voyage of the wonderful conversion of the Gentiles, it is a

---

[1] "Abortivis," abortive.   [2] "Facessat," may be dismissed

testimony and token that they came not to Jerusalem fraught with fear; but that they did even without fear stoutly profess that which they had taught before. Therefore, they come not to plead their cause before their judges; but that they may, with common consent and judgment, on both sides, approve that which was commanded by God touching the abolishing of ceremonies. For though they did not despise the judgment of the apostles, yet because they knew that it was not lawful for them, neither for the apostles, to decree otherwise concerning the cause, it did not become them to stand as men whose matter is handled at the bar.[1] Thence cometh the boldness of rejoicing; to this end[2] tendeth the joy of the godly, whereby they subscribe both to the doctrine of Paul and also the calling of the Gentiles.

4. *They were received of the Church.* By this word *Church* he meaneth the multitude itself and the whole body; that done, he assigneth a peculiar place to the apostles and elders, by whom Paul and Barnabas were specially received. Furthermore, because the apostles had no certain place of abode at Jerusalem, but went ever now and then sometimes to one place and sometimes to another, whithersoever occasion did call them, that church had elders to whom the ordinary government of the Church was committed; and what the one function differeth from the other we have before declared, (Acts xiv. 23.) And hereby it appeareth what brotherly courtesy there was in the apostles and elders, because they do not only courteously receive Paul and Barnabas, but so soon as they hear what success they had with their pains they took, they magnify the grace of God. Luke repeateth again that form of speech which we had before in the chapter next going before, when he saith, that they declared whatsoever things God had done with them. Wherein we must remember that which I said before, that God is not made a fellow-labourer, but all the whole praise of the work is ascribed to him. Therefore it is said, that he did that

---

[1] " Reos," as men accused, defenders. added.

[2] " Huc accedit," to this is

with Paul and Barnabas which he did by them, as he is said to deal mercifully with us when he helpeth our miseries.

5. *Certain of the sect of the Pharisees.* It is not without cause that Luke expresseth what kind of men they were which went about to trouble or hinder Paul, even at Jerusalem also. And it is to be thought that the evil flowed from that fountain; and that Luke doth now more plainly express, that there brake out now also fans [disturbers] out of that very same sect, from whence the authors of that wicked dissension came. For though they had given Christ their names, yet there remained relics of their former nature. We know how proud the Pharisees were, how haughty, how lofty their looks were;[1] all which they would have forgotten if they had truly put on Christ. Like as there remained no Phariseeism in Paul, but a great part had gotten the habit of stubbornness by long custom, which they could not shake off so easily by and by. Forasmuch as there reigned most of all among them hypocrisy, they were too much addicted to external rites, which are coverings for vices. They were likewise puffed up with pride, so that they did tyrannously covet to make all other men subject to their decrees. It is well-known how sore sick the monks are of both diseases. Whereby it cometh to pass, that nothing is more cruel than they to oppress the Church, nothing is more wicked or froward than they to despise the Word of God. Moreover, we see many of them which came out of those dens which have cast from them their cowl, and yet can they never forget those conditions which they learned there.[2]

6. *And the apostles and elders came together, that they might look to this business.*

7. *And after there had been great disputing, Peter arose and said to them, Men and brethren, ye know how that of old time God did choose in us, that by my mouth the Gentiles should hear the word of the gospel and believe.*

---

[1] " Quanta confidentia, quale supercilium," how confident, how supercilious. [2] " Quos illic imbiberunt mores," the habits which they contracted there.

8. *And God, who is knower of the hearts, bare witness to them, giving them his Holy Spirit, as to us.*

9. *And he put no difference between them and us, after that by faith he had purified their hearts.*

10. *Therefore, why do ye now tempt God to lay a yoke upon the necks of the disciples, which neither our fathers nor we were able to bear?*

11. *But we believe that we have salvation through the grace of our Lord Jesus Christ, even as they.*

6. *The apostles and elders met together.* Luke saith, not that all the whole Church was gathered together, but those who did excel in doctrine and judgment, and those who, according to their office, were competent[1] judges in this matter. It may be, indeed, that the disputation was had in presence of the people. But lest any man should think that the common people were suffered hand over head to handle the matter, Luke doth plainly make mention of the apostles and elders, as it was more meet that they should hear the matter and to decide it.[2] But let us know, that here is prescribed by God a form and an order in assembling synods, when there ariseth any controversy which cannot otherwise be decided. For seeing that many did daily gainstand Paul, this disputation alone, by reason whereof there was great ruin like to ensue, and which was already come to hot combats, did enforce him to go to Jerusalem.

7. *And when there had been great disputation.* Though there were choice made of grave men, and such as were public teachers of the Church, yet could not they agree by and by.[3] Whereby appeareth how the Lord did exercise his Church, even then, by the infirmity of men, that it might learn to be wise with humility. Moreover, he suffered (even in that company and assembly wherein he was chief) the principal point of Christian doctrine to be diversely tossed and handled, lest we should wonder, if at any time it so fall

---

[1] "Legitimi," lawful. [2] "Sicut magis idonei erant cognitores," as they were more fit to take cognisance of it. [3] "Ne inter eos quidem statim convenire potuit," not even could they come instantly to an agreement.

out, that men, who are otherwise learned and godly, do, through unskilfulness, fall into an error. For some were not so quick witted [acute] that they could thoroughly see into the greatness of the matter. So that when they judge that the law ought to be kept, being unadvisedly carried away with the zeal of the law, they see not into how deep a labyrinth they throw the consciences of other men, and their own also. They thought that circumcision was an eternal and inviolable token of God's covenant; the same opinion had they of all the whole law. Wherefore Peter standeth chiefly upon this, to show the state of the question, which the most of them knew not. And his oration hath two members. For, first, he proveth by the authority of God that the Gentiles must not be enforced to keep the law; secondly, he teacheth that all man's salvation is overthrown, if the conscience be once caught in this snare. Therefore, the former part (wherein he declareth that he was sent of God to teach the Gentiles, and that the Holy Spirit came down upon them) tendeth to this end, that men did not unadvisedly disannul the ceremonies of the law, but that God is the author of that disannulling. And so soon as the authority of God is brought forth, all doubting is taken away, because this is all our wisdom, to stay ourselves upon the authority, government, and commandment of God,[1] and to make more account of his beck and pleasure than of all reasons. Now, it is meet that we ponder the words of Peter, whereby he proveth that this was granted to the Gentiles by God, to be free from the yoke of the law.

You know. He calleth them to bear witness, (and unto them he appealeth,) lest any man should think that he is about to speak of some dark and doubtful thing. The history was well known to them all. That which remained, he showeth that they were blind even in most clear light, yea, because they had not long ago learned that which was openly showed. He calleth the beginning of the preaching of the gospel old days, or the old time, as if he should say,

---

[1] " Dei imperio acquiescere," to acquiesce in the command of God.

long ago, as it were since the first beginning of the Church, after that Christ began to gather to himself any people.

God did choose in us. The word *choose* doth signify to appoint or decree. Though Peter doth comprehend as well the free election of God as the choice whereby God did adopt the Gentiles to be his people; therefore, he chose, that is, as it were, making choice, that he might show a token of his free election in the Gentiles, he would that by my mouth they should hear the doctrine of the gospel. These words, *in us,* do import as much as in our sight, or we being witnesses, or among us.[1] For his meaning is, that he declareth nothing but that which they knew full well; to wit, which was done before their eyes. The phrase is common enough both among the Grecians, and also among the Hebretians, [Hebrews,] unless we had liefer resolve it as some other do, He hath chosen me out of this company.

And believe. This was a seal to confirm the calling of the Gentiles. The office of teaching was enjoined Peter by an oracle; but the fruit which came of his doctrine doth make his ministry noble and authentical, as they call it. For, seeing that the elect are illuminate into the faith by a peculiar grace of the Spirit, doctrine shall bring forth no fruit, unless the Lord show forth his power in his ministers, in teaching the minds of those inwardly which hear, and in drawing their hearts inwardly. Therefore, seeing the Lord commanded that the doctrine of the gospel should be brought unto the Gentiles, he did sanctify them to himself, that they might be no longer profane. But the solemn consecration was then perfect in all points, when he imprinted in their hearts, by faith, the mark of their adoption. The sentence which followeth immediately is to be understood as set down by way of exposition;[2] for Peter annexeth the visible graces of the Spirit unto faith, as, assuredly, they were nothing else but an addition thereof. Therefore, seeing that the Gentiles are ingrafted into the people of God without circumcision and ceremonies, Peter gathereth that it was not

---

[1] "In medio nostri," in the midst of us.   [2] "Exegetice," exegetically.

well done to lay upon them any necessity to keep the law. Yet it seemeth to be but a weak argument to prove their election withal, because the Holy Ghost came down upon them. For they were such gifts that they could not reason from the same, that they were reckoned in the number of the godly. But it is the Spirit of regeneration alone which distinguisheth the children of God from strangers. I answer, Though men, who were otherwise vain, were endued with the gift of tongues and such like, yet doth Peter take for a thing which all men grant, that which was known, that God had sealed in Cornelius and his cousins [relatives] his free adoption by the visible grace of the Spirit, as if he should point out his children with his finger.

The knower of the hearts. He applieth this adjunct to God, according to the circumstance of the present matter; and it hath under it a secret contrariety,[1] that men are more addicted to external purity, because they judge according to their gross and earthly sense and understanding; but God doth look into the heart. Therefore, Peter teacheth that they judge preposterously in this matter according to man's understanding, seeing that the inward pureness of the heart alone is here to be esteemed, which we know not.[2] And by this means doth he bridle our rashness, lest, taking to ourselves more than we ought, we murmur against the judgment of God. As if he should say, if thou see no reason of that testimony which God gave them, think with thyself what great difference there is between him and thee. For thou art holden with external pomp according to thy gross nature, which must be abandoned when we come to the throne of God,[3] where the hearts of men are known spiritually. But, in the mean season, we must note a general doctrine, that the eyes of God do not look upon the vain pomp of men,[4] but upon the integrity of men's hearts, as it is written, (Jer. v. 3.) Whereas the old interpreter and Erasmus translate it, that God knoweth the hearts, it doth

---

[1] " Tacita antithesis," a tacit antithesis. [2] " Quæ nobis occulta est," which is hidden from us. [3] " Ad cœleste tribunal," to the heavenly tribunal. [4] " Operum," of works.

not sufficiently express that which Luke saith in Greek; for when he calleth God καρδιαγνωστην, he setteth him against[1] men, who judge rather for the most part by the outward appearance; and therefore they may be called προσωπογνωσται, or *knowers of the face,* if they be compared with God.

9. *And he put no difference.* There was indeed some difference, because the Gentiles who were uncircumcised were suddenly admitted unto the covenant of eternal life; whereas the Jews were prepared by circumcision unto faith. But Peter's meaning is, that they were both chosen[2] together by God unto the hope of the same inheritance, and that they were extolled into the like degree of honour, that they might be the children of God and members of Christ, and, finally, the holy seed of Abraham, a priestly and princely generation. Whereupon it followeth, that they cannot without sacrilege be counted unclean, sithence God hath chosen them to be a peculiar people, and hath consecrated them to be holy vessels of his temple. For the wall of separation being pulled down, whereby the Gentiles and Jews were divided among themselves, he hath joined the Gentiles to the Jews, that they might grow together into one body, (Ephes. ii. 14;) and that I may so say, he hath mixed circumcision and uncircumcision together, that as well those of the household as strangers may be one in Christ, and may make one Church; and that there may not be any longer either Jew or Grecian.

Seeing that by faith he hath purified. This member is answerable to that former adjunct which he applieth to God; as if he should say, that God, who knoweth the hearts, did inwardly purge the Gentiles, when he vouchsafed to make them partakers of his adoption, that they might be endued with spiritual cleanness. But he addeth farther, that this purity did consist in faith. Therefore he teacheth, first, that the Gentiles have true holiness without ceremonies, which may suffice before God's judgment-seat.

---

[1] "Eum opponit," he opposes him to, or contrasts him with

[2] "Utrosque pariter allectos esse," that both were in like manner allured.

Secondly, he teacheth that this is attained unto by faith, and from it doth it flow. In like sort, Paul gathereth, that uncircumcision doth not hinder a man but that he may be counted holy and just before God, (Rom. iv. 10;) because circumcision did follow after righteousness in the person of Abraham, and by order of time it was latter, [posterior.]

But here ariseth a question, whether that purity which the fathers had in times past were unlike to that which God gave now to the Gentiles? For it seemeth that Peter distinguisheth the Gentiles from the Jews by this mark, because, being content with the cleanness of the heart alone, they need no help of the law. I answer, that the one of them differ from the other, not in substance, but in form, [only.] For God had respect always unto the inward cleanness of the heart; and the ceremonies were given to the old [ancient] people only for this cause, that they might help their faith. So that cleanness, as touching figures and exercises, was only for a time, until the coming of Christ, which hath no place among us at this day; like as there remaineth from the very beginning of the world unto the end the same true worship of God, to wit, the spiritual worship; yet is there great difference in the visible form. Now, we see that the fathers did not obtain righteousness by ceremonies, neither were they therefore pure before God, but by the cleanness of the heart. For the ceremonies of themselves were of no importance to justify them; but they were only helps, which did accidentally (that I may so term it) purge them; yet so that the fathers and we had the same truth. Now, when Christ came, all that which was accidental did vanish away; and, therefore, seeing the shadows be driven away, there remaineth the bare and plain pureness of the heart.

Thus is that objection easily answered which the Jews think cannot possibly be answered. Circumcision is called the eternal covenant, or of the world, (Gen. xvii. 13;) therefore, say they, it was not to be abolished. If any man shall say that this is not referred unto the visible sign, but rather unto the thing figured, it shall be well answered;

but there is another answer besides this. Seeing that the kingdom of Christ was a certain renewing of the world, there shall no inconvenience follow if he made an end of[1] all the shadows of the law, forasmuch as the perpetuity of the law is grounded in Christ. I come now unto the second member, where Peter placeth the cleanness [purity] of the Gentiles in faith. Why doth not he say, In perfection of virtues, or holiness of life, save only because men have righteousness from another, and not from themselves? For, if men, by living well and justly, should purchase righteousness, or if they should be clean before God by nature, this sentence of Peter should fall to the ground. Therefore, the Spirit doth in these words plainly pronounce that all mankind is polluted, and with filthiness defiled; secondly, that their blots can by no other means be wiped away than by the grace of Christ. For, seeing that faith is the remedy whereby the Lord doth freely help us, it is set as well against the common nature of all men, as against every man's own merits. When I say that all mankind is polluted, my meaning is, that we bring nothing from our mother's womb but mere filthiness, and that there is no righteousness in our nature which can reconcile us to God. Man's soul was indeed endued with singular gifts at the first; but all parts thereof are so corrupt with sin, that there remaineth in it no drop of pureness any longer; therefore we must seek for cleanness without ourselves.

For if any man allege that it may be recovered by merits of works, there is nothing more absurd than to imagine that wicked and froward nature can deserve anything. Therefore, it resteth that men seek elsewhere for that which they shall never be able to find within themselves. And surely it is the office of faith to translate that unto us which is proper to Christ, and to make it ours by free participation. So that there is a mutual relation between faith and the grace of Christ. For faith doth not make us clean, as

---

[1] "Nihil esse absurdi si finem . . imposuerit," there is no absurdity in his having put an end to.

a virtue or quality poured into our souls; but because it receiveth that cleanness which is offered in Christ. We must also note the phrase, that God purifieth the hearts; whereby Luke doth both make God the author of faith, and he teacheth also that cleanness is his benefit. To make short, he signifieth unto us, that that is given to men by the grace of God which they cannot give to themselves. But forasmuch as we said that faith taketh that of Christ which it transpoureth [transferreth] into us; we must now see how the grace of Christ doth make us clean, that we may please God. And there is a double manner of purging, because Christ doth offer and present us clean and just in the sight of his Father, by putting away our sins daily, which he hath once purged by his blood; secondly, because, by mortifying the lusts of the flesh by his Spirit, he reformeth us unto holiness of life. I do willingly comprehend both kinds of purging under these words; because Luke doth not touch one kind of purging only, but he teacheth that the whole perfection thereof consisteth without the ceremonies of the law.

10. *Now, therefore, why tempt ye?* This is the other part of the sermon wherein Peter showeth how deadly that doctrine is which Paul's enemies sought to bring in; to wit, which might drown godly souls in despair. He inferreth and gathereth out of the former member, that God is tempted if the Gentiles be enforced to keep the law of necessity;[1] he riseth higher, and pierceth even unto the very fountain. For he reasoneth hitherto, that the Gentiles should have injury done them if there be more required at their hands than God will; and seeing that he made them equal with the holy people, and did vouchsafe them the honour of adoption, it was an unmeet and inconvenient [absurd] matter that they should be rejected, and so his liberality should be restrained. For he saith

---

[1] " Ad necessitatem servandæ legis," to a necessity of observing the law.

last of all, that this faith is sufficient for them, though they want ceremonies. And now he taketh an higher principle, that those who tie men's salvation to the works of the law leave them no good hope; but rather throw the whole world headlong into horrible destruction, if it can obtain salvation by no other means but by keeping the law. With what arguments he proveth this we shall see in their place. As touching the words, seeing the Scripture saith, that God is tempted divers ways, Peter's meaning is, in this place, that God is provoked as it were of set purpose, when there is an heavier burden laid upon men than they be able to bear; and that his power is brought within bounds [1] when that yoke is bound which he doth loose, which is nothing else but by striving against nature to match ourselves with giants, as they say.

That the yoke should be laid upon their necks. The meaning of the words is plain, that God is tempted when there is laid upon men's consciences a sorer burden than they are able to bear, and by this means the salvation of men's souls is sore shaken; seeing that they must needs by this means be drowned in despair, which cannot be without their destruction. But that injury which is done to God is no whit more tolerable, when as he is robbed of his right that he may not have liberty to deliver us. But we may easily gather out of the thing itself that he doth not speak of the ceremonies only. The servitude of the old training up under the law was hard and laborious; but yet it were too absurd to call it a yoke that cannot be borne; and we know that not only holy men, but also even most hypocrites, did well and exactly accomplish the outward observation of the rites.

Moreover, it were not any hard matter to satisfy the moral law, if it were content with corporeal obedience only, and did not require spiritual righteousness; for it is granted to many to bridle their hands and feet; but to

---

[1] " Circumscribi," is circumscribed.

moderate all the affections so that there may reign perfect abstinence and purity, as well in the soul as in the body, this is too hard a matter.

Therefore, those be too foolish who restrain unto ceremonies Peter's words, whereby the weakness of men to perform the righteousness of the heart is expressed; which doth not only far pass their strength, but is altogether contrary to nature. These men were, I warrant you, deceived by one reason, because the question was moved concerning ceremonies only; but they do remember that Peter did more attentively and more wisely consider as became him, what a labyrinth this error (to look to, but light) did bring with it. The false apostles did avouch, that no man could attain unto salvation unless he did keep the ceremonies. If man's salvation be tied to works, it shall be no longer grounded in the grace of Christ, and so, by this means, free reconciliation shall fall flat to the ground. Now, seeing that man's strength is unable to keep the law, all men are subject to the curse which the Lord there denounceth against the transgressors; and so, by this means, all men shall come in danger of despair, seeing that they see themselves guilty of eternal death by the law. Peradventure the false apostles understood these things craftily. But Peter pierceth the very fountain, that he may bring to light the deadly poison of that doctrine; and thus must we do, so often as Satan doth craftily thrust in wicked errors.

At this day we seem to some to be too contentious, when as we do so stoutly stand in this, that men must not pray for the dead; for it is both a most ancient custom, neither is it a thing to look to very dangerous, though men pour out superfluous prayer; yet [nay] it is a plausible opinion, because it carrieth some colour of human godliness.

Furthermore, unskilful men judge thus, because they seek not out the head spring. For, if we grant that men may pray for the dead, we must also admit this, that they are now punished by the judgment of God, because they made not satisfaction in this life for their sins. And so, by this means the force of Christ's satisfaction is translated unto the works of men. Secondly, the rule of praying aright is overthrown, if men may pray at all adventure, without the word of God. This is also a greater absurdity than that we ought lightly to pass over it. In sum, we can never give true judgment of any question, unless, having thoroughly ript up the fountain of that doctrine which is called in question, we deduct all consequences which it bringeth with it. Therefore, it is no marvel if Peter, to the end he may pull the false apostles out (by the ears,) as it were out of their lurking dens, do generally dispute touching the whole law; because he doth nothing else but open the matter itself, whereof the simple were ignorant; that they may all see what a deadly doctrine it is, which doth both extinguish the grace of Christ, and drown souls in the horrible dungeon of despair.[1]

Neither we nor our fathers. Peter doth not only dispute what men have done indeed, but what they were able to do; neither doth he speak only of the common riff-raff,[2] but of the holy fathers. Seeing that he denieth that they were able to bear the yoke of the law, it is manifest that the law cannot possibly be kept. I know that Jerome's saying is so generally received, that it is, as it were, an undoubted and most certain maxim, If any man say that it is a thing impossible to keep the law, let him be accursed; but we must not hearken to any voice of man which is contrary to the judgment of the Spirit of God. We hear what the Spirit pronounceth in this place by the mouth of Peter, not concerning the will and works of men, but touching their ability and power. And hereunto agreeth Paul, affirming that it was an impossible thing that the law should give us life, forasmuch as it was weak through the flesh. Indeed, if any man were able to fulfil the law, he should find the life which is there promised; but forasmuch as Paul denieth that life can be gotten by the law, it follow-

---

[1] " In horrendæ desperationis abyssum," in the abyss of horrible despair.
[2] " Vulgo hominum," of the vulgar.

eth that there is farther and higher righteousness required there than man is able to perform. I confess, indeed, that Jerome doth not wholly grant to the strength of nature power to fulfil the law, but partly also to the grace of God, as he doth afterward expound himself, that a faithful man, holpen by the grace of the Spirit, may be said to be able to fulfil the law. But even that mitigation is not true. For, if we do weigh the strength of nature only, men shall not only be unable to bear the yoke of the law, but they shall not be able to move so much as a finger to perform the least jot of the law. And surely if that be true, that all the cogitations of man's mind are wicked from his childhood, (Gen. viii. 21;) that all the understandings of flesh[1] are enemies to God, (Rom. viii. 7;) that there is none which seeketh after God, (Psalm xiv. 3;) and other such places, which are common in the Scripture, tending to the same end, but especially which are cited by Paul in the third to the Romans, (Rom. iii. 11,) man's power and ability to fulfil the law shall not only be weak and lame, but altogether none to begin.[2]

Therefore, we must thus think, that even the very faithful, after they being regenerate by the Spirit of God, do study to attain unto the righteousness of the law, do perform, notwithstanding, but the half, and far less than half, not the whole. For doubtless Peter speaketh not in this place of the epicure[3] or profane men; but of Abraham, of Moses, and of other holy fathers which were the most perfect in the world; and yet he saith that these fainted under the burden of the law, because it did pass their strength. It is hatefully objected that the Spirit of God is blasphemed when as ability to fulfil the law is taken away from his grace and help; but we may readily answer, because the question is not what the grace of the Spirit is able to do, but what that measure of grace is able to do which God doth divide to every one in this life. For we must always

---

[1] "Carnis sensus," carnal propensities. [2] "Sed ad inchoandum prorsus nulla," but that he shall have no power at all to begin. [3] "De Epicuro," of Epicurus.

consider what God doth promise to do; neither let us unadvisedly ask this question, whether that can be done which he himself doth testify shall never be, and which he will not have done? He promiseth the grace and aid of the Spirit to the faithful, whereby they may be able to resist the lusts of the flesh, and to subdue them; yet shall they not quite abolish and drive them away. He promiseth them grace, whereby they may walk in newness of life; yet shall they not be able to run so swiftly as the law requireth. For he will have them kept under during their whole life, that they may fly to beg pardon. If it be unlawful to separate from the power of God's counsel, and the order by him set down, it is a foolish and vain cavil, whereby the adversaries go about to burden us, when as they say that we diminish the power of God; nay rather, they transform God, when they hold that his counsel and purpose can be altered.

The Pelagians did in times past, in like sort, burden[1] Augustine. He answereth, that though it be a thing possible that the law should be fulfilled, yet is that sufficient for him, that no man did ever fulfil it, and that the Scripture doth not testify that it shall be fulfilled until the end of the world. By which words he delivereth himself from their importunate subtilty. But there was no cause why he should doubt, but freely and flatly grant that it might be fulfilled, the Holy Ghost being the author. For we must limit the grace of the Spirit, that it may agree with the promises. Furthermore, we have already declared how far the promises reach. There is no man which moveth any question concerning this, whether God be not able if he will to make men perfect; but they dote foolish which separate his power from his counsel, whereof they have an evident and plain testimony in the Scripture. God doth plainly declare a hundred times what he will, and what he hath determined to do: to go any farther is sacrilege.

Jerome was enforced by reason of philosophy to hurl out the thunderbolt of his curse against Peter and Paul;[2] be-

---

[1] "Premebant," pressed [2] "Ut sui anathematis fulmen Petro et Paulo infligeret," to thunder out an anathema against Peter and Paul

cause the laws must be applied unto their hability for whom they be appointed; which, as I confess to take place in man's laws, so I utterly deny that it is good as touching the law of God, which, in exacting righteousness, doth not respect what man is able to do, but what he ought to do.

Though here ariseth a harder question, "Whether the law were not given to this end, that it might enforce men to obey God? And this should be in vain, unless the Spirit of God should direct the faithful to keep it; and that the solemn protestation of Moses seemeth to put the matter out of doubt, when he saith that he giveth precepts to the Jews, not such as they may read, but indeed fulfil, (Deut. xxx. 12;) whence we gather that the yoke was laid upon the neck of the Jews when the law was given, that it might make them subject to God, that they might not live as them lusted." I answer, that the law is counted a yoke two ways. For, inasmuch as it bridleth the lusts of the flesh, and delivereth a rule of godly and holy life, it is meet that the children of God take this yoke upon them; but, inasmuch as it doth exactly prescribe what we owe to God, and doth not promise life without adding the condition of perfect obedience, and doth again denounce a curse if we shall in any point offend, it is a yoke which no man is able to bear. I will show this more plainly.

The plain doctrine of good life, wherein God doth invite us unto himself, is a yoke which we must all of us willingly take up; for there is nothing more absurd than that God should not govern man's life, but that he should wander at pleasure without any bridle. Therefore, we must not refuse the yoke of the law, if the simple doctrine thereof be considered. But these sayings do otherwise qualify (that I may so term it) the law. "He which shall do these things shall live in them," &c., (Levit. xviii. 5.) Again, "Cursed is he which continueth not in all things which are written," (Deut. xxvii. 26,) that it may begin to be a yoke which no man can bear.

For, so long as salvation is promised to the perfect keeping of the law alone, and every transgression is called into judgment, mankind is utterly undone. In this respect doth Peter affirm that God is tempted, when man's arrogance doth burden the consciences of men with the law; for it is not his purpose to deny but that men must be governed by the doctrine of the law, and so he granteth that they be under the law[1] not simply[2] to teach, but also to humble men with the guilt of eternal death. Considering that that quality was annexed unto doctrine, he affirmeth that the souls of the godly must not be tied with the yoke of the law, because by this means it should of necessity come to pass that they should be drowned in eternal destruction. But, when as not only the grace of the Holy Spirit is present to govern us, but also free forgiveness of sins to deliver and acquit us from the curse of the law; then is that of Moses fulfilled, that the commandment is not above us, (Deut. xxx. 11;) and then do we also perceive how sweet the yoke of Christ is, and how light his burden is, (Matth. xi. 30.) For, because we know that through the mercy of God that is forgiven us, which is wanting through the infirmity of the flesh, we do cheerfully, and without any grief,[3] take upon us that which he enjoineth us. Wherefore, so that the rigour of the law be taken away, the doctrine of the law shall not only be tolerable, but also joyful and pleasant; neither must we refuse the bridle which doth govern us mildly, and doth not urge us sorer than is expedient.

11. *By the grace of Jesus Christ.* Peter compareth these two together as contrary the one to the other; to have hope[4] in the grace of Christ, and to be under the yoke of the law; which comparison doth greatly set out the justification of Christ, inasmuch as we gather thereby, that those are justified by faith who, being free and quit from the yoke of the law, seek for salvation in the grace of Jesus

---

[1] " Jugo," yoke.   [2] " Verum quia legis officium est " but because it is the office of the law, omitted.   [3] " Sine molestia," without trouble, repugnance.   [4] " Spem salutis," hope of salvation

Christ. Furthermore, I said before that the yoke of the law is made of two cords. The former is, " He which doth these things shall live in them;" the other is, " Cursed is every one which doth not continue in all the commandments." Let us return unto the contrary member. If we cannot otherwise attain unto salvation by the grace of Christ, unless the yoke of the law be taken away, it followeth that salvation is not placed in keeping the law, neither are those which believe in Christ subject to the curse of the law; for if he could be saved through grace, who is as yet enwrapped in the yoke of the law, then should Peter's reasoning be but foolish, which is drawn from contraries: thus, We hope for salvation by the grace of Christ; therefore we are not under the yoke of the law. Unless there were a disagreement between the grace of Christ and the yoke of the law, Peter should deceive us.[1]

Wherefore, those must needs depart from the righteousness of the law, whosoever desire to find life in Christ; for this contrariety appertaineth not unto doctrine, but unto the cause of justification.

Whereby is also refuted their surmise,[2] who say that we are justified by the grace of Christ, because he regenerateth us by his Spirit, and giveth us strength to fulfil the law. Those who imagine this, though they seem to ease the yoke of the law a little, yet they keep souls bound with the cords thereof. For this promise shall always stand in force, He which shall do these things shall live in them; on the other side, The curse shall come upon all which shall not absolutely fulfil the law. Wherefore, we must define the grace of Christ far otherwise (whereunto the hope of salvation leaneth) than they dream; to wit, that it be free reconciliation gotten by the sacrifice of his death; or, which is all one, free forgiveness of sins, which, by pacifying and appeasing God, doth make him of an enemy or severe judge,[3] and which cannot be pleased nor entreated, a merciful

---

[1] " Fucum faceret," should make a gloss
[2] " Commentum," fiction.
[3] " Vel severo et implacabili judice," or a severe and implacable judge.

Father. I confess, indeed, that we be regenerate into newness of life by the grace of Christ; but when we are about assurance of salvation, then must we call to mind the free adoption alone, which is joined with the purging [expiation] and forgiveness of sins. For, if works be admitted, that they may make us righteous in part only, the yoke of the law shall not be broken, and so Peter's contrariety [antithesis] shall fall to the ground, or else be dissolved.

Even as they. Peter doth testify in this place, that though the servitude of the law were laid upon the fathers as touching the external show, yet were their consciences free and quit; whereby is put away that absurdity, which might otherwise have troubled godly minds not a little. For, seeing that the covenant of life is eternal, and the same which God made with his servants from the beginning until the end of the world, it were an absurd thing, and intolerable, that any other way to obtain salvation should be taught at this day than that which the fathers had in times past. Therefore, Peter affirmeth that we agree very well with the fathers, because they no less than we reposed hope of salvation in the grace of Christ; and so, reconciling the law and the gospel together, as touching the end of the doctrine, he taketh from the Jews the stumbling-block which they feigned to themselves by reason of the discord.

Whereby it appeareth that the law was not given to the fathers that they might thereby purchase salvation, neither were the ceremonies added, that, by the observing thereof, they might attain unto righteousness; but this was the only end of all the whole law, that, casting from them all confidence which they might repose in works, they might repose all their hope in the grace of Christ. Whereby is also refuted the doting of those who think that the old people, inasmuch as they were content with earthly goods, did think no whit of the heavenly life. But Peter maketh the fathers partners with us of the same faith; and doth make salvation common to both; and yet there be some which delight in that brain-sick fellow, Servetus, with his so filthy sacrileges. Furthermore, we must note that Peter teacheth that the faith of the fathers [ancients] was always grounded in Christ, seeing that they could neither find life anywhere else, neither was there any other way for men to come unto God. Therefore, this place agreeth with that saying of the apostle, " Christ yesterday, and to-day, and for ever," (Heb. xiii. 8.)

12. *And all the multitude kept silence, and heard Barnabas and Paul declare what signs and wonders God had wrought by them among the Gentiles.*
13. *And after they had done speaking, James answered, saying, Men and brethren, hear me :*
14. *Simeon hath showed how at the first God hath visited, that he might take of the Gentiles a people in his name.*
15. *And hereunto agree the words of the prophets, as it is written,*
16. *After these things I will return, and will build again the tabernacle of David, which is decayed ; and I will restore the ruins thereof, and will set it up ;*
17. *That the men which remain may seek the Lord, and all nations which call upon my name, saith the Lord, which doth all these things.*
18. *Known from the beginning [to God] are all his works.*

12. *All the multitude held their peace.* By these words, Luke giveth us to understand that the Spirit of God did so reign in that assembly, that they yielded forthwith to reason. The disputation was hot before; but now, after that Peter hath laid open the counsel of God, and hath handled the question according to the doctrine of the Scripture, by and by all noise being stayed, they are quiet and whist who did of late unadvisedly defend the error. This is a lively image of a lawful Council, when the truth of God alone, so soon as it is once come to light, maketh an end of all controversies ; and assuredly it is effectual enough to appease all discord when the Spirit beareth the chief sway ; because he is again

a fit governor, as well to moderate their tongues who must speak before others, as to keep the rest under obedience, that they be not too much addicted to themselves and wedded to their own wills, but that, laying away stubbornness, they may show themselves obedient to God. Neither is it to be doubted but that there was some few which would not yield, as it falleth out in a great assembly; yet the truth of God had the upper hand, so that the silence whereof Luke speaketh was a manifest testimony of common obedience. And this was no small moderation in Peter, in that having suffered every one to say for himself what he could, he deferred his judgment (lest it should be prejudicial to others) so long, until the question had been thoroughly discussed to and fro.

They heard Barnabas and Paul. We may gather by these words that they were not heard with silence before. For seeing that the more part was persuaded that they did wickedly admit the profane Gentiles into the Church, there should nothing which they should have said have been patiently received until this false opinion were corrected and reformed; but all should have been taken at the worst. We see what a poison displeasure conceived for no cause is, which doth so possess men's minds, that it stoppeth the way, so that the truth can never have entrance. Hereby we learn how true that saying is, All things are sound to the sound, (Tit. i. 15,) for there is nothing so wholesome but corrupt affection do turn the same into that which is hurtful. And to this end tendeth the narration made by Paul and Barnabas, that they may show and prove that God doth allow their apostleship among the Gentiles; forasmuch as it was ratified and confirmed by miracles, which are, as it were, certain seals thereof.

13. *James answered, saying.* Some old writers of the Church think that this James was one of the disciples, whose surname was Justus and Oblia, whose cruel death is recorded by Josephus in the Twentieth Book of his Antiquities. But would to God the old writers had travailled rather

to know the man, than to set forth, with feigned praises, the holiness of a man whom they knew not. It is a childish toy and surmise, in that they say that it was lawful for him alone to enter into the most holy place. For if in that entering in there had been any religion, he had done it contrary to the law of God, forasmuch as he was not the highest priest. Secondly, it was a superstitious thing thus to foster the shadowish worship of the Temple. I omit other trifles. And they are greatly deceived in that they deny that he was one of the twelve apostles. For they are enforced to confess that it is he whom Paul commendeth so honourably, that he maketh him the chief among the three pillars of the Church, (Gal. ii. 9.) Assuredly, a man inferior in order and degree could never have excelled the apostles so far; for Paul giveth him the title of an apostle. Neither is that worth the hearing which Jerome bringeth, [viz.] that the word is general there, seeing that the dignity of the order is there handled; forasmuch as Christ did prefer the apostles before other teachers of the Church.

Moreover, we may gather out of this place, that they made no small account of James, (Acts xxi. 18;) forasmuch as he doth with his voice and consent so confirm the words of Peter, that they are all of his mind. And we shall see afterwards how great his authority was at Jerusalem. The old writers think that this was because he was bishop of the place; but it is not to be thought that the faithful did at their pleasure change the order which Christ had appointed. Wherefore, I do not doubt but that he was son to Alpheus, and Christ's cousin, in which sense he is also called his brother. Whether he were bishop of Jerusalem or no, I leave it indifferent; neither doth it greatly make for the matter, save only because the impudency of the Pope is hereby refuted, because the decree of the Council is set down rather at the appointment, and according to the authority of James than of Peter. And assuredly Eusebius, in the beginning of his Second Book, is not afraid to call James, whosoever he were, the Bishop of the Apostles. Let the men of Rome go now and boast that their Pope is head of the Universal

Church, because he is Peter's successor, who suffered another to rule him,[1] if we believe Eusebius.

Men and brethren, hear me. James' oration consisteth upon [of] two principal members; for, first, he confirmeth and proveth the calling of the Gentiles by the testimony of the prophet Amos; secondly, he showeth what is best to be done to nourish peace and concord among the faithful; yet so that the liberty of the Gentiles may continue safe and sound, and that the grace of Christ may not be darkened. Whereas Peter is in this place called Simeon, it may be that this name was diversly pronounced then. Whereas he saith that God did visit to take a people of the Gentiles, it is referred unto the mercy of God, whereby he vouchsafed to receive strangers into his family. It is, indeed, a harsh phrase, yet such as containeth a profitable doctrine; because he maketh God the author of the calling of the Gentiles, and pronounceth that it is through his goodness that they began to be reckoned among his people, when he saith that they were taken by him; but he proceedeth further, when he saith that he did visit that he might take. For this is his meaning, That at such time as the Gentiles were turned away from God he did mercifully look upon them; because we can do nothing but depart farther and farther from him, until such time as his fatherly look prevent us of his own accord.

In his name. The old interpreter hath, To his name, which is almost all one, though the preposition επι may be otherwise translated, to wit, For his name, or Upon his name.[2] Neither shall the sense disagree, that the salvation of the Gentiles is grounded in the power or name of God, and that God did respect no other thing in calling them but his own glory; yet did I retain that which is more usual; to wit, that, in numbering them among his people, he would have them counted in his name, like as it shall be said shortly after, that his name is called upon by all those whom he gathereth together into his Church. The adverb of time,

---

[1] "Sibi præesse," to take precedence of him

[2] "Propter," on account of

πρῶτον, may be expounded two ways; if you read it, first, as the old interpreter and Erasmus have it, the sense shall be, that Cornelius and others were, as it were, the first fruits at whom God began the calling of the Gentiles; but it may be taken also comparatively, because there was already some token of the adoption of the Gentiles showed in Cornelius and his cousins, before that Barnabas and Paul preached the gospel to the Gentiles. And I do better like this latter sense.

15. *Hereto agree the words of the prophets.* We see now how the apostles took nothing to themselves imperiously, but did reverently follow that which was prescribed in the word of God. Neither did it grieve them, neither did they count it any disgrace to them to profess themselves to be the scholars of the Scripture. Also we must here note, that the use of the doctrine of the prophets is yet in force, which some brain-sick men would banish out of the Church. By citing the prophets, in the plural number, to be witnesses, whereas he doth allege one place only, he signifieth that there is such an agreement among them, that that which is spoken by one is the common testimony of them all, because they speak all with one mouth, and every one speaketh as in the person of all, or rather the Spirit of God speaketh in them all. Moreover, the oracles of all the prophets were gathered together, that they might make one body. Wherefore that might worthily and fitly be ascribed to all the prophets in general, which was taken out of some one part of the general book.

16. *After these things I will return.* Because the place is not cited word for word as it is in the prophet, we must see what difference there is, though it be not necessary to examine straitly what diversity there is in the words, so it appear that the prophecy doth fitly agree with the matter which is in hand. After that God hath promised the restoring of the tabernacle of David, he saith also, that he will bring to pass that the Jews shall possess the remnants

of Edom. In all that text, there appeareth nothing as yet
whence the calling of the Gentiles can be fet[1] or gathered;
but that which followeth immediately after in the prophet,
concerning the remnant of the Gentiles which shall call upon the name of the Lord, doth plainly show that the Jews
and Gentiles shall make one Church, because that which
was then proper to the Jews alone is given to both in general. For God placeth the Gentiles in like degree of honour
with the Jews, when he will have them to call upon his
name. Those of Idumea, and the people thereabout, were
in times past under David subject to the Jews; but though
they were tributaries to the people of God, yet were they
nevertheless strangers from the Church. Therefore, this was
news and a strange thing, in that God reckoneth them up
with the holy people, that he may be called[2] the God of them
all; seeing that it is certain that they are all made equal in
honour among themselves by this means. Whereby it doth
plainly appear how well the testimony of the prophet agreeth
with the present purpose. For God promiseth to restore
the decayed tabernacle, wherein the Gentiles shall obey the
kingdom of David, not only that they may pay tribute, or
take [to arms] weapon at the king's commandment, but that
they may have one God, and that they may be one family to
him.

Yet there may a question be moved, why he had rather
cite this prophecy, than many other which contain more
plentiful proof of the matter which he hath in hand, of
which sort Paul citeth many? (Rom. xv. 9, 10, 11.) I answer, first, that the apostles were not ambitious in heaping
up places of Scripture; but they did simply aim at this,
which was sufficient for them, to wit, that they might prove
that their doctrine was taken out of the word of God; secondly, I say that this prophecy of Amos is more plain than
it is commonly taken to be. The prophet intreateth of the
restoring of an house which was decayed;[3] he describeth
the miserable ruin thereof. Therefore, the promise, which

---

[1] " Elici," inferred.   [2] " Pariter," in like manner.   [3] " Collapsa
erat," had fallen down.

is added immediately, that the seat and throne shall be set up again, from of which kings of the posterity of David shall rule over the Gentiles, doth properly appertain unto Christ. Therefore, so soon as the kingdom of Christ is set up, that must needs follow which the prophet saith also, that the Gentiles shall call upon the name of God. Now, we see that James did not unadvisedly make choice of this place; for if the kingdom of Christ cannot be otherwise established, unless God be called upon everywhere throughout the whole world, and the Gentiles grow together to be one with his holy people, it is an absurd thing that they should be driven from hope of salvation, and the middle wall must fall to the ground, wherewith the one was separate from the other under the law,[1] (Eph. ii. 14.) The first word, *I will return*, is not in the prophet, but the change of the state which he denounceth is very well expressed by this means.

The tabernacle of David, which was decayed. It is not without cause that that evil-favoured wasteness and ruin of the king's house is set before our eyes by the prophet; for unless the godly should have been persuaded that Christ should notwithstanding come, though the kingdom of David were brought to nought, who should not only restore to their old order things which were decayed, but should exalt even unto the heavens the glory of his kingdom with incomparable success, they should have despaired a hundred times in a day. After they were returned from the exile wherein they lived at Babylon, they were brought by continual destructions almost unto utter destruction. Afterward that which remained was consumed by little and little with civil[2] discord, yea, when God did relieve their miseries, that kind of help which they had was a certain matter of despair;[3] for that rule which the Maccabees took upon them was

---

[1] " Hunc enim finem inter alios habebant ceremoniæ, ut sanctum Dei populum a profanis Gentilus discernerent, nunc sublato discrimine, ceremonias quoque abrogari convenit," for ceremonies had this, among other ends, that they might distinguish the holy people of God from the profane Gentiles; the distinction being now removed, ceremonies must also be abolished The whole of this passage is omitted in the translation   [2] " Intestinis," intestine.
[3] " Quædam erat desperationis materia," was a kind of material for despair.

then taken away from the tribe of Juda. For these causes the Spirit of God doth diligently beat in [inculcate] this by the prophet, that Christ shall not come until the kingdom of David shall perish, that they may not despair of salvation even amidst greatest miseries. So Isaiah saith, that there shall a branch arise out of the contemptible and base stock,[1] (Isaiah xi. 1;) and let us also remember, that God doth observe this wonderful way in restoring the Church, that he doth build it up[2] when it is decayed.

Furthermore, this place teacheth when the Church is best ordered, and what is the true and right constitution thereof, to wit, when the throne of David is set up, and Christ alone hath the pre-eminence, that all may meet together in his obedience.[3]

Though the Pope have oppressed the Church with his sacrilegious tyranny, yet doth he make boast of the title of the Church; yea, he deceiveth men under the vain title of the Church, that he may put out the clear light of sound doctrine. But if we shall come thoroughly to examine the matter, we may easily refute such a gross mock, because he alone beareth rule, having deposed Christ. He doth in word confess that he is Christ's vicar; but in very deed after that he hath by a beautiful banishment[4] sent Christ into the heavens, he taketh to himself all his power; for Christ reigneth by the doctrine of his gospel alone, which is wickedly trodden under foot by this abominable idol. But let us remember that this shall be the lawful estate of the Church among us, if we do all in general[5] obey Christ, the King of kings, that there may be one sheepfold and one Shepherd, (John x. 16.)

17. *That those which remain may seek.* James added this word *seek* by way of exposition, which is not found nor read in the prophet; and yet it is not superfluous, because,

---

[1] " Ex contempto et ignobili trunco," from an ignoble and despised trunk.
[2] " Ex ruinis," out of ruins.   [3] " In ejus obsequium conveniant," may accord in obeying him   [4] " Specioso exilio," a specious exile.
[5] " Omnes ad unum," all to a man.

to the end we may be numbered among the people of God, and that he may take us for his own, we must, on the other side, [in our turn,] be encouraged to seek him. And it is to be thought that Luke did summarily comprehend those things whereof James did dispute in his own language among the Jews; whereby it came to pass that the exposition of the matter was mixed with the words of the prophet. Instead of the *relics of the Gentiles* which Amos useth, Luke, out of the Greek translation, (which was more familiar,) putteth the *rest of the men* in the same sense, to wit, that there must go before the purging of the filthiness of the world a cutting, or paring, as it came to pass. And this doctrine must be also applied unto our time. For, because the corruption of the world is worse than that it can be wholly brought to obey Christ, he bloweth away, with divers fans of tribulations, the chaff and weeds, that he may at length gather unto himself that which shall remain.

18. *Known from the beginning.* This is a prevention,[1] to put away the hatred which might have risen upon the novelty; for the sudden change might have been suspected, and therefore did it trouble weak minds. Therefore James preventeth, showing that this was no new thing with God, though it fell out suddenly otherwise than men thought; because God saw, before the world was created, what he would do, and the calling of the Gentiles was hidden in his secret counsel. Whereupon it followeth, that it must not be esteemed according to the sense of man. Furthermore, James hath respect unto the words of the prophet, when he affirmeth that God, who should do all these things, was also the author of the prophecy. Therefore, his meaning is, that, seeing God speaketh by his prophet, he saw then, yea, from the very beginning,[2] that neither uncircumcision nor anything else should let him,

---

[1] "Prolepsis," an anticipation.   [2] "Ab ultima æternitate," from the remotest eternity.

but that he would choose the Gentiles into his family. Nevertheless, there is comprehended under this a general exhortation, that men do not take upon them to measure, with the small measure of their wit, the works of God, the reason whereof is oftentimes known to none but to himself; but rather let them cry, being astonished [1] that his ways are past finding out, and that his judgments are too deep a depth, (Romans xi. 33.)

19. *Wherefore, I think that we ought not to trouble those who of the Gentiles are turned to God:*
20. *But that we must write unto them, that they abstain from the filthiness of images, and from fornication, and from strangled, and from blood.*
21. *For Moses of old time hath those in every city which preach him, when he is read in the synagogues every Sabbath day.*

19. *That we must not trouble.* He denieth that the Gentiles must be driven from the Church through the disagreement about ceremonies, seeing they were admitted by God; yet it [he] seemeth contrary to himself, when he denieth that they ought to be troubled, and yet prescribeth certain rites. The answer is easy, which I will hereafter more at large prosecute. First, he requireth nothing at their hands but that which they were bound to do by brotherly concord; secondly, these precepts could no whit trouble or disquiet their consciences, after that they knew that they were free before God, and that false and perverse religion was taken away, which the false apostles sought to bring in. The question is now, why James doth enjoin the Gentiles these four things alone? Some say that this was fet [derived] from the ancient custom of the fathers, who did not make any covenant [2] with any people which they could enforce to obey them but upon

---

[1] " Exclament cum stupore," exclaim in amazement
[2] " Qui non soldant fœdus percutere," who were not accustomed to enter into any covenant.

this condition; but because there is no fit author of that thing brought to light, I leave it in doubt and undecided.

But here appeareth a manifest reason why they gave particular commandment concerning things offered to idols, blood, and that which was strangled. They were, indeed, of themselves things indifferent; yet such as had some special thing in them more than other rites of the law. We know how straitly the Lord commandeth to eschew those things which are contrary to the external profession of faith, and wherein there is any appearance or suspicion of idolatry. Therefore, lest there should any blot of superstition remain in the Gentiles, and lest the Jews should see anything in them which did not agree with the pure worship of God, no marvel if, to avoid offence, they be commanded to abstain from things offered to idols.

The word αλισγημα, which Luke useth, doth signify all manner of profanation; therefore I have not changed the common translation, which hath pollution or filthiness. Yet it is sometimes taken for sacrifices; which sense should not disagree with James' purpose; and, peradventure, it shall be more plain and natural so to expound it in this place; because, where Luke doth shortly after repeat the same decree, he will put ειδωλοθητα, or things sacrificed to idols.

As concerning blood and that which was strangled, not only the Jews were forbidden by the law of Moses to eat them, (Deut. xii. 23;) but this law was given to all the world after the flood, (Gen. ix. 4,) whereby it came to pass, that those which were not quite grown out of kind[1] did loathe blood. I do not speak of the Jews, but of many of the Gentiles. I confess, indeed, that even that commandment was but temporal; yet, notwithstanding, it was extended farther than unto one people. No marvel, therefore, if there might arise greater offence thereupon, which to cure seemed good to the apostles. But there ariseth a harder question concerning fornication; because James seemeth to reckon the same among things indifferent, whereof they

---

[1] "Qui non prorsus erant degeneres," who were not wholly degenerate.

must beware only in respect of offence ; but there was another cause for which he placed fornication among those things which were not of themselves unlawful. It is well known what unbridled liberty to run a-whoring did reign and rage everywhere; and this disease had got the upper hand principally among the men of the east country, as they be more given to lust. Assuredly the faith and chastity of wedlock was never less observed and kept any where than among them. Moreover, he doth not intreat indifferently, in my judgment, in this place of all manner [of] fornication or whoredom, as of adultery, and wandering, and unbridled lusts, whereby all chastity is violate and corrupt ; but I think he speaketh of concubineship, as they call it; which was so common among the Gentiles, that it was almost like to a law.

Therefore, whereas James reckoneth up a common corruption among things which are of themselves not corrupt, there is therein no inconvenience ;[1] so that we know that it was not his meaning to place those things in one order which are very far unlike among themselves. For, whereas unclean men do thereby colour and cloak their filthiness, they may easily be refuted. James, say they, coupled eating of blood with whoredom; but doth he compare them together as things that are like, at least which disagree not in any point. Yea, he doth only respect[2] the wicked and corrupt custom of men, which was fallen away from the first law and order of nature appointed by God. As concerning the judgment of God, the knowledge thereof must be fet [sought] out of the continual doctrine of the Scripture ; and it is nothing doubtful what the Scripture saith; to wit, that whoredom is accursed before God, and that the soul and body are thereby defiled, that the holy temple of God is polluted, and Christ is rent in pieces; that God doth daily punish whoremongers, and that he will once pay them home.[3] The filthiness of whoredom, which the heavenly

---

[1] " In eo nihil absurdi," in that there is an absurdity. [2] " Respicit," refers to   [3] " Et horrendum semel fieri ultorem," and that he will one day take fearful vengeance on them.

Judge doth so sore condemn, can be covered with no cloaks by the patrons of whoredom, how witty and eloquent soever they be.

21. *For Moses hath.* This place, in my judgment, hath been badly expounded, and drawn into a contrary sense. For interpreters think that James addeth this, because it were superfluous to prescribe anything to the Jews, who were well acquainted with the doctrine of the law, and to whom it was read every Sabbath-day; and they pick out this meaning, Let us be content to require these few things at the hands of the Gentiles, which are not accustomed to bear the yoke of the law; as touching the Jews they have Moses, out of whom they may learn more. Some do also gather out of this place, that circumcision, with its appurtenances, ought to be observed even at this day among the Jews. But they reason unfitly and unskilfully, though that exposition which I have set down[1] were true. But James had a far other meaning; to wit, he teacheth that it cannot be that ceremonies can be abolished so quickly, as it were, at the first dash; because the Jews had now a long time been acquainted with the doctrine of the law, and Moses had his preachers; therefore, it stood them upon to redeem concord for a short time, until such time as the liberty gotten by Christ might, by little and little, appear more plainly. This is that which is said in the common proverb, That it was meet that the old ceremonies should be buried with some honour. Those who are skilful in the Greek tongue shall know that that last member, When he is read every Sabbath-day in the synagogues, was by me changed not without cause, for avoiding of doubtfulness.[2]

22. *Then it seemed good to the apostles and elders, with the whole church, to send chosen men of them to Antioch, with Paul and Barnabas, Judas, surnamed Barsabas, and Silas, chief men among the brethren.*

[1] "Quam retuli," to which I have referred.   [2] "Nempe, vitandæ ambiguitatis causa," namely, for the purpose of avoiding ambiguity.

23. *Sending letters by their hands after this form : The apostles, and elders, and brethren, to those brethren which are at Antioch, and in Syria and Cilicia, which are of the Gentiles, greeting :*
24. *Because we have heard that certain which went out from us have troubled you with words, subverting your souls, commanding you to be circumcised, and to keep the law, to whom we gave no commandment ;*
25. *It seemed good to us, being gathered together with one mind, to send chosen men to you, with our beloved Barnabas and Paul ;*
26. *Men which have ventured their souls for the name of our Lord Jesus Christ.*
27. *Therefore we have sent Judas and Silas, who shall also tell you the same things by word of mouth.*
28. *For it seemed good to the Holy Ghost and us, to lay no greater burthen upon you than these necessary things,*
29. *That ye abstain from those things which are sacrificed to images, and from blood, and from that which is strangled, and from fornication ; from which things, if you shall keep yourselves, ye shall do well. Fare ye well.*

22. *It pleased the apostles.* That tempest was made calm not without the singular grace of God, so that after the matter was thoroughly discussed, they did all agree together in sound doctrine. Also the modesty of the common people is gathered by this, because, after that they had referred the matter to the judgment of the apostles and the rest of teachers, they do now also subscribe to their decree ; and, on the other side, the apostles did show some token of their equity, in that they set down nothing concerning the common cause of all the godly without admitting the people. For assuredly, this tyranny did spring from the pride of the pastors, that those things which appertain unto the common state of the whole Church are subject (the people being excluded) to the will, I will not say lust, of a few.[1] We know what a hard mat-

[1] " Prudenter vero Apostoli et Presbyteri Judam et Silam mittendos censuerunt, quo res minus suspecta esset," but the apostles prudently deemed it

ter it is to suppress the slanders of the wicked, to satisfy most men who are churlish and forward, to keep under the light and unskilful, to wipe away errors conceived, to heal up hatred, to appease contentions, [and] to abolish false reports. Peradventure, the enemies of Paul and Barnabas might have said that they had gotten letters by fair and flattering speeches; they might have invented some new cavil; the rude and weak might, by and by, have been troubled; but when chief men come with the letters, that they may gravely dispute the whole matter in presence, all sinister suspicion is taken away.

24. *Certain which went out from us.* We see that there was no respect of persons among these holy men, which doth always corrupt sound and right judgments. They confess that there were knaves of their own company; and yet they do no whit flatter them, or, through corrupt favour, incline to cover their error; yea, rather in condemning them freely, they spare not even themselves. And, first, they pluck from their faces that visure [mask] which they had abused, to deceive withal. They boasted that they were privy to the meaning of the apostles.[1] The apostles reprove them, and condemn them of and for lying in that false pretence, when they utterly deny that they did command any such thing. Again, they accuse them far more sharply, that they troubled the Church and subverted souls. For by this means they bring them in contempt and detestation with the godly, because they cannot be admitted but to their destruction. But false teachers are said to subvert souls, because the truth of God doth edify or build them up, and so this speech containeth a [this] general doctrine, Unless we will willingly have our souls drawn headlong from being any longer temples of the Holy Ghost, and unless we desire their ruin, we must beware of those which

proper to send Judas and Silas, that there might be less ground for suspicion, omitted.

[1] " Se apostolorum mentem tenere," that they knew the mind of the apostles.

go about to lead us away from the pure gospel. That which they say touching the keeping of the law doth only appertain unto ceremonies, though we must always remember, that they did so intreat of ceremonies; that [as if] both the salvation and also the righteousness of men did therein consist. For the false apostles did command that they should be kept, as if righteousness came by the law, and salvation did depend upon works.

25. *With our beloved Barnabas and Paul.* They set these praises against the slanders wherewith the false apostles had essayed to bring Paul and Barnabas out of credit.[1] And, first, to the end they may remove the opinion of disagreement which had possessed the minds of many, they testify their consent; secondly, they commend Paul and Barnabas for their ferventness in zeal and most manlike courage, that they were not afraid to venture or lay down their souls for Christ's sake. And this is an excellent virtue in a minister of the gospel, and which deserveth no small praise, if he shall not only be stout and courageous to execute the office of teaching, but also be ready to enter danger which is offered in defence of his doctrine. As the Lord doth thus try the faith and constancy of those which be his, so he doth, as it were, make them noble with the ensigns of virtue, that they may excel in his Church. Therefore, Paul holdeth forth the marks of Christ which he did bear in his body, (Gal. vi. 17,) as a buckler to drive back those knaves which did trouble his doctrine. And though it do not so fall out with most stout and courageous teachers and preachers of the gospel, that they strive for the gospel until they come in danger of life, because the matter doth not so require, yet is this no let but that Christ may purchase authority for his martyrs, so often as he bringeth them into worthy and renowned conflicts.

Nevertheless, let even those who are not enforced to enter combat by any necessity be ready to shed their blood,

---

[1] " Paulo et Barnabas aspergeri," to asperse Paul and Barnabas

if God see it good at any time that it should be so. But the apostles commend the fortitude of Paul and Barnabas only in a good cause; because, if it were sufficient to enter dangers manfully, the martyrs of Christ should nothing differ from troublesome and frenzied men, from cutters and roysters.[1] Therefore, Paul and Barnabas are commended, not because they laid open themselves simply to dangers, but because they refuse not to die for Christ's sake. Peradventure, also, the apostles meant to nip[2] those knaves by the way, who, having never suffered any thing for Christ's sake, came out of their roust and dainties[3] to trouble the churches, which cost the courageous soldiers of Christ dearly.

28. *It seemed good to the Holy Ghost and to us.* Whereas the apostles and elders match and join themselves with the Holy Ghost, they attribute nothing to themselves apart therein; but this speech importeth as much as if they should say, that the Holy Ghost was the captain, guide, and governor, and that they did set down, and decreed that which they write as he did indite it to them.[4] For this manner of speech is used commonly in the Scripture, to give the ministers the second place after that the name of God is once expressed. When it is said that the people believed God and his servant Moses, (Exod. xiv. 31,) faith is not rent in pieces, as if it did addict itself partly to God, and partly to mortal man. What then? to wit, whereas the people had God for the sole author of their faith, they believed or gave credence to his minister, from whom he could not be separate. Neither could they otherwise believe God than by believing the doctrine set before them by Moses, as they did shake off the yoke of God after that they had once rejected and despised Moses. Whereby the wicked-

---

[1] " Nihil a tumultuosis et phreneticis, nihil a gladiatoribus differrent," should differ in no respect from tumultuous and frenzied men, or from gladiators   [2] " Oblique perstringere," indirectly to lash   [3] " Ex sua umbra et deliciis prodierant," had come forth from their luxurious retirement   [4] " Seque eo dictante statuisse quod scribunt," and that which they write was resolved on his dictation.

ness of those men is also refuted, who, making boast of faith with full mouth, do no less wickedly than proudly contemn the ministry. For, as it were a sacrilegious partition, if faith should depend even but a very little upon man, so those men do openly mock God who feign that they have him to be their teacher, when they set nought by the ministers by whom he speaketh. Therefore, the apostles deny that they invented that decree of their own brain which they deliver to the Gentiles, but that they were only ministers of the Spirit, that they may, with the authority of God, make them commendable, which (proceeding from him) they do faithfully deliver. So, when Paul maketh mention of his gospel, he doth not enforce upon them a new gospel, which is of his own inventing, but he preacheth that which was committed to him by Christ.

And the Papists are doltish who go about, out of these words, to prove that the Church hath some authority of her own; yea, they are contrary to themselves. For, under what colour do they avouch that the Church cannot err, save only because it is grounded immediately by the Holy Spirit? Therefore, they cry out with open mouth, that those things be the oracles of the Spirit which we prove to be their own inventions. Therefore, they do foolishly urge this cause, *it seemed good to us;* because, if the apostles decreed any thing apart from the Spirit, that principal maxim shall fall to ground, that Councils decree nothing but which is indited by the Spirit.

Besides these necessary things. The Papists do forwardly triumph under colour of this word, as if it were lawful for men to make laws which may lay necessity upon the conscience. That (say they) which the Church commandeth must be kept under pain of mortal sin, because the apostles say that that must necessarily be observed which they decree. But such a vain cavil is quickly answered. For this necessity reached no farther than there was any danger lest the unity should be cut asunder. So that, to speak properly, this necessity was accidental or external; which was placed not in the thing itself, but only in avoiding of the offence, which appeareth more plainly by abolishing of the decree. For laws made concerning things which are of themselves necessary must be continual. But we know that this law was foredone[1] by Paul so soon as the tumult and contention was once ended, when he teacheth that nothing is unclean, (Rom. xiv. 14;) and when he granteth liberty to eat all manner [of] meats, yea, even such as were sacrificed to idols, (1 Cor. x. 25.) Wherefore, in vain do they gather any cloak or colour out of this word to bind men's consciences, seeing that the necessity spoken of in this place did only respect men in the external use, lest there should any offence arise thereupon, and that their liberty before God might stand whole and sound. Also, in vain do they gather out of all the whole place, and in vain do they go about out of the same to prove that the Church had power given to decree anything contrary to the word of God. The Pope hath made such laws as seemed best to him, contrary to the word of God, whereby he meant to govern the Church; and that not ten or twenty, but an infinite number, so that they do not only tyrannously oppress souls, but are also cruel torments to vex and torment them.

To the end the hired brabblers [wranglers] of the Pope may excuse such cruelty, they do object that even the apostles did forbid the Gentiles that which was not forbidden in the word of God. But I say flatly, that the apostles added nothing unto the word of God; which shall plainly appear if we list to mark their drift. I said of late that they meant nothing less[2] than to set down a perpetual law, whereby they might bind the faithful. What then? They use that remedy which was fit for the nourishing of brotherly peace and concord among the Churches, that the Gentiles may for a time apply themselves[3] to the Jews. But if we will grant anything, we must assuredly confess that this is according to the word of God, that love bear the sway in things in-

---

[1] "Refixam," remodelled. that the last thing they meant was to accommodate themselves.

[2] "Nihil minus in animo illis fuisse,"

[3] "Se . . . accommodent,"

different; that is, that the external use of those things which are of themselves free be bent unto the rule of charity.

In sum, if love be the bond of perfection and end of the law; if God command that we study to preserve mutual unity among ourselves, and that every man serve his neighbour to edify, no man is so ignorant which doth not see that that is contained in the word of God which the apostles command in this place, only they apply a general rule to their time. Furthermore, let us remember that which I said before, that it was a politic law which could not ensnare the conscience, neither bring in any feigned worship of God; which two vices the Scripture condemneth everywhere in men's traditions. But admit we should grant (which is most false) that that did not accord with the word of God which was decreed in that council, yet that maketh nothing for the Papists. Let the councils decree anything contrary to [beyond, in addition to] the express word of God, according to the revelation of the Spirit; yet none but lawful councils may have this authority given them. Then let them prove that their councils were godly and holy, to the decrees whereof they will have us subject. But I will not any farther prosecute this point, because it was handled in the beginning of the chapter. Let the readers know (which is sufficient for this present place) that the apostles pass not the bounds of the word of God when they set down an external law, as time requireth, whereby they may reconcile the Churches among themselves.

30. *Therefore, when they were let go, they came to Antioch: and when they had assembled the multitude together, they delivered the epistle:*
31. *Which, when they had read, they rejoiced over the consolation.*
32. *And Judas and Silas, seeing they were also prophets, did with many words exhort* [or they did comfort] *the brethren, and strengthened them.*
33. *And they tarried there for a time, and then they were let go by the brethren in peace unto the apostles.*

34. *But it seemed good to Silas to stay there.*
35. *And Paul and Barnabas stayed at Antioch, teaching and preaching with many more the word of the Lord.*

30. *When the multitude was gathered.* This was the most lawful kind of dealing to admit the whole multitude unto the reading of the epistle. For if there fall out any controversy in the doctrine of faith, it is meet that the judgment be referred over unto the learned and godly, and to such as are exercised in the Scripture; and, chiefly, to the pastors rightly ordained. Notwithstanding, because it belongeth to all alike to know for a surety what they must hold, the godly and learned teachers must make known[1] to the whole Church what they have set down out of the word of God. For there is nothing more unfitting for holy and Christian order than to drive away the body of the people from common doctrine, as if it were a herd of swine, as they use to do under the tyranny of Popery. For because the Pope and the horned bishops did think that the people would never be obedient enough until they were brought into gross ignorance, they imagined that this was the best summary of faith, to know nothing, but to depend wholly upon their decrees. But, on the contrary, there must be a mean observed, that lawful governments may continue;[2] and that, on the other side, the people may have that liberty which unto them belongeth, lest they be oppressed like slaves.

31. *They rejoiced over the consolation.* Seeing that the epistle is so short, and containeth nothing but a bare narration, what consolation could they have by it? But we must note, that there was no small matter of consolation therein, because, when they knew the consent of the apostles, they were all pacified, and also whereas before there was variance among them, they are now reconciled one to another. Seeing there went a false report about, that all the apostles were against Paul and Barnabas, this same had

[1] " Fraterne communicare," must fraternally communicate.   [2] " Salvæ maneant," may continue safe.

shaken some who were too light of belief, many did stand in doubt; the wicked abused this occasion to speak evil; others some were pricked forward[1] with love of novelty and with curiosity, and one was set against another. But now, after that they see that the judgment of the first Church doth agree with the doctrine of Paul and Barnabas, they obtain that for which the children of God ought most to wish, that being established in the right faith, and being of one mind among themselves, they may with quiet minds have peace one with another.

32. *Judas and Silas.* These two brethren were sent for this cause, that they might also testify the same thing by word which was contained in the letters, and more also; otherwise the apostles would not have sent such short letters concerning so great and weighty a matter; and they would have also spoken somewhat touching the mysteries of faith, and would have made some long exhortation, wherein they would have persuaded them unto the study of godliness. Now, Luke showeth some farther things by them done; to wit, that being furnished with the gift of prophecy, they edify the Church in general, as if he should say, they did not only do their duty faithfully in the cause which was now in hand, but they did also take good and profitable pains in teaching and exhorting the Church And we must note that he saith that they exhorted the Church, because they were prophets; for it is not a thing common to all men to enter such an excellent function. Therefore, we must beware, lest any man pass[2] his bounds; as Paul teacheth, 1 Cor. vii. 20; and Ephesians iv. 1, that every one keep himself within the measure of grace received. Wherefore, it is not in vain that Luke saith that the office of teaching is peculiar; lest any man, through ambition, being void of ability, or through rash zeal, or through any other foolish desire, coveting to put out his head, trouble the order of the Church.

[1] "Titillibat," tickled with.
[2] "Temere transiliat," rashly overleap

They were prophets. Whereas the word hath divers significations, it is not taken in this place for those prophets to whom it was granted to foretel things to come; because this title should come in out of season[1] when he intreateth of another matter; but Luke's meaning is, that Judas and Silas were endued with excellent knowledge and understanding of the mysteries of God, that they might be good interpreters of God; as Paul, in the fourteenth of the First to the Corinthians, (1 Cor. xiv. 3,) when he intreateth of the prophecy, and preferreth it before all other gifts, speaketh not of foretelling of things to come; but he commendeth it for this fruit, because it doth edify the Church by doctrine, exhortation, and consolation. After this manner doth Luke assign exhortation to the prophets, as being the principal point of their office.

33. *They were let go in peace.* That is, when they departed, the brethren, in taking their leave of them, did wish them well, as friends use to do. And there is *synecdoche* in this member; because the one of the two did only return to Jerusalem. And in the text there is a correction added immediately, that it seemed good to Silas to tarry there; but when Luke joineth them both together, his meaning is only to declare that the Church was quiet before they thought upon any returning. At length he addeth that Paul and Barnabas, so long as they were at Antioch, gave themselves to teaching, and did continue in this work,[2] and yet did they give place to many more.[3] Whereby it appeareth, that they had all one and the same desire without grudging,[4] so that they joined hand in hand to do good; though it seemeth that he maketh mention of many more of set purpose, lest we should think that, after

---

[1] "Parum opportune interpositum esset," should have been inappropriately interposed. [2] "Intentos fuisse ad docendum, et in hoc opere assiduos," were intent on teaching, and assiduous in the work. [3] "Aliis compluribus," to several other persons. [4] "Sine æmulatione," without rivalship.

that Paul and Barnabas were departed, that Church was destitute, which did flourish in abundance of teachers. Moreover, the blessing of God, which began straightway to appear again in that Church, is now again commended and extolled, which Church Satan went about[1] by his ministers miserably to scatter and lay waste.

> 36. *And after a few days Paul said to Barnabas, Returning, let us now visit our brethren throughout all cities wherein we have preached the word of the Lord, and see how they do.*
> 37. *And Barnabas counselled to take John, whose surname was Mark.*
> 38. *But Paul besought him, that he which slid back from them in Pamphylia, and had not gone with them to the work, might not be taken to their company.*
> 39. *And the contention waxed so hot between them, that they parted company; and Barnabas having taken to him Mark, sailed to Cyprus.*
> 40. *But Paul having chosen Silas, journeyed, being committed to the grace of God by the brethren.*
> 41. *And he went through Syria and Cilicia, establishing the churches.*

36. *Let us visit our brethren.* In this history we must first note how careful Paul was for the churches which he had ordained. He laboureth, indeed, at Antioch profitably, but because he remembered that he was an apostle ordained of God, and not the pastor of one particular place, he keepeth the course of his calling. Secondly, as it did not become him to be tied to one place, so he thinketh with himself, that he was bound to all whom he begat in the Lord; therefore, he will not suffer them to want his help. Moreover, the work that was begun in those places could not be neglected; but it would shortly after decay. Yet it is to be thought that Paul stayed still in the church of Antioch, until he saw the estate thereof well ordered, and con-

---

[1] " Nuper molitus erat," had lately plotted.

cord established. For we know and try[1] what great force principal churches[2] have to keep other lesser churches in order. If there arise any tumult in an obscure street, or if there fall out any offence, the rumour goeth not so far, neither are the neighbours so much moved; but if any place be excellent, it cannot quail without great ruin, or, at least, but that the lesser buildings shall be therewith sore shaken, both far and wide. Therefore, Paul, in staying a time at Antioch, did provide for other churches; and so we must no less look unto his wisdom than his diligence in this example, because oftentimes the immoderate heat of the pastors in going about matters doth no less hurt than their sluggishness.

How they do. Paul knew that amidst so great lightness and inconstancy of men, and as their nature is inclined to vice, if there be any thing well ordered among them, it doth seldom continue stable, and for any long time; and especially that churches do easily decay or grow out of kind, unless they be looked to continually. There ought nothing under heaven to be more firm than the spiritual building of faith, whose stability is grounded in the very heaven; yet there be but few in whose minds the word of the Lord doth thoroughly take lively root; therefore, firmness is rare in men. Again, even those who have their anchor firmly fixed in the truth of God, do not cease notwithstanding to be subject to divers tossings, whereby, though their faith be not overturned, yet hath it need of strengthening, that it may be underpropped and stayed. Moreover, we see how Satan doth assault, and with what subtile shifts he goeth about privily to pull down sometimes whole churches, sometimes every one of the faithful particularly. Therefore, it is not without cause that Paul is so careful for his scholars, lest they behave themselves otherwise than is to be wished; and therefore is he desirous in time to prevent, if there be any inconvenience risen, which cannot be until he have taken view.[3]

[1] " Experimur," we know by experience
[2] " Quantum habeant momenti primariæ ecclesiæ," how great weight principal churches have.
[3] " Sine inspectione," without inspection.

37. *And Barnabas gave counsel.* Luke doth here set down that doleful disagreement which ought to make all the godly afraid for just causes. The society of Paul and Barnabas was consecrated by the heavenly oracle. They had long time laboured, being of one mind, under this yoke whereunto the Lord had tied them; they had, by many experiences, tried [felt] the excellent favour of God, yea, that wonderful success mentioned heretofore by Luke was a manifest blessing of God. Though they had been almost drowned so often in so many tempests of persecution, and were set upon so sore[1] by infinite enemies, though domestical sedition were everywhere kindled against them, yet they were so far from being pulled in sunder, that their agreement was then most of all tried, [proved.] But now, for a light matter, and which might easily have been ended, they break that holy bond of God's calling.

This could not fall out without great perturbance to all the godly. Seeing that the heat of the contention was so great and vehement in these holy men, who had long time accustomed themselves to suffer all things, what shall befal us, whose affections being not as yet so brought to obey God, do oftentimes rage[2] without modesty? Seeing that a light occasion did separate them, who had long time, amidst so great trials, retained unity holily, how easily may Satan cause those to be divided who have either none, or, at least, a cold desire to foster peace? What great pride was it for Barnabas, who had no more honourable thing than to be Paul's companion, that he might behave himself like a son towards his father, so stubbornly to refuse his counsel? Peradventure, also, some might think that Paul was not very courteous in that he did not forgive a faithful helper this fault. Therefore, we be admonished by this example, that unless the servants of Christ take great heed, there be many chinks through which Satan will creep in, to disturb that concord which is among them.

But now we must examine the cause itself, for some there

---

[1] "Subinde," ever and anon.   [2] "Subinde lasciviant," do every now and then wanton.

be who lay the blame of the disagreement upon Paul;[1] and, at the first hearing, the reasons which they bring seem probable. John Mark is rejected, because he withdrew himself from Paul's company; but he fell not away from Christ. A young man, being as yet unacquainted with bearing the cross, returned home from his journey. He was somewhat to be borne with for his age, being a fresh-water soldier [a tyro] he fainted in troubles even at the first dash; he was not, therefore, about to be a slothful soldier during his whole life. Now, forasmuch as his returning to Paul is an excellent testimony of repentance, it seemeth to be a point of discourtesy[2] to reject him; for those must be handled more courteously, who punish themselves for their own offences of their own accord. There were also other causes which ought to have made Paul more courteous. The house of John Mark was a famous inn,[3] (Acts xii. 12;) his mother had entertained the faithful in most grievous persecution; when Herod and all the people were in a rage, they were wont to have their secret meetings there, as Luke reported before. Surely he ought to have borne with such a holy and courageous woman, lest immoderate rigour should alienate her. She was desirous to have her son addicted to preach the gospel; now, what a great grief might it have been to her that his pains and industry should be refused[4] for one light fault? And now whereas John Mark doth not only bewail his fault, but in very deed amend the same, Barnabas hath a fair colour why he should pardon him.[5]

Yet we may gather out of the text, that the Church did allow Paul's counsel. For Barnabas departeth, and with his companion he saileth into Cyprus. There is no mention made of the brethren, (as if he had departed privily without taking his leave;) but the brethren commend Paul in their prayers to the grace of God; whereby appeareth that the Church stood on his side. Secondly, whereas God showeth

---

[1] "Nimio Pauli rigori," on Paul's excessive rigour [2] "Minime humanum," contrary to humanity [3] "Celebre erat Ecclesiæ hospitium," was celebrated for its hospitality to the Church. [4] "Ejus operam respui," that his assistance should be spurned away. [5] "Speciosum colorem . . cur ignoscat," a specious excuse for pardoning him.

forth the power of his Spirit in blessing Paul, and doth bless his labours with happy success of his grace, and leaveth Barnabas, as it were, buried, there may a probable reason be drawn thence, that it pleased him that such an example of severity should be showed. And surely the offence of John Mark was greater than it is commonly taken for. He slid not back, indeed, from the faith of Christ, yet did he forsake his calling, and was a revolt [apostate] from the same; therefore, it was a matter which might have given evil example, if he had been straightway received again into the calling from which he was slid back. He had given himself over to serve Christ upon this condition, that he should be free no longer. It was no more lawful for him to break his promise made in this behalf, than it is for a husband to leave his wife, or for a son to forsake his father. Neither doth infirmity excuse his unfaithfulness, whereby the holiness of the calling was violated.

And we must note, that he was not altogether rejected of Paul; he counted him as a brother, so he would be content with the common order; he refused to admit him unto the common [public] function of teaching, from whence he fell filthily through his own fault. And there is no great difference between these two, whether he which hath offended be quite excluded from pardon, or he have only public honour denied him; though it may be that they did both exceed measure, as accidents do oftentimes mar a matter which is otherwise good. It was well done of Paul, and according to the right of discipline profitably, not to admit him to be his companion, whose inconstancy he had once tried, [experienced;] but when he saw Barnabas so importunate, he might have yielded to his desire. We ought to make more account of the truth than of the favour of all the whole world; but it is convenient that we ponder wisely what great weight there is in the matter which is in hand. For if, in a matter of no weight or edification, a man vaunt of his constancy, prepare himself for the conflict, and cease not to defend that until the end, wherein he did once take delight, it shall be but foolish and perverse obstinacy. There was also some middle way and means whereby Paul might have granted somewhat to the importunateness of his fellow [colleague] in office, and yet have not revolted from the truth. It was not for him to flatter Mark, or to cloak his offence, yet was he not letted by religion, but that after he had freely professed what he thought, he might suffer himself to be overcome in that matter, which did neither indamage true doctrine, nor endanger man's salvation; which I say for this cause, that we may learn to moderate our desire, even in the best causes, lest it pass measure, and be too fervent.

CHAPTER XVI.

1. *And he came to Derbe and Lystra; and, behold, there was there a certain disciple named Timotheus, the son of a certain faithful woman, a Jewess, and his father was a Grecian.*
2. *He was well reported of by the brethren which were at Lystra and Iconium.*
3. *Paul would have him to go with him; and when he had taken him he circumcised him, because of those Jews which were in those places. For they all knew that his father was a Grecian*
4. *And as they passed through the cities, they delivered to them to be kept the decrees which were decreed by the apostles and elders which were at Jerusalem.*
5. *And so the churches were confirmed in the faith, and abounded in number daily.*

1. Luke doth now begin to declare what were the proceedings of Paul after that Barnabas and he were separate. And first he showeth, that he took to his company at Lystra Timothy to be his companion. But, to the end we may know that Paul did nothing rashly, or without good consideration, Luke saith plainly, that Timothy was such a

man as the brethren did well like of, and that they gave testimony of his godliness; for thus doth he speak word for word. And so Paul himself observeth the like choice, which he elsewhere commandeth to be made in choosing ministers, (1 Tim. iii. 7.) Neither is it to be thought, that those prophecies did even then come to light wherewith Timothy was set forth and adorned by the Spirit, as Paul doth testify elsewhere, (1 Tim. i. 18.) But there seemeth to be some disagreement in that, in that Luke saith that Timotheus was well reported of amongst the brethren; and Paul will have him to have a good report of those who are without, who is chosen to be a bishop. I answer, that we must principally look unto the judgment of the godly, as they be sole meet witnesses, and do alone rightly discern well and wisely according to the Spirit of God; and that we ought to attribute no more to the wicked than to blind men. Therefore it appeareth that godliness and holiness of life must be judged according to the will and consent of godly men; that he be counted worthy to be a bishop whom they commend. Notwithstanding, I confess that even this also is required in the second place, that the very infidels be enforced to commend him; lest the Church of God come in danger[1] of their slanders and evil speaking, if it commit [permit] itself to be governed by men of evil report.

3. *He circumcised him, because of the Jews.* Luke doth plainly express that Timothy was not circumcised, because it was necessary it should be so, or because the religion of that sign did continue as yet, but that Paul might avoid an offence. Therefore, there was respect had of men, whereas the matter was free before God. Wherefore, the circumcising of Timothy was no sacrament, as was that which was given to Abraham and his posterity, (Gen. xvii. 13;) but an indifferent ceremony which served only for nourishing of love, and not for any exercise of godliness.

---

[1] " Obnoxia sit," be subjected to.

Now, the question is, whether it were lawful for Paul to use a vain sign, whose signification and force was abolished; for it seemeth a vain thing when there is a departure made from the institution of God. But circumcision was commanded by God to continue only until the coming of Christ. To this question I answer, that circumcision did so cease at the coming of Christ, that, notwithstanding the use thereof was not quite abolished by and by; but it continued free, until all men might know that Christ was the end of the law, by the more manifest revelation of the light of the gospel.

And here we must note three degrees. The first is, that the ceremonies of the law were so abolished by the coming of Christ, that they did neither any longer appertain unto the worship of God, neither were they figures of spiritual things, neither was there any necessity to use them. The second is, that the use thereof was free, until the truth of the gospel might more plainly appear. The third, that it was not lawful for the faithful to retain them, save only so far forth as the use thereof served for edification, neither was there any superstition thereby fostered; though that free power to use them, whereof I have spoken, be not without exception, because there was a divers respect to be had of ceremonies. For circumcision was not in the same place wherein the sacrifices were, which were ordained for the purging [expiating] of sins. Wherefore it was lawful for Paul to circumcise Timotheus; it had not been lawful for him to offer a sacrifice for sin. This is, indeed, a general thing, that all the worship of the law did cease at the coming of Christ, (because it was to continue but for a time,) as touching faith and conscience; but concerning the use we must know this, that it is indifferent, and left in the liberty of the godly for a short time, so far as it was not contrary to the confession of faith. We must note the shortness of time whereof I speak, to wit, until the plain manifestation of the Gospel; because some learned men are grossly deceived in this point, who think that circumcision doth yet take place[1] among the Jews; whereas Paul teacheth, that it is superfluous when we are buried with Christ by baptism, (Colos. ii. 11, 12.) It was better and more truly said in the old proverb, That the synagogue was to be buried with honour.

Now it resteth that we declare how far forth the use of circumcision was indifferent. That shall easily appear by the manner of the liberty. Because the calling of the Gentiles was not as yet generally known, it was meet that the Jews should have some prerogative granted them. Therefore, until it might be better known that the adoption was deducted from the lineage and kindred of Abraham unto all the Gentiles, it was lawful, so far as edification did require, to retain the sign of difference. For seeing that Paul would not circumcise Titus, and doth avouch that the same was well done, (Gal. ii. 3,) it followeth that it was not lawful to use this ceremony always and without choice. Therefore they were to have respect unto edification, and unto the public commodity of the Church. Because he could not circumcise Titus, unless he would betray the doctrine[2] of the Gospel, and lay himself open to the slanders of the adversaries, he abstained from the free use of the ceremony, which he did use in Timotheus, when he saw that it was profitable for the Church. Hereby it doth easily appear what horrible confusion doth reign in Popery. There is there a huge heap of ceremonies, and to what end but that they may have instead of one veil of the old temple an hundred. God did abrogate those ceremonies which he had commanded, that the truth of the Gospel might shine more clearly. Men durst take upon them to bring in new, and that without keeping any measure. After this came in a wicked surmise, that all these serve for the worship of God. At length followed the devilish confidence of merit. Now, forasmuch as it is evident enough that such ceremonies are neither veils nor sepulchres wherewith Christ is covered,

---

[1] "Locum adhuc habere apud Judæos," is still binding on the Jews.
[2] "Puram doctrinam," the pure doctrine.

but rather stinking dunghills wherein faith[1] and religion are choked, those who make the use thereof generally free do ascribe more to the Pope than the Lord granteth to his law. It is to no end to speak of the mass and of such filthiness which contain in themselves manifest idolatry.

They all knew this. Luke telleth us that this was Paul's drift, to make an entrance for Timotheus unto the Jews, lest they should abhor him as a profane man. They knew all (saith he) that his father was a Grecian. Therefore, because the mothers had no power over their children, they were fully persuaded that he was uncircumcised. Let the readers note here by the way, how miserable the bondage of the people of God was then. Eunice, mother to Timotheus, was one of the small remnant which the very Jews themselves counted a monster, and yet, being married to a man which was an infidel, she durst not consecrate her children to God. No, she durst not so much as give them the external sign of grace, and yet she ceased not therefore to instruct her son of a child holily in the fear of God, and in his true worship—an example surely worthy to be followed of women, whom their husbands affray with their tyrannous government, from keeping and training up their children and families chastely in true godliness. Grecian is taken in this place for a Gentile, after the old and common custom of the Scripture.

4. *They delivered them the decrees to keep.* In these words Luke doth signify unto us how desirous Paul was of peace. The best and strongest bond to keep and foster peace among the churches, was to keep that which was set down by the apostles. When Paul taketh great pains about that, he taketh great heed lest through his fault there arise any trouble. And let us remember that that continued but for a time. Because, so soon as he seeth the danger of offence cease, he doth quite unburthen the churches, and setting apart the decree, he maketh that free which the apostles

---

[1] " Sincera fides," sincere faith.

had there forbidden. And yet doth he not cancel or violate by that abrogation that which the apostles had decreed, or contemn the authors themselves; because they were not determined to establish a perpetual law, but only to mitigate for a short time that which might hurt weak consciences; as I did more at large declare in the former chapter. Whereby the folly of the Papists is sufficiently refuted, who do grievously lay to our charge that we be far unlike Paul, because we will have the consciences of the godly governed by the Word of God alone, setting light by the decrees of the Church, as they call them, and not to be subject to the will of men. But, as I have already said, Paul meant nothing less than to ensnare men's consciences in the snare of necessity, for he is not contrary to himself, when he crieth in other places, that "all things are clean to the clean," (Tit. i. 15.) And again, "He which is clean eateth all things," (Rom. xiv. 2.) And again, "The kingdom of God is not meat and drink," (Rom. xiv. 17.) And again, " Meat doth not commend us to God," (1 Cor. viii. 8.) Again, "Eat all things which are sold in the shambles, asking no question for conscience sake," (1 Cor. x. 25.) But in one word he reconcileth those things which might otherwise seem to disagree, when he commanded to abstain from things sacrificed to idols, for another man's conscience sake. Nevertheless, he taketh great heed that he bind not godly souls with the laws of men.

Therefore we attempt nothing at this day which is contrary to or disagreeing with Paul. But the Papists mock us too grossly when they compare their laws with the decrees of the apostles. The apostles invented no new worship of God, they had erected no new spiritual government; but for the desire they had to maintain peace, they exhorted the Gentiles that they would yield a little to the Jews. Before the Pope can excuse his laws under this colour, he must first change them wholly. And as for us, seeing that the Papists do place the spiritual worship of God in man's inventions, and translate the right which belongeth to God alone unto men, that they may reign as lords over souls; we are enforced manfully to withstand them, unless through treacherous silence we will betray the grace gotten by the blood of Christ. Now, what likelihood can there be between three decrees set down for the help and comfort of the weak, and an infinite heap of laws, which doth not only oppress miserable souls with the weight thereof, but also swallow up faith? We know the complaint of Augustine writing to Januarius, that the Church was wickedly laden even then with too great a burden of traditions. Could he, I pray you, suffer the bondage of these times, which is almost a hundred times harder and heavier?

5. *The churches were confirmed.* By this we gather, that that which Luke setteth down, or rather toucheth concerning the decrees of the apostles, was, as it were, put in by the way, being not much appertinent unto the matter.[1] For he commendeth a far other fruit of Paul's doctrine, when he saith that the churches were confirmed in the faith. Therefore Paul did so order external things, that he was principally careful for the kingdom of God, which consisteth in the doctrine of the gospel, and doth far surpass and surmount external order. Therefore those decrees were mentioned, inasmuch as they were expedient for maintaining concord, that we might know that the holy man had a care thereof. But religion and godliness hath the former place, whose sole foundation is faith; which again doth stay itself upon the pure Word of God, and doth not depend upon men's laws. Now, by this example, Luke pricketh us forward to proceed continually, lest, at the beginning, sloth or neglect of profiting come upon us. Also the way to increase faith is expressed, to wit, when the Lord doth stir us up by the industry of his servants; as at that time he used the labour and diligence of Paul and his companions. When he addeth immediately that they were also increased in number, he commendeth another fruit of preaching, and yet he doth therewithal

[1] "Accessorium," accessory.

signify unto us, that the more those profit in faith who are first called, the more do they bring unto Christ; as if faith did creep abroad unto others by branches.[1]

> 6. *And when they had gone through Phrygia and the country of Galatia, they were forbidden of the Holy Ghost to speak the word in Asia ;*
> 7. *And going into Mysia, they essayed to go into Bithynia: and the Spirit suffered them not.*
> 8. *And when they had passed through Mysia, they came down to Troada,* [Troas.]
> 9. *And Paul saw a vision by night ; There was a certain man of Macedonia, standing and praying him, and saying, Coming into Macedonia, help us.*
> 10. *And so soon as he saw the vision, we sought straightway to go into Macedonia, being surely confirmed that the Lord had called us to preach the gospel to them.*

6. *When they had gone throughout.* Luke showeth here how diligent and careful Paul and his companions were in the office of teaching; for he saith that they journeyed through divers regions of the Lesser Asia that they might preach the gospel. But he reciteth one thing which is worth the remembering, that they were forbidden by the Spirit of God to speak of Christ in some places, which serveth not a little to set forth the apostleship of Paul; as undoubtedly he was not a little encouraged to proceed, when he knew that the Spirit of God was his guide in his way, and the governor of his actions. And whereas whithersoever they came they prepared themselves to teach, they did that according to their calling, and according to the commandment of God. For they were sent to preach and publish the gospel to the Gentiles without exception; but the Lord revealed his counsel in governing the course of their journey which was before unknown, even in a moment.

Notwithstanding, the question is, If Paul taught no-

---

[1] " Propagine," by propagation.

where but whither he was led by the Spirit, what certainty shall the ministers of the Church have at this day of their calling, who are certified by no oracles when they must speak or hold their peace? I answer, Seeing that Paul's province and charge was so wide, he had need of the singular direction of the Spirit. He was not made the apostle of one particular place, or of a few cities, but he had received commandment to preach the gospel through Asia and Europe; which was to sail in a most wide sea. Wherefore, there is no cause why we should wonder that in that confused wideness God beckoned unto him, as it were by reaching forth his hand, how far he would have him go, or whither.

But here ariseth another harder question, why the Lord did forbid Paul to speak in Asia, and suffered him not to come into Bithynia? For, if answer be made that these Gentiles were unworthy of the doctrine of salvation, we may again demand why Macedonia was more worthy? Those who desire to be too wise, do assign the causes of this difference in men, that the Lord vouchsafeth every man of his gospel, as he seeth him bent unto the obedience of faith; but he himself saith far otherwise, to wit, that he appeared plainly to those which sought him not, and that he spake to those who asked not of him. For whence cometh aptness to be taught, and a mind to obey, but from his Spirit? Therefore, it is certain that some are not preferred before other some by their merit, seeing that all men are naturally like backward and wayward from faith. Therefore, there is nothing better than to leave free power to God to vouchsafe and deprive of his grace whom he will. And surely as his eternal election is free, so his calling is also free which floweth thence, and is not grounded in men, seeing that he is not indebted to any.

Wherefore, let us know that the gospel springeth and issueth out to us out of the sole fountain of mere grace. And yet God doth not want a just reason, why he offereth his gospel to some, and passeth over other some. But I say that that reason lieth hid in his secret counsel. In the mean season, let the faithful know that they were called freely when others were set aside, lest they take that to themselves which is due to the mercy of God alone. And in the rest, whom God rejecteth for no manifest cause, let them learn to wonder at the deep depth of his judgment, which they may not seek out. And here the word Asia is taken for that part which is properly so called. When Luke saith that Paul and his companions essayed to come into Bithynia until they were forbidden of the Spirit, he showeth that they were not directed by oracles, save only when need required, as the Lord useth to be present with his in doleful[1] and uncertain matters.

9. *A vision by night.* The Lord would not that Paul should stay any longer in Asia; because he would draw him into Macedonia. And Luke expresseth the manner of the drawing, that a man of Macedonia appeared to him by night. Where we must note that the Lord did not always observe the same manner of revelation, because divers kinds are more convenient for confirmation. And it is not said that this vision was offered in a dream, but only in the night season. For there be certain night visions which men see when they be awake.

Help us. This speech setteth forth the ministry committed to Paul. For, seeing that the gospel is the power of God to salvation, (Rom. i. 16,) those which are the ministers of God are said to help those who perish; that having delivered them from death, they may bring them unto the inheritance of eternal life. And this ought to be no small encouragement for godly teachers to stir up the heat of their study and desire, when they hear that they call back miserable souls from destruction, and that they help those who should otherwise perish, that they may be saved. Again, all people unto whom the gospel is brought are taught reverently to embrace the ministers thereof as deliverers, unless they will maliciously reject the grace of God; and yet this

---

[1] " Dubiis," doubtful.

commendation and title is not so translated unto men, that God is robbed even of the best part of his praise; because, though he by his ministers give salvation, yet is he the only author thereof, as if he reached out his hands to help.

10. *Being fully persuaded.* Hence we gather, that it was no bare vision, but that it was also confirmed by the testimony of the Spirit. For Satan doth oftentimes abuse ghosts and visures [masks] to deceive withal, that he may mock and cozen the unbelievers. Whereby it cometh to pass, that the bare vision leaveth man's mind in doubt; but such as are divine indeed, those doth the Spirit seal by a certain mark, that those may not doubt nor waver whom the Lord will have certainly addicted to himself. A wicked spirit appeared to Brutus, inviting him to enter that unhappy combat and battle which he had at Philippi, even in the very same place whereunto Paul was afterwards called. But as the cause was far unlike, so the Lord dealt far otherwise with his servant, so that he put him out of doubt, and left him not astonished with fear. Now, in Paul and his companions the desire to obey ensued immediately upon the certainty; for, so soon as they understand that the Lord called them, they address themselves to their journey. The termination of the participle which is here used is active; and though it have divers significations, I do not doubt but that Luke's meaning is, that Paul and the rest, after that they had conferred [compared] this vision with the former oracles, were fully persuaded that the Lord had called them into Macedonia.

11. *Therefore, when we had loosed from Troas, we came with a straight course into Samothracia, and the day following to Neapolis;*
12. *And from thence to Philippi, which is the chief city of the parts of Macedonia, being a free city; and we stayed in the same city certain days.*
13. *And on the day of the Sabbaths we went out of the city beside a river, where was wont to be prayer; and sitting, we spake to the women which came together.*
14. *And a certain woman named Lydia, a seller of purples, of*

the city of the Thyatirans, which worshipped God, heard; whose heart the Lord opened, that she might take heed to those things which were spoken of Paul.

15. *And when she was baptized, and her house, she besought us, saying, If ye judge me faithful to the Lord, enter into my house and tarry. And she enforced us.*

11. This history doth, as it were in a glass, show how sharply the Lord did exercise the faith and patience of his, by bringing them in great straits which they could not have overcome unless they had been endued with singular constancy; for the entrance of Paul into Macedonia is reported to be such, as that it might have caused him to give but small credence to the vision. These holy men, leaving the work which they had in hand, did cross the seas with great haste, as if the whole nation of the Macedonians would have come to meet them with earnest desire to be helped. Now, the success is so far from being answerable to their hope, that their mouths are almost quite stopped. When they enter the chief city, they find none there with whom they may take any pains; therefore they are enforced to go into the field, that they may speak in an obscure corner and wilderness. Yea, even there they cannot have one man which will hearken to their doctrine; they can only have one woman to be a disciple of Christ, and that one which was an alien. Who would not have said that this journey was taken in hand foolishly which fell out so unhappily? But the Lord doth thus bring to pass his works under a base and weak kind,[1] that his power may shine more clearly at length; and it was most meet that the beginnings of the kingdom of Christ should be so ordered, that they might taste [savour] of the humility of the cross. But we must mark the constancy of Paul and his companions, who being not dismayed with such unprosperous beginnings, try whether any occasion will offer itself contrary to their expectation. And assuredly the servants of Christ must wrestle with all lets, neither must they be discouraged, but go forward to-mor-

---

[1] " Specie," appearance.

row, if this day there appear no fruit of their labour, for there is no cause why they should desire to be more happy than Paul. When Luke saith that they abode in that city, some had rather have it, that they conferred or disputed, but the other translation is more plain. And the text persuadeth us to make choice thereof, because Luke will shortly after declare that Lydia was the first-fruits of that Church; and we may easily guess that the apostles went out of the city, because there was no gate opened to them in it.

13. *In the day of the Sabbaths.* No doubt the Jews sought some place which was solitary and by the way, when they were disposed to pray, because their religion was then everywhere most odious. And God, by their example, meant to teach us what great account we ought to make of the profession of faith; that we do not forsake it either for fear of envy or of danger. They had, indeed, in many places synagogues, but it was not lawful for them to assemble themselves publicly at Philippi, which was a free city of Rome.[1] Therefore, they withdraw themselves into a secret corner, that they may pray to God where they could not be espied; and yet there were those who did grudge even at this, so that they might think that it might both cause trouble and danger, but they prefer the worship of God before their own quietness and commodity. Furthermore, we may gather by this word Sabbath, that Luke speaketh of the Jews. Secondly, forasmuch as he commendeth the godliness of Lydia, it must needs be that she was a Jewess, which matter needeth no long disputation, forasmuch as we know that it was an heinous offence for the Grecians and Romans to celebrate the Sabbath, or to take up Jewish rites. Now, we understand that the Jews made choice of the river's bank, that they might there pray, not for any superstition's sake, but because they shunned the company of men, and the sight of the people. If any man object, why did not every man pray in his house privately? The an-

---

[1] " Colonia Romana," a Roman colony.

swer is ready, that this was a solemn rite of praying, to testify godliness; and that being far[1] from the superstitions of the Gentiles, they might one exhort another to worship God alone, and that they might nourish the religion received of the fathers among themselves. As touching Paul and his fellows who were lately come,[2] it is to be thought that they came thither not only to pray, but also because they hoped to do some good. For it was a fit place for them to teach in, being far from noise; and it was meet that they should be more attentive to hear the word who came thither to pray. Luke putteth the day of the Sabbaths instead of the Sabbath; where, following Erasmus, I have translated it, *There was wont* to be prayer; the old interpreter hath, *did seem.* And the word νομιζεσθαι hath both significations among the Grecians. Yet this sense is more fit for this present place, that they did commonly use to have prayer there.

We spake to the women. Either that place was appointed for the assemblies of women,[3] or else religion was cold among men, so that they came more slowly. Howsoever it be, we see that the holy men omit no occasion or opportunity, because they vouchsafe to offer the gospel even to women alone. Furthermore, forasmuch as it seemeth likely to me that men and women made their prayers there together, I suppose that Luke omitted the men either because they would not hear, or else because they profited nothing by hearing.

14. *A woman named Lydia.* If they had been heard of a few women, yet this had been but to enter in, as it were, by a strait chink; but now whereas one only heareth attentively and with fruit, might it not have seemed that the way was stopt before Christ?[4] But afterward there sprung a noble Church of that one small graft, which Paul setteth out with many excellent commendations; yet it may be

---

[1] " Remoti," removed, at a distance from guests.   [2] ' Novi hospites," new guests.   [3] " Tantum," only, omitted.   [4] " Obstructos esse Christo ingressus," that the entrance of Christ was hindered.

that Lydia had some companions, whereof there is no mention made, because she did far excel them all. And Luke doth not assign that for the cause why this one woman did show herself apt to be taught, because she was more witty[1] than the rest, or because she had some preparation of herself; but he saith that the Lord opened her heart that she might give ear and take heed to the speech of Paul. He had of late commended her godliness; and yet he showeth that she could not comprehend the doctrine of the gospel, save only through the illumination of the Spirit. Wherefore, we see that not faith alone, but all understanding and knowledge of spiritual things, is the peculiar gift of God, and that the ministers do no good by teaching and speaking unless the inward calling of God be thereunto added.

By the word heart, the Scripture meaneth sometimes the mind, as when Moses saith, " God hath not given thee hitherto a heart to understand." So likewise in this place, Luke doth not only signify unto us that Lydia was brought by the inspiration of the Spirit, with affection of heart to embrace the gospel, but that her mind was lightened, that she might understand it. By this let us learn that such is the blockishness, such is the blindness of men, that in seeing they see not, in hearing they hear not, until such time as God doth give them new eyes and new ears. But we must note the speech, that the heart of Lydia was opened that she might give ear to the external voice of the teacher. For as preaching alone is nothing else but the dead letter, so we must beware lest a false imagination, or a show of secret illumination, lead us away from the word whereupon faith dependeth, and wherein it resteth. For many, to the end they may amplify the grace of the Spirit, feign to themselves certain inspired persons,[2] that they may leave no use of the external word. But the Scripture doth not suffer any such divorce to be made which joineth the ministry of men with the secret inspiration of the Spirit. Unless the mind of Lydia had been opened, Paul's preaching should

---

[1] " Acutiori ingenio," of acuter intellect. [2] " Ενθουσιασμους," inspirations.

have been only literal;[1] and yet the Lord doth not inspire her with bare revelations only, but he giveth her the reverence of his word, so that the voice of man, which might otherwise have been uttered in vain, doth pierce into a mind endued with heavenly light.

Therefore, let those brain-sick fellows be packing, [begone,] who, under colour [pretext] of the Spirit, refuse external doctrine. For we must note the temperature or moderation which Luke setteth down here, that we can have or obtain nothing by the hearing of the word alone, without the grace of the Spirit; and that the Spirit is given us, not that he may bring contempt of the word, but rather that he may dip [instil] into our minds, and write in our hearts the faith thereof.

Now, if the cause be demanded why the Lord opened one woman's heart alone, we must return unto that principle, that so many believe as are ordained[2] to life. For the fear of God, which went before the plain and manifest knowledge of Christ in Lydia, was also a fruit of free election. The describers of situations of places[3] say, that Thyatira is a city of Lydia situate upon the side of the river called Hermus, and that it was sometimes called Pelopia; but some there be who attribute it to Phrygia, some to Mysia.

15. *When she was baptized.* Hereby it appeareth how effectually God wrought in Lydia even in a short moment. For it is not to be doubted but that she received and embraced the faith of Christ sincerely, and gave him her name, before Paul would admit her unto baptism. This was a token of mere readiness; also, her holy zeal and godliness do therein show themselves, in that she doth also consecrate her family to God. And, surely, all the godly ought to have this desire, to have those who are under them to be partakers of the same faith. For he is unworthy to be numbered among the children of God, and to be a ruler over

---

[1] "Literalis," literal, (gone no farther than the letter.) [2] "Præordinati," preordained. [3] "Geographi," geographers.

others, whosoever is desirous to reign and rule in his own house over his wife, children, servants, and maids, and will cause them to give no place to Christ. Therefore, let every one of the faithful study to govern and order his house so, that it may be an image of the Church. I grant that Lydia had not in her hand the hearts of all those which were of her household, that she might turn unto Christ whomsoever she would;[1] but the Lord did bless her godly desire, so that she had all her household obedient. The godly (as we have already said) must endeavour, with might and main, to drive from their houses all manner of superstition; secondly, that they have not profane families, but that they keep them under the fear of the Lord. So Abraham, the father of the faithful, was commanded to circumcise all his servants with him; and he is commended for the care he had to govern his house, and to instruct his family. Furthermore, if this duty be required at the hands of the householder, much more of a prince, that he suffer not so much as in him lieth the name of God to be profaned in his realm.

She besought them, saying. This hath the force of an adjuration, when she saith, if ye have judged me faithful; as if she should say, I beseech you by that faith which you have approved by baptism, that ye refuse not to lodge with me; and Lydia did by such an earnest desire testify how entirely she loved the gospel. Nevertheless, it is not to be doubted but that the Lord gave her such an affection, to the end Paul might be the more encouraged to proceed, not only because he saw that he was liberally and courteously entertained, but also because he might thereby judge of the fruit of his doctrine. Therefore, this was not the woman's inviting only, but also God's, to keep Paul and his company there, to which end that tendeth also that Lydia enforced them, as if God did lay hand upon them, and stay them in the woman's person.

16. *And it happened, as we went to prayer, a certain maid, having*

---

[1] " Suo arbitrio," at her own will.

a spirit of divination, did meet us, which brought her masters much gain by divining.
17. *She followed Paul and us, and cried, saying, These men are the servants of the most high God, which preach to us the way of salvation.*
18. *And this she did many days. And Paul, taking it grievously, and turning back, said to the spirit, I command thee, in the name of the Lord Jesus Christ, that thou come out of her. And he came out the same hour.*
19. *And when her masters saw that the hope of their gain was gone, having taken Paul and Silas, they drew them into the market-place to the rulers.*
20. *And when they had presented them to the magistrates, they said, These men trouble our city, seeing they be Jews:*
21. *And they preach ordinances, which we may not receive nor keep, seeing we are Romans.*
22. *And the multitude came together against them; and when the magistrates had rent their garments, they commanded them to be beaten with rods.*

16. Luke prosecuteth the increase of the Church; for though he do not straightway in a word express that thing, yet is it easily gathered out of the text, that many were brought unto the faith, or at least that the Church was somewhat augmented, and Paul did not frequent the assemblies in time of prayer in vain. Notwithstanding, Luke doth also report that Satan did interrupt this course; to wit, because after that the apostles were beaten with rods, and cast in [into] prison, they were at length enforced to depart the city; yet we shall see in the end of this chapter, that when Satan had done his worst, there was some body of the Church gathered before they did depart.

Having a spirit of divination, (or of Python.) The poets do feign that the serpent called Python was slain with the darts of Phœbus; hereupon rose another invention;[1] that they said, that those who were possessed were inspired with the spirit of Python, and, peradventure, they were thereupon

---

[1] " Figmento," fiction.

called Phœbades, in honour of Apollo. But Luke followeth the common custom of speaking, because he showeth the error of the common people, and not through what inspiration the maid did prophesy. For it is certain that the devil did deceive men under the visor of Apollo, as all idolatry and subtilty was invented and forged in his shop. But some men may marvel that the devil (through whose motion and persuasion the maid did cry) was the author of such an honourable commendation, wherewith she adorned Paul and Silas, and the rest. For, seeing that he is the father of lying, how could the truth proceed from him? Secondly, how is it that he gave place willingly to the servants of Christ, by whom his kingdom was destroyed? how can this hang together, that he prepared the minds of the people to hear the gospel, whose mortal enemy he is? Assuredly, there is nothing more proper to him than to turn away the minds of the people from the word of the gospel, which he doth now will and wish them to hear.

Whence cometh such a sudden change, or unwonted motion? But the devil is the father of lying in such sort, that he covereth himself under the false and deceivable colour of truth. There he played another person through his crafty subtilty, than was agreeable to his nature,[1] that by creeping in craftily he might do the more hurt; and, therefore, whereas he is called the father of lies, we must not so take it as if he did always lie manifestly and without any colour. Yea, rather we must beware of his crafty subtilty, lest when he pretendeth the colour of truth he deceive us under a vain show. We see, also, how he useth like subtilty daily. For what can bear a fairer show than the Pope's titles, wherein he doth not boast himself to be the adversary of Christ, but his vicar? What can be more plausible than that solemn preface, In the name of the Lord, Amen? Notwithstanding, we know, that whilst the hypocritical ministers of Satan do thus pretend the truth, they corrupt it, and, with a deadly

---

[1] " Egit igitur callido artificio aliam personam quam ferret ejus natura," therewith cunning artifice he played a character different from that which naturally belonged to him.

corruption, infect it. Seeing that Satan hath a double way to resist the gospel, to wit, because he doth sometimes rage openly, and sometimes he creepeth in craftily under lies, he hath also two kinds of lying and deceiving, either when he overthroweth the Word of God with false doctrines and gross superstitions, or else when he doth craftily feign that he is a friend of the Word, and so doth insinuate himself subtilely;[1] yea, he doth never hurt more deadly than when he transformeth himself into an angel of light. Now, we perceive to what end that so gorgeous a title did tend, wherewith he did extol Paul and his companions, namely, because it was not so convenient for him to make open war against the gospel, he went about to overthrow the credit thereof by secret shifts. For if Paul had admitted that testimony, there should have been no longer any difference between the wholesome[2] doctrine of Christ and the mocks of Satan. The light and brightness of the gospel should have been entangled in the darkness of lying, and so quite put out.

But the question is, why God doth grant Satan so great liberty, as to suffer him to deceive miserable men, and to bewitch them with true divinations? For, omitting the disputations which some men move concerning his foresight, I take this for a plain case, that he doth prophesy and foretel things to come, and which are hidden only through God's sufferance. But God seemeth by this means to lay open men who are reckless or careless to his subtilty, so that they cannot beware. For seeing that prophecies breathe out divine power, men's minds must needs be touched with reverence so often as they come abroad, unless they contemn God. I answer, that Satan hath never so much liberty granted him of God, save only that the unthankful world may be punished, which is so desirous of a lie, that it had rather be deceived than obey the truth. For that is a general evil, whereof Paul complaineth in the first chapter to the Romans, (Rom. i. 21,) That men do not glorify God, being

---

[1] " Quasi per cuniculos obrepit," creeps in as if by burrowing.
[2] " Salvificam," saving.

known naturally by the creation of the world, and that they suppress his truth unjustly.

It is a just reward for so great unthankfulness, that Satan hath the bridle given him, that through divers jugglings he may work the ruin of those who turn away maliciously from the light of God. Therefore, so often as you read the divinations of Satan, think upon the just judgment of God.

Now, if God so sharply punish the contempt of his light in the profane Gentiles, who have no other teachers but the heaven and earth, how much more sharp punishment do those deserve who wittingly and willingly choke the pure doctrine of salvation, revealed to them in the law and the gospel? No marvel, therefore, if Satan have long bewitched the world so freely with his subtilty, since that the truth of the gospel hath been wickedly contemned, which was made most manifest. But it is objected again, that no man is free from danger when false divinations fly to and fro so fast. For even as well the good as the evil seem to be subject to the cozenage of Satan when the truth is darkened and overcast. The answer is ready, though Satan set snares for all men in general, yet are the godly delivered by the grace of God, lest they be caught together with the wicked. There is also a more manifest distinction set down in the Scripture, because the Lord doth by this means try the faith and godliness of his, and doth make blind the reprobate, that they may perish as they be worthy. Therefore Paul saith plainly, that Satan hath not leave granted him to lead any into error save those who will not obey God and embrace the truth, (2 Thes. ii. 11, 12.)

Whereby is also reproved their wicked ungodliness, who, under this colour, excuse the profane contempt of all doctrine; whither shall we turn ourselves, (say they,) seeing that Satan is so expert to deceive? Therefore, it is better for us to live without any religion at all, than, through the desire of religion, to run headlong into destruction. Neither do they object and pretend this fear for their excuse in earnest; but, seeing they desire nothing more than to wander carelessly, like beasts, without any fear of God, they can be content with any excuse, so they be not tied to any religion. I confess, indeed, that Satan doth no less craftily than wickedly abuse the sacred name of God; and that that proverb is too true which Papistry hath brought forth, that, In the name of the Lord beginneth all evil; but seeing that the Lord doth pronounce that he will be the teacher of the humble, and hath promised that he will be nigh to those which are right in heart; seeing that Paul teacheth that the Word of God is the sword of the Spirit; seeing that he doth testify that those who are well-grounded in the faith of the gospel are not in danger to be seduced by man; seeing that Peter calleth the Scripture a light shining in a dark place; seeing that courteous exhortation, or inviting of Christ, can never deceive us, " Seek, and ye shall find; knock, and it shall be opened to you;" let Satan do what he can, and let the false prophets seek to darken the truth so much as they are able, we need not be afraid lest the Spirit of wisdom and discretion [discernment] forsake us, who ruleth[1] Satan at his pleasure, and maketh us triumph over him by the faith of his word.

18. *Paul took it grievously.* It may be that at the first Paul neglected, and did not greatly regard the crying of the maid, because he hoped that there would be no account made thereof, and had rather that it should vanish away of itself. But the continual repetition doth at length make him weary; because, if he had any longer dissembled, Satan would have waxed more and more insolent through his silence and patience. Secondly, he ought not to have broken out into this prohibition rashly, until he knew for a certainty that he was furnished with the power of God. For Paul's commandment[2] had been foolish and vain without the commandment of God. And this must be noted, lest any man condemn Paul of too great hastiness, because he encountered so valiantly with the unclean spirit. For he did not conceive any grief or indignation, save only that he saw

---

[1] " Compescit," quelleth.   [2] " Imprecatio," imprecation, anathema.

that the stability of Satan would increase, unless he did betimes prevent it; neither did he attempt any thing without the motion of the Spirit; neither did he enter the conflict until he was armed with power from heaven. Notwithstanding, he seemeth to be contrary to himself, seeing that he saith elsewhere that he rejoiceth upon what occasion soever he see the gospel preached, (Phil. i. 18,) even by wicked men, and such as did study of set purpose to bring him in contempt. I answer, that he had another more apt reason for himself in this place;[1] because all men would have thought that the spirit of the maid had played with Paul;[2] so that by that means the doctrine of the gospel should not only have come in [into] suspicion, but should also have come into great contempt.[3] And to this end was it that Christ also did command the devil to hold his peace, (Mark i. 25,) whereas notwithstanding he suffered his name to be extolled by unmeet and unworthy men, (Luke iv. 35.)

I command thee. We must note the form of speech; for as the miracle was about to have a double use, namely, that the power of Christ might be known; secondly, that he might declare that he had no fellowship with Satan's jugglings; so Paul, in giving the authority and power to Christ alone, doth declare that he is only a minister; that done, he doth openly set Christ against the devil,[4] to the end that, by the conflict, all men may see that they be deadly enemies. For it was profitable that many should be awaked who had been given to such gross seducing, that being well purged, they might come to the true faith.

19. *But when her masters.* The same devil who of late did flatter Paul by the mouth of the maid, doth now drive her masters into fury, that they may put him to death; so that, having changed his coat, he doth now play a tragedy,

---

[1] " Hic diversam rationem," that here there was a different reason.
[2] " Colludere puellæ dæmonum cum Paulo," that the demon of the damsel was in collusion with Paul.   [3] " Sed recidisset in merum ludibrium," but become a mere laughing-stock.   [4] " Opponit Christum dæmoni," he opposes Christ to the demon.

who could not speed well before by his fair speech and flattery. And though the heat of zeal wherewith Paul was provoked to anger did raise the whirlwind of persecution, yet is he not therefore to be blamed; neither did it any whit repent Paul that he had wrought the miracle, so that he did wish that that were undone which was done, because he knew full well through what motion he had driven the devil out of the maid. Whereby we are taught that we must not rashly condemn things which are well done, and that which is taken in hand at the commandment of God, though an unhappy success follow; because God doth then examine [test] the constancy of those which be his, until a more joyful and prosperous end drive away all sorrow. As touching the men, Luke expresseth the cause why they were so mad upon Paul; to wit, because their hope of filthy gain was gone. But though they were pricked forward with covetousness only to persecute the Gospel and the ministers thereof; yet they pretend a fair colour, that it grieveth them that the public state should be perverted, that their ancient laws should be broken, and peace troubled. So, though the enemies of Christ behave themselves wickedly and unhonestly, yet they always invent some cause for their sin. Yea, though their wicked desire appear plainly, yet, with an impudent face, they always bring in somewhat to cover their filthiness withal. So at this day those Papists which are more zealous over their law,[1] have nothing else in their minds besides their gain and government. Let them swear and forswear by all their saints and sacrifices, that they are enforced only with a godly affection; yet the matter itself doth plainly show, that it is the coldness of their kitchens which maketh their zeal so hot, and that ambition is the fan[2] thereof. For they be either hungry dogs pricked forward with greediness, or furious lions breathing out nothing but cruelty.

20. *These men trouble our city.* This accusation was

[1] " Acerrimi zelotæ legis suæ," the fiercest zealots for their law.
[2] " Flabellum," bellows

craftily composed to burden the servants of Christ. For on the one side they pretend the name of the Romans, than which nothing was more favourable ; on the other, they purchase hatred, and bring them in contempt, by naming the Jews, which name was at that time infamous ; for, as touching religion, the Romans were more like to any than to the Jewish nation. For it was lawful for a man which was a Roman to do sacrifice either in Asia or in Grecia, or in any other country where were idols and superstitions. I warrant you Satan did agree with himself very well, though he put on divers shapes, but that which was religion only, than which there was no other in the world, was counted among the Romans detestable. They frame a third accusation out of the crime of sedition ;[1] for they pretend that the public peace is troubled by Paul and his company. In like sort was Christ brought in contempt,[2] (Luke xxiii. 5 ;) and even at this day the Papists have no more plausible thing wherewith they may bring us to be hated, than when they cry that our doctrine tendeth to no other end but to procure tumults, that at length there may follow a filthy confusion of all things. But we must valiantly contemn this filthy and false infamy as did Christ and Paul, until the Lord bring to light the malice of our enemies, and refute their impudence.

21. *Ordinances which.* They lean to a prejudice, lest the cause should come to be disputed ; as the Papists deal with us at this day, this was decreed in a General Council ; it is a more ancient and common opinion, than that it may be called in question ; custom hath long time approved this; this hath been established by consent more than a thousand years ago. But to what end tend all these things, save only that they may rob the Word of God of all authority ? They make boast of man's decrees, but in the mean season they leave no place at all for the laws of God. We may see by

[1] " Tertiam calumniam ex erimine seditionis concinnant," they concoct a third calumny out of the charge of sedition
[2] " Odiose traductus fuit," was hatefully traduced

this place what force these prejudices ought to have. The laws of the Romans were excellent, but religion doth depend upon the Word of God alone. Therefore in this matter we must take great heed, that men being brought under, the authority of God alone do prevail, and that he make all things which in the world are excellent subject to him.

22. *The multitude came together.* When Luke declareth that there was great concourse of the people made, after that a few men of no reputation, to wit, such as did juggle and cozen to get gain, and whose filthiness was well known, had made some stir; he teacheth with what fury the world rageth against Christ. Foolishness and inconstancy are indeed common vices among all people, and almost continual, but the wonderful force of Satan doth therein betray itself, in that those who are in other matters modest and quiet, are for a matter of no importance in a heat,[1] and become companions of most vile persons, when the truth must be resisted. There was never a whit more modesty to be found in the judges themselves, if we consider what was their duty. For they ought, by their gravity, to have appeased the fury of the people, and to have set themselves stoutly against their violence, they ought to have aided and defended the guiltless; but they lay hands on them outrageously, and renting their garments, they command them to be stripped naked and whipt before they know the matter. Surely the malice of men is to be lamented;[2] whereby it came to pass, that almost all the judgment-seats of the world, which ought to have been sanctuaries of justice, have been polluted with the wicked and sacrilegious oppugning of the gospel.

Notwithstanding, the question is, why they were cast in prison, seeing they were already punished, for the prison was ordained for the keeping of men? They used this kind of correction, until they might know more; and so

---

[1] " Repente effervent," suddenly effervesce, break out.   [2] " Deploranda," desperate, deplorable.

we see the servants of Christ more sharply handled than adulterers, robbers, and other most vile persons.[1] Whereby appeareth more plainly that force of Satan in stirring up the minds of men, that they observe no show of judgment in persecuting the gospel. But though the godly be more hardly handled for defending the truth of Christ, than are the wicked for their wickedness; yet it goeth well with the godly, because they triumph gloriously before God and his angels in all injuries which they suffer. They suffer reproach and slander; but because they know that the marks of Christ are in greater price and more esteemed in heaven than the vain pomps of the earth, the more wickedly and reproachfully the world doth vex them, the greater cause have they to rejoice. For if profane writers did so honour Themistocles, that they preferred his prison before the seat and court of judges; how much more honourably must we think of the Son of God, whose cause is in hand so often as the faithful suffer persecution for the gospel? Therefore, though the Lord suffered Paul and Silas to be scourged and imprisoned by the wicked judges, yet he did not suffer them to be put to any shame, but that which turned to their greater renown. For seeing that those persecutions, which we must suffer for the testimony of the gospel, are remnants of the sufferings of Christ; like as our Prince turned the cross, which was accursed, into a triumphant [triumphal] chariot, so he shall, in like sort, adorn the prisons and gibbets of his, that they may there triumph over Satan and all the wicked.

Renting their garments. Because the old interpreter had truly translated this, it was evil done of Erasmus to change it, that the magistrates did rent their own garments. For this was Luke's meaning only, that the holy men were outrageously[2] beaten, the lawful order of judgment being neglected, and that they laid hands on them with such violence that their garments were rent. And this had

---

[1] " Et alios quosvis sceleratos." and villains of any description.
[2] " Tumultuose," tumultuously.

been too far disagreeing with the custom of the Romans, for the judges to cut [rend] their own garments publicly in the market-place; especially seeing the question was concerning an unknown religion, for which they did not greatly care; but I will not long stand about a plain matter.

23. *And when they had given them many stripes, they did cast them into prison, commanding the keeper of the prison to keep them safe:*
24. *Who, seeing he had received such commandment, did put them in the inner prison, and made fast their feet in the stocks.*
25 *And at midnight Paul and Silas praying, did praise God: and those which lay bound heard them.*
26. *And suddenly there was a great earthquake, so that the foundations of the prison were shaken: and by and by all the doors were opened, and all their hands* [chains] *were loosed.*
27. *And when the keeper of the prison awaked, and saw all the prison doors open, drawing out his sword, he was about to slay himself, thinking that those which lay bound were fled.*
28. *And Paul cried with a loud voice, saying, Do thyself no harm: for we be all here.*

23. *That he should keep them safe.* Whereas the magistrates command that Paul and Silas should be kept so diligently, it was done to this end, that they might know more of the matter. For they had already beaten them with rods to appease the tumult. And this is that which I said of late, that the world doth rage with such blind fury against the ministers of the gospel, that it doth keep no mean in severity. But as it is very profitable for us, for example's sake, to know how uncourteously and uncomely the witnesses of Christ were entertained in times past; so it is no less profitable to know that which Luke addeth immediately concerning their fortitude and patience. For even when they lay bound with fetters, he saith that in prayer they lauded God, whereby it appeareth that

neither the reproach which they suffered, nor the stripes which made their flesh smart, nor the stink of the deep dungeon, nor the danger of death, which was hard at hand, could hinder them from giving thanks to the Lord joyfully and with glad hearts.

We must note this general rule, that we cannot pray as we ought, but we must also praise God. For though the desire to pray arise of the feeling of our want and miseries, and therefore it is, for the most part, joined with sorrow and carefulness;[1] yet the faithful must so bridle their affections, that they murmur not against God; so that the right form of prayer doth join two affections together, (to look too contrary,) [viz.] carefulness and sorrow, by reason of the present necessity which doth keep us down, and joyfulness, by reason of the obedience whereby we submit ourselves to God, and by reason of the hope which, showing us the haven nigh at hand, doth refresh us even in the midst of shipwreck. Such a form doth Paul prescribe to us. Let your prayers (saith he) be made known to God with thanksgiving, (Phil. iv. 6.) But in this history we must note the circumstances. For though the pain of the stripes were grievous, though the prison were troublesome, though the danger were great, seeing that Paul and Silas cease not to praise God, we gather by this how greatly they were encouraged to bear the cross. So Luke reported before that the apostles rejoiced, because they were counted worthy to suffer reproach for the name of the Lord, (Acts v. 41.)

And those which lay bound. We must know that Paul and Silas prayed aloud, that they might make the boldness of a good conscience known to others who were shut up in the same prison; for they might have made their prayer with secret groaning and sighing of heart as they were wont, or they might have prayed unto the Lord quietly and softly. Why do they then exalt their voice? Assuredly, they do not that for any ambition; but that they may profess, that, trusting to the goodness of their cause, they fly without fear

---

[1] " Anxietate animi," anxiety of mind

unto God. Therefore, in their prayers was included a confession of faith, which did appertain unto a common example, and prepared as well the malefactor's as the jailor's house to consider the miracle.

26. *There was an earthquake.* The Lord, in showing this visible sign, meant chiefly to provide for his servants, that they might more manifestly know that their prayers were heard; yet he had respect also of the rest. He could have loosed the fetters of Paul and Silas without an earthquake, and also have opened the gates. But that addition served not a little to confirm them, seeing that the Lord, for their sakes, did shake both the air and also the earth. Again, it was requisite that the keeper of the prison and the rest should feel the presence of God, lest they should think that the miracle came by chance. Neither is it to be doubted, but that the Lord did then show a token of his power, which should be profitable for all ages; so that the faithful may fully assure themselves that he will be nigh unto them so often as they are to enter[1] combats and dangers for the defence of the gospel. Nevertheless, he doth neither always keep the same course, to testify his presence by manifest signs; neither is it lawful for us to prescribe him a law. For he did help his by manifest miracles then for this cause, that we may be content with his hidden grace at this day; concerning which matter we have spoken more upon the second chapter.

27. *When the keeper of the prison was awaked.* He would have slain himself that he might prevent punishment; for it had been a foolish answer to have said that the doors were opened of their own accord. But this question may be asked, Seeing that Paul seeth that they might have some hope to escape if he should slay himself, why doth he hinder him? for he seemeth by this means to refuse the deliverance which was offered by God; yea, it seemeth to have

[1] "Subeunda," undergo

been a mere toy,[1] in that the Lord would have the jailor awaked, lest there should be any use[2] of the miracle. I answer, that we must in this place have respect unto his counsel and purpose. For he did not loose Paul and Silas, and the rest, from their fetters, neither did he, therefore, open the doors, that he might straightway let them go free; but that, by showing the power of his hand, he might seal up the faith of Paul and Silas, and might make the name of Christ glorious among others. Therefore, he doth so yield to the petitions of Paul and Silas, that he showeth that he is able enough to deliver them so often as he shall think it good; and that nothing can hinder him, but that he is able to enter not only into prisons, but also into graves, that he may deliver those that be his.[3] He opened the gates of the prison to Peter to another end, as we saw chapter xii. But now, forasmuch as he had another way in readiness to deliver Paul and Silas, he meant not so much to deliver them for the present time by miracle, as to confirm them against the time to come. Again, we must call that to mind which I said of late, that the opening of the prison appertained unto others, that it might be known to many witnesses that God did favour the doctrine, which was now burthened with an unjust prejudice. Undoubtedly, Paul perceived this; and, therefore, though his bands were loosed, he did not once wag from his place.[4] He might have gone away, if he had been so disposed. Why doth he not? Was it because he contemned the grace of God? or because, through his slothfulness, he will make the miracle frustrate? None of all these is probable; whence we gather that he was holden by God, as the Lord useth to direct the minds of those which be his in doubtful matters, that they may follow sometimes ignorantly, sometimes wittingly, that which is expedient to be done, and not pass their bounds.

29. *And calling for a light he sprang in, and, trembling, he fell down at the feet of Paul and Silas.*

[1] " Merum ..ludicrum," a mere absurdity that there might be no use [2] " Ne quis esset usus," that there might be no use [3] " A morte," from death. [4] " Pedem loco non movit," he did not stir a foot from the place.

30. *And when he had brought them forth, he saith, Sirs, what must I do to be saved?*
31. *And they said, Believe in the Lord Jesus Christ, and thou shalt be saved, and thy household.*
32. *And they spake to him the word, and to all that were in his house.*
33. *And taking them at the same hour of the night, he washed their stripes; and was himself baptized, and all his household, forthwith.*
34. *And when he had brought them into his house, he set meat before them; and he rejoiced that he and all his whole house believed in God.*

29. *Being astonished, he fell down.* This keeper was no less brought under with fear to show obedience to God than with the miracle prepared.[1] Hereby it appeareth what a good thing it is for men to be thrown down from their pride, that they may learn to submit themselves to God. He was hardened in his superstitions; therefore, he might with a lofty stomach[2] have despised whatsoever Paul and Silas should have said, whom he had also reproachfully[3] thrust into the innermost part of the prison. Now, fear maketh him apt to be taught and gentle. Therefore, so often as the Lord shall strike us or cast us down,[4] let us know that this is done that we may be brought in [to] order from our too much haughtiness.

But it is a wonder that he was not reproved for falling down at their feet. For why did Paul wink at that which (as Luke recordeth) Peter would not suffer in Cornelius? (Acts x. 26.) I answer, that Paul doth therefore bear with the keeper, because he knoweth that he was not moved with superstition, but with fear of God's judgment so to humble himself. It was a kind of worship common enough; but chiefly among the Romans it was a solemn thing when they would humbly crave any thing, or crave pardon, they fell

---

[1] " Quam miraculo præparatus," than prepared by the miracle.
[2] " Sprevisset igitur alto animo," hence he might have shown high contempt for.   [3] " Probrose," disgracefully.   [4] " Aliqua consternatione tanget," or throw us into consternation.

down at their knees to whom they put up their supplication. Therefore, there was no cause why Paul should be displeased with a man whom he saw simply humbled of God. For if there had been any thing committed contrary to the glory of God, he had not forgotten that zeal which he showed before among the men of Lycaonia. Therefore, by his silence, we gather that in this kind of worship there was nothing contrary to godliness or the glory of God.

30. *Sirs, what must I do?* He doth so ask counsel, that he showeth therewithal that he will be obedient. By this we see that he was thoroughly[1] touched, so that he was ready to do what they should command him, whom not many hours before he had bound uncourteously. The wicked oftentimes when they see wonders, though they tremble for a time, yet are they straightway made more obstinate, as it befel Pharaoh, (Exod. viii. 8, 32;) at least they are not so tamed that they give over themselves to God. But in this place the keeper (acknowledging the power of God) was not only a little afraid, so that he returned straightway unto his former cruelty, but he showeth himself obedient to God, and desirous of sound and wholesome doctrine. He demandeth how he may obtain salvation; whereby it appeareth more plainly that he was not suddenly taken with some light[2] fear of God only, but truly humbled to offer himself to be a scholar to his ministers. He knew that they were cast in prison for no other cause, save only because they did overthrow the common estate of religion. Now he is ready to hear their doctrine which he had before contemned.

31. *Believe in the Lord Jesus.* This is but a short, and, to look to, a cold and hungry definition of salvation, and yet it is perfect to believe in Christ. For Christ alone hath all the parts of blessedness and eternal life included in him, which he offereth to us by the gospel; and by faith we re-

---

[1] " Serio," seriously [2] " Evanido," evanescent.

ceive them, as I have declared, (Acts xv. 9.) And here we must note two things; first, that Christ is the mark[1] whereat faith must aim; and, therefore, men's minds do nothing else but wander when they turn aside from him. Therefore, no marvel if all the divinity of Popery be nothing else but an huge lump[2] and horrible labyrinth; because, neglecting Christ, they flatter themselves in vain and frivolous speculations. Secondly, we must note, that after we have embraced Christ by faith, that alone is sufficient to salvation. But the latter member, which Luke addeth by and by, doth better express the nature of faith, Paul and Silas command the keeper of the prison to believe in the Son of God. Do they precisely stay in this voice [word] only? Yea, it followeth in Luke, in the text, [context,] that they preached the word of the Lord. Therefore, we see how that faith is not a light or dry opinion concerning unknown things, but a plain and distinct knowledge of Christ conceived out of the gospel. Again, if the preaching of the gospel be absent, there shall no faith remain any longer. To conclude, Luke coupleth faith with preaching and doctrine; and after that he hath briefly spoke of faith, he doth, by way of exposition, show the true and lawful way of believing. Therefore, instead of that invention of entangled faith, whereof the Papists babble, let us hold faith unfolded in the word of God, that it may unfold to us the power of Christ.

33. *He was baptized, and all his household.* Luke doth again commend the godly zeal of the keeper, that he did consecrate all his whole house to the Lord; wherein doth also appear the grace of God, in that he brought all his whole family unto a godly consent. And we must also note the notable exchange: he was of late about to murder himself, because he thought that Paul and the rest were escaped; but now laying aside all fear, he bringeth them home.[3]

---

[1] "Unicum scopum," the only mark. [2] "Immane chaos," immense chaos. [3] "Sponte," of his own accord.

So that we see how faith doth animate and encourage those to behave themselves stoutly who before had no heart. And surely, when we droop[1] through fear and doubtfulness, there is no better matter of boldness than to be able to cast all our cares into God's bosom; that no danger may terrify us from doing our duty, whilst that we look for an end at God's hand, such as he shall see to be most profitable.

34. *He rejoiced that he believed.* The external profession of faith was before commended in the jailor; now the inward fruit thereof is described. When he did lodge the apostles,[2] and was not afraid of punishment, but did courteously entertain them in his own house, otherwise than he was enjoined by the magistrate, he did testify that his faith was not idle. And that joy whereof Luke speaketh in this place is a singular good thing, which every man hath from his faith. There is no greater torment than an evil conscience; for the unbelievers, though they seek by all means to bring themselves into a certain amazedness, yet because they have no peace with God, they must needs quake and tremble. But admit they perceive not their present torments, yea, they rage and play the madmen through mad and unbridled licentiousness; yet are they never quiet, neither do they enjoy quiet joy.[3] Therefore, sincere and quiet stable joy proceedeth from faith alone, when we perceive that God is merciful to us. In this respect, Zacharias saith, "Rejoice and be glad, O daughter of Sion, behold, thy King cometh." Yea, this effect is everywhere in the Scripture attributed to faith, that it maketh the souls joyful. Therefore, let us know that faith is not a vain or dead imagination, but a lively sealing [sense] of the grace of God, which bringeth perfect joy by reason of the certainty of salvation, whereof it is meet that the wicked be void, who do both fly from the God of peace, and disturb all righteousness.

---

[1] "Torpeamus," become torpid. [2] "Hospitalıter,' hospitably.
[3] "Nec sereno gaudio potıuntur," nor do they obtain serene joy.

35. *And when it was day, the magistrates sent the apparitors,* [officers,] *saying, Let those men go.*
36. *And the keeper of the prison told these words to Paul, The magistrates have sent to loose you : now therefore going out, depart in peace.*
37. *And Paul said to them, After that they have beaten us openly, before our cause was known, seeing that we be Romans, they have cast us into prison ; and now they cast us out privily ? No, surely ; but let them come themselves and fetch us out.*
38. *And the apparitors* [officers] *told these words to the magistrates : who feared, after that they heard that they were Romans.*
39. *And they came and besought them ; and when they had brought them out, they requested them that they would depart out of the city.*
40. *And coming out of the prison, they entered in unto Lydia : and when they had seen the brethren, they comforted them, and departed.*

35. *When it was day.* The question is, how it came to pass that the judges did so suddenly change their purpose? The day before they had commanded that Paul and Silas should be bound with fetters, as if they meant to punish them cruelly, now they let them go free. At least, if they had heard them, it might have been that the knowledge of the cause had brought them to be more gentle and better minded.[1] But it appeareth that, forasmuch as the matter stood as yet still in one state, they were brought unto repentance of their own accord. I answer, that there is no other thing here set down but that which falleth out most commonly when sedition is once raised. For not only the minds of the common people begin to rage, but also the tempest carrieth away the governors also, no doubt perversely. For we know that of Virgil,—

"And as amidst a mighty rout, when discord oft is bred,
And baser froward-minded men with furious rage are led ;

---

[1] "Ad mansuetudinem et sanam mentem," to mildness and a sound mind.

Forthwith flies fire, and stones are flung, madness doth tools supply,
Then if on the sudden they do any one espy
Whom love to commonwealth and just deserts have reverent made,
They hush, and eke attentive stand, to hear what will be said.
He governs both their will and rage,
With words their wrath he doth assuage."

Therefore, there can be nothing more unseemly than that in a hot tumult the judges should be set on fire [along] with the people; but it falleth out so for the most part. Therefore, when those officers saw the people up, they thought there was cause enough why they should beat the apostles with rods. But now they are caused with shame and infamy to suffer punishment for their lightness, [levity.] Peradventure also, when they inquire of the beginning of the tumult, they find those who had deceived the people[1] in the fault. Therefore, when they had found out that Paul and Silas were innocent, they let them go, though too late. By which example, those which bear rule are taught to beware of too much haste. Again, we see how carelessly magistrates flatter[2] themselves in their own offences, which they know full well they have committed, especially when they have to do with unknown and base persons. When these men grant free liberty to Paul and Silas to depart, they are not ignorant that they had before done them injury; yet they think it will be sufficient if they do not continue to do them injury still, and to be more cruel upon them.[3] The apparitors [officers] are called ῥαβδουχοι, of the staves which they did bear; whereas the ensigns of the sergeants [lictors] were hatchets bound about with rods.

After that they have beaten us openly. Their defence consisteth upon [of] two points, that they raged against, and cruelly intreated, the body of a man that was a Roman; secondly, that they did that contrary to the order of law. We shall see afterwards that Paul was a citizen of Rome. But it was straitly provided by Portius' law, by the laws of

---

[1] "Circulatores," the circulators (of the charge.)   [2] "Condonent," forgive.   [3] "Si non pergant usque in 1·los esse injusti et crudeles," if they do not persist to the last in injustice and cruelty towards them

Sempronius, and also by many more, that no man should have power of life or death over any citizen of Rome but the people. Notwithstanding, it may seem to be a strange thing that Paul did not maintain [assert] his right before he was beaten with rods; for the judges might honestly excuse themselves by his silence; but it is to be thought that he was not heard in the midst of the tumult. If any man object that he doth now seek remedy too late, and out of season, yea, that he doth catch at a vain and foolish comfort,[1] when he requireth that the magistrates come themselves, we may readily answer, Paul was like to fare never a whit the better therefore; but we must mark that he meant nothing less than to provide for his own private commodity; but that he might ease the brethren somewhat afterward,[2] that the magistrates might not be so bold as to rage so freely against the good and innocent brethren. Because he had gotten their heads under his girdle,[3] he translated his right to help the brethren, that they might be borne with. This was the cause for which he did chide them. And so Paul did wisely use the opportunity offered him; as we must neglect nothing which may make for the bridling of the enemies, that they take not to themselves so much liberty to oppress or vex the innocent, forasmuch as the Lord bringeth to our hands such helps not in vain. Notwithstanding, let us remember that if we have been injured in anything, we must not repay injuries, but we must only endeavour to stay their lust, lest they hurt others in like sort.

38. *They were afraid, because they were Romans.* They are not once moved with the other point, because they had handled innocents cruelly without discretion;[4] and yet that was the greater reproach. But because they did not fear that any man would punish them, they were not moved with God's judgment. This is the cause that they do care-

---

[1] "Solatium," solace, compensation. [2] "Aliquid levationis in posterum afferret," produce some alleviation in future. [3] "Quia illos jam sibi tenebat obnoxios," because he now had them in his power. [4] "Nulla interposita cognitione,' without any previous cognisance.

lessly pass over that which was objected concerning injury done by them, only they are afraid of the officers[1] of the Romans, and lest they should be beheaded for violating the liberty in the body of a citizen. They knew that this was death if any of the chief governors [prefects] should commit it, then what should become of the officers of one free city?[2] Such is the fear of the wicked, because they have an amazed[3] conscience before God, they do long time flatter themselves in all sins, until the punishment[4] of men hang over their heads.

40. *When they saw, &c.* They were desired to part presently; yet it became them to regard the brethren, lest the tender seed of the gospel should perish, and undoubtedly they would have tarried longer if they had been suffered, but the prayers and requests of the magistrates were imperious and armed, which they are enforced to obey. Nevertheless, they foreslow [neglect] not their necessary duty, but they exhort the brethren to be constant. And whereas they went straight to Lydia, it is a token, that though the Church were increased, yet that woman was the chief even of a great number, as touching diligence in duties of godliness;[5] and that appeareth more plainly thereby, because all the godly were assembled in her house.

CHAPTER XVII.

1. *And when they had journeyed through Amphipolis and Appollonia, they came to Thessalonica, where was a synagogue of the Jews.*

---

[1] " Securibus," axes.   [2] " Coloniæ," colony.   [3] " Stupidam," stupid, dull   [4] " Ultro," vengeance.   [5] " In officiis pietatis," in offices of piety.

2. *And as his manner was, Paul entered in unto them, and three Sabbaths disputed with¹ them out of the Scriptures,*
3. *Opening and alleging that Christ must have suffered and rise again from the dead; and that this is Christ, whom, saith he, I preach to you.*
4. *And certain of them believed, and were joined to Paul and Silas, and of religious Grecians a great multitude, and of chief women not a few.*

1. *They came to Thessalonica.* We know not why Paul attempted nothing at Amphipolis and Appollonia, which were, notwithstanding, famous cities, as appeareth by Pliny; save only because he followed the Spirit of God as his guide; and took occasion by the present matter, as occasion was offered, to speak or hold his peace; and, peradventure, he did also essay to do some good there, but because it was without any good success, therefore Luke passeth over it. And whereas being beaten at Philippos, [Philippi,] and scarce escaping out of great danger, he preacheth Christ at Thessalonica, it appeareth thereby how courageous he was to keep the course of his calling, and how bold he was ever now and then to enter into new dangers.

This so invincible fortitude of mind, and such patient enduring of the cross, do sufficiently declare, that Paul laboured not after the manner of men, but that he was furnished with the heavenly power of the Spirit. And this was all so wonderful patience in him, in that, entering in unto the Jews, whose unbridled frowardness he had so often tried, [experienced,] he proceedeth to procure their salvation. But because he knew that Christ was given to the Jews for salvation, and that he himself was made an apostle upon this condition, that he should preach repentance and faith, first to the Jews and then to the Gentiles, committing the success of his labour to the Lord, he obeyeth his commandment, (though he had no great hope to do good.) He seemed before to have taken his last farewell of the Jews, when he said, It was behoveful that the kingdom of God should be

---

¹ " Disserebat," discoursed to.

first preached to you; but because ye receive it not, behold, we turn to the Gentiles; but that harder sentence must be restrained to that company who had wickedly rejected the gospel when it was offered unto them, and made themselves unworthy [of] the grace of God. And toward the nation itself Paul ceaseth not to do his embassage; by which example we are taught, that we ought to make so great account of the calling of God, that no unthankfulness of men may be able to hinder us, but that we proceed to be careful for their salvation, so long as the Lord appointeth us to be their ministers. And it is to be thought that even now there were some who on the first Sabbath refused sound doctrine, but their frowardness[1] did not hinder him, but that he came again upon other Sabbaths.

2. *He disputed.* Luke setteth down first what was the sum of the disputation; to wit, that Jesus, the son of Mary, is Christ, who was promised in times past in the law and the prophets, who, by the sacrifice of his death, did make satisfaction for the sins of the world, and brought righteousness and life by his resurrection; secondly, how he proved that which he taught. Let us handle this second member first. Luke saith that he disputed out of the Scriptures; therefore the proofs of faith must be fet from [sought at] the mouth of God alone. If we dispute about matters which concern men, then let human reasons take place; but in the doctrine of faith, the authority of God alone must reign, and upon it must we depend.

All men confess that this is true, that we must stay ourselves upon God alone; yet there be but a few which hear him speak in the Scriptures. But and if that maxim take place among us,[2] that the Scripture cometh of God, the rule either of teaching or of learning ought to be taken nowhere else. Whereby it doth also appear with what devilish fury the Papists are driven, when they deny that there can

---

[1] " Pravitas," depravity, perverseness.   [2] " Valet inter nos," is held good among us

any certainty be gathered out of the Scriptures; and, therefore, they hold that we must stand to the decrees of men. For I demand of them whether Paul did observe a right order in disputing or no? at least, let them blush for shame, that the Word of the Lord was more reverenced in an unbelieving nation than it is at this day among them. The Jews admit Paul, and suffer him when he disputeth out of the Scriptures; the Pope and all his count it a mere mock when the Scripture is cited; as if God did speak doubtfully there, and did with vain boughts[1] mock men. Hereunto is added, that there is at this day much more light in the Scripture, and the truth of God shineth there more clearly than in the law and the prophets. For in the gospel, Christ, who is the Sun of righteousness, doth shed out his beam with perfect brightness upon us; for which cause the blasphemy of the Papists is the more intolerable, whilst that they will make the Word of God as yet uncertain. But let us know, as faith can be grounded nowhere else than in the Word of the Lord, so we must only stand to the testimony thereof in all controversies.

3. *Opening.* In this place he describeth the sum or subject of the disputation, and he putteth down two members concerning Christ, that he must have died and risen again, and that the son of Mary which was crucified is Christ. When the question is concerning Christ, there come three things in question, Whether he be, who he is, and what he is. If Paul had had to deal with the Gentiles, he must have fet his beginning farther;[2] because they had heard nothing concerning Christ; neither do profane men conceive that they need a Mediator. But this point was out of doubt among the Jews, to whom the Mediator was promised; wherefore Paul omitteth that as superfluous, which was received by common consent of all men. But because there was nothing more hard than to bring the Jews to confess

---

[1] "Ambagibus," ambiguities. [2] "Necesse fuisset altius sumere exordium," it would have been necessary to go farther back with his exordium.

that Jesus who was crucified was the Redeemer, therefore Paul beginneth with this, that it was meet that Christ should die, that he may remove the stumbling-block of the cross. And yet we must not think that he recited the bare history, but he taketh an undoubted principle, that the causes were showed why Christ must have suffered and rise again; to wit, because he preached of the ruin of mankind, of sin and of the punishment thereof, of the judgment of God, and of the eternal curse wherein we are all enwrapped. For even the Scripture calleth us hither, when it foretelleth the death of Christ. As Isaias saith not simply that Christ should die, but plainly expressing, because [that] we have all erred, and every one hath gone his own way, he assigneth the cause of his death, that God hath laid upon him all our iniquities; that the chastisement of our peace is upon him, that by his stripes we may be healed; that by making satisfaction for us, he hath purchased righteousness for us, (Isaiah liii. 4–8.) So doth Daniel show the force and fruit of his death in his 9th chapter, (Dan. ix. 24,) when he saith that sin must be sealed up, that eternal righteousness may succeed.

And, surely, there is no more apt or effectual way to prove the office of Christ, than when men, being humbled with the feeling of their miseries, see that there is no hope left, unless they be reconciled by the sacrifice of Christ. Then laying away their pride, they humbly embrace his cross, whereof they were before both weary and ashamed. Therefore, we must come unto the same fountains at this day, from which Paul fetteth [fetcheth] the proof of the death and resurrection of Christ. And that definition brought great light to the second chapter. It had not been so easy a matter for Paul to prove, and certainly to gather, that the Son of Mary is Christ, unless the Jews had been taught before what manner of Redeemer they were to hope for. And when that doth once appear, it doth only remain that those things be applied to Christ which the Scripture doth attribute to the Mediator. But this is the sum of our faith, that we know that the Son of Mary is that Christ and Mediator which God promised from the beginning; that done, that we know and understand why he died and rose again; that we do not feign to ourselves any earthly king, but that we seek in him righteousness, and all parts of our salvation; both which things Paul is said to have proved out of the Scriptures. We must know that the Jews were not so blockish, nor so impudent, as they be at this day. Paul might have drawn arguments from the sacrifices and from all the worship of the law, whereat the Jews gnarl at this day like dogs. It is well known how unseemly they rent and corrupt other places of Scripture. At that day they had some courtesy[1] in them; also they did somewhat reverence the Scripture, so that they were not altogether such as would not be taught; at this day the veil is laid over their hearts, (2 Cor. iii. 15,) so that they can see no more in the clear light than moles.

4. *Certain of them believed.* We see here the fruit of Paul's disputation. He proved flatly [plainly] that Jesus was Christ, who, by his death, did appease the Father's wrath for us, and whose resurrection is the life of the world. Yet only certain of the Jews believe; the rest are blind at noonday, and with deaf ears refuse the certain and plain truth. This is also worth the noting, that whereas only a few Jews believed, a great multitude of the Grecians, who were far farther off, came unto the faith. To what end can you say they were nousled [trained] up in the doctrine of the law from their childhood, save only that they might be more estranged from God? Therefore, the Lord doth now begin to show some tokens of that blindness in them which the prophets do oftentimes denounce unto them. Notwithstanding, he declareth by this that his covenant was not in vain, because he did at least gather some of that people unto himself, that the sparkles of the election may shine in the remnant which was saved freely. Luke doth moreover teach, that they did not believe the sayings of Paul, only so far forth that they subscribed unto them with a cold consent, but that they did testify their earnest affection, because they

[1] " Ingenuitas," ingenuousness

had joined themselves to Paul and Silas as companions, and provoked against themselves the hatred of their nation by the free profession of the gospel.[1] For what meaneth this adjoining, save only because they professed that they allowed [approved] that doctrine which he delivered, and that they took his part? For there is nothing more contrary to faith, than if, when we know [recognise] the truth of God, we stand notwithstanding in doubt, and are loath to join ourselves to any side. If any man had rather expound it, that they did join themselves to Paul and Silas, because they were desirous to learn, that they might be better instructed at home; thereby doth also appear the lively heat of faith; and that doth always continue unmoveable, that no man doth truly believe in Christ, save only he which doth give over himself to him, and doth freely and willingly fight under his banner.

Of religious Grecians a multitude. Because they had learned [imbibed] the first principles of godliness, they were nearer to the kingdom of God than others who had always [lain] laid in the filth of superstition. Notwithstanding, the question is, how the Grecians came by religion, who, being bewitched with wicked errors and dotings, were without God? as Paul teacheth, (Ephes. ii. 12.) But we must know, that whither soever the Jews were exiled, there went with them some seed of godliness,[2] and there was some smell [savour] of pure doctrine spread abroad. For their miserable scattering abroad was so turned unto a contrary end by the wonderful counsel of God, that it did gather those unto the true faith who did wander in error. And though religion were also corrupt among them with many wicked inventions, yet because most of the Gentiles were weary of their madness, they were by this short sum[3] enticed unto Judaism, that nothing is more safe than the worship of one and the true God. Therefore, by religious Grecians understand those who had some taste of the true and lawful worship of God,

---

[1] "Ingenua," frank, ingenuous.
[2] "Dispersum fuisse aliquod prelatis semen," some seed of piety was spread.
[3] "Hoc compendio," by this compendious argument, viz

so that they were not any longer given to gross idolatry. Though, as I have said, it is to be thought that it was only a light and obscure taste, which was far from true instruction. Wherefore, Luke doth improperly give them such an honourable title. But as the Spirit of God doth sometimes vouchsafe [to give] some rude beginning and first exercise of faith, or the only [mere] preparation, the name of faith, so they are called in this place religious, who, having taken their leave of idols, had begun to acknowledge one God.

And though that confused or obscure persuasion doth not deserve of itself to be counted religion, yet because it is a step whereby we come nearer unto God, it taketh the name of the consequent, as they call it, or of that which followeth. Yea, the blind and superstitious fear of God is sometimes called religion; not because it is so indeed, but improperly, to note the difference between a mean worship of God,[1] and gross and Epicurish contempt. Nevertheless, let us know that the truth and the sound doctrine of the word of God is the rule of godliness, so that there can be no religion without the true light of understanding.

> 5. *And the unbelieving Jews being moved with envy, [zeal,] and taking to them certain vagabonds, froward fellows, and having assembled the multitude, they made a tumult in the city; and besetting the house of Jason, they sought to bring them out unto the people.*
> 6. *And when they had not found them, they drew Jason and certain brethren unto the governors of the city, crying, Those who have troubled the whole world are come hither also,*
> 7. *Whom Jason hath received privily; and all these do contrary to the decrees of Cæsar, saying that there is another king, one Jesus.*
> 8. *And they troubled* [stirred up] *the multitude and the magistrates of the city when they heard these things:*
> 9. *And when they had received sufficient assurance of Jason and the rest, they let them go.*
> 10. *And forthwith the brethren sent forth Paul and Silas by*

---

[1] "Qualemcunque Dei cultum," any kind of divine worship.

night unto Berea, who, when they were come, they went into the synagogue of the Jews.

5. *And being moved with envy.* We see how Paul could nowhere erect the kingdom of Christ without some conflict, for so soon as any fruit of doctrine appeared, there arose persecution therewithal; but because he knew that he was to war against Satan and the wickedness of the world, he was not only hardened against all assaults, but he was more encouraged more courageously to proceed. Therefore, all the servants of Christ must be content with this one example of him, if they see that their labour doth yield some fruit, they must recompense all manner of persecutions with this reward. And this place teacheth that the zeal wherewith the unbelievers are carried headlong, and set on fire, is nothing else but furious force,[1] because it is not governed by the prudence of the Spirit, neither yet with righteousness or equity. And though they do always pretend the name of God for an excuse of their disordered zeal, yet this history doth plainly declare, that mere hypocrisy doth reign inwardly, and that all corners of their hearts are stuffed with poisoned malice. These enemies of Paul did boast that they were defenders of the law of God; and that they did hate Paul, and contend with him only in defence thereof.

Why do they then arm the wicked, and conspire together with them to raise tumult? Why then do they also before a profane magistrate bring the gospel in that contempt which might have redounded to the contempt of the law? Such sedition doth plainly declare, that they were moved with nothing less than with desire to please God, to be thus hot against Paul, for to what end do they beset Jason's house, and strive disorderly[2] to pluck out Paul thence, save only that they may set him before the people to be stoned? Therefore, let us know that wicked zeal, which is hot [boils] in superstitious men, is always infected with hypocrisy and malice; and this is the cause that it breaketh out into cruelty without keeping any measure.

Taking to them certain vagabonds. The Greek word

[1] " Rabiosum . . . impetum," a rabid impulse.   [2] " Tumultuose," tumultuously.

which Luke useth doth signify sluggards, and men whereof there ought no account to be made, who, having nothing wherewith they could keep themselves occupied at home, did run up and down idle ;[1] or bold [audacious] fellows and hungry, who are ready to forswear themselves to raise tumults, and to be at one end of [2] every wicked fact. Whereby it doth likewise appear that their own consciences told them that they did amiss, seeing they got wicked men to take their part, and to give them their consent. For seeing the magistrate did favour them, what did move them to raise that tempest, save only because they had no hope to have any success, unless (matters should be out of order and) all should be in an uproar? And Luke describeth how such fans did raise sedition ; to wit, they gathered the people together in troops, and spread abroad their poison here and there, until they were strong enough to make an assault ;[3] which policy [artifice] is too common among seditious fellows, as those cities which are subject to this mischief do full well know.

6. *Those men who have troubled the whole world.* This is the state of the gospel, to have those uproars which Satan raiseth imputed to it. This is also the maliciousness of the enemies of Christ, to lay the blame of tumults upon holy and modest teachers, which they themselves procure. Assuredly, the gospel is not preached to this end that it may set men together by the ears ;[4] but rather that it may keep them in peace, being reconciled to God. When Christ doth meekly will us[5] there to come unto him, Satan and the wicked rage ;[6] therefore, Paul and Silas might easily have defended themselves; but it was requisite for them to suffer this false slander for a time ; and so long as they were not heard, to put it up quietly. And the Lord meant by their example to teach

---

[1] " Per forum," through the market-place   [2] " Operam suam locare," hire out their assistance in   [3] " Donec ad vim inferendam sufficerent," until they were able to offer violence.   [4] " Ut homines ad mutuos conflictus accendat," that it may inflame men to mutual conflict.   [5] " Ad se benigne invitet," benignity invite us to himself.   [6] " Tumultuantur," make a tumult.

us, that we must not give place to slanders and false reports; but we must stand stoutly in maintaining the truth, being ready to hear evil for things done well. Wherefore, away with the perverse wisdom of some, who, to the end they may escape false slanders, cease [hesitate] not to betray Christ and his gospel through their treacherous moderation, as though their good name were more precious than Paul's and such like, yea, than the sacred name of God, which is not free from blasphemies.

7. *All these men, &c.* The second point of the accusation is this, that they violate the majesty of the empire of Rome. A great and grievous crime, yet too impudently forged. Paul and Silas sought to erect the kingdom of Christ, which is spiritual. The Jews knew well that this might be done without doing any injury to the Roman empire. They knew that they meant nothing less than to overthrow the public estate, or to take from Cæsar his authority. Therefore, the Jews catch at the pretence of treason, that they may oppress the innocent with the envy of the crime alone.[1]

Neither doth Satan cease at this day to blear men's eyes with such smokes and mists. The Papists know full well, and they be sufficiently convict before God, that that is more than false which they lay to our charge, That we overthrow all civil government; that laws and judgments are quite taken away; that the authority of kings is subverted by us; and yet they be not ashamed to the end they may make all the whole world offended with us, falsely to report that we be enemies to public order; for we must note that the Jews do not only allege that Cæsar's commandments were broken, because Paul and Silas durst presume to alter and innovate somewhat in religion, but because they said there was another king. This crime was alto-

---

[1] " Sed colorem hunc malitiose obtendunt quærendæ invidiæ causa. Non tanti erat apud Macedones religio, præsertim Judaica, ut ejus causa homines ignotos, protinus ad cædem raperent," but maliciously use this pretext for the purpose of producing obloquy. There was not so much religion, especially Jewish, among the Macedonians, that for its sake they would hurry off strangers to execution Omitted.

gether forged; but if at any time religion enforce us to resist tyrannical edicts and commandments which forbid us to give due honour to Christ, and due worship to God; we may then justly say for ourselves, that we are not rebellious against kings, for they be not so exalted, that they may go about like giants to pull God out of his seat and throne. That excuse of Daniel was true, that he had not offended the king, whereas notwithstanding he had not obeyed his wicked commandment, neither had he injured mortal man, because he had preferred God before him. So let us faithfully pay to princes the tributes which are due to them, let us be ready to give them all civil obedience; but if, being not content with their degree, they go about to pluck out of our hands the fear and worship of God, there is no cause why any should say that we despise them, because we make more account of the power and majesty of God.

8. *They raised the multitude.* We see how unjustly the holy men were handled. Because they had no place granted them to defend themselves, it was an easy matter to oppress them, though they were guiltless. We see, likewise, that it is no new matter for magistrates to be carried away with the rage of the people as with a tempest, especially when the injury toucheth those who are strangers and unknown, at whose hands they look for no reward; because they will not come in danger for nothing. For then they care not for reason or equity, neither do they hear the matter,[1] but one driveth forward another without any resistance, and all things are done out of order, as when they run unto some great fire. But it came to pass, by the singular goodness of God, that so great heat was stayed by and by; for so soon as the magistrates profess that they will know farther of the matter, the multitude is appeased; assurance [security] is taken; and, at length, the matter is ended.

---

[1] " Nec suscipitur causæ cognitio," nor do they take cognisance of the cause.

10. *They sent them out to Berea.* Hereby it appeareth that Paul's labour brought forth fruit in a small time; for though the brethren send forth him and Silas, yet they adjoin themselves as voluntary companions to their danger and cross by this duty. But the constancy of Paul is incredible, because, having had such experience of their stubbornness and malice of his nation, he doth never cease to try whether he can bring any to Christ, namely, seeing he knew that he was bound both to Jews and Gentiles, no injury of men could lead him away from his calling. So all the servants of Christ must so wrestle with the malice of the world, that they shake not off Christ's yoke with what injuries soever they be provoked.

11. *And those were noblemen among the Thessalonians, who had received the word with all readiness of mind, daily searching the Scriptures whether these things were so.*
12. *And many of them believed; and honest women which were Grecians, and men not a few.*
13. *But when the Jews of Thessalonica knew that Paul did also preach the word of God at Berea, they came thither also, moving the multitudes.*
14. *And then straightway the brethren sent forth Paul that he might go as it were unto the sea: but Silas and Timotheus remained there.*
15. *Moreover, those which guided Paul brought him even unto Athens: and when they had received commandment to Silas and Timotheus that they should come to him with speed, they departed*

11. *Did excel in nobility.* Luke returneth again unto the men of Thessalonica. The remembrance of Christ might have been thought to have been buried by the departure of Paul, and surely it is a wonder that that small light, which began to shine, was not quite put out, and that the seed of sound doctrine did not wither away, which had need continually to be watered that it might spring up. But after Paul's departure, it appeared how effectual and fruitful his preaching had been. For those who had only

tasted of the first principles of godliness do nevertheless profit and go forward, though he be absent, and exercise themselves in the continual reading of the Scripture. And, first, Luke saith that they were of the chief families. For the nobility whereof he maketh mention is referred not unto the mind, but unto the nation. Some think that the men of Berea are compared with the men of Thessalonica, because he saith ευγινεστερους, and not in the superlative degree ευγενεστατους. But I think that that manner of speech is usual and common among the Grecians, which the Latins could not so well digest.[1] Moreover, he had said a little before, that certain principal women believed at Thessalonica, and it is not to be thought that the men of Berea were preferred before those of this city. And there is a threefold reason why Luke maketh mention of their excellency of birth. We know how hardly men come down from their high degree, what a rare matter it is for those who are great in the world to undertake the reproach of the cross, laying away their pride, and rejoice in humility, as James commandeth, (James i. 10.)

Therefore Luke commendeth the rare efficacy and working of the Spirit of God, when he saith that these noblemen were no whit hindered by the dignity of the flesh, but that embracing the gospel, they prepared themselves to bear the cross, and preferred the reproach of Christ before the glory of the world. Secondly, Luke meant to make known unto us, that the grace of Christ standeth open for all orders and degrees. In which sense Paul saith, that God would have all men saved, (1 Tim. ii. 4;) lest the poor and those who are base do shut the gate against the rich, (though Christ did vouchsafe them the former place.) Therefore we see that noblemen, and those who are of the common sort,[2] are gathered together, that those who are men of honour, and which are despised, grow together into

---

[1] " Quæ Latinis auribus esset durior," which would have sounded harsher to Latin ears   [2] " Nobiles et plebeios," that nobles and plebeians.

one body of the Church, that all men, in general, may humble themselves, and extol the grace of God. Thirdly, Luke seemeth to note the cause why there were so many added, and the kingdom of Christ was, in such short time, so spread abroad and enlarged at Thessalonica; to wit, because that was no small help, that chief men, and men of honour, did show other men the way, because the common sort is for the most part moved by authority. And though this were no meet stay for faith and godliness, yet is it no strange thing for God to bring the unbelievers (who wander as yet in error) to himself, by crooked and byways.[1]

Received the word. This is the first thing which he commendeth in the men of Thessalonica, that with a willing and ready desire they received the gospel. Secondly, that they confirmed their faith [2] by diligent inquisition; so that their faith and godliness are commended in the beginning for forwardness,[3] and in process they are praised for their constancy and fervent desire they had to profit. And surely this is the first entrance into faith that we be ready to follow, and that, abandoning the understanding and wisdom of the flesh,[4] we submit ourselves to Christ, by him to be taught and to obey him. Also Paul himself, in adorning the Thessalonians with this title, doth agree with Saint Luke, (1 Thes. ii. 13.)

As touching the second member, this diligence is no small virtue, whereunto Luke saith the faithful were much given for confirmation of their faith. For many who at the first break out[5] give themselves straightway to idleness, while that they have no care to profit, and so lose that small seed[6] which they had at the first.

But two inconveniences[7] may be in this place objected; for it seemeth to be a point of arrogancy in that they inquire that they may judge; and it seemeth to be a thing

---

[1] " Per obliquas vias," through winding paths   [2] " Quotidie," daily
[3] " Initio a promptitudine," at the commencement for promptitude or readiness   [4] " Proprio carnis sensu," our own carnal sense.
[5] " Ebulliunt," spring forth.   [6] " Fidei semen," seed of faith.
[7] " Absurda," absurdities.

altogether disagreeing with that readiness whereof he spake of late ; secondly, forasmuch as inquisition is a sign of doubtfulness, it followeth that they were before endued with no faith, which hath always assurance and certainty joined and linked with it. Unto the first objection I answer, that Luke's words ought not so to be understood, as if the Thessalonians took upon them to judge, or as though they disputed whether the truth of God were to be received; they did only examine Paul's doctrine by the rule and square of the Scripture, even as gold is tried in the fire; for the Scripture is the true touchstone whereby all doctrines must be tried. If any man say that this kind of trial is doubtful, forasmuch as the Scripture is oftentimes doubtful, and is interpreted divers ways, I say, that we must also add the judgment of the Spirit, who is, not without cause, called the Spirit of discretion, [discernment.] But the faithful must judge of every doctrine no otherwise than out of, and according to, the Scriptures, having the Spirit for their leader and guide. And by this means is refuted that sacrilegious quip [quibble] of the Papists, Because there can be nothing gathered certainly out of the Scriptures, faith doth depend only upon the determination of the Church. For when the Spirit of God doth commend the men of Thessalonica, he prescribeth to us a rule in their example. And in vain should we search the Scriptures, unless they have in them light enough to teach us.

Therefore, let this remain as a most sure maxim, that no doctrine is worthy to be believed but that which we find to be grounded in the Scriptures. The Pope will have all that received without any more ado, whatsoever he doth blunder out at his pleasure ; but shall he be preferred before Paul, concerning whose preaching it was lawful for the disciples to make inquisition ? And let us note that this is not spoken of any visured [pretended] Council, but of a small assembly of men, whereby it doth better appear that every man is called to read the Scripture. So likewise, making of search doth not disagree with the forwardness of faith ; for so soon as any man doth hearken, and being desirous to learn, doth show himself attentive, he is now bent and apt to be taught, though he do not fully[1] give his consent. For example's sake, an unknown teacher shall profess that he doth bring true doctrine: I will come, being ready to hear, and my mind shall be framed unto the obedience of the truth. Nevertheless, I will weigh with myself what manner [of] doctrine it is which he bringeth; neither will I embrace anything but the certain truth, and that which I know to be the truth. And this is the best moderation, when, being fast bound with the reverence of God, we hear that willingly and quietly which is set before us, as proceeding from him. Nevertheless, we beware of the seducing subtilty of men; neither do our minds throw themselves headlong with a blind rage[2] to believe every thing without advisement. Therefore, the searching mentioned by Luke doth not tend to that end that we may be slow and unwilling to believe, but rather readiness with judgment is made the mean between lightness and stubbornness.

Now must we answer the second objection. Faith is contrary to doubtfulness: he which inquireth doubteth; therefore it followeth, that forasmuch as the Thessalonians inquire and make search touching the doctrine of Paul, they were void of faith as yet. But the certainty of faith doth not hinder the confirmation thereof. I call that confirmation when the truth of God is more and more sealed up in our hearts, whereof, notwithstanding, we did not doubt before. For example's sake, I hear out of the gospel that I am reconciled to God through the grace of Christ, and that my sins are purged [expiated] through his holy blood: there shall be some testimony uttered which shall make me believe this. If afterward I examine and search the Scriptures more thoroughly, I shall find other testimonies oftentimes which shall not only help my faith, but also increase it and establish it, that it may be more sure and settled. In like sort, as concerning understanding, faith is in-

---

[1] "Statim plane," plainly, and at once. with a blind and giddy impulse.
[2] "Cæco levitatis impetu,"

creased by reading the Scriptures. If any man object again, that those men do attribute but small authority to Paul's doctrine, who search the Scriptures whether these things be so, I answer, that such are the proceedings of faith, that they sometimes seek for that in the Scripture whereof they are already persuaded by God, and have the inward testimony of the Spirit. And Luke doth not say that the faith of the Thessalonians was in all points perfect; but he doth only declare how they were brought to Christ,[1] and how they did profit in faith, until the absolute building of godliness might be erected among them.

12. *And many believed.* This is not referred unto the sentence next going before, as if those of whom he spake began to believe, making choice of some of them : for that were an absurd thing. But Luke's meaning is, because many were added by their example, the Church was increased in that city. And hitherto hath Luke declared the first beginning of the church of Thessalonica, lest any man should think that Paul's labours did perish through his sudden and violent departure; for unless I be much deceived, he showeth for this purpose what fruit his preaching brought forth in the other city, before he came to the exile of Berea.

13. *And when the Jews.* We see how the Jews were carried to and fro with such hatred of the gospel as could never be appeased. For they do not only expel Christ furiously when he is offered unto them at home; but when they hear that he is preached elsewhere, they run thither like mad men. But we must not so much in this place consider the fury of the nation as the desperate malice of Satan, who pricketh forward those which be his to trouble the kingdom of Christ, and to destroy man's salvation ; and he useth them as fans to raise sedition. Wherefore, let us know, that when at this day so many furious enemies do set themselves against the faithful ministers of Christ, it is not

---

[1] " Qualiter initiati fuerint Christo," how they were initiated in Christ

men which procure the war, but it is Satan, the father of lying, who doth go about all these things that he may overthrow the kingdom of Christ, (John viii. 44.) And though there be not always the same form in fighting and encountering, yet will Satan never cease to make weary those whom he knoweth to serve Christ faithfully, either with open war, or secret lying in wait, or domestical combats.

16. *And as Paul waited for them at Athens, his spirit was sore grieved in him, forasmuch as he saw the city given to idolatry.*
17. *Therefore he disputed in the synagogue with the Jews and religious men, and in the market daily with those which lit upon him.*
18. *And certain Epicures,* [Epicureans,] *and philosophers of the Stoics, disputed with him, and some said, What will this babbler say? and other some, He seemeth to be a declarer of new devils,* [or gods,] *because he preached to them Jesus and the resurrection.*
19. *And when they had caught him, they led him to Mars' Street, saying, May we know what new doctrine this is which thou utterest?*
20. *For thou bringest certain new things to our ears: Therefore, we will know what these things mean.*
21. *And all the men of Athens, and the strangers which were there, gave themselves to nothing else but to speak or hear some new thing.*

16. *Was sore grieved.* Though Paul, whithersoever he came, did stoutly execute that function of teaching which he knew was enjoined him, yet Luke showeth that he was more incensed and moved at Athens, because he saw idolatry reign more there than in any other place for the most part. The whole world was then full of idols; the pure worship of God could be found nowhere; and there were everywhere innumerable monsters of superstitions, but Satan had made the city of Athens more mad than any other city, so that the people thereof were carried headlong with greater madness unto their wicked and perverse rites. And

this example is worth the noting, that the city, which was the mansion-house of wisdom, the fountain of all arts, the mother of humanity, did exceed all others in blindness and madness. We know with what commendations witty and learned men did set forth the same, and she had conceived so great good liking of herself that she counted those rude[1] whom she had not polished. But the Holy Ghost condemning the whole world of ignorance and blockishness, saith that those masters of liberal sciences were bewitched with an unwonted madness. Whence we gather what man's wit can do in matters which concern God. Neither need we doubt of this, but that the Lord suffered the men of Athens to fall into extreme madness, that all the world might learn by them, and that they might teach all ages that the foresight and wit of man's mind being holpen with learning and instruction, doth altogether dote, and is mere foolishness when it cometh to the kingdom of God. They had undoubtedly their cloaks and colours, wherewith they did excuse their worshippings, how preposterous and corrupt soever they were. And yet, notwithstanding, it is certain that they did not only deceive men with childish and frivolous toys, but that they themselves were deluded shamefully with gross and filthy jugglings, as if they were deprived of common sense, and were altogether blockish and brutish. And as we learn what manner [of] religion proceedeth from man's understanding, and that man's wisdom is nothing else but a shop of all errors, so we may know that the men of Athens, being drunk with their own pride, did err more filthily than the rest. The antiquity, the pleasantness, and beauty of the city, did puff them up, so that they did boast that the gods came thence. Therefore, forasmuch as they did pull down God from heaven, that they might make him an inhabitant of their city, it was meet that they should be thrust down into the nethermost hell. Howsoever it be, the vanity of man's wisdom is here marked with eternal infamy by the Spirit of God; because, where it

---

[1] " Barbaros," barbarians.

was principally resident, there was the darkness more thick. Idolatry did reign most of all there; and Satan carried men's minds to and fro more freely by his mocks and juggling.

Now, let us come unto Paul. Luke saith, forasmuch as he saw the city so given to idolatry, his spirit waxed hot, or was moved. Where he doth not attribute unto him indignation only, neither doth he only say that he was offended with that spectacle, but he expresseth the unwonted heat of holy anger, which sharpened his zeal, so that he did address himself more fervently unto the work. And here we must note two things. For in that Paul was wroth when he saw the name of God wickedly profaned, and his pure worship corrupted, he did thereby declare, that nothing was to him more precious than the glory of God. Which zeal ought to be of great force among us, as it is in the Psalm, (Psalm lxix. 9,) "The zeal of thine house hath eaten me up." For it is a common rule of all the godly, that so soon as they see their heavenly Father blasphemed, they be sore vexed, as Peter teacheth that the godly man Lot, because he could not cure most filthy facts, did vex his heart, (2 Pet. ii. 8.) And teachers must, above all others, be fervent, as Paul saith, that he is jealous that he may retain the Church in true chastity, (2 Cor. xi. 2.) And those who are not touched when they see and hear God blasphemed, and do not only wink thereat, but also carelessly pass over it, are not worthy to be counted the children of God, who at least do not give him so much honour as they do to an earthly father. Secondly, we must note that he was not so grieved, that being cast down through despair, he was quite discouraged, as we see most men to be far from waxing hot, or being moved, when they see the glory of God wickedly profaned, that in professing and uttering sorrow and sighing, they do, notwithstanding, rather wax profane with others than study to reform them. Nevertheless, they have a fair cloak for their sluggishness, that they will not procure any tumult when they are like to do no good.[1] For they think

---

[1] "Quod nolunt sine profectu tumultuare," that they are unwilling to excite tumult to no good purpose.

that their attempts shall be in vain if they strive against the wicked and violent conspiracy of the people. But Paul is not only not discouraged with wearisomeness, neither doth he so faint by reason of the hardness of the matter, that he doth cast from him his office of teaching; but he is pricked forward with a more sharp prick to maintain godliness.

17. *With the Jews and religious men.* It was an ordinary thing with Paul, wheresoever the Jews had synagogues, there to begin, and to offer Christ to his own nation. After that he went to the Gentiles, who, having tasted of the doctrine of the law, though they were not as yet thoroughly nousled up in [imbued with] true godliness, did, notwithstanding, worship the God of Israel, and being desirous to learn, did not refuse those things which they knew were taken out of Moses and the prophets; and because such aptness to be taught was an entrance unto faith, yea, was a certain beginning of faith, the Spirit vouchsafeth them an honourable title, who being only lightly sprinkled with the first rudiments, drew nearer unto the true God; for they be called religious. But let us remember that they be distinguished from others by this mark, that all the religion of the world may be brought to nought. Those are called worshippers of God spiritually who gave their name to the God of Israel. Religion is attributed to them alone; therefore there remaineth nothing else for the rest but the reproach of atheism, howsoever they toil and moil[1] in superstition. And that for good considerations; for of whatsoever pomp the idolaters make boast, if their inward affection be examined, there shall be nothing found there but horrible contempt of God, and it shall appear that it is a mere feigned colour wherewith they go about to excuse their idols.

18. *They reasoned with him.* Luke addeth now that Paul had a combat with the philosophers; not that he set upon

---

[1] " Anxie se torqucant," anxiously torment themselves

them of set purpose, forasmuch as he knew that they were even born only to brawl and cavil; but he was enforced to enter such a conflict contrary to his purpose, as Paul himself commandeth godly teachers to be furnished with spiritual weapons, wherewith they may valiantly defend the truth if any enemies set themselves against it, (Titus i. 9.) For it is not always in our choice to make choice of those with whom we will deal; but the Lord doth often suffer stubborn and importunate men to arise to exercise us, that by their gainsaying the truth may more plainly appear. Neither is it to be doubted but that the Epicures, [Epicureans,] according to their wonted frowardness, did trouble the holy man; and that the Stoics, trusting to their subtile quips and cavils, did stubbornly deride him;[1] yet the end shall show that he did not dispute sophistically, neither was he carried away unto any unprofitable and contentious disputation, but did observe that modesty which he himself commandeth elsewhere. And thus must we do, that by refuting meekly and modestly vain cavillings, we may utter that which is sound and true; and we must always avoid this danger, that ambition or desire to show our wit do not inwrap us in superfluous and vain contentions.

Furthermore, Luke maketh mention of two sects, which, though they were the one contrary to the other,[2] had, notwithstanding, their contrary vices. The Epicures [Epicureans] did not only despise liberal arts, but were also open enemies to them. Their philosophy was to feign that the sun was two feet broad, that the world was made *ex atomis*, [of atoms,] (or of things which were so small that they could not be divided or made smaller,) and by deluding men thus, to blot out the wonderful workmanship which appeareth in the creation of the world. If they were a thousand times convict, they were as impudent as dogs. Though they did, in a word, confess that there be gods, yet they did imagine that they were idle in heaven, and that they were wholly set upon pleasure, and

---

[1] "Contumaciter insultaverint," did contumaciously insult him

[2] "Ex diametro inter se essent oppositæ," were diametrically opposed to each other.

that they were blessed only because they were idle. As they did deny that the world was created by God, as I have said of late, so they thought that man's affairs were tossed to and fro without any governing, and that they were not governed by the celestial providence. Pleasure was their felicity,[1] not that unbridled and filthy pleasure; yet such as did more and more corrupt men by her enticements, being already, of their own accord, bent to pamper the flesh They counted the immortality of their souls but a fable, whereby it came to pass that they gave themselves liberty to make much of their bodies.

As for the Stoics, though they said that the world was subject to the providence of God, yet did they afterwards, through a most filthy surmise, or rather doting, corrupt that point of their doctrine. For they did not grant that God did govern the world by counsel, justice, and power, but they forged a labyrinth of the compass or agreement of the causes, that God himself being bound with the necessity of fate or destiny, might be carried violently with the frame of heaven, as the poets do tie and fetter their Jupiter with golden fetters, because the Fates or Destinies do govern when he is about something else. Though they placed felicity [the chief good] in virtue, they knew not what true virtue was, and they did puff up men with pride,[2] so that they did deck themselves with that which they took from God. For though they did all abase the grace of the Holy Ghost, yet was there no sect more proud. They had no other fortitude, but a certain rash and immoderate fierceness.[3]

Therefore there was in Paul wonderful force of the Spirit, who standing amidst such beasts, which sought to pull him to and fro, stood firm in the sound sincerity of the gospel, and did valiantly withstand and endure, as well the dogged malapertness [petulance] of the former sect, as the pride and crafty cavillings of the other. And hereby we see more plainly what small agreement there is between the heavenly

---

[1] "Summum bonum," the supreme good. [2] "Superba confidentia," with proud confidence. [3] "Ferrea immanitus," iron-hearted cruelty.

wisdom and the wisdom of the flesh. For though the whole multitude were offended with the gospel, yet the philosophers were captains and standard-bearers in assaulting the same. For that did principally appear in them which Paul himself speaketh of the wisdom of the flesh, that it is an enemy to the cross of Christ, (1 Cor. i. 26,) so that no man can be fit to learn the principles of the gospel unless he first abandon the same.

Other some said. Luke setteth before us two sorts of men, which both were far from godliness; and yet the one sort is worse than the other. Those who are desirous to hear that again which they call new, first, they are moved not with any right desire to learn, but with vain curiosity; secondly, they think unhonourably of the Word of God, in that they count it profane novelty; yet because they give ear, and that being in doubt until they may know farther of the matter, they are not quite past hope. But the rest who proudly refuse that which is offered, yea, condemn it reproachfully, do shut the gate of salvation against themselves. For this railing did proceed from monstrous pride; what meaneth this babbler? Because they neither vouchsafe to hear Paul, and also reproachfully refuse him, as if he were some common jester.[1] Moreover, they do not loathe his doctrine through rash zeal, but do openly tread under foot that which is brought unto them concerning religion, though as yet they know it not; because these are ashamed to learn any thing of a base and obscure fellow, who had hitherto professed themselves to be teachers of all the whole world.

A declarer of new devils. They do not take devils [deities] in evil part, as the Scripture useth to do; but for the lesser gods or angels, who they thought were in the midst between the highest God and men, whereof Plato maketh mention oftentimes. As touching the sum of the matter, we must note that those things which Paul spake concerning Christ and the resurrection seemed to them to be new devils. Whence we gather, that our faith is principally distinguished

---

[1] " Trivialis nugator," silly or paltry trifler.

and discerned from the superstitions of the Gentiles by these marks; because it setteth forth Christ to be the sole Mediator; because it teacheth us to seek for salvation only at his hands; because it commandeth us to seek remission of our sins in his death, whereby we may be reconciled to God; because it teacheth that men are renewed and fashioned again by his Spirit, who were before profane, and slaves to sin, that they may begin to live righteously and holy. Again, because from such beginnings as do plainly declare that the kingdom of God is spiritual, it lifteth up our minds at length unto the hope of the resurrection to come. For as concerning other things, though the philosophers do not reason purely, yet they say somewhat. Yea, they speak much concerning eternal life and the immortality of the soul; but as touching faith, which showeth free reconciliation in Christ; and regeneration, whereby the Spirit of God doth restore in us the image of God; concerning calling upon God, and the last resurrection, not a word.

19. *They brought him to Mars' Street.* Though this were a place appointed for judgment, yet Luke doth not mean that Paul was brought before the seat of the judges, that he might plead his cause before the judges of Mars' Street.[1] But that he was brought thither, where was most commonly a great assembly of people, that the serious disputation might be had before a great and famous audience. And admit we grant that he was brought before the judgment-seat, yet the end doth declare that he was not presented to the judges, but that he had free liberty to speak as before an audience. And that which followeth shortly after, touching the nature and conditions [manners] of the men of Athens, doth sufficiently declare that their curiosity was the cause; that Paul had such audience given him, that he had such a famous place granted him to preach Christ in, that so many came together. For in any other place it had been a crime worthy of death, to speak in the market or in any other public

---

[1] " Areopagitis," the Areopagites

place, having gathered a company of people together; but there, because those who did carry about trifles had liberty granted them to prate, by reason of the immoderate desire they had to hear news, Paul was permitted to intreat of the mysteries of faith, being requested.

Gave themselves to nothing else. The two vices which Luke reciteth do almost always go together. For it falleth out seldom that those who are desirous of novelties are not also babblers. For that saying of Horace is most true, "Fly a demander of questions, for the same is also a blab." And surely we see that curious men are like rent barrels.[1] Furthermore, both vices came of idleness; not only because the philosophers spent whole days in disputing, but because the common sort was too much set upon novelty; neither was there any craftsman so base there, which would not thrust in himself to set in order the state of Grecia. And surely that which Luke saith here is witnessed by all writers, both Greek and Latin, that there was nothing more light, covetous, or froward than that people. Wherefore, there could never be any certain government set down in that city, which was, notwithstanding, the mistress of sciences. Therefore, in principal power,[2] they had, notwithstanding, no long liberty; neither did they ever cease off from attempting things and making many hurly-burlies, until they brought themselves and all Grecia to utter ruin. For when their state was decayed, yet did not they forsake their boldness. Therefore, Cicero doth laugh at their folly, because they did no less fiercely set forth their decrees then, than when they were lords over Grecia. Now, though there were small hope to do any good among curious men, yet Paul did not neglect the opportunity, if, peradventure, he might gain some of a great company to Christ. Neither was this any small praise for the gospel in the most noble place of the city, and, as it were, in a common theatre, to refute and

---

[1] "Doliis pertusis," broken, leaking casks.   [2] "In summa potentia," though in supreme power, (an independent state.)

openly to reprove all forged and false worshippings, which had reigned there even until this day.

> 22. *And, standing in the midst of Mars' Street, he saith, Men of Athens, I see you in all things, as it were, more superstitious.*
> 23. *For, passing by and beholding your manner of worshipping, I found also an altar wherein was written,* To the unknown God. *Therefore, whom you worship ignorantly, him do I preach unto you.*
> 24. *God, who hath made the world, and all things which are therein, seeing he is Lord both of heaven and earth, dwelleth not in temples made with hands:*
> 25. *Neither is he worshipped with men's hands, needing any thing, seeing that he giveth to all life and breath through all things.*

22. *Men of Athens.* We may divide this sermon of Paul into five members. For though Luke doth only briefly touch those things which he set down in many words, yet I do not doubt but that he did comprehend the sum, so that he did omit none of the principal points. First, Paul layeth superstition to the charge of the men of Athens, because they worship their gods all at a very venture;[1] secondly, he showeth by natural arguments who and what God is, and how he is rightly worshipped; thirdly, he inveigheth against the blockishness of men, who, though they be created to this end, that they may know their Creator and Maker, yet do they wander and err in darkness like blind men; fourthly, he showeth that nothing is more absurd than to draw any portraiture of God,[2] seeing that the mind of man is his true image; in the first place, he descendeth at length unto Christ and the resurrection of the dead. For it was requisite to handle those four points generally, before he did descend unto the faith of the gospel.

As it were, more superstitious. The Grecians do oftentimes

---

[1] "Fortuito," fortuitously.   [2] "Deum statuis vel picturis figurare," to figure God by pictures or statues.

take δεισιδαιμονια in good part; notwithstanding it doth sometimes signify immoderate fear, wherewith superstitious men do carefully torment themselves, whilst that they forge to themselves vain doubts. And this seemeth to be the meaning of this place, that the men of Athens pass all measure in worshipping God, or that they do not perceive what manner [of] work moderation should be; as if he should say, that they deal very undiscreetly in that they weary themselves in going byways. Thus much touching the words; now to the matter. He proveth by this one reason, that all the worshippings of the men of Athens are corrupt, because they be uncertain what gods they ought to worship, because they take in hand rashly and unadvisedly divers rites, and that without measure. For in that they had set up an altar to the unknown God, it was a token that they knew no certainty. They had, indeed, a great company of gods whereof they spake much, but when as they mix them with unknown gods, they confess by this that they know nothing of the true divinity. Furthermore, whosoever doth worship God without any certainty, he worshippeth his own inventions instead of God. Howsoever credulous men do flatter themselves, yet neither doth God allow any religion without knowledge and truth, neither ought it to be counted holy and lawful. Yea, how proud soever they be, yet because they doubt[1] in their consciences, they must needs be convict by their own judgment. For superstition is always fearful, and doth ever now and then coin some new thing.

Therefore we see how miserable their condition is who have not the certain light of the truth, because they do both always doubt in themselves, and lose their labour before God. Notwithstanding, we must note that the unbelievers, whilst that they sometimes make themselves blind through voluntary stubbornness, and are sometimes amidst divers and manifold doubts, [yet] strive and fight with themselves. Oftentimes they do not only flatter themselves, but if any man dare mutter against their folly, they rage cruelly against

---

[1] " Perplexi hærent," remain perplexed

him; the devil doth so bewitch them, that they think nothing to be better than that which pleaseth them. Nevertheless, if there arise any doubt, if any seducer put up his head, if any new folly [delirium] begin to appear, they do not only waver, being in doubt, but also of their own accord offer themselves to be carried hither and thither. Whereby it appeareth, that neither in judgment, neither in quiet state of mind, they stay and rest in the common custom of worshipping God, but that they droop like drunken men. But carefulness and doubtfulness, [anxiety,] which doth not suffer the unbelievers to flatter and please themselves, is better than amazedness.[1] Finally, though superstition be not always fearful, yet forasmuch as it is inwrapt in divers errors, it disquieteth men's minds, and doth prick them with divers blind torments. This was the cause that the men of Athens did mix their domestical gods (whom they thought they knew, because in their vain opinion they had invented them) with unknown gods. For thereby appeareth their unquietness, because they confess that they have not as yet done as they ought, when they have done sacrifice to the familiar[2] gods, which they had received of their fathers, and whom they called their country gods.[3] Therefore, to the end Paul may pluck out of their minds all vain and false persuasions, he taketh this maxim, that they know not what they worship, neither have they any certain divine power, [deity.] For if they had known any god at all, being content with him, they would never have fallen away unto unknown gods, forasmuch as the knowledge of the true God alone is sufficient for the abolishing of all idols.

23. *To the unknown God.* I can well grant that this altar was dedicated to all strange gods; yet I cannot yield to that which Jerome saith, that Paul did, by a certain holy wiliness, attribute that to one God which was written of many. For seeing the superscription [inscrip-

---

[1] " Tali stupore magis tolerabilis est," is more tolerable than such stupor.
[2] " Popularibus," popular. [3] " Indigetas et patrios," native and country gods.

tion] was common in every man's mouth, there was no place for subtilty, [craft;] why did he then change the plural number? Surely, not that he might deceive the men of Athens, but because the matter did so require, he said, that he brought doctrine concerning an unknown god. And after he hath showed that they are deceived, because they knew not what god they ought to worship, and had no certain godhead in a great heap of gods, he doth now insinuate himself, and doth purchase favour for his doctrine. Because it was an unjust thing to reject that which was uttered concerning a new god, to whom they had already given over themselves; and it was far better first to know him, than rashly to worship him whom they knew not. Thus doth Paul return again to that principle, that God cannot be worshipped rightly unless he be first made known.

But here may a question be moved: how he saith that God was worshipped at Athens, who doth refuse all worshippings which are not agreeable to the prescript of his law, yea, he pronounceth that all that is idolatry which men invent without his Word? If God allow no worship but that which is agreeable to his Word, how doth Paul give this praise to men, who did dote without measure that they worshipped God? For Christ, in condemning the Samaritans, is content[1] with this one principle, in that they worship God without knowledge, (John iv. 22;) and yet they did boast that they worshipped the God of Abraham. Then, what shall we say of the men of Athens, who, having buried and quite put out the remembrance of the true God, had put in place of him Jupiter, Mercury, Pallas, and all that filthy rabble? I answer, that Paul doth not in this place commend that which the men of Athens had done; but taketh from their affection, though it were corrupt, free matter for teaching.

24. *God, who hath made the world.* Paul's drift is to teach what God is. Furthermore, because he hath to deal with

---

[1] "Nititur et contentus est," founds on, and is contented with.

profane men, he draweth proofs from nature itself; for in vain should he have cited[1] testimonies of Scripture. I said that this was the holy man's purpose, to bring the men of Athens unto the true God. For they were persuaded that there was some divinity; only their preposterous religion was to be reformed. Whence we gather, that the world doth go astray through bending crooks and boughts, yea, that it is in a mere labyrinth, so long as there remaineth a confused opinion concerning the nature of God. For this is the true rule of godliness, distinctly and plainly to know who that God whom we worship is. If any man will intreat generally of religion, this must be the first point, that there is some divine power or godhead which men ought to worship. But because that was out of question, Paul descendeth unto the second point, that the true God must be distinguished from all vain inventions. So that he beginneth with the definition of God, that he may thence prove how he ought to be worshipped; because the one dependeth upon the other. For whence came so many false worshippings, and such rashness to increase the same oftentimes, save only because all men forged to themselves a God at their pleasure? And nothing is more easy than to corrupt the pure worship of God, when men esteem God after their sense and wit.

Wherefore, there is nothing more fit to destroy all corrupt worshippings, than to make this beginning, and to show of what sort the nature of God is. Also our Saviour Christ reasoneth thus, John iv. 24, "God is a Spirit." Therefore he alloweth no other worshippers but such as worship him spiritually. And surely he doth not subtilely dispute of the secret substance [essence] of God; but by his works he declareth which is the profitable knowledge of him. And what doth Paul gather thence, because God is the creator, framer, and Lord of the world? to wit, that he dwelleth not in temples made with hands. For, seeing that it appeareth plainly by the creation of the world, that the

---

[1] "Pugnasset," contended with them by citing.

righteousness, wisdom, goodness, and power of God doth reach beyond the bounds of heaven and earth ; it followeth, that he can be included and shut up within no space of place.

Notwithstanding this demonstration seemeth to have been in vain, because they might readily have said, that images and pictures were placed in temples to testify God's presence; and that none was so gross but that he knew that God did fulfil [fill] all things. I answer, that that is true which I said a little before, that idolatry is contrary to itself. The unbelievers said, that they worshipped the gods before their images; but unless they had tied the Godhead and power of God to images, and had hoped[1] to be holpen thereby, would they have directed their prayers thither ? Hereby it came also to pass, that one temple was more holy than another. They ran to Delphos that they might fet [fetch] the oracles of Apollo thence. Minerva had her seat and mansion at Athens. Now we see that Paul doth touch that false opinion, whereby men have always been deceived; because they feigned to themselves a carnal God.

This is the first entrance into the true knowledge of God, if we go without ourselves, and do not measure him by the capacity of our mind; yea, if we imagine nothing of him according to the understanding of our flesh,[2] but place him above the world, and distinguish him from creatures. From which sobriety the whole world was always far; because this wickedness is in men, naturally to deform God's glory with their inventions. For as they be carnal and earthy, they will have one that shall be answerable to their nature. Secondly, after their boldness they fashion him so as they may comprehend him. By such inventions is the sincere and plain knowledge of God corrupt; yea, his truth, as saith Paul, is turned into a lie, (Rom. i. 25.) For whosoever doth not ascend high above the world, he apprehendeth vain shadows and ghosts instead of God.

---

[1] " An inde sperassent," could they have hoped ?
carnis nostiæ," according to our carnal sense.

[2] " Pro sensu

Again, unless we be carried up into heaven with the wings of faith, we must needs vanish away in our own cogitations. And no marvel if the Gentiles were so grossly deluded and deceived, to include God in the elements of the world, after that they had pulled him out of his heavenly throne; seeing that the same befel the Jews, to whom notwithstanding the Lord had showed his spiritual glory. For it is not without cause that Isaiah doth chide them for including God within the walls of the temple, (Isaiah lxvi. 1.) And we gather out of Stephen's sermon, that this vice was common to all ages; which sermon is set down by Luke in the 7th chapter and 49th verse.

If any man asked the Jews, whose grossness the Holy Ghost reproveth, if they thought that God was included in their temple, they would stoutly have denied that they were in any such gross error. But because they did only behold the temple, and did rise no higher in their minds, and trusting to the temple, did boast that God was as it were bound to them, the Spirit doth for good causes reprehend them, for tying him to the temple as if he were a mortal man. For that is true which I said even now, that superstition is contrary to itself, and that it doth vanish away into divers imaginations. Neither have the Papists at this day any defence, saving that wherewith the Gentiles went about in times past to paint or cover their errors after a sort. In some, superstition doth feign that God dwelleth in temples made with hands, not that it will shut him up as it were in a prison;[1] but because it doth dream of a carnal (or fleshly) God, and doth attribute a certain power to idols, and doth translate the glory of God unto external shows.

But if God do not dwell in temples made with hands, (2 Kings xix. 15,) why doth he testify in so many places of Scripture, that he sitteth between the cherubims, and that the temple is his eternal rest? (Psalm lxxx. 1; cxxxii. 14.) I answer, As he was not tied to any place, so he meant nothing less than to tie his people to earthly signs,

---

[1] " In ergastulis," in houses of hard labour.

but rather he cometh down to them that he might lift them up unto himself. Therefore, those men did wickedly abuse the temple and the ark, who did so behold those things that they stayed still upon earth, and did depart from the spiritual worship of God. Hereby we see that there was great difference between those tokens of God's presence which men invented to themselves unadvisedly, and those which were ordained by God, because men do always incline downwards, that they may lay hold upon [apprehend] God after a carnal manner; but God by the leading of his word doth lift them upward. Only he useth middle signs and tokens, whereby he doth insinuate himself with slow men,[1] until they may ascend into heaven by degrees (and steps.)

25. *Neither is he worshipped with man's hands.* The same question which was answered of late concerning the temple, may now be objected touching ceremonies. For it seemeth that that may be translated unto the worshippings of the law of Moses, which Paul condemneth in the ceremonies of the Gentiles. But we may readily answer, that the faithful did never properly place the worship of God in ceremonies; but they did only count them helps wherewith they might exercise themselves according to their infirmity. When they did slay beasts, offered bread and drink offerings, light torches and other lights, they knew that godliness was not placed in these things, but being holpen by these,[2] they did always look unto the spiritual worship of God, and they made account of it alone. And God himself saith plainly in many places, that he doth not pass for any external or visible thing, that ceremonies are of themselves of no importance, and that he is worshipped no otherwise but by faith, a pure conscience, by prayer and thankfulness. What did the Gentiles then? to wit, when they erected images, they offered incense, they set forth plays, and laid their cushions

---

[1] " Familiariter . se insinuet," he may familiarly insinuate himself.
[2] " Talibus rudimentis," by such rudiments.

before their idols, they thought they had fulfilled the offices of godliness excellent well. Not only the philosophers, but also the poets, do sometimes deride the folly of the common people, because they did disorderly place the worship of God in the pomp and gorgeousness of ceremonies. That I may omit infinite testimonies, that of Persius is well known:

" Tell me, ye priests to sacred rites, what profit gold doth bring?
The same which Venus' puppets fine, certes no other thing.
Why give not we to gods that which the blear-eyed issue could
Of great Messala never give from out their dish of gold?
Right justly deem'd a conscience clear, and heavenly thoughts of mind,
A breast with mildness such adorn'd, as virtue hath assign'd,
  Let me in temples offer these,
  Then sacrifice the gods shall please."

And, undoubtedly, the Lord caused profane men to utter such speeches, that they might take away all colour of ignorance. But it doth plainly appear, that those who spake thus did straightway slide back again unto common madness; yea, that they did never thoroughly understand what this meant. For though those who pass the common people in wit be enforced to confess that bare ceremonies are in no estimation, yet it is impossible to pull from them this persuasion, but that they will think that they be a part of the divine worship. Therefore, the more diligently they give themselves to such vanities, they do not doubt but that they do the duties of godliness well. Therefore, because all mortal men, from the highest to the lowest, do think that God is pacified with external things, and they will, with their own works, fulfil their duty towards him, that doth Paul refute. There is also a reason added, because, seeing he is Lord of heaven and earth, he needeth nothing, because, seeing that he giveth breath and life to men, he can receive nothing of them again. For what can they bring of their own, who, being destitute of all good things, have nothing but of his free goodness, yea, who are nothing but by his mere grace, who shall forthwith be brought to nought, if he withdraw the Spirit whereby they live? Whereupon it followeth, that they are not only dull, but too proud, if they thrust in themselves to worship God with the works of their own hands.

For whereas he saith, that alms and the duties of love are sweet-smelling sacrifices, that must be distinguished from the matter which we have now in hand, where Paul doth only intreat of the ceremonies which the unbelievers put in place of the spiritual worship of God. By life and breath is meant the life which men live so long as the soul and body are joined together. Touching the end of the sentence, though some Greek books[1] agree in this reading, κατα παντα, "through all things;" yet that seemeth to me more agreeable which the old interpreter hath, και τα πανια, "and all things," because it is both plainer, and doth also contain a more perfect and full doctrine. For thence we do better gather that men have nothing of their own; and also certain Greek copies agree thereto.

26. *And hath made of one blood all mankind to dwell upon all the face of the earth, and hath appointed the times before determined, and the bounds of their habitation.*
27. *That they might seek God, if peradventure they may grope* [after] *him, and find him, though he be not far from every one of us.*
28. *For in him we live, move, and have our being; as certain of your poets said, For we be also his generation.*
29. *Therefore, seeing we be the generation of God, we must not think that the Godhead is like to gold, or silver, or to stone, graven by the cunning cogitation of man.*

26. *And he hath made of one blood.* Paul doth now show unto the men of Athens to what end mankind was created, that he may by this means invite and exhort them to consider the end of their life. This is surely filthy unthankfulness of men, seeing they all enjoy the common life, not to consider to what end God hath given them life; and yet this beastly blockishness doth possess the more part, so that

---

[1] "Codices," manuscripts.

they do not consider to what end they be placed in the world, neither do they remember the Creator of heaven and earth, whose good things they do devour. Therefore, after that Paul hath intreated of the nature of God, he putteth in this admonition in due season, that men must be very careful to know God, because they be created for the same end, and born for that purpose; for he doth briefly assign unto them this cause of life, to seek God. Again, forasmuch as there was not one kind of religion only in the world, but the Gentiles were distract into divers sects, he telleth them that this variety came from corruption. For to this end, in my judgment, tendeth that when he saith, that all were created of one blood. For consanguinity and the same original ought to have been a bond of mutual consent among them; but it is religion which doth most of all join men together, or cause them to fly one another's company. Whereupon it followeth, that they be revolted from nature who disagree so much in religion and the worship of God; because, wheresoever they be born, and whatsoever place [clime] of the world they inhabit, they have all one Maker and Father, who must be sought of all men with one consent. And surely neither distance of places, nor bounds of countries, nor diversity of manners, neither any cause of separation among men, doth make God unlike to himself. In sum, he meant to teach that the order of nature was broken, when as religion was pulled in pieces among them, and that that diversity, which is among them, is a testimony that godliness is quite overthrown, because they are fallen away from God the Father of all, upon whom all kindred dependeth.

To dwell upon the face of the earth. Luke doth briefly gather, as he useth to do, the sum of Paul's sermon; and it is not to be doubted, but that Paul did first show that men are set here as upon a theatre, to behold the works of God; and, secondly, that he spake of the providence of God, which doth show forth itself in the whole government of the world. For when he saith, that God appointeth the times ordained before, and the bounds of men's habitations, his meaning is, that this world is governed by his hand and counsel, and that men's affairs fall not out by chance, as profane men dream. And so we gather out of a few words of Luke, that Paul did handle most weighty matters. For when he saith that the times were ordained before by him, he doth testify that he had determined, before men were created, what their condition and estate should be. When we see divers changes in the world; when we see realms come to ruin, lands altered, cities destroyed, nations laid waste, we foolishly imagine, that either fate or fortune beareth the swing in these matters; but God doth testify in this place by the mouth of Paul, that it was appointed before in his counsel how long he would have the state of every people to continue, and within what bounds he would have them contained. But and if he have appointed them a certain time, and appointed the bounds of countries, undoubtedly he hath also set in order the whole course of their life.

And we must note, that Paul doth attribute to God not only a bare foreknowledge and cold speculation, as some men do indiscreetly, but he placeth the cause of those things which fall out, in his counsel and beck. For he saith not that the times were only foreseen, but that they were appointed and set in such order as pleased him best. And when he addeth also that God had appointed from the beginning those things which he had ordained before, his meaning is, that he executeth by the power of his Spirit those things which he hath decreed in his counsel according to that: "Our God is in heaven; he hath done whatsoever he would," (Psalm cxv. 3.) Now, we see, as in a camp, every troop and band hath his appointed place, so men are placed upon earth, that every people may be content with their bounds, and that among these people every particular person may have his mansion. But though ambition have oftentimes raged, and many, being incensed with wicked lust, have past their bounds, yet the lust of men hath never brought to pass, but that God hath governed all events from out of his holy sanctuary. For though men, by raging upon earth, do seem to assault heaven, that they may overthrow God's providence, yet they are enforced, whether they will or no, rather to establish the same. Therefore, let us know that the world is so turned over through divers tumults, that God doth at length bring all things unto the end which he hath appointed.

27. *That they might seek God.* This sentence hath two members; to wit, that it is man's duty to seek God; secondly, that God himself cometh forth to meet us, and doth show himself by such manifest tokens, that we can have no excuse for our ignorance. Therefore, let us remember that those men do wickedly abuse this life, and that they be unworthy to dwell upon earth, which do not apply their studies to seek him; as if every kind of brute beasts should fall from that inclination which they have naturally, which should for good causes be called monstrous. And, surely, nothing is more absurd, than that men should be ignorant of their Author, who are endued with understanding principally for this use. And we must especially note the goodness of God, in that he doth so familiarly insinuate himself, that even the blind may grope after him. For which cause the blindness of men is more shameful and intolerable, who, in so manifest and evident a manifestation, are touched with no feeling of God's presence. Whithersoever they cast their eyes upward or downward, they must needs light upon lively and also infinite images of God's power, wisdom, and goodness. For God hath not darkly shadowed his glory in the creation of the world, but he hath everywhere engraven such manifest marks, that even blind men may know them by groping. Whence we gather that men are not only blind but blockish, when, being helped by such excellent testimonies, they profit nothing.

Yet here ariseth a question, whether men can naturally come unto the true and merciful[1] knowledge of God. For Paul doth give us to understand, that their own sluggishness is the cause that they cannot perceive that God is pre-

---

[1] "Liquidam," clear.

sent; because, though they shut their eyes, yet may they grope after him. I answer, that their ignorance and blockishness is mixed with such frowardness, that, being void of right judgment, they pass over without understanding all such signs of God's glory as appear manifestly both in heaven and earth. Yea, seeing that the true knowledge of God is a singular gift of his, and faith (by which alone he is rightly known) cometh only from the illumination of the Spirit, it followeth that our minds cannot pierce so far, having nature only for our guide. Neither doth Paul intreat in this place of the ability of men, but he doth only show that they be without excuse, when as they be so blind in such clear light, as he saith in the first chapter to the Romans, (Rom. i. 20.) Therefore, though men's senses fail them in seeking out God, yet have they no cloak for their fault, because, though he offer himself to be handled and groped, they continue, notwithstanding, in a quandary;[1] concerning which thing we have spoken more in the fourteenth chapter, (Acts xiv. 17.)

Though he be not far from every one of us. To the end he may the more touch the frowardness of men, he saith that God is not to be sought through many crooks, neither need we make any long journey to find him; because every man shall find him in himself, if so be that he will take any heed. By which experience we are convicted that our dulness is not without fault, which we had from the fault of Adam. For though no corner of the world be void of the testimony of God's glory, yet we need not go without ourselves to lay hold upon him. For he doth affect and move every one of us inwardly with his power in such sort, that our blockishness is like to a monster, in that in feeling him we feel him not. In this respect certain of the philosophers called man *the little world*, [a microcosm;] because he is above all other creatures a token of God's glory, replenished with infinite miracles.

---

[1] " Attoniti," in stupid amazement.

28. *For in him.* I grant that the apostles, according to the Hebrew phrase, do oftentimes take this preposition *in* for *per*, or *by* or *through*; but because this speech, that we live in God, hath greater force, and doth express more, I thought I would not change it; for I do not doubt but that Paul's meaning is, that we be after a sort contained in God, because he dwelleth in us by his power. And, therefore, God himself doth separate himself from all creatures by this word *Jehovah*, that we may know that in speaking properly he is alone, and that we have our being in him, inasmuch as by his Spirit he keepeth us in life, and upholdeth us. For the power of the Spirit is spread abroad throughout all parts of the world, that it may preserve them in their state; that he may minister unto the heaven and earth that force and vigour which we see, and motion to all living creatures. Not as brain-sick men do trifle, that all things are full of gods, yea, that stones are gods; but because God doth, by the wonderful power and inspiration of his Spirit, preserve those things which he hath created of nothing. But mention is made in this place properly of men, because Paul said, that they needed not to seek God far, whom they have within them.

Furthermore, forasmuch as the life of man is more excellent than motion, and motion doth excel essence, [mere existence,] Paul putteth that in the highest place which was the chiefest, that he might go down by steps unto essence or being, thus, We have not only no life but in God, but not so much as moving; yea, no being, which is inferior to both. I say that life hath the pre-eminence in men, because they have not only sense and motion as brute beasts have, but they be endued with reason and understanding. Wherefore, the Scripture doth for good causes give that singular gift which God hath given us, a title and commendation by itself. So in John, when mention is made of the creation of all things, it is added apart, not without cause, that life was the light of men, (John i. 4.)

Now, we see that all those who know not God know not

themselves; because they have God present with them not only in the excellent gifts of the mind, but in their very essence; because it belongeth to God alone to be, all other things have their being in him. Also, we learn out of this place that God did not so create the world once that he did afterward depart from his work; but that it standeth by his power, and that the same God is the governor thereof who was the Creator. We must well think upon this continual comforting and strengthening, that we may remember God every minute.

Certain of your poets. He citeth half a verse out of Aratus, not so much for authority's sake, as that he may make the men of Athens ashamed; for such sayings of the poets came from no other fountain save only from nature and common reason. Neither is it any marvel if Paul, who spake unto men who were infidels and ignorant of true godliness, do use the testimony of a poet, wherein was extant a confession of that knowledge which is naturally engraven in men's minds. The Papists take another course. For they so lean to the testimonies of men, that they set them against the oracles of God; and they do not only make Jerome, or Ambrose, and the residue of the holy fathers, masters of faith, but they will no less tie us to the stinking [vile] answers of their Popes than if God himself should speak. Yea, that which more s, they have not been afraid to give so great authority to Aristotle, that the apostles and prophets were silent in their schools rather than he.

Now, that I may return unto this sentence which I have in hand, it is not to be doubted but that Aratus spake of Jupiter; neither doth Paul, in applying that unto the true God, which he spake unskilfully of his Jupiter, wrest it unto a contrary sense. For because men have naturally some perseverance of God,[1] they draw true principles from that fountain. And though so soon as they begin to think upon God, they vanish away in wicked inventions, and so

---

[1] " Aliquo Dei sensu imbuti sunt," are imbued with some knowledge of God.

the pure seed doth degenerate into corruptions; yet the first general knowledge of God doth nevertheless remain still in them. After this sort, no man of a sound mind can doubt to apply that unto the true God which we read in Virgil touching the feigned and false joy, that *All things are full of joy.* Yea, when Virgil meant to express the power of God, through error he put in a wrong name.

As touching the meaning of the words, it may be that Aratus did imagine that there was some parcel of the divinity in men's minds, as the Manichees did say, that the souls of men are of the nature of God.[1] So when Virgil saith concerning the world, *The Spirit doth nourish within, and the mind being dispersed through all the joints, doth move your whole huge weight,* he doth rather play the philosopher, and subtilely dispute after the manner of Plato, than purely mean that the world is supported by the secret inspiration of God. But this invention ought not to have hindered Paul from retaining a true maxim, though it were corrupt with men's fables, that men are the generation of God, because by the excellency of nature they resemble some divine thing. This is that which the Scripture teacheth, that we are created after the image and similitude of God, (Gen. i. 27.) The same Scripture teacheth also, in many places, that we be made the sons of God by faith and free adoption when we are ingrafted into the body of Christ, and being regenerate by the Spirit, we begin to be new creatures, (Gal. iii. 26.) But as it giveth the same Spirit divers names because of his manifold graces, so no marvel if the word sons be diversely taken. All mortal men are called sons in general, because they draw near to God in mind and understanding; but because the image of God is almost blotted out in them, so that there appear scarce any slender lines, [lineaments,] this name is by good right restrained unto the faithful, who having the Spirit of adoption given them, resemble their heavenly Father in the light of reason, in righteousness and holiness.

[1] "Ex traduce Dei," are transferred from God.

29. *Therefore seeing that.* He gathereth that God cannot be figured or resembled by any graven image, forasmuch as he would have his image extant in us. For the soul wherein the image of God is properly engraven cannot be painted; therefore it is a thing more absurd to go about to paint God. Now, we see what great injury they do to God which give him a bodily shape; when as man's soul, which doth scarce resemble a small sparkle of the infinite glory of God, cannot be expressed in any bodily shape.

Furthermore, forasmuch as it is certain that Paul doth in this place inveigh against the common superstition of all the Gentiles, because they would worship God under bodily shapes, we must hold this general doctrine, that God is falsely and wickedly transfigured, and that his truth is turned into a lie so often as his Majesty is represented by any visible shape; as the same Paul teacheth in the first chapter to the Romans, (Rom. i. 23.) And though the idolaters of all times wanted not their cloaks and colours, yet that was not without cause always objected to them by the prophets which Paul doth now object, that God is made like to wood, or stone, or gold, when there is any image made to him of dead and corruptible matter. The Gentiles used images that, according to their rudeness, they might better conceive that God was nigh unto them. But seeing that God doth far surpass the capacity of our mind, whosoever attempteth with his mind to comprehend him, he deformeth and disfigureth his glory with a wicked and false imagination. Wherefore, it is wickedness to imagine anything of him according to our own sense. Again, that which worse is, it appeareth plainly that men erect pictures and images to God for no other cause, save only because they conceive some carnal thing of him, wherein he is blasphemed.

The Papists also are at this day no whit more excusable. For what colours soever they invent to paint and colour those images, whereby they go about to express God, yet because they be inwrapped in the same error, wherein the men of old time were entangled, they be urged with the testimonies of the prophets. And that the heathen did use the same excuses in times past, wherewith the Papists go about to cover themselves at this day, it is well known out of their own books. Therefore, the prophets do not escape the mocks of certain, as if they laid too great grossness to their charge, yea, burthen them with false accusations; but when all things are well weighed, those who will judge rightly shall find, that whatsoever starting holes [evasions] even the most witty men have sought, yet were they taken with this madness, that God is well pleased with the sacrifice done before images. Whereas we, with Erasmus, translate it *numen*, Luke putteth θειον in the neuter gender for divinity or godhead. When Paul denieth that God is like to gold, or silver, or stone, and addeth afterward, *graven* by cunning or invention of man, he excludeth both matter and form, and doth also condemn all inventions of men, which disfigure the true nature of God.

30. *And though God have winked at the times of this ignorance hitherto, he willeth all men everywhere to repent now:*
31. *Because he hath appointed a day, wherein he will judge the world in righteousness, by that man whom he hath appointed; having fulfilled his promise to all men, when he raised him up from the dead.*
32. *And when they had heard the resurrection of the dead, some mocked; and other some said, We will hear thee of this again.*
33. *So Paul went out from among them; yet certain joining themselves to him believed: among whom was both Dionysius, Areopagita, and a woman named Damaris, and others with them.*

30. *And the times of this ignorance.* Because that is commonly thought to be good which hath been used of long time, and is approved by the common consent of all men; it might have been objected to Paul, why dost thou disannul those things which have been received, and used continually since the beginning of the world? and whom canst thou persuade that the whole world hath been deceived so long? as

there is no kind of abomination so filthy, which the Papists do not think to be well fortified with this buckler. Paul preventeth[1] this question; showing that men went astray so long therefore, because God did not reach out his hand from heaven, that he might bring them back again into the way. It may seem an inconvenient [a strange] thing, that men endued with reason and judgment should err so grossly and filthily in a most weighty matter. But Paul's meaning is, that men do never make an end of erring, until God do help them. And now he assigneth no other cause why he did not redress this any sooner, save only his good pleasure.

And assuredly we be not able to comprehend the reason why God did at a sudden set up the light of his doctrine, when he suffered men to walk in darkness four thousand years; at least seeing the Scripture doth conceal it, let us here make more account of sobriety than of preposterous wisdom. For they go about to bring God within bounds, which is a most unseemly thing, and contrary to nature herself, whosoever they be that will not suffer him to speak or hold his peace at his pleasure. Again, those that will not be content with his wisdom and secret counsel, must needs murmur against Paul, who teacheth manifestly that ignorance did reign in the world, so long as it pleased God to wink at it. Other some interpret it otherwise, that God did spare ignorance, as if he did wink, being unwilling to punish it; but that surmise is altogether contrary to Paul's meaning and purpose, who meant not to lessen man's fault, but to magnify the grace of God which did appear at a sudden, and it is proved to be false out of other places, because those who have sinned without law shall notwithstanding perish without law, (Rom. ii. 12.)

In some, Paul's words carry with them this meaning only, that men were set upon blindness, until God did reveal himself unto them; and that we ought not too curiously and boldly to demand and require the cause why he put away darkness no sooner; but that whatsoever pleased him ought

---

[1] " Anticipat," anticipates.

to seem to us right and equal without making any more ado. For though this be a hard speech that men were miserably deceived long time, whilst that God made as though he saw it not, yet must we be content with, and stay ourselves upon his providence. And if at any time there come upon us a vain and perverse desire to know more than is meet for us, let us straightway call to mind that which Paul teacheth in many places, that it was a mystery hid since the beginning of the world, in that the light of the gospel did appear to the Gentiles at a sudden, (Rom. xvi. 25; Ephes. iii. 9;) and that this is a token of the manifold wisdom of God, which swalloweth up all the senses of men. Again, let us remember that it doth not lessen the fault of men, because God would not heal their errors; forasmuch as their own conscience shall always hold them convict, that they cannot escape just damnation. And Paul (not that he might lay the fault and blame upon God, but that he might cut off occasion of curious and hurtful questions) said, that the world did err whilst God did wink. And hereby we learn how reverently we ought to think of God's providence, lest any man should be so bold, as man's nature is proud, to demand a reason of God of his works.

Furthermore, this admonition is no less profitable for us than for the men of that time. The enemies of the gospel, when it beginneth to spring again, count it a great absurdity that God did suffer men to go astray so long under the apostacy of the Pope, as if (though there appear no reason) it were not as lawful for him now to wink at men's ignorance as in times past. And we must principally note to what end he saith this; to wit, that the ignorance of former times may not hinder us from obeying God without delay when he speaketh. Most men think that they have a fair colour for their error, so they have their fathers to keep them company, or so they get some patronage or defence by long custom; yea, they would willingly creep out here,[1] that they may not obey the word of God. But Paul saith, that we

---

[1] " Imo libenter et cupide hoc captant effugium," nay, they willingly and eagerly catch at this subterfuge.

must not fet [seek] an excuse from our fathers' ignorance when God speaketh unto us; because, though they be not guiltless before God, yet our sluggishness is more intolerable if we be blind at noonday, and lie as deaf, or as if we were asleep, when the trumpet of the gospel doth sound.[1]

Now he willeth all men. In these words Paul teacheth that we must give ear to God so soon as he speaketh, as it is written, " To-day, if ye will hear his voice, harden not your hearts," (Psalm xcv. 7, 8; Heb. iii. 7, 8.) For the stubbornness of those men is without excuse, who foreslow [neglect] this opportunity when God doth gently call them unto him. Also, we gather out of this place to what end the gospel is preached, to wit, that God may gather us to himself from the former errors of our life. Therefore, so oft as the voice of the gospel doth sound in our ears, let us know that God doth exhort us unto repentance. We must also note that he attributeth to God the person of the speaker, though he do it by man. For otherwise the gospel hath not so full authority as the heavenly truth deserveth, save only when our faith doth look unto him who is the governor of the prophetical function, and doth depend upon his mouth.

31. *Because he hath appointed a day.* He maketh mention of the last judgment, that he may awake them out of their dream. For we know how hard a matter it is for men to deny themselves. Therefore, they must be violently enforced unto repentance, which cannot be done better than when they be cited to appear before God's judgment-seat, and that fearful judgment is set before them, which they may neither despise nor escape. Therefore, let us remember that the doctrine of repentance doth then take place, when men, who would naturally desire to flatter themselves, are awaked with fear of God's judgment, and that none are fit teachers of the gospel but those who are the criers or apparitors of the highest Judge, who bring those who are to come

---

[1] " Clangente evangelii tuba," during the clang of the gospel trumpet.

before the Judge to plead their cause, and denounce the judgment hanging over their heads, even as if it were in their own hand. Neither is this added in vain, *in righteousness,* or *righteously.* For though all men in the world confess that God is a just Judge, yet we see how they, for the most part, pamper and flatter themselves; for they will not suffer God to demand an account farther than their knowledge and understanding doth reach. Therefore, Paul's meaning is, that men do profit themselves nothing by vain flattery; because they shall not prejudice God's justice by this means, which showeth that all that is an abomination before God which seemeth goodly in the sight of men, because he will not follow the decrees of men, but that form which himself hath appointed.

By the man whom he hath appointed. It is not to be doubted but that Paul spake more largely concerning Christ, that the Athenians might know that he is the Son of God, by whom salvation was brought to the world, and who had all power given him in heaven and earth; otherwise this speech, which we read here, should have had but small force to persuade. But Luke thought it sufficient to gather the sum of the sermon briefly. Yet is it to be thought that Paul spake first concerning the grace of Christ, and that he did first preach him to be the Redeemer of men, before he made him a Judge. But because Christ is oftentimes contemned, when he offereth himself to be a Redeemer, Paul denounceth that he will once sharply punish such wicked contempt, because the whole world must be judged by him. The word ὁρίζειν may be referred, as well unto the secret counsel of God, as unto external manifestation. Yet because the former exposition is more common, I do willingly embrace the same; to wit, that God, by his eternal decree, hath ordained his Son to be the Judge of the world; and that to the end the reprobate, who refuse to be ruled by Christ, may learn that they strive but in vain against the decree of God, which cannot be broken. But because nothing seemeth more strange to men, than that God shall judge in the person of man, Paul addeth afterward, that this dignity of Christ, which were hard to be believed, was approved by his resurrection.

The will of God alone ought to be so reverenced among us, that every man for himself subscribe to his decrees without delay. Because the cloak and colour of ignorance useth oftentimes to be objected, therefore Paul saith plainly, that Christ was by his resurrection openly showed to be the Judge of the world, and that that was revealed to the eyes of men, which God had before determined with himself concerning him. For that point of doctrine, which Luke toucheth briefly in few words, was handled by Paul at large. He said not only in a word that Christ rose from death, but he did also intreat of the power of his resurrection as was meet. For to what end did Christ rise, but that he might be the first fruits of those which rise again? (1 Cor. xv. 23.) And to what end shall we rise again, but either to life or death? Whereupon it followeth, that Christ by his resurrection is declared and proved to be the Judge of the world.

32. *Some mocked.* By this we see how great the carelessness of men is, whom neither the tribunal-seat of God, nor the majesty of the highest [supreme] Judge, doth make afraid, (Acts xxvi. 23.) We have said that this is a most sharp prick, wherewith men's minds are pricked forward to fear God, when his judgment is set before their eyes; but there is such unspeakable hardness in the contemners, that they are not afraid to count that a fable or lie which is spoken concerning the giving of an account of our life once.[1]

Notwithstanding, there is no cause why the ministers of the gospel should omit[2] the preaching of the judgment which is enjoined them. Though the wicked do laugh and mock, yet this doctrine, which they go about to make of none effect, shall so gird them, that they shall at length perceive that they have striven in vain with their snare.[3] And no marvel if this point of Paul's doctrine were derided at

---

[1] " De reddenda semel vitæ ratione," about one day rendering an account of our lives [2] " Supersedeant," supersede [3] " Laqueo," snare or fetter

Athens; for it is a mystery hid from men's minds, whereon the chiefest philosophers did never think, neither can we otherwise comprehend it, than when we lift up the eyes of faith unto the infinite power of God. And yet Paul's sermon was not altogether without fruit; because there were some of the hearers which were desirous to profit and go forward. For when they say that they will hear him again, their meaning is, that though they were not as yet thoroughly persuaded, yet had they some taste, which did provoke them to be desirous to profit. Surely this desire was contrary to loathsomeness.[1]

34. *Among whom was also Dionysius.* Seeing that Luke doth name one man and one woman only, it appeareth that there was but a small number of those which believed at the first. For those other of whom he maketh mention remained indifferent; because they did neither wholly despise Paul's doctrine, neither were they so thoroughly touched, that they joined themselves unto him that they might be his scholars. Luke maketh mention of Dionysius above the rest, because he was in no small authority among his citizens. Therefore, it is likely that Damaris was also a woman of some renown, [rank.]

Furthermore, it is ridiculous in that the Papists [have] made of a judge an astrologer. But this is to be imputed partly to their ignorance, partly to their boldness,[2] who, seeing they knew not what Areopagus or Mars' Street meant, took to themselves liberty to feign whatsoever they would. And their rudeness is too gross, who ascribe the books of the heavenly and ecclesiastical hierarchy, and of the names of God, to this Dionysius. For the heavenly hierarchy is stuffed not only with many doltish and monkish trifles, but also with many absurd inventions, and wicked speculations. And the books of the Ecclesiastical Hierarchy do themselves declare that they were made many years after, when as the purity of Christianity was corrupt with an huge heap of

---

[1] " Fastidio," fastidiousness or disdain   [2] " Audaciæ," effrontery

ceremonies. As for the book of the names of God, though it have in it some things which are not altogether to be despised, yet it doth rather breathe out subtilties than sound godliness.

CHAPTER XVIII.

1. *After this Paul departed from Athens, and came to Corinthus.*
2. *And having gotten a certain Jew called Aquila, born in Pontus, who came [had come] lately from Italy, and Priscilla, his wife, (because Claudius had commanded all Jews to depart from Rome,) he came unto them.*
3. *And because he was of the same craft, he abode with them, and wrought; and they were tent-makers.*
4. *And he disputed in the synagogue every Sabbath day, and persuaded both Jews and Greeks.*
5. *And when Silas and Timotheus were come from Macedonia, Paul was forced in the spirit, testifying to the Jews that Jesus was Christ.*

1. This history is worthy to be remembered even for this one cause, because it containeth the first beginning of the Church of Corinthus, which, as it was famous for good causes, both because of the multitude of men, and also because of the excellent gifts bestowed upon them, so there were in it gross and shameful vices. Furthermore, Luke showeth in this place with what great labour, and how hardly, Paul did win the same to Christ. It is well known what a rich city Corinthus was by reason of the noble mart, how populous, how greatly given to pleasure. And the old proverb doth testify that it was sumptuous and full of riot: All men cannot go to Corinthus. When Paul entereth the same, what hope, I pray you, can he conceive? He is a simple man, unknown, having no eloquence or pomp, showing no wealth or power. In that that huge gulf doth not swallow up his

confidence and desire which he had to spread abroad the gospel, by this we gather that he was furnished with wonderful power of the Spirit of God; and also that God wrought by his hand after a heavenly manner, and not after any human manner. Wherefore he boasteth not without cause, that the Corinthians are the seal of his apostleship, (1 Cor. ix. 2.) For they be twice blind, who do not acknowledge that the glory of God did more plainly appear in such a simple and base kind of dealing; and he himself showed no small token of invincible constancy, when, being vexed with the mocks of all men, (as the proud did contemn him,) he did notwithstanding stay himself upon God's help alone. But it is worth the labour to note all the circumstances, as Luke setteth down the same in order.

2. *A Jew called Aquila.* This was no small trial, in that Paul findeth none at Corinthus to lodge him save Aquila, who had been twice exiled. For being born in Pontus, he forsook his country, and sailed over the sea, that he might dwell at Rome. He was compelled to depart thence again by the commandment of Claudius Cæsar. Though the commodiousness of the city was such, the plenty so great, the situation so pleasant, and there were also so many Jews there, yet Paul found no more fit host than a man that had been banished out of his own country, and also out of another soil.[1] If we compare the great fruit which ensued immediately upon his preaching with such a base entrance, the power of the Spirit of God shall [more] plainly appear. Also, we may see how the Lord, by his singular counsel, turneth those things to his glory, and the salvation of the godly, which seem contrary to the flesh, and unhappy.[2] Nothing is more miserable than exile, according to the sense of the flesh. But it was far better for Aquila to be Paul's companion, than to be in the highest office either at Rome or in his country. Therefore, this happy calamity of Aquila doth teach us, that the Lord doth often better provide for

---

[1] "Alieno solo," a foreign soil. [2] "Infausta," ill-omened, unpropitious.

us when he doth sharply punish[1] us, than if he should most gently entreat us, and when he tosseth us to and fro in most extreme exile,[2] that he may bring us unto the heavenly rest.

All Jews to depart from Rome. The estate of that nation was then very miserable, so that it is a wonder that they did not almost all depart from the worship of God. But this is a greater wonder, that the religion wherein they had been brought up prevailed against Cæsar's tyranny, and that so soon as Christ, the Sun of righteousness, did arise, few were turned unto him. Notwithstanding, I do not doubt but that the Lord suffered them[3] to pass through many troubles, that they might the more willingly, yea, the more greedily receive the grace of redemption offered them; but the more part[4] became dull in their misery,[5] few did submit themselves to be taught when the Lord did punish them, as did Aquila and Priscilla. Yet, if Suetonius say the truth, they were expelled through hatred of the name of Christ, and so calamity might have more provoked and angered a great part, because they were wrongfully accused for that religion which they did detest.

3. *They were of the same trade.* This place teacheth that Paul, before he came to Corinth, was wont to work with his hands; and that not upon pleasure, but that he might get his living with his handywork. It is not known where he first learned his occupation; notwithstanding it appeareth by his own testimony that he wrought principally at Corinth. And he showeth a reason, because the false apostles taught freely without taking any thing, that they might craftily creep in, therefore the holy man would not give place to them in that point, lest he should cause the gospel of Christ to be evil spoken of, (1 Cor. ix. 12, 15.) But we may easily gather out of this

---

[1] " Affligit," afflict. [2] " Per dura exilia," through the hardships of exile [3] " Consulto...passus fuerit," purposely suffered. [4] " Ut fieri solet," as is usual, omitted. [5] " In suis malis obstupuit," were stupified by their calamities.

place, that whithersoever he came, (until he was occupied in the continual labour of teaching,) he wrought of his occupation, that he might get his living. When Chrysostom saith that Paul was a cordiner, he doth no whit dissent from Luke, because they were wont at that time to make tents of skins.

4. *He disputed in the synagogue.* It is a wonder how that crept in which is in the Latin books,[1] that Paul put in the name of Christ: unless it were because some reader would supply the want of the general sentence. For Luke setteth down two things in this place: to wit, that Paul disputed among the Jews; secondly, that he began more plainly to profess Christ after that Silas and Timotheus were come. And though it be likely that he began to speak of Christ even at the first entrance, because he could not omit the principal point of the heavenly doctrine, yet that doth not hinder but that he might use some other manner of disputation. Therefore I take πειθειν, that is, to *persuade,* for *to induce by little and little.* For, in my judgment, Luke doth signify, that forasmuch as the Jews did handle the law coldly and foolishly, Paul spake of the corrupt and wicked nature of man, of the necessity of grace, of the Redeemer which was promised, of the means to obtain salvation, that he might awake them; for this is a fit and brief[2] preparation unto Christ. Again, when he saith that he was forced in spirit to teach that Jesus was Christ, his meaning is, that he was enforced with greater vehemency to intreat and speak of Christ freely and openly. So that we see that Paul did not utter all things at one time, but he tempered his doctrine as occasion did serve.

And because like moderation is profitable at this day, it is convenient for faithful teachers wisely to consider where to begin, lest a preposterous and confused order do hinder the proceeding of doctrine. Furthermore, though there

---

[1] " Mirum est unde repserit quod legitur in Latinis codicibus," it is strange how the reading crept into the Latin manuscripts.   [2] " Concinna," appropriate.

were ferventness enough in Paul, yet it is no inconvenient thing that he was made more courageous by some new help, not that he was encouraged by shame, or the hope which he reposed in his fellows, but because he considered that this help was sent him, as it were, from heaven. But this forcing in the spirit is not taken for a violent or external impulsion, (as they say,[1]) as those which were called Phœbades and frantic men were wont to be carried away with devilish madness; but there was more ferventness added unto the wonted inspiration of the Spirit which was in Paul, so that he was moved with new power of God, and yet did he of his own accord follow the Spirit as his guide. Whereas Paul did testify that Jesus is Christ, I expound it thus: when he had thoroughly taught the Jews concerning the office of the Redeemer, he declared by testimonies of Scripture that this is he which was to be hoped for, because all those things agree to him which the law and the prophets attribute to Christ. Therefore, he did not simply affirm, but using a solemn testification, he proved Jesus, the Son of Mary, to be that Christ who should be the Mediator between God and men, that he might restore the world from destruction to life.

6. *And when they gainsayed him, and railed upon him, shaking his garments, he said unto them, Your blood be upon your own head ; I will go henceforth clean unto the Gentiles*
7. *And going thence, he entered into the house of a certain man named Justus, a worshipper of God, whose house joined to the synagogue.*
8. *And Crispus, the chief ruler of the synagogue, believed in the Lord with all his household : and many of the Corinthians which heard believed, and were baptized.*
9. *And the Lord said by night, by a vision, to Paul, Fear not, but speak, and hold not thy peace :*
10. *Because I am with thee, and no man shall lay hand on thee to hurt thee : because I have much people in this city.*

---

[1] " Pro violento impulsu et extrinseeo ut loquuntur," for a violent and extrinsic impulse, as it is called.

11. *And he remained there a year and six months, teaching them the word of the Lord.*

6. *When they gainsayed.* The Jews suffered Paul after a sort until he came unto the manifest preaching of Christ. And here brake out their rage. And we must note the speech, that they go from gainsaying unto blaspheming and railing. For it falleth out thus for the most part, when men take to themselves such liberty, that the devil doth inflame them by little and little unto greater madness. For which cause, we must take good heed that no wicked lust or desire provoke us to resist the truth; and, above all, let that horrible judgment terrify us which the Spirit of God thundereth out by the mouth of Paul against all rebels. For undoubtedly, in that Paul by shaking his garments gave some token of detestation, it was no human or private indignation, but zeal kindled by God in his heart; yea, God raised him up to be a preacher and setter forth of his vengeance, to the end the enemies of the word might know that they should not escape scot free for their stubbornness. We spake somewhat touching this sign of execration or cursing in the thirteenth chapter, (Acts xiii. 51.) Let the readers repair thither. The sum is, that God is sorer displeased with contempt of his word than with any wickedness. And surely, men be quite past hope when they tread under foot, or drive from them, the only remedy of all evils and maladies. Now, as the Lord cannot abide rebellion against his word, so it ought to sting and nettle us full sore. My meaning is this, that when the wicked enter combat with God, and, as it were, arm themselves to resist, we are called, as it were, by the heavenly trumpet unto the conflict, because there is nothing more filthy than that the wicked should mock God to his face, whilst we say nothing, and that they should even break out into reproaches and blasphemies.

Your blood. He denounceth to them vengeance, because they be without excuse. For they can shift no part of their fault from themselves, after that despising the calling of

God they have endeavoured to put out the light of life. Therefore, seeing they bear the blame of their own destruction, he doth also affirm that they shall be punished. And in saying that he is clean, he testifieth that he hath done his duty, it is well known what the Lord giveth all his ministers in charge in Ezekiel, (Ezek. iii. 18,) If thou show not unto the wicked that he may convert,[1] I will require his blood at thy hand. Therefore Paul (because he did what he could to bring the Jews to repentance) doth acquit himself of all guiltiness. And by these words, teachers are warned that unless they will be guilty of blood before the Lord, they must do what in them lieth to bring those which go astray into the way, and that they suffer nothing to perish through ignorance.

I will go unto the Gentiles. Though the Jews had showed themselves to be most ready to be taught, yet ought Paul to have employed himself to teach the Gentiles, whose apostle and minister he was made; but here he expresseth the passage whereby he withdrew himself from the stubborn Jews for all. For he observed this course in teaching, that beginning with the Jews he might couple the Gentiles with them in the society of faith, and so might make of both together one body of the Church. When there remained no hope to do any good among the Jews, then the Gentiles only remained. Therefore, the sense is this, that they must be deprived of their own inheritance, that it may be given to the Gentiles, and so be wounded, partly that being stricken with fear, yea, being cast down,[2] they might come to soundness of mind; partly that the emulation or striving of the Gentiles might prick them forward unto repentance. But because they were incurable, reproach and shame served for this purpose only to bring them into despair.

7. *Departing thence.* Paul did not change his lodging which he had with Priscilla and Aquila, because he was

---

[1] " Si non annunciaveris impio ut se convertat," if you do not warn the wicked to be converted.   [2] " Confusi," confounded.

weary of their company; but that he might more familiarly insinuate himself and come in favour with the Gentiles. For I suspect that this Justus, of whom Luke maketh mention, was rather a Gentile than a Jew. Neither doth the nighness of the synagogue any whit hinder; for the Jews were scattered abroad, so that they had no certain place of the city to dwell in. Yea, it seemeth that Paul did make choice of the house which did join to the synagogue, that he might the more nettle the Jews. The title and commendation ascribed to Justus confirmeth this opinion; for it is said that he was a worshipper of God. For though the Jews had not sincere religion, yet because they did all profess the worship of God, it might have seemed that godliness took place commonly in all the whole nation. But because it was a rare matter among the Gentiles to worship God if any drew near unto true godliness, he hath this singular testimony given him which is set against idolatry. Also, I think that the Corinthians, of whom Luke speaketh shortly after, were Gentiles. Nevertheless, lest we should think that Paul's labour was altogether fruitless which he bestowed among the Jews, Luke reckoneth up two of them which believed, Crispus and Sosthenes, of whom Paul himself speaketh in the first chapter of the First Epistle to the Corinthians, (1 Cor. i. 1, 14.) For in his salutation he maketh Sosthenes his fellow in office, after that he saith that he baptized Crispus. I take it that he is called the ruler of the synagogue, not as if he alone did bear rule and had the government, because Sosthenes hath the same title given him shortly after, but because he was one of the chief men.

9. *And the Lord said.* Though the fruit of Paul's doctrine (in that he gained some daily to Christ) might have encouraged him to go forward, yet is the heavenly oracle added for his farther confirmation. Whence we gather that there were great combats set before him, and that he was sore tossed divers ways. For the Lord did never,

without cause,[1] pour out his oracles; neither was it an ordinary thing with Paul to have visions, but the Lord used this kind of remedy when necessity did so require; and the thing itself doth show that there laid upon the holy man a great weight of business, under which he might not only sweat but almost faint, unless he had been set on foot again, and refreshed with some new help. And it is not without cause that he saith that his coming was base and contemptible, and that he was conversant there in fear and trembling, (1 Cor. ii. 3.) For mine own part, I think thus, that the wonderful power of the Spirit, wherewith Paul was endued before, was holpen with the oracle. Furthermore, forasmuch as the Scripture distinguisheth visions from dreams, as it appeareth by the twelfth chapter of the book of Numbers, (Numbers xii. 6,) Luke meaneth by this word *vision*, that when Paul was in a trance he saw a certain shape or form whereby he knew that God was present with him. Assuredly, it is not to be doubted but that God appeared by some sign.

Fear not. This exhortation showeth that Paul had cause of fear ministered unto him; for it had been a superfluous thing to correct fear, or to will him not to fear when all was well and quiet, and especially in a man so willing and ready.

Furthermore, when the Lord (to the end he may have his servant to do his duty faithfully and stoutly) beginneth with restraining fear, by this we gather that nothing is more contrary to the pure and free preaching of the gospel than the straits of a faint heart. And surely experience doth show that none are faithful and courageous ministers of the word whom this fault doth hinder; and that those only are rightly prepared and addressed to teach to whom it is granted with boldness and courage of heart to overcome all manner [of] danger. In which respect, he writeth to Timothy that the spirit of fear is not given to the preachers of the gospel, but of power, and love, and sobriety, (2 Tim. i. 7.) There-

---

[1] " Temere," at random

fore, we must note the connection of words, Fear not, but speak, which is all one as if he should have said, Let not fear let thee to speak. And because fear doth not only make us altogether without tongue, but doth so bind us that we cannot purely and freely speak that which is needful. Christ touched both briefly. Speak, (saith he,) and hold not thy peace; that is, speak not with half thy mouth, as it is in the common proverb. But in these words there is prescribed to the ministers of the word of God a common rule, that they expound and lay open plainly, and without colour or dissimulation, whatsoever the Lord will have made known to his Church; yea, let them keep back nothing which may make for the edifying or increase of God's Church.

10. *Because I am.* This is the former reason why Paul, having subdued fear, must manfully and stoutly do his duty, because he hath God on his side. Whereto answereth the rejoicing of David, "If I shall walk in the midst of the shadow of death, I shall fear none ill: because thou art with me," (Psalm xxiii. iv.) Again, "If tents be pitched about me," &c., (Psalm xxvii. 3.) The question is, whether he did not perceive that God was present with him elsewhere, as he had had experience of his help in divers places. For the promise is general, "I am with you until the end of the world," (Matth. xxviii. 20.) Neither is it lawful for us to mistrust so often as we obey his calling, but that he will be present with us. But it is an usual thing with the Lord to apply that unto certain kinds when the matter so requireth, which he hath promised to do in all affairs; and we know that when we come to the push, then are we most desirous of help. Moreover, these two members are joined together, "I am with thee, and no man shall hurt thee." For it falleth out sometimes that God doth help us, and yet doth he, to look to, suffer us to be oppressed, as he forsook not Paul even in the midst of death; and here he promiseth the peculiar defence of his hand, whereby he shall be preserved from the violence of his enemies.

But the question is, whether Paul needed any such confirmation, who ought to have been willing to enter [undergo] all manner [of] dangers. For what if he had been to suffer death, should he therefore have fainted through fear? I answer, that if at any time God pronounce that his servants shall be safe for a time, that doth no whit hinder, but that they may prepare themselves to suffer death valiantly; but as we distinguish between profitable and necessary, so we must note that there be some promises, which, if the faithful want, they must needs faint and sink down;[1] and that other some are added when it is expedient so to be, which, though they be taken away, (because the grace of God doth nevertheless remain firm and sure,) the faith of the godly doth not fail. After this sort, Paul is commanded not to fear, because his enemies shall not touch him; and if so be he should have been oppressed even then with their violence, yet would he not have been afraid, but God would have his boldness and courage to increase even by this, because he should be without danger. If at any time the Lord bear with us so far forth, we are not to despise such a comfort of our infirmity. In the mean season, let this be sufficient for us to tread under foot all corrupt fear of the flesh, that so long as we fight under his banner we cannot be forsaken of him. And when it is said, "No man shall gainstand thee to do thee hurt," the Lord doth not mean that he shall be free from violence and tumult whom the Jews did afterward deadly invade; but his meaning is, that their attempts shall be frustrate, because the Lord had determined to deliver him out of their hands Therefore, we must fight stoutly that we may win the field.[2]

Because I have much people. The second reason why he should take a good heart is, because the Lord will raise up a great and populous church there, though it be to be doubted whether this member depend upon that which goeth next before; for the text will run fitly thus, Because the Lord determined by the hand of Paul to gather together a great church, he would not suffer the enemies to interrupt the

---

[1] " Penitus," altogether   [2] " Victoria," victory

course of his labours, as if he should have said, I will help thee, that thou mayest not fail my people whose minister I have appointed thee to be. I do willingly embrace this exposition, that divers reasons are not inferred which are to be read apart, but that they be so distinguished that they agree together. Furthermore, the Lord calleth those his people, who, though they might then for good causes be counted strangers, yet because they were written in the book of life, and were forthwith to be admitted into his family, they have this title given them not improperly. For we know that many sheep wander without the flock for a time, as the sheep have many wolves among them. Therefore whom the Lord determined shortly after to gather to himself, those doth he take for his people in respect of their future faith. But let us remember, that those are ingrafted into the body of Christ who appertain unto the same by the eternal adoption of God; as it is written, "Thine they were, and thou gavest them me," (John xvii. 6.)

11. *He continued there a year.* We do not read that Paul stayed so long anywhere else save there; and yet it appeareth by his two epistles that he was not only likely to suffer much troubles, but that he had suffered many unjust and unmeet things by reason of the pride and unthankfulness of the people, so that we see that there was no part of warfare wherein the Lord did not wonderfully exercise him. Also, we gather what a hard and laborious matter the edifying of the Church is, seeing that the most excellent workmaster spent so much time about the laying of the foundation of one church only. Neither doth he boast that he had finished the work, but that the Lord had put others in his place, that they might build upon his foundation; as he saith afterwards that he had planted, and that Apollos had watered, (1 Cor. iii. 6.)

12. *Now when Gallio was deputy of Achaia, the Jews rose with one accord against Paul, and brought him before the judgment-seat,*

13. *Saying, This man persuadeth men to worship God contrary to the law.*
14. *And when Paul was about to open his mouth, Gallio said unto them, If it were any injury or wicked fact, O Jews, I would according to reason maintain you:*
15. *But if it be a question of words and names, and your law, look ye to it yourselves; for I will be no judge in these matters.*
16. *And he drave them from the judgment seat.*
17. *And when all the Greeks had caught Sosthenes, the ruler of the synagogue, they smote him before the judgment-seat. Neither did Gallio care for any of these things.*

12. *When Gallio.* Either the change of the deputy did encourage the Jews to wax more proud and insolent, as froward men use to abuse new things that they may procure some tumult, or else hoping that the judge would favour them, they brake the peace and silence at a sudden, which had continued one whole year. And the sum of the accusation is, that Paul went about to bring in a false kind of worship contrary to the law. Now, the question is, whether they spake of the law of Moses or of the rites used in the empire of Rome. Because this latter thing seemeth to me to be cold,[1] I do rather receive that, that they burdened Paul with this crime, that he brake and altered the worship prescribed in the law of God, and that to the end they might hit him in the teeth with novelty or innovation. And surely Paul had been worthy to have been condemned if he had gone about any such thing; but forasmuch as it is most certain that they did treacherously and wickedly slander the holy man, they endeavoured to cover an evil cause with an honest excuse. We know how straitly the Lord commandeth in the law, how he will have his servants to worship him. Therefore, to depart from that rule is sacrilege. But forasmuch as Paul never meant to add to, or take away anything from the law, he is unjustly accused of this fault. Whence we gather, that though the faithful

---

[1] " Et coactum," and forced.

behave themselves never so uprightly and blamelessly, yet can they not escape false and slanderous reports until they be admitted to purge themselves. But Paul was not only unworthily and falsely slandered by the adversaries, but when he would have refuted their impudency and false reports, his mouth was stopt by the deputy. Therefore he was enforced to depart from the judgment-seat without defending himself. And Gallio refuseth to hear the cause, not for any evil will he bare to Paul, but because it was not agreeable to the office of the deputy to give judgment concerning the religion of every province. For though the Romans could not enforce the nations which were subject to them to observe their rites, yet lest they should seem to allow that which they did tolerate, they forbade their magistrates to meddle with this part of jurisdiction.

Here we see what the ignorance of true godliness doth in setting in order the state of every commonwealth and dominion. All men confess that this is the principal thing that true religion be in force and flourish. Now, when the true God is known, and the certain and sure rule of worshipping him is understood, there is nothing more equal[1] than that which God commandeth in his law, to wit, that those who bear rule with power (having abolished contrary superstitions) defend the pure worship of the true God. But seeing that the Romans did observe their rites only through pride and stubbornness, and seeing they had no certainty where there was no truth, they thought that this was the best way[2] they could take if they should grant liberty to those who dwelt in the provinces to live as they listed. But nothing is more absurd than to leave the worship of God to men's choice. Wherefore, it was not without cause that God commanded by Moses that the king should cause a book of the law to be written out for himself, (Deut. xvii. 18;) to wit, that being well instructed, and certain of his faith, he might with more courage take in hand to maintain that which he knew certainly was right.

---

[1] "Aequum," equitable or just.
[2] "Optimum compendium," the best and shortest way

15. *Of words and names.* These words are not well packed together. Yet Gallio speaketh thus of the law of God by way of contempt, as if the Jewish religion did consist only in words and superfluous questions. And surely (as the nation was much given to contention) it is not to be doubted but that many did trouble themselves and others with superfluous trifles. Yea, we hear with what Paul hitteth them in the teeth[1] in many places, especially in the Epistle to Titus, (Cap. i. 14, and iii. 9.) Yet Gallio is not worthy to be excused who doth mock the holy law of God together with their curiosity. For as it behoved him to cut off all occasion of vain contentions in words, so we must, on the other side, know that when the worship of God is in hand, the strife is not about words, but a matter of all other most serious is handled.

17. *All the Grecians having taken Sosthenes.* This is that Sosthenes whom Paul doth honourably couple with himself as his companion in the beginning of the former Epistle to the Corinthians. And though there be no mention made of him before among the faithful, yet it is to be thought that he was then one of Paul's companions and advocates. And what fury did enforce the Grecians to run headlong upon him, save only because it is allotted to all the children of God to have the world set against them, and offended with them and their cause, though unknown? Wherefore, there is no cause why such unjust dealing should trouble us at this day when we see the miserable Church oppugned on every side. Moreover, the frowardness of man's nature is depainted out unto us as in a table, [picture.] Admit we grant that the Jews were hated everywhere for good causes, yet why are the Grecians rather displeased with Sosthenes, a modest man, than with the authors of the tumult, who troubled Paul without any cause? Namely, this is the reason, because, when men are not governed with the Spirit of God, they are carried headlong unto evil, as it were, by the secret in-

[1] " Quid illis exprobret Paulis,' how Paul upbraideth them

spiration of nature, notwithstanding it may be that they bare Sosthenes such hatred, thinking he had lodged wicked men to raise sedition.

Neither did Gallio care for any of these things. This looseness[1] must be imputed not so much to the sluggishness of the deputy as to the hatred of the Jewish religion. The Romans could have wished that the remembrance of the true God had been buried. And, therefore, when as it was lawful for them to vow their vows, and to pay them to all the idols of Asia and Greece, it was a deadly fact[2] to do sacrifice to the God of Israel. Finally, in the common liberty[3] of all manner [of] superstition, only true religion was accepted. This is the cause that Gallio winketh at the injury done to Sosthenes. He professed of late that he would punish injuries if any were done; now he suffereth a guiltless man to be beaten before the judgment-seat. Whence cometh this sufferance, save only because he did in heart desire that the Jews might one slay another, that their religion might be put out[4] with them? But forasmuch as, by the mouth of Luke, the Spirit condemneth Gallio's carelessness, because he did not aid a man who was unjustly punished,[5] let our magistrates know that they be far more inexcusable if they wink at injuries and wicked facts, if they bridle not the wantonness of the wicked, if they reach not forth their hand to the oppressed. But and if the sluggish are to look for just damnation, what terrible judgment hangeth over the heads of those who are unfaithful and wicked,[6] who, by favouring evil causes, and bearing with wicked facts, set up, as it were, a banner of want of punishment,[7] and are fans to kindle boldness to do hurt?

18. *And when Paul had tarried there many days, having taken his leave of the brethren, he sailed into Syria, Priscilla*

---

[1] "Cessatio," non-interference offence. [2] "Capitale erat," it was a capital offence. [3] "In communi... licentia," while there was a common licence. [4] "Extingueretur," might be extinguished. [5] "Afflictum," afflicted, oppressed. [6] "Perfidis et malignis," malignant and perfidious. [7] "Impunitatis," of impunity.

and Aquila accompanying him, when he had shaven his head at Cenchrea: for he had a vow

19. And he came to Ephesus, when he left them. And when he had entered into the synagogue, he disputed with the Jews.

20. And when they desired him that he would stay longer time with them, he did not consent;

21. But took his leave, saying, I must needs keep the feast which is at hand in Jerusalem: but I will return to you again, God willing. And he loosed from Ephesus.

22. And when he was come down to Cæsarea, and was gone up, and had saluted the Church, he came down to Antioch.

23. And when he had tarried there some time, he departed, walking through the country of Galatia and Phrygia in order, strengthening all the disciples.

18. *And when he had tarried there many days.* Paul's constancy appeareth in this, in that he is not driven away with fear, lest he should trouble the disciples, who were as yet ignorant and weak, with his sudden and untimely departure. We read in many other places, that when persecution was raised against him elsewhere he fled forthwith. What is the cause, then, that he stayeth at Corinthus? to wit, when he saw that the enemies were provoked with his presence to rage against the whole Church, he did not doubt but that the faithful[1] should have peace and rest by his departure; but now, when he seeth their malice bridled, so that they cannot hurt the flock of God, he had rather sting and nettle them, than by departing minister unto them any new occasion of rage. Furthermore, this was the third journey which Paul took to Jerusalem. For going from Damascus, he went once up that he might be made known to the apostles. And he was sent the second time with Barnabas, that he might handle and end the controversy about ceremonies. But Luke doth not set down for what cause he now took such a long and laborious journey, determining with all speed to return.

When he had shorn his head. It is uncertain whether that

[1] " Pacem et quietem fidelibus redimere," to purchase the peace and quiet of the faithful.

be spoken of Aquila or of Paul: neither skilleth it much. Though I interpret it willingly of Paul, because it seemeth to me a likely thing that he did this for because of the Jews, unto whom he was about to come. Assuredly, I think this to be a thing which all men grant, that he made not any ceremonial vow for his own cause, only that he might do some worship to God. He knew that that was to continue only for a time which God commanded under the law to the old people; and we know how diligently he teacheth that the kingdom of God consisteth not in these external elements, and how straitly he urgeth the abrogating thereof. It had been an absurd thing for him to bind his own conscience with that religion from which he had loosed all other men.

Therefore, he did shear his head for no other cause, save only that he might apply himself[1] to the Jews, who were as yet ignorant, and not thoroughly taught; as he doth testify that he took upon him the voluntary observing of the law, from which he was freed, that he might gain those who were under the law, (1 Cor. ix. 20.) If any man object that it was not lawful for him to make semblance of a vow which he had not made from his heart, we may easily answer, that as touching the substance of purifying he did not dissemble, and that he used the ceremony which was as yet free, not as if God did require such worship, but that he might somewhat bear with the ignorant.

Therefore, the Papists are ridiculous when they fet[2] from hence an example of making vows. Paul was moved with no religion to make his vow; but these men place a feigned worship of God in vows. Respect of time enforced Paul to keep the rites of the law. These men do nothing else but entangle in superstition the Church of Christ, which was set free long ago. For it is one thing to bring in use again old ceremonies used long ago, and another to tolerate the same being as yet used, until such time as they may by little and little grow out of use. I omit that the Papists in

---

[1] "Se accommodaret," accommodate himself   [2] "Eliciunt," extract.

vain and foolishly compare the shaving of their priests with the sign of purifying which God had allowed in the law. But because we need not stand any longer to refute them, let this one thing suffice us, that Paul bound himself with a vow that he might bring those which were weak to Christ, at least that he might not offend them, which vow he knew was of no importance before God.

19. *Entering into the synagogue.* In that he shook his garment at Corinthus,[1] it was [not] done for that cause, (as this place teacheth,) that he might cast off the whole nation, but only such as he had already tried [experienced] to be of desperate obstinacy. Now, he cometh afresh unto the Ephesians, that he might try whether he could find any more obedience among them. Furthermore, it is a wonder, that seeing it appeareth by Luke's report that he was heard more patiently in this synagogue than in any other place, and also that he was requested to tarry, he did not grant their request. Hence we may easily gather that which I said before, that he had some great cause to go up to Jerusalem in haste. Also, he himself showeth that he must make haste, saying, I must keep the feast which is at hand at Jerusalem. Neither is it to be doubted but that after he had set things in good order there, he departed with their good leave; and we may gather out of Luke's words that they did admit his excuse lest the repulse should offend them. And this is worth the noting, that when better hope to do good is offered us than we were wont to have, we are drawn unto divers affairs, as it were, by the hand of God, that we may learn to give over ourselves to be governed at his pleasure.

The feast. That which I said of late touching the vow doth also appertain unto the feast day. For Paul meant not to do thereby any duty of godliness[2] to God, but to be at the assembly, wherein he might do more good than at any other time of the year. For the Epistle to the Gala-

---

[1] " In signum detestationis," in token of detestation officio," office of piety.

[2] " Pietatis

tians doth sufficiently testify what account he made of difference of days, (Gal. iv. 10.) And we must note that he maketh no promise touching his return without using this exception, if it please the Lord. We do all confess that we be not able to stir one finger without his direction; but because there reigneth in men so great arrogancy everywhere, that they dare determine anything (passing over God) not only for the time to come, but also for many years, we must oftentimes think upon this reverence and sobriety, that we may learn to make our counsels subject to the will and providence of God; lest, if we be deliberate and take counsel as those use to do who think that they have fortune at their commandment, we be justly punished for our rashness. And though there be not so great religion in words but that we may at our pleasure say that we will do this or that, yet is it good to accustom ourselves to use certain forms in our speeches, that they may put us in mind that God doth direct all our doings.

22. *When he came down to Cæsarea.* Though Luke saith in a word that Paul saluted the Church at Jerusalem, yet is it certain that he was drawn thither with some great necessity. And yet we may gather by this text that he stayed not long at Jerusalem, peradventure because things fell not out as he would. Moreover, he declareth that his journey in his return was not idle or barren, in that he saith that he strengthened all the disciples, undoubtedly not without great pains-taking, because he was enforced to go hither and thither, and oft to turn out of his way; for this word καθεξῆς doth signify a continual course. Now, we have already declared (Acts ix. 36) in what respect those be called disciples who had given their names to Christ, and professed the name of Christ; to wit, because there is no godliness without true instruction. They had, indeed, their pastors under whom they might profit. Yet the greater Paul's authority was, and the more excellent spirit he had given him, so they were not a little strengthened by his

passing by them, especially seeing he was the chief workmaster in the founding of all these churches.

24. *And a certain Jew named Apollos, born in Alexandria, an eloquent man, came to Ephesus, being mighty in the Scriptures.*
25. *He was instructed in the way of the Lord, and being fervent in the spirit, he spake and taught diligently those things which are the Lord's, knowing only the baptism of John.*
26. *And he began to speak freely in the synagogue : whom when Priscilla and Aquila had heard, they took him to their company, and showed him the way of the Lord more perfectly.*
27. *And when he was determined to go into Achaia, the brethren exhorting him, wrote to the disciples that they should receive him : who, when he was come, he helped them much who had believed through grace.*
28. *For he overcame the Jews mightily, and that openly, showing by the Scriptures that Jesus was Christ.*

24. *A certain Jew.* This ought for good causes to be ascribed to the providence of God, in that whilst Paul is enforced to depart from Ephesus, Apollos cometh in his place to supply his absence. And it is very expedient to know the beginning of this man of what sort it was, forasmuch as he was Paul's successor among the Corinthians, and did behave himself so excellently, and did his faithful endeavour, and took great pains, so that Paul commendeth him honourably as a singular fellow in office. "I have planted, (saith he,) Apollos hath watered," (1 Cor. iii. 6.) Also, these things have I figuratively appointed unto myself and Apollos, (1 Cor. iv. 6.) Luke giveth him first two titles of commendation, that he was eloquent and mighty in the Scriptures; afterward he will add his zeal, faith, and constancy. And though Paul do truly deny that the kingdom of God consisteth in words, and he himself was not commended for eloquence, yet dexterity in speaking and reasoning[1] (such as Luke doth here commend) is not to be de-

---

[1] " Sermocinandi," sermonising, haranguing.

spised, especially when no pomp or vain boasting is sought after, by using fine words and great eloquence; but he which is to teach counteth it sufficient for him, without fraud or ambition, without lofty words and curious cunning, plainly to lay open the matter he hath in hand. Paul was without eloquence; the Lord would have the chief apostle to want this virtue, to the end the power of the Spirit might appear more excellent in his rude and homely speech. And yet was he furnished with such eloquence as was sufficient to set forth the name of Christ, and to maintain the doctrine of salvation. But as the distribution of the gifts of the Spirit is divers and manifold, Paul's infancy,[1] that I may so call it, did no whit let but that the Lord might choose to himself eloquent ministers. Furthermore, lest any man should think that Apollos' eloquence was profane or vain,[2] Luke saith that it was joined with great power,[3] namely, that he was mighty in the Scriptures. Which I expound thus, that he was not only well and soundly exercised in the Scriptures, but that he had the force and efficacy thereof, that, being armed with them, he did in all conflicts get the upper hand. And this (in my judgment) is rather the praise of the Scripture than of man,[4] that it hath sufficient force both to defend the truth, and also to refute the subtilty of Satan.

25. *He was instructed.* That which Luke addeth shortly after seemeth not to agree with this commendation, to wit, that he knew only the baptism of John. But this latter member is added by way of correction. Nevertheless, these two agree very well together; that he understood the doctrine of the gospel, because he both knew that the Redeemer was given to the world, and also was well and sincerely instructed concerning the grace of reconciliation; and yet had he been trained up only in the principles of the gospel, so much as could be had out of John's institution.[5] For we

---

[1] "Pauli infantia," Paul's want of utterance.
[2] "Vel inanem et fulinem," or futile and vain.
[3] "Cum majore...virtute," with a greater virtue or excellence
[4] "Scripturæ potius quam hominis laus est," is greater praise to Scripture than to the man
[5] "Institutio," instruction.

know that John was in the midst between Christ and the prophets; and of his office doth both his father Zacharias intreat in his tongue, (Luke i. 76; Luke i. 16 and 17;) and also the angel out of the prophecy of Malachi, (Mal. iii. 1.) Surely, seeing that he carried the light before Christ, and did highly extol his power, his disciples are for good causes said to have had knowledge of Christ. Moreover, the speech is worth the noting, that he knew the baptism of John. For thence we gather the true use of the sacraments; to wit, that they enter[1] us in some certain kind of doctrine, or that they establish that faith which we have embraced. Surely, it is wickedness and impious profanation to pull them away[2] from doctrine. Wherefore, that the sacraments may be rightly administered, the voice of the heavenly doctrine must sound there. For what is the baptism of John? Luke comprehendeth all his ministry under this word, not only because doctrine is annexed unto baptism, but also because it is the foundation and head thereof, without which it should be a vain and dead ceremony.

Being fervent in spirit he spake. Apollos hath another commendation given him in these words, that he was inflamed with an holy zeal to teach. Doctrine without zeal is either like a sword in the hand of a madman, or else it lieth still as cold and without use, or else it serveth for vain and wicked boasting. For we see that some learned men become slothful; other some (which is worse) become ambitious; other some (which is of all the worst) trouble the Church with contention and brawling. Therefore, that doctrine shall be unsavoury which is not joined with zeal. But let us remember that Luke putteth the knowledge of the Scripture in the first place, which must be the moderation of zeal,[3] for we know that many are fervent without consideration, as the Jews did rage against the gospel, by reason of a perverse affection which they did bear toward the law; and even at this day we see what the Papists be, who

---

[1] "Initient," initiate.   [2] "Avelli," to dissever.   [3] "Quæ esset zeli moderatio," to moderate zeal.

are carried headlong with furious violence, being pricked forward with an opinion unadvisedly conceived. Therefore, let knowledge be present that it may govern zeal. And now it is said that zeal was the cause of diligence, because Apollos gave himself to teach diligently. But and if that man, being not yet thoroughly and perfectly taught in the gospel, did preach Christ so diligently and freely, what excuse do those men hope to have, who know that more perfectly and fully, which he knew not as yet, if they do not endeavour so much as in them lieth to further and advance the kingdom of Christ? Luke doth attribute zeal to the Spirit, therefore, because it is a rare and peculiar gift; neither do I so expound it that Apollos was moved and pricked forward with the instinct of his mind, but by motion of the Holy Spirit.

26. *Whom, when Priscilla.* By this it appeareth how far Priscilla and Aquila were from the love of themselves, and from envying another man's virtue, in that they deliver those things familiarly and privately to an eloquent man, which he may afterward utter publicly. They excelled not in the same grace wherein he did excel, and, peradventure, they might have been despised in the congregation. Moreover, they most diligently help him, whom they see better furnished as well with eloquence as the use of the Scripture; so that they keep silence, and he alone is heard.

Again, this was no small modesty which was in Apollos, in that he doth suffer himself to be taught and instructed not only in [by] an handy-craftsman, but also by a woman. He was mighty in the Scripture, and did surpass[1] them; but as touching the accomplishment of the kingdom of Christ, those do polish and trim him who might seem to be scarce fit ministers. Also, we see that at that time women were not so ignorant of the word of God as the Papists will have them; forasmuch as we see that one of the chief teachers of the Church was instructed by a woman. Notwithstanding, we must remember that Priscilla did execute this function

---

[1] " Illis longe superior," and far superior to them.

of teaching at home in her own house, that she might not overthrow the order prescribed by God and nature.

27. *When he was determined.* Luke doth not express for what cause Apollos would go to Achaia. Notwithstanding, we gather out of the text [context] that he was not allured with any private commodity, but because more plentiful fruit in spreading abroad the gospel did show itself there; because the brethren did more encourage him with their exhortation, and did spur him when he did already run. Which they would not have done, unless it had been for the common profit of the Church. For it had been an absurd thing to entreat a man to depart to another place, whose faithful industry they already used, and did know that they should have need of him afterward, unless there had been some better recompence offered. And I take it that the brethren of Ephesus wrote to those of Achaia, not only that they should provide lodging for the man, but also that they should suffer him to teach. This is holy commendation indeed, when we study to extol every good man with our testimony and consent, [suffrage,] lest the gifts of the Holy Ghost, which he hath given to every man for the edifying of the Church, lie buried.

When he came. The brethren foresaw this, who had already had experience thereof, when they exhorted him to address himself to that journey which he had already in mind conceived. And whereas it is said that he helped the faithful much, we may take it two ways; either that he helped those who were not so well furnished, and that he did support them to beat down the pride of their enemies; for every man was not able to have weapon in readiness, to undertake a hard combat against old[1] enemies, who would never have yielded, unless they had been enforced; or that he aided them, lest their faith should fail, being shaken with the gainsaying of the enemies, which thing doth oftentimes befall the weak. I take it that they were helped both ways;

---

[1] "Veteranos," veteran.

that having a skilful and practised captain, they got[1] the victory in the conflict. Secondly, that their faith was fortified with a new prop, that it might be without danger of wavering. Furthermore, Luke seemeth to note that the brethren were helped with this stoutness and constancy, when as he saith that he disputed publicly with the Jews. For this was a sign of zeal and boldness not to fly the light. Whereas, in the end of the sentence, these words are used, *through grace;* it doth either agree with the word going before, *they believed;* or else it must be referred unto the help wherewith he helped the brethren. The former interpretation is nothing hard. For the meaning thereof shall be this, that the faithful were illuminate by the grace of God, that they might believe; as if he had said, The brethren, who were already called by the benefit of God unto faith, were furthered. Yet the other text seemeth to agree better, that Apollos, in imparting that grace which he had received with the brethren, did help them. So that, *through grace,* shall import as much as according to the measure of the grace received.

28. *He overcame the Jews.* By this it appeareth to what use that ability which Apollos had (in that he was mighty in the Holy Scriptures) did serve; to wit, because he had a strong and forcible proof to reprove and overcome the enemies withal. Also, the state of the disputation is briefly set down, that Jesus is Christ. For this was out of question among the Jews, that Christ was promised to be the deliverer; but it was a hard matter to persuade them that Jesus, the Son of Mary, was this Christ, through whom salvation was offered. Therefore, it was expedient for Apollos so to dispute concerning the office of Christ, that he might prove that the testimonies of the Scripture were fulfilled in the Son of Mary; and that he might thereby gather that he was Christ.

Also, this place doth testify, that the Scripture is profit-

---

[1] " Superiores essent," might be victorious.

able not only to teach, but also to break the obstinacy of those which do not obey and follow willingly. For our faith should not otherwise be firm enough, unless there were an evident demonstration extant there of those things which are necessary to be known for salvation. Surely, if the law and the prophets had so great light, that Apollos did thereby prove manifestly that Jesus is Christ, as if he did point out the matter with his finger, the adding of the gospel must bring this to pass at least, that the perfect knowledge of Christ may be fet [sought] from the whole Scripture.

Wherefore it is detestable blasphemy against God in that the Papists say, that the Scripture is dark and doubtful. For to what end should God have spoken, unless the plain and invincible truth should show itself in his words? And whereas they infer, that we must stand to the authority of the Church, and they are not to dispute with heretics out of the Scriptures; their cavil is sufficiently refuted by Luke. For, seeing there was nothing more stubborn than the Jews, we need not to fear but that those weapons whereto Apollos trusted, and overcame them, shall suffice us against all heretics, seeing that by them we get the victory of the devil, the prince of all errors.

CHAPTER XIX.

1. *And it came to pass when Apollos was at Corinthus, that Paul, having gone through the upper parts, came to Ephesus, and having found certain disciples, he said unto them,*
2. *Have ye received the Holy Ghost since ye believed? But they said unto him, Yea, we have not so much as heard whether there be any Holy Ghost.*
3. *And he said unto them, Wherewith were ye then baptized? And they said, With the baptism of John.*
4. *And Paul said, John truly baptized with the baptism of re-*

pentance, speaking to the people, that they should believe in Him who should come after him ; that is, in Christ Jesus.
5. *When they heard these things, they were baptized in the name of the Lord Jesus.*
6. *And when Paul had laid his hands upon them, the Holy Ghost came upon them ; and they spake with tongues, and did prophesy.*
7. *And all the men were about twelve.*

1. Luke showeth here that the Church of Ephesus was not only confirmed and increased by Paul's return, but also that there was a miracle wrought there, because the visible graces of the Spirit were given to certain rude and new disciples. Furthermore, it is not known whether they were inhabitants of the city or strangers; neither doth it greatly skill. It is not to be doubted but that they were Jews, because they had received the baptism of John; also, it is to be thought that they dwelt at Ephesus when Paul found them there.

2. *Whether they had received the Holy Ghost.* The end of the history doth show that Paul doth not speak in this place of the Spirit of regeneration, but of the special gifts which God gave to divers at the beginning of the gospel, for the common edifying of the Church. But now upon this interrogation of Paul ariseth a question, whether the Spirit were common to all everywhere at that time ? For if he were given only to a few, why doth he join him with faith, as if they were so linked together that they could not be separate ? Peradventure, they were none of the common sort; or because they were an indifferent number, that is, twelve, Paul demandeth whether they were all without the gifts of the Spirit. Notwithstanding, I think thus, that so many Jews were offered in presence of the Gentiles, not by chance, but by the counsel of God; and that at one time being disciples, that is, of the number of the faithful, who did notwithstanding confess that they were ignorant of the principal glory of the gospel, which was apparent in spiritual gifts,

that by them Paul's ministry might be beautified and set forth. For it is unlike that Apollos left so few disciples at Ephesus; and he might have taught them better, since that he learned the way of the Lord perfectly of Priscilla and Aquila.

Moreover, I do not doubt but that the brethren of whom Luke spake before were other than these. In sum, when Paul seeth that these men do profess the name of Christ, to the end he may have a more certain trial of their faith, he asketh them whether they have received the Holy Ghost. For it appeareth by Paul himself that this was a sign and token of the grace of God to establish the credit of doctrine; I would know of you whether ye received the Holy Ghost by the works of the law, or by the hearing of faith, (Gal. iii. 2.)

We know not whether there be any Holy Ghost. How could it be, that men being Jews heard nothing of the Spirit, concerning which the prophets speak everywhere, and whose commendations and titles are extant in the whole Scripture? Surely we gather by this that Paul did neither speak generally of the Spirit; and that these men, as they were asked, did deny that they knew those visible graces wherewith God had beautified the kingdom of his Son. Therefore, they confess that they know not whether God give such gifts. Therefore, there is in the word *Spirit* the figure *metonymia*. And this sense doth that confirm, that if they had altogether denied that they knew anything concerning the Spirit of God, Paul would not have passed over with silence such a gross error; yea, an error altogether monstrous. When he demandeth to what end, or how they were baptized, he showeth therewithal, that wheresoever Christ had been soundly and thoroughly preached, the visible graces did also appear, that such worship[1] might be common to all churches. Wherefore, no marvel if Paul wonder that the faithful are ignorant of such glory of Christ, which God would have to be apparent everywhere at that time; and

---

[1] " Decus," honour.

adding a correction immediately, he telleth them that they must not stay in those rudiments which they had learned; because it was John's office to prepare disciples for Christ.

4. *John truly.* Paul's admonition tended to this end, that these men being convict of their ignorance might desire to go forward. He saith that John preached of Christ who was to come. Therefore he sent out his disciples,[1] that running in the course they might go towards Christ, who was not as yet revealed. Wherefore, to the end these men may not flatter themselves, and refuse to go forward, he showeth that they be yet far from the mark. For the feeling of want doth enforce men to desire that which is as yet lacking. The sum cometh to this end, as if Paul had said, Before Christ was glorified, this power of his did not appear[2] in the world; when he was ascended into heaven he would have his kingdom to flourish thus. Therefore the graces of the Spirit were much less shed out when John was as yet in the course of his embassage, which do now declare that Christ sitteth at the right hand of his Father, forasmuch as he had not as then openly showed himself to be the Redeemer of the world. Therefore know ye that you must go farther forward; because ye be far from the mark. So that he doth plainly show that the faith of the godly who had been taught by John, ought to have looked unto Christ who was to come, lest these men should stand still, being newly entered, without going any farther.

And even by this also are we taught that the baptism of John was a token of repentance and remission of sins, and that our baptism at this day doth not differ any thing from it, save only that Christ is already revealed, and in his death and resurrection our salvation is made perfect: and so baptism was brought unto his [its] effect; because out of that fountain of Christ's death and resurrection, whereof I have spoken, floweth repentance, and thither is faith referred again that it may thence fet [seek] free righteousness. In

---

[1] " Ex carceribus," from the goal.   [2] " Viguit," flour sh

sum, Paul showeth plainly that that was the baptism of regeneration and renovation as is ours. And because both purging and newness of life doth flow from Christ alone, he saith that it was grounded in his faith, by which words we be also taught, that hereupon dependeth all the force of baptism, that we lay hold upon by faith in Christ whatsoever baptism doth figure; so far off is it, that the outward sign doth derogate from or diminish the grace of Christ any iota.

5. *When they heard these things.* Because the men of old had conceived an opinion that the baptism of John and of Christ were diverse, it was no inconvenient[1] thing for them to be baptized again, who were only prepared with the baptism of John. But that that diversity was falsely and wickedly by them believed, it appeareth by this, in that it was a pledge and token of the same adoption, and of the same newness of life, which we have at this day in our baptism; and, therefore, we do not read that Christ did baptize those again who came from John unto him. Moreover, Christ received baptism in his own flesh, that he might couple himself with us by that visible sign, (Matth. iii. 15;) but if that feigned diversity be admitted, this singular benefit shall fall away and perish, that baptism is common to the Son of God and to us, or that we have all one baptism with him. But this opinion needeth no long refutation, because to the end they may persuade that these two baptisms be diverse, they must needs show first wherein the one differeth from the other; but a most excellent likelihood answereth on both parts, and also the agreement and conformity of the parts,[2] which causeth us to confess that it is all one baptism.

Now the question is, whether it were lawful to repeat the same; and furious men in this our age, trusting to this testimony, went about to bring in baptizing again.[3] Some take

---

[1] "Absurdum," absurd   [2] "Atqui utrumque respondet optima similitudo et partium omnium symmetria et conformitas," but there is perfect resemblance, and a complete symmetry and conformity of all the parts.
[3] "Anabaptismum invehere," to introduce Anabaptism

baptism for new institution or instruction, of whose mind I am not, because, as their exposition is too much racked, so it smelleth of a starting-hole.[1]

Other some deny that baptism was repeated; because they were baptized amiss by some foolish enemy[2] of John. But because their conjecture hath no colour; yea, the words of Paul do rather import that they were the true and natural disciples of John, and Luke doth honourably call them disciples of Christ; I do not subscribe to this opinion, and yet I deny that the baptism of water was repeated, because the words of Luke import no other thing, save only that they were baptized with the Spirit. First, it is no new thing for the name of baptism to be translated unto the gifts of the Spirit, as we saw in the first and in the eleventh chapters, (Acts i. 5, and xi. 6,) where Luke said, that when Christ promised to his apostles to send the Spirit visible, he called it baptism.

Also, that when the Spirit came down upon Cornelius, Peter remembered the words of the Lord, "Ye shall be baptized with the Holy Ghost." Again, we see that those visible gifts are spoken of by name in this place, and that the same are given with baptism. And whereas it followeth immediately, that when he had laid his hands upon them, the Spirit came, I take it to be added by way of interpretation; for it is a kind of speaking much used in the Scripture, first to set down a thing briefly, and afterwards to make it more plain. Therefore, that which by reason of brevity was somewhat obscure, doth Luke better express and lay more open, saying, that by laying on of hands the Spirit was given them. If any man object, that when baptism is put for the gifts of the Spirit, it is not taken simply, but having somewhat added to it. I answer, that Luke's meaning doth sufficiently appear by the text; and again, that Luke doth allude unto the baptism whereof he spake. And surely if you understand it of the external sign, it shall be an absurd thing that it was given them without using

---

[1] " Effugium sapit," savours of evasion.   [2] " Æmulatore," rival.

any better doctrine. But and if you take it metaphorically for institution, the speech shall be as yet harsh; and the narration should not agree, that after they were taught the Holy Ghost came down upon them.

Furthermore, as I confess that this laying on of hands was a sacrament, so I say that those fell through ignorance who did continually imitate the same. For seeing that all men agree in this, that it was a grace which was to last only for a time, which was showed by that sign, it is a perverse and ridiculous thing to retain the sign since the truth is taken away. There is another respect of baptism and the supper, wherein the Lord doth testify that those gifts are laid open for us, which the Church shall enjoy even until the end of the world. Wherefore we must diligently and wisely distinguish perpetual sacraments from those which last only for a time, lest vain and frivolous visures [semblances] have a place among the sacraments. Whereas the men of old time did use laying on of hands, that they might confirm the profession of faith in those who were grown up,[1] I do not mislike it; so that no man think that the grace of the Spirit is annexed to such a ceremony, as doth Jerome against the Luciferians.

But the Papists are worthy of no pardon, who being not content with the ancient rite, durst thrust in rotten and filthy anointing, that it might be not only a confirmation of baptism, but also a more worthy sacrament, whereby they imagine that the faithful are made perfect who were before only half perfect,—whereby those are armed against the battle, who before had their sins only forgiven them. For they have not been afraid to spew out these horrible blasphemies.

> 8. *And going into the synagogue, he spake freely about three months, disputing and persuading concerning the kingdom of God.*
> 9. *And when some waxed hard-hearted that they could not believe, speaking evil of the way before the multitude, de-*

---

[1] " In adultis," in adults.

parting from them he did separate the disciples, and disputed daily in the school of one Tyrannus.

10. *And this he did by the space of two years, so that all which dwelt in Asia heard the word of the Lord Jesus, both Jews and Greeks.*

11. *And the Lord showed no small miracles by the hands of Paul.*

12. *So that from his body were brought napkins and partlets unto those that were sick, and the diseases departed from them, and the evil spirits came out of them.*

8. *Going into the synagogue.* By this we gather that Paul began with the company of the godly, who had already given their names to Christ. Secondly, that he came into the synagogue, that he might gather together into one body of the Church the rest of the Jews who knew not Christ as yet, or at least who had not as yet received him. And he saith that Paul behaved himself boldly, that we may know that he was not therefore heard by the space of three months, because he did craftily cover the doctrine of the gospel, or did insinuate himself by certain dark crooks. Luke doth also by and by express some token of boldness, showing that he disputed and persuaded touching the kingdom of God. And we know that by this word is oftentimes noted that restoring which was promised to the fathers, and which was to be fulfilled by the coming of Christ. For seeing that without Christ there is an evil-favoured and confused scattering abroad and ruin of all things, the prophets did attribute this not in vain to the Messias who was to come, that it should come to pass that he should establish the kingdom of God in the world. And now, because this kingdom doth bring us back from falling and sliding back, unto the obedience of God, and maketh us sons of enemies; it consisteth—First, in the free forgiveness of sins, whereby God doth reconcile us to himself, and doth adopt us to be his people: Secondly, in newness of life, whereby he fashioneth and maketh us like to his own image. He saith that he disputed and persuaded, meaning that Paul did so dispute, that he proved that with sound reasons which he

did allege; that done, he used the pricks of godly exhortations, whereby he pricked forward his hearers.[1] For no profound disputations[2] shall make us obedient to God, unless we be moved with godly admonitions.

9. *Seeing their hearts were hardened.* We do not read that Paul was heard so patiently and so favourably by the Jews at any place as at Ephesus at his first coming. For whereas others raising tumults did drive him away, he was requested by these to tarry longer. Now, after that he had endeavoured, by the space of three months, to erect the kingdom of God among them, the ungodliness and stubbornness of many doth show itself. For Luke saith that they were hardened; and surely such is the power of the heavenly doctrine, that it doth either make the reprobate mad or else more obstinate; and that not of nature, but accidentally, as they say, because, when they be urged by the truth, their secret poison breaketh out.

Luke addeth that they spake evil of the way before the people. For the contemners of the gospel[3] do resist that deadlily among others which they will not embrace. And this do they to no other end, save only because they be desirous (if it can be) to have all men partners in their impiety. It is well known that every ordinance is understood by this word *way;* but here it is referred unto the gospel of Christ. Now, Luke saith that Paul departed from them, and did separate the brethren, by which example we are taught, that when we have experience of desperate and incurable stubbornness, we must lose our labour no longer. Therefore, Paul admonisheth Titus to avoid a man that is an heretic, after once or twice admonition, (Tit. iii. 10.) For the word of God is unjustly blasphemed,[4] if it be cast to dogs and swine. Also, we must provide for the weak, lest through wicked backbitings and

---

[1] "Ut januam regno Dei aperirent," that they might open a door for the gospel.   [2] "Argutiæ," subtle reasonings   [3] "Hac tandem se projiciunt," at length proceed to such extremes that they.   [4] "Indigna contumelia afficitur," is grossly insulted.

slandering of sound doctrine, their godliness be subverted. Therefore, Paul did separate the disciples, lest the goats should with their stink infect the flock of sheep; secondly, that the pure worshippers of God might make profession freely.

Disputing daily. This place showeth how continual Paul's diligence was in teaching; and that they be too churlish and dainty who are straightway weary of learning. For we see how few come daily, who are ready and apt to hear. And though he had a particular care for the household flock which he had gathered as into a sheepfold, yet he doth not suffer strangers to be destitute of his industry; but continuing the course of his disputation, he trieth whether he can find any which are apt to be taught. He calleth it the school of Tyrannus, meaning no such man as had gotten the government of Asia; for the Romans bare rule throughout all Asia, but it is to be thought that the school was built at the charge of one Tyrannus, and given to the city. Therefore, the faithful did use a public place, which bare the name of the builder, where they had their assemblies.

10. *All which dwelt.* Luke doth not mean that the men of Asia came thither to hear Paul; but that the smell [savour] of his preaching went throughout all Asia, and that the seed was sown far and wide; so that his labour was fruitful not only to one city, but also to places which were far off; and that cometh to pass oftentimes, that when the truth of God is preached in one place, it soundeth where the voice of the minister cannot sound, being spread abroad far and wide; because it is delivered from hand to hand, and one doth teach another. For one man were not sufficient, unless every man were for himself diligent to spread abroad the faith.

11. *No small miracles.* He calleth miracles *virtutes* or *powers*, after the common custom of the Scripture, which were testimonies of the extraordinary power of God. And

he showeth that Paul's apostleship was set forth with these ensigns, that his doctrine might have the greater authority. For it is a common speech, That wonders and signs are showed by the hand of men. So that the praise thereof is ascribed to God alone as to the author; and man is only the minister. And that he may the more amplify the miracles, he saith that handkerchiefs and partlets[1] were brought unto the sick, which so soon as they touched they were healed. It is not unknown[2] to what end Paul had such power given him, to wit, that he might prove himself to be a true apostle of Christ, that he might make the gospel to be believed, and might confirm his ministry. And here it is expedient to call to mind those things which we had before, touching the lawful use of miracles. And whereas God did heal the sick with Paul's handkerchiefs, it tended to that end, that even those who had never seen the man might, notwithstanding, reverently embrace his doctrine, though he himself were absent. For which cause the Papists are more blockish, who wrest this place unto their relics; as if Paul sent his handkerchiefs that men might worship them and kiss them[3] in honour of them; as in Papistry, they worship Francis' shoes and mantle, Rose's girdle, Saint Margaret's comb, and such like trifles. Yea, rather, he did choose most simple[4] things, lest any superstition should arise by reason of the price or pomp. For he was fully determined to keep Christ's glory sound and undiminished.

> 13. *And certain of the vagabond Jews, exorcists, essayed to name over those which had evil spirits the name of the Lord Jesus, saying, We adjure you by Jesus whom Paul preacheth.*
> 14. *And there were certain sons of Sceva, a Jew, the chief of the priests, who did this.*
> 15. *And the evil spirit answered and said, Jesus I know, and Paul I know; but who are ye?*

---

[1] "Semicinctia," girdles.   [2] "Non obscurum est," it is clear.
[3] "Oscularentur venerabundi homines," men given to veneration might kiss them.   [4] "Vilissimas," most worthless

16. *And the man in whom the evil spirit was ran upon them, and overcame them, and prevailed against them, so that they escaped out of that house naked and wounded.*

17. *And this was known to all both Jews and Grecians which dwelt at Ephesus; and fear came upon them all, and the name of the Lord Jesus was magnified.*

13. To the end it may more plainly appear that the apostleship of Paul was confirmed by those miracles whereof mention was made of late, Luke doth now teach that when certain did falsely pretend the name of Christ, such abuse was most sharply punished. Whereby we gather that such miracles were wrought by the hand of Paul, to no other end, save only that all men might know that he did faithfully preach Christ to be the power of God; forasmuch as the Lord did not only not suffer them to be separate from the pure doctrine of the gospel; but did so sharply punish those who did draw them preposterously unto their enchantments; whence we gather again, that whatsoever miracles do darken the name of Christ, they be juggling casts of the devil; and that those be cozeners and falsifiers who draw the true miracles of God to any other end, save only that true religion may be established.[1]

Certain exorcists. I do not doubt but that this office did proceed of foolish emulation. God was wont to exercise his power divers ways among the Jews; and he had used the prophets in times past as ministers to drive away devils; under colour hereof they invented conjuration,[2] and hereupon was erected unadvisedly an extraordinary function without the commandment of God. Also, it may be that (God appointing it so to be) it did somewhat;[3] not that he favoured it preposterously, but that they might more willingly retain the religion of their fathers, until the coming of Christ. Under the reign of Christ, wicked ambition caused strife between the Christians and the Jews. For exorcists were made after the will of men; after that (as

---

[1] "Sanciatur," sanctioned or confirmed   [2] "Exorcismos," exorcisms   [3] "Aliquid perfecerint," they accomplished somewhat.

superstition doth always wax worse and worse) the Pope would have this common to all his clerks, who were to be promoted unto an higher degree. For after that they be made door-keepers, forthwith the conjuring of devils is committed to them; and by very experience they set themselves to be laughed at. For they are enforced to confess that they give a vain title, and such as is without effect, for where is the power they have to conjure devils? and the very exorcists themselves do take upon them, to their own reproach, an office which they never put in practice. But this falleth out justly, that there is no end of erring, when men depart from the word of God. As touching these men, we gather that they were wandering rogues, and such as went from door to door, of which sort we see many at this day in Popery; for he saith that they went about. By which words he giveth us to understand, that they went to and fro as occasion was offered them to deceive men.

We adjure you by Jesus. It is a thing like to be true, [probable,] that these deceivers flee unto the name of Christ, that they might get new power, whereof they had falsely boasted before, or because the power which they had did cease, that they might darken the gospel. This invocation had two faults; for whereas they were enemies[1] to Paul's doctrine, they abuse the colour thereof without faith, as it were, unto magical enchantments; secondly, they take to themselves without the calling of God that which is not in man's hand. But the lawful calling upon the name of God and Christ is that which is directed by faith, and doth not pass the bounds of a man's calling. Wherefore, we are taught by this example, that we must attempt nothing, unless we have the light of the word of God going before us, lest we suffer like punishment for our sacrilege. The Lord himself commandeth us to pray. Whosoever they be which have not the gift of miracles given them, let them keep themselves within these bounds. For when the apostles

---

[1] " Alieni," aliens from, strangers to.

made the unclean spirits come out of men, they had God for their author, and they knew that they did faithfully execute the ministry which he had enjoined them.

16. *The man running upon them.* That is attributed to the man which the devil did by him. For he had not been able to do such an act of himself, as to put to flight seven strong young men being wounded and naked. And to set down for a certainty how the devil doth dwell in men, we cannot, save only that there may be[1] a contrariety between the Spirit of God and the spirit of Satan. For as Paul teacheth that we be the temples of God, because the Spirit of God dwelleth in us; so he saith again that Satan worketh effectually in all unbelievers. Notwithstanding, we must know that Luke speaketh in this place of a particular kind of dwelling; to wit, when Satan hath the bridle so much that he doth possess the whole man.

Furthermore, God meant to show such a token, that he might declare that his power is not included in the sound of the voice, and that it is not lawful superstitiously to abuse the name of his Son. And when he suffereth Satan to deceive us, let us know that we be more sharply punished than if he should wound us in the flesh. For the false show and colour of miracles is an horrible enchantment to bewitch and besot the unbelievers, that they may be drowned in deeper darkness, because they refused the light of God.

17. *There came fear.* The fruit of that vengeance which God brought upon those who did wickedly abuse the name of Christ is this, in that they were all touched with reverence, lest they should contemn that doctrine, whose revenger the Lord hath showed by an evident token and testimony he would be, and they were brought to reverence Christ. For, besides that God doth invite us by all his

---

[1] " Nisi quod statui potest," unless that it may be held there is.

judgments to come thus far, that they may terrify us from sinning, in this example peculiarly was the majesty of Christ set forth, and the authority of the gospel established. Wherefore, there is more heavy and grievous punishment prepared for deceivers, who, with their enchantments, profane the name of Christ wittingly, lest they promise to themselves that they shall escape unpunished for such gross sacrilege. Whereas he saith that it was made known to all men, it signifieth as much as commonly or everywhere. For his meaning is, that the matter was much talked of among the people, to the end the name of Christ might be made known to more men.

18. *And many of those which believed came, confessing, and showing their works.*
19. *And many of those which used curious arts, bringing their books, burnt them before them all; and when they had cast the price of them, they found it fifty thousand pieces of silver.*
20. *So mightily grew the word of the Lord, and was confirmed.*
21. *And when these things were accomplished, Paul purposed in spirit, having passed over Macedonia and Achaia, to go to Jerusalem, saying, After that I have been there, I must also see Rome.*
22. *And when he had sent two of those which ministered to him into Macedonia, to wit, Timotheus and Erastus, he stayed for a time in Asia.*

18. *Many which believed.* Luke bringeth forth one token of that fear whereof he spake. For they did indeed declare that they were thoroughly touched and moved with the fear of God, who, of their own accord, did confess the faults and offences of their former life, lest, through their dissimulation, they should nourish the wrath of God within. We know what a hard matter it is to wring true confession out of those who have offended, for seeing men count nothing more precious than their estimation, they make more account of shame than of truth; yea, so much as in them

lieth, they seek to cover their shame. Therefore, this voluntary confession was a testimony of repentance and of fear. For no man, unless he be thoroughly touched, will make himself subject to the slanders and reproaches of men, and will willingly be judged upon earth, that he may be loosed and acquitted in heaven. When he saith, *Many*, by this we gather that they had not all one cause, for it may be that these men had corrupt consciences a long time; as many are oftentimes infected with hidden and inward vices. Wherefore, Luke doth not prescribe all men a common law; but he setteth before them an example which those must follow who need like medicine. For why did these men confess their facts, save only that they might give testimony of their repentance, and seek counsel and ease at Paul's hands? It was otherwise with those who came unto the baptism of John, confessing their sins, (Matth. iii. 6.) For by this means they did confess that they did enter into repentance without dissimulation.

But in this place Luke teacheth by one kind, after what sort the faithful were touched with the reverence of God, when God set before them an example of his severity. For which cause the impudence of the Papists is the greater, who colour their tyranny by this fact. For wherein doth their auricular confession agree[1] with this example? First, the faithful confessed how miserably they had been deceived by Satan before they came to the faith, bringing into the sight of men certain examples. But by the Pope's law it is required that men reckon up all their words and deeds and thoughts. We read that those men confessed this once; the Pope's law commandeth that it be repeated every year at least. These men made confession of their own accord; the Pope bindeth all men with necessity. Luke saith there came many, not all; in the Pope's law there is no exception. These men humbled themselves before the company of the faithful; the Pope giveth a far other commandment, that the sinner confess his sins, whispering in the ear of one

[1] " Quid enim . affine habet," for what affinity has.

priest.[1] Lo, how well they apply[2] the Scriptures to prove their subtilty.

19. *Who used curious crafts.* Luke doth not only speak of magical jugglings, but of frivolous and vain studies, whereof the more part of men is for the most part too desirous. For he useth the word περιεργα, under which the Grecians comprehend whatsoever things have in themselves no sound commodity, but lead men's minds and studies through divers crooks unprofitably. Such is judicial astrology, as they call it, and whatsoever divinations men[3] invent to themselves against the time to come. They burn their books, that they may cut off all occasion of erring, both for themselves and for others. And whereas the greatness of the price doth not call them back from endamaging themselves so much, they do thereby better declare the study [zeal] of their godliness. Therefore, as Luke did of late describe their confession in words, so now he setteth down the confession they make in deeds. But because the Grecians take αργυριον for all kind of money, it is uncertain whether Luke doth speak of pence or sestertians.[4] Notwithstanding, because it is certain that he expressed a sum, that we might know that the faithful did valiantly contemn gain, I do nothing doubt but that he meaneth pence, or some other better kind of coin.[5] And fifty thousand pence (denarii) make about nine thousand pound of French money, [French livres.]

20. *Grew mightily,* [*lions.*] The word κατα κρατος doth signify that the word increased not a little, (or that these proceedings were not common;) as if he should say, that in those increasings appeared rare efficacy, and such as was greater than it used commonly to be. The word *grew* do

---

[1] "Ut clanculariis susurris in aurem proprii sacerdotes obmurmuret peccator," that the sinner mutter secret whispers into the ear of his own priest.
[2] "Quam dextre accommodent," how dexterously they accommodate.
[3] "Stulti homines," foolish men. [4] "Sestertios an denarios," "sestertii an denarios" [5] "Denarios vel aliquod etiam præstantius numismatis genus," denarii, or even some more valuable species of coin.

I refer unto the number of men, as if he should have said, that the Church was increased, new disciples being gathered together daily, because doctrine is spread abroad. And I interpret that, that the word was confirmed in every one thus, to wit, that they did profit in the obedience of the gospel and in godliness more and more, and that their faith took deeper root.

21. *He purposed in spirit.* His meaning is, that Paul purposed to take his journey through the instinct and motion of the Spirit; that we may know that all his whole life was framed according to God's will and pleasure. And therefore hath he the Spirit to be the governor of his actions, because he did both give over himself by him to be ruled, and did also depend upon his government. Neither skilleth that which followeth, that he had not that success in his journey which he did hope for; for God doth oftentimes govern and rule his faithful servants, suffering them to be ignorant of the end.[1] For he will have them so far forth addicted to him, that they follow that which he hath showed them by his Spirit, even shutting their eyes when matters be doubtful. Moreover, it is certain that he was wholly addicted to profit the churches, omitting and foreslowing [neglecting] his own commodity, in that he had rather deprive himself of Timotheus, a most excellent to him of all, most faithful, most dear, finally, a most fit companion, than not to provide for the Macedonians.

23. *And at that time there happened no small tumult about that way.*
24. *For a certain man named Demetrius, a silversmith, which made silver shrines for Diana, brought no small gains to the men of that occupation;*
25. *Whom, when he had called together, and those who were makers of like things, he said, Men, ye know that by this craft we have advantage.*[2]

---

[1] " De exitu ipsos celans," concealing the issue from them.
[2] " Nobis suppetit facultas,' our living is derived.

26. *And ye see and hear that not only at Ephesus, but almost throughout all Asia, this Paul hath persuaded and turned away much people, saying that they be not gods which are made with hands:*
27. *And not only this part cometh in danger to us, lest it be set at nought; but also lest the temple of the great goddess Diana be despised, and it come to pass that her majesty be destroyed, whom all Asia and the world worshippeth.*
28. *When they heard these things, they were full of wrath, and cried out, saying, Great is Diana of the Ephesians.*

23. Tumult about that way. Concerning this word *way*, let the readers understand thus much, that it is here taken for that which the Latins call *sect;* the Greek philosophers call it *heresies* or *heresy.* But because in the Church of God, where the unity of faith ought to reign, there is nothing more odious or detestable than for every man to choose, at his pleasure, that which he will follow, I think that Luke did fly that name which was, for good causes, infamous among the godly, and that after the Hebrew phrase, he put *way* instead of *ordinance.* And as touching the sum of the matter, we see how wonderfully the Lord did exercise his servant. He did hope when he did address himself for his journey, that the Church would be quiet after his departure, and, lo, there ariseth an uproar at a sudden where he did least fear. But in Demetrius it appeareth what a hurtful plague covetousness is. For one man, for his own gain's sake, is not afraid[1] to trouble a whole city with sedition. And the craftsmen, who were as firebrands kindled by him, and do spread abroad the fire everywhere, do teach us what an easy matter it is to cause filthy [sordid] men, and whose belly is their God, to commit all manner [of] wickedness; especially if they live only by gains evil gotten,[2] and the hope of gain be taken from them.

Moreover, in his history we see a lively image of our time. Demetrius and his band raised a tumult; because, if

---

[1] "Non dubitat," does not hesitate. [2] "Si ex illiberali quæstu in diem vivunt," if they live from day to day by the gain of a mean occupation.

superstition whereby they were wont to get gains be taken away, their craft will fall to the ground. Therefore they fight as if it were for their life, lest Demetrius go without his fat prey, and the rest want their daily living. What zeal doth at this day prick forward the Pope, the horned bishops, the monks, and all the rabblement of the Popish clergy? Yea, what fury doth drive them so sore[1] to resist the gospel? They boast that they strive for the Catholic faith; neither did Demetrius want an honest colour, pretending the worship of Diana. But the matter itself doth plainly declare, that they fight not so much for the altars as for the fires, to wit, that they may have hot kitchens. They can well wink at filthy blasphemies against God, so they lack nothing of their revenues, only they are more than courageous in maintaining such superstitions as are meetest for their purpose.[2]

Therefore, being taught by such examples, let us learn to make choice of such a kind of life as is agreeable to the doctrine of Christ; lest desire of gain[3] provoke us to enter a wicked and ungodly combat. And as for those who, through ignorance or error, are fallen unto any ungodly occupation, or are entangled in any other impure and wicked kind of life, let them, notwithstanding, beware of such sacrilegious rashness. And as touching godly teachers, let them learn by this example, that they shall never want adversaries, until the whole world, through denial of itself, offer peace, which we know will never come to pass. Because Paul's doctrine taketh away Demetrius and the rest of the silversmiths' gains, they leap out furiously to put out [destroy] the same, will not they do the same whom the gospel shall contrary? But there is no man who hath not occasion to fight. For all the affections of the flesh are enemies to God. So that it must needs be, that how many lusts of the flesh there be [reign] in the world, there are as many armed enemies to resist Christ. It will, indeed, often-

---

[1] " Tam acriter," so keenly help the meal chest, (larder) gain

[2] " Quæ ad farinas valent," as

[3] " Lucri cupiditas," eagerness for

times fall out, that God will bridle the wicked, lest they raise some tumult, or break out into open rage. Yet, whosoever is not tamed and brought down to bear Christ's yoke, he shall always hate his gospel. So that faithful and godly teachers must persuade themselves that they shall always have to deal with great store of enemies. Demetrius' covetousness is manifest. Nevertheless, we must also know this, that he was Satan's fan, [bellows,] who, seeking by all means to overthrow Paul's doctrine, found this fit instrument. Now, forasmuch as we know that Satan is a deadly enemy to Christ and the truth, do we think that he shall ever want ministers, who shall rage through his motion and persuasion, either with open rage, or else seek to work the overthrow of the gospel by secret practices, or spew out the poison of their hatred, or else, at least, show some token of enmity by fretting and murmuring?

25. *By this craft.* Demetrius doth in this place filthily betray his malice. It is lawful for a man, in some measure, to provide for his private profit; but to trouble common [the public] peace for a man's own gain, to overthrow[1] equity and right, to give over a man's self to do violence and commit murder, to extinguish that of set purpose which is just and right; that is too great wickedness. Demetrius confesseth that this is the state of the cause, because, [viz. that] Paul denieth that those are gods which are made with men's hands. He doth not inquire whether this be true or no; but being blinded with a desire to get gain, he is carried headlong to oppress true doctrine. The same blindness doth drive him headlong to seek violent remedies. Also the craftsmen, because they be afraid of poverty and hunger, run headlong as violently; for the belly is blind and deaf, so that it can admit no equity. For which cause, every one of us ought more to suspect himself, when the question is touching our own gain and profit, lest the same covetous desire which made these men so mad take away

---

[1] "Pervertere," to pervert

all difference of justice and injustice, of that which is filthy and that which is honest.

27. *Not only this part.* This is first disorderly handled in[1] that Demetrius is careful for religion after other things;[2] because nothing is more absurd than to prefer the belly before the goddess; but even this is also vain, in that he pretendeth that the worship of Diana is in hazard. For if he had suffered no loss by Paul's doctrine, he would have sat quietly at home; he would neither have taken thought for the worship of Diana, neither would he have troubled others. What is the cause, then, he is so diligent and so earnest in his business? even this, because he was plagued at home; and because he saw that he and his copartners had no honest or probable cause to make any stir, he goeth about to colour [gloss] the matter with some other colour. Therefore, to the end he may cover the shame of his wicked fact, he cloaketh it with the title of religion, which is plausible. So that the wicked, howsoever they strive frowardly against God, yet they gather here and there honest excuses[3] impudently; but God doth not suffer himself to be mocked, but doth rather pull them out of their starting-holes, [subterfuges.] There needeth no other witness to refute Demetrius' hypocrisy, because he cutteth his own throat with his own words, when he betrayeth the sorrow which he had conceived, because of the loss which he sustained.[4] In like state do the Papists stand at this day; they boast with full mouth that they be patrons of the Catholic faith and of the holy mother the Church, but when they have spoken[5] thus touching their zeal, in the very handling of the cause they breathe out with open throat the smell of their kitchens. But if we have a desire to handle the cause of godliness purely and in earnest, let

---

[1] " Hoc primum præpostere," this is, in the first place, preposterous.
[2] " Secundo tandem loco," only in the second place.   [3] " Captant honestos prætextus," catch at specious pretexts.   [4] " Dum privatæ jacturæ dolorem prodit," while he betrays grief for a private loss.
[5] " Sic præfati," premised this much

us forget our commodities, that the glory of God may have the chief place. For the show of profit doth so tie all our senses with enticements, that though we wander through all manner of wickedness, yet do we flatter ourselves so long as we be determined to provide for our own commodity.

Whom all Asia and the world doth worship. It seemeth to Demetrius an unmeet thing that Diana her majesty should be brought to naught, which all the world doth reverence and worship, and this is a common starting-hole [subterfuge] for all superstitious persons, to pretend the consent of the multitude. But true religion requireth a more stedfast stay than in the will and pleasure of men. There is nothing which at this day doth more keep back the simple and unskilful, than that they dare not cast from them (such ancient) errors as are commonly received everywhere. Because they feign and imagine that that which pleased many, though foolishly and rashly, is to be counted lawful. For which cause they be not afraid boldly to set the very name of custom against God himself. But the Lord doth prescribe to us another manner of rule, to wit, that being content with his authority alone, we do not pass either for the opinion of men, nor for our own commodity, nor for the custom of many nations.

29. *And all the city was full of confusion. And they rushed into the common place* [theatre] *with one consent, having caught Gaius and Aristarchus, men of Macedonia, Paul's companions.*
30. *And when Paul would have entered in unto the people, the disciples would not suffer him.*
31. *And certain also of the chief of Asia, which were his friends, sent unto him, requesting him that he would not enter into the place,* [theatre.]
32. *Some therefore cried one thing, and some another for the assembly was out of order, and the more part knew not for what cause they came together.*
33. *And some of the company drew forth Alexander, the Jews thrusting him forward. And when Alexander had re-*

quired silence with the hand, he would have excused the matter[1] *to the people.*

34. *Whom when they knew to be a Jew, there arose a shout of all men almost for the space of two hours, crying, Great is Diana of the Ephesians.*

29. Luke setteth down in this place the nature of the people, as if it were depainted in a table.[2] Like as if a thousand houses should be set on fire at a sudden, so all the city was on an uproar in one moment; and when such a tempest is once raised, it is not easily stayed. And forasmuch as the servants of Christ cannot avoid this mischief, they must be armed with invincible constancy, that they may boldly suffer the tumults raised among the people, and that they may not be troubled as with some new and strange matter, when they see that the people is unquiet. So Paul himself doth elsewhere triumph that he went valiantly through the midst of sedition, (2 Cor. vi. 5.) Nevertheless, the Lord doth uphold the ministers of his word with an excellent comfort, when as they be tossed amidst divers storms and garboils, and with excellent boldness doth he establish them, when he doth testify that he holdeth the helm of his Church; and not that only, but that he is the governor and moderator of all tumults and storms, so that he can stay the same so soon as it seemeth good to him. Therefore, let us know that we must sail as it were in a tempestuous sea; yet that we must suffer this infamy, as if we ourselves were the procurers of trouble;[3] neither may anything lead us away from the right course of our duty. So that in sailing we shall be sore troubled; yet will not the Lord suffer us to suffer shipwreck. Furthermore, we see that though sedition be confused, yet doth the people always take the worse part; as the men of

---

[1] "Rationem reddere," have rendered an account   [2] "In tabula," in a picture.   [3] "Quasi turbas ipsi concitemus," as if we ourselves excited the disturbance

Ephesus do now catch Gaius and Aristarchus, and they drive back Alexander with their furious outcries. Whence cometh this, save only because Satan doth reign in their hearts, so that they rather favour an evil cause? There is also another reason, because a prejudice conceived upon a false report doth possess their minds, so that they cannot abide to sift the cause any farther.

30. *And when Paul would.* We may see that Paul's constancy was coupled with modesty. When as he might well have kept himself out of sight, of his own accord was he prepared to put himself in hazard. And yet he doth not refuse to follow their counsel, who knew the state of matters better than he. If he had not been kept back, that which he determined to do could not have been imputed to rashness. There was no sedition raised through his fault. Why should he not venture his life, especially seeing that he did not despair of better success? But when the brethren, and such friends as were more skilful, dissuade him, his modesty is worthy to be commended, in that he doth not stand stoutly in his purpose.

33. *They drew out Alexander.* It is to be thought that the Jews did not send forth this Alexander to plead the common cause of the nation, but that they were desirous to bring him before the people that he might be murdered. Nevertheless, the name Jew made him to be so hated, that they did outrageously refuse whatsoever he was about to speak in the matter and cause; yea, he did hardly escape with his life in such an uproar. Moreover, it is uncertain whether this be that Alexander of whom Paul maketh mention elsewhere, (1 Tim. i. 20; and 2 Tim. iv. 14;) yet the conjecture seemeth to me allowable. But and if we believe that it is he, let us learn by this fearful example to walk circumspectly, lest Satan carry us away into like falling away, [defection.] For we see that he who was at the point to suffer martyrdom, became a treacherous and wicked revolt, [apostate.]

34. *Great is Diana of the Ephesians.* This was a clamorous confession, but without any soundness; neither did it proceed from the faith of the heart. For whence came that great divinity of Diana whereof they spake, save only because like mad men they furiously defend that error which they had once received? It fareth otherwise with true godliness, that we believe with the heart unto righteousness, and then doth the confession of the mouth follow to salvation. Therein doth the distemperature and mad stubbornness of all mad men and brain-sick fools differ from the constancy and zeal of the martyrs. And yet, notwithstanding, our sluggishness is shameful if we be not as ready and stout in the confession of a sure faith as are they in their filthy error. For we see what the Spirit of God prescribeth unto us by the mouth of David, "I believed, and therefore will I speak," (Psalm cxvi. 10.)

> 35 *And when the town-clerk had pacified the multitude, he said, Ye men of Ephesus, what man is he that knoweth not the city of the Ephesians is a worshipper of the great goddess Diana, and of the image that came down from Jupiter?*
> 36. *And seeing these things are out of question, you must be quiet, and do nothing rashly.*
> 37. *For ye have brought men which are neither church-robbers, nor yet blasphemers of your goddess.*
> 38. *But and if Demetrius and the craftsmen that are with him have a matter against any man, there be open assemblies, and there be deputies: let them accuse one another.*
> 39. *But and if there be any other matter in question, it shall be decided in a lawful assembly.*
> 40. *For it is to be doubted*[1] *lest we be accused of this day's sedition, seeing there is no cause whereby we may give a reason of this concourse. And when he had thus spoken, he let the assembly depart.*

35. Luke showeth in this place that the tumult was so appeased, that yet, notwithstanding, superstition prevailed with the mad people, and the truth of God was not heard.

---

[1] "Periculum est," there is a danger

For the town-clerk, as politic men use to do, counteth it sufficient for him if he can by any means appease the outrageous multitude. Nevertheless, the cause itself is oppressed. He saw undoubtedly Demetrius' malice, and how he had troubled the city, abusing the pretence of religion for his own private gain; but he toucheth not that wound which he knew to be unknown to the unskilful. Nevertheless, to the end he may stay the uproar and contention, he extolleth the feigned power of Diana, and maintaineth her superstitious worship. If Paul had been in the common place[1] at that time, he would rather have suffered death an hundred times than have suffered himself to be delivered from danger paying so dear for it. For though the town-clerk had not been by him commanded to speak thus, yet it should have been treacherous dissimulation in a public witness and preacher of heavenly doctrine. The scribe affirmeth that the image which the Ephesians did worship came down from heaven, and that Paul and his companions spake no blasphemy against their goddess. Could he have holden his peace, but he must needs by his silence have allowed his false excuse? And this had been to shake hands with idolatry. Therefore, it was not without cause that Luke said before that Paul was kept back by the brethren, and not suffered to enter into the common place, [theatre.]

37. *Men which are neither church-robbers.* He doth both truly and well deny that they be church-robbers; but he doth shortly after falsely define the kind of church-robbery to speak blasphemously against Diana. For seeing that all superstition is profane and polluted, it followeth that those be sacrilegious persons who translate the honour which is due to God alone unto idols. But the wisdom of the town-clerk, and that carnal, is here commended, and not his godliness. For he had respect unto this alone to extinguish the heat of the uproar; and therefore doth he at length conclude, if Demetrius have any private matter, there be

---

[1] " In theatro," in the theatre.

judgment-seats and magistrates. And that public affairs must be handled in a lawful, and not in a disordered assembly—in an assembly gathered by the commandment of the magistrates, and not in a concourse which is without consideration, run together through the motion of one man, and to satisfy his appetite.[1] He calleth them deputies,[2] in the plural number, not that Asia had more than one, but because legates did sometimes keep courts in the place of the deputies. Also, he appeaseth them by putting them in fear, because the deputy had occasion offered to punish and fine the city sore.[3]

CHAPTER XX.

1. *And after the tumult was ceased, when Paul had called unto him the disciples, and had embraced them, he took his journey that he might go into Macedonia.*
2. *And when he had walked through those parts, and had with much speech exhorted them, he came into Greece.*
3. *And when he had spent three months there, when the Jews laid in wait for him as he was about to loose into Syria, he purposed to return through Macedonia.*
4. *And there accompanied him into Asia Sopater of Berea; and of the Thessalonians, Aristarchus and Secundus; and Gaius of Derbe, and Timotheus; and of Asia, Tychicus and Trophimus.*
5. *When these were gone before, they stayed for us at Troas.*
6. *And we sailed away after the day of sweet [unleavened] bread from Philippi, and came to them to Troas within five days, where we stayed seven days.*

1. Luke declareth in this chapter how Paul, loosing from

---

[1] "Unius hominis impulsu et libidine," at the instigation and caprice of one man   [2] "Proconsules," proconsuls   [3] "Quia proconsuli oblatu erat occasio urbis male mulctandæ," because an opportunity was given to the proconsul to impose a heavy fine on the city.

Asia, did again cross the seas to go to Jerusalem. And though whatsoever is written in this narration be worthy of most diligent meditation and marking, yet doth it need no long exposition. It appeareth that the Church was preserved in safety by the wonderful power of God amidst those troublesome tumults. The church of Ephesus was as yet slender and weak: the faithful having had experience of a sudden motion [commotion] once, might for just causes fear, lest like storms should ever now and then arise. We need not doubt that Paul did with much ado depart from them; yet because greater necessity doth draw him unto another place, he is enforced to leave his sons who were lately begotten, and had as yet scarce escaped shipwreck in the midst of the raging sea. As for them, though they be very loath to forego Paul, yet, lest they do injury to other churches, they do not keep him back nor stay him. So that we see that they were not wedded to themselves, but that they were careful for the kingdom of Christ, that they might provide as well for their brethren as for themselves. We must diligently note these examples, that one of us may study to help another in this miserable dispersing; but if it so fall out at any time that we be bereft of profitable helps, let us not doubt nor waver, knowing that God doth hold the helm of our ship. And we must also note this, that Paul doth not depart until he have saluted the brethren, but doth rather strengthen them at his departure. As Luke saith straightway of the Macedonians, that Paul exhorted them with many words, that is, not overfields,[1] as if it were sufficient to put them only in mind of their duty; but as he commandeth elsewhere that others should do, he urged importunately, and beat in [inculcated] thoroughly things which were needful to be known, that they might never be forgotten, (2 Tim. iv. 2.)

3. *Because the Jews laid wait for him.* The Lord did exercise his servant so diversely and continually that he set

---

[1] "Defunctorie," perfunctorily.

before us in him an example of most excellent constancy. It is not sufficient for him to be wearied with the labour and trouble of a long and wearisome journey, unless he be also brought in danger of his life by those which lay in wait for him. Let all the servants of Christ set this mirror before their eyes, that they may never faint through the wearisomeness of straits. Notwithstanding, when Paul doth journey another way that he may avoid their laying in wait, he showeth that we must have regard of our life so far forth that we throw not ourselves headlong into the midst of dangers. And those who accompany him give no small testimony of their godliness; and we see how precious his life was to the faithful, when as a great many being chosen out of divers countries to be his companions, do for his sake take a hard and sharp journey not without great charges. Luke saith that Paul tarried at Philippos so long as the days of unleavened bread did last, because he had at that time better opportunity offered to teach. And forasmuch as it was unknown as yet that the law was disannulled, it stood him upon to beware, lest by neglecting the feast-day he should be thought among the rude to be a contemner of God. Though, for mine own part, I think that he sought principally opportunity to teach, because the Jews were then more attentive to learn.

7. *And upon one day of the Sabbaths, when the disciples were come together to break bread, Paul disputed with them, being about to take his journey on the morrow; and he prolonged his speech until midnight.*
8. *And there were many lights in an upper chamber, where they were gathered together.*
9. *And a certain young man named Eutychus, sitting in a window, being fallen into a deep sleep, as Paul disputed long time, being more overcome with sleep, he fell down from the third loft downward, and was taken up dead.*
10. *And when Paul came down, he fell upon him, and embracing him, said, Be not ye troubled, for his soul is in him.*
11. *And when he was gone up, and had broken bread, and had*

eaten, *having had long conference until it was day, he departed.*
12. *And they brought the boy alive, and were not a little comforted.*
13. *But when he had taken ship, we loosed to Assos, thence to receive Paul, for so had he appointed, being about to go by land.*

7. *And in one day.* Either doth he mean the first day of the week, which was next after the Sabbath, or else some certain Sabbath. Which latter thing may seem to me more probable; for this cause, because that day was more fit for an assembly, according to custom. But seeing it is no new matter for the Evangelists to put one instead of the first, according to the custom of the Hebrew tongue, (Matth. xxviii. 1; Luke xxiv. 1; John xx. 1,) it shall very well agree, that on the morrow after the Sabbath they came together. Furthermore, it were too cold to expound this of any day. For to what end is there mentioned of the Sabbath, save only that he may note the opportunity and choice of the time? Also, it is a likely matter that Paul waited for the Sabbath, that the day before his departure he might the more easily gather all the disciples into one place. And the zeal of them all is worth the noting, in that it was no trouble to Paul to teach until midnight, though he were ready to take his journey, neither were the rest weary of learning. For he had no other cause to continue his speech so long, save only the desire and attentiveness of his auditory.

To break bread. Though breaking of bread doth sometimes signify among the Hebrews a domestical banquet, yet do I expound the same of the Holy Supper in this place, being moved with two reasons. For seeing we may easily gather by that which followeth that there was no small multitude gathered together there, it is unlikely that there could any supper be prepared in a private house. Again, Luke will afterward declare that Paul took bread not at supper time, but after midnight. Hereunto is added that, that he saith not that he took meat that he might eat, but that he might only taste. Therefore, I think thus, that they had appointed a solemn day for the celebrating of the Holy Supper of the Lord among themselves, which might be commodious for them all. And to the end Paul might remedy after a sort the silence of longer absence, he continueth his speech longer than he did commonly use to do. That which I spake of the great number of men is gathered thence, because there were many lights in the upper chamber, which was not done for any pomp or ostentation, but only for necessity's sake. For when there is no need, it is ambition and vanity which maketh men bestow cost. Furthermore, it was meet that all the whole place should shine with lights, lest that holy company might be suspected of some wickedness or dishonesty. Add also another conjecture, if the chamber had been empty, those which were present would not have suffered Eutychus to sit upon a window. For it had been filthy licentiousness in despising[1] the heavenly doctrine to depart aside into a window, seeing there was room enough elsewhere.

9. *When he was fallen into a deep sleep.* I see no cause why some interpreters should so sore and sharply condemn the drowsiness of the young man, that they should say that he was punished for his sluggishness by death. For what marvel is it, if, seeing the night was so far spent, having striven so long with sleep, he yielded at length? And whereas, against his will, and otherwise than he hoped for, he was taken and overcome with deep sleep, we may guess by this that he did not settle himself to sleep. To seek out a fit place wherein to sleep had been a sign of sluggishness, but to be overcome with sleep, sitting at a window, what other thing is it but without fault to yield to nature ?[2] As if a man should faint through hunger or too much wearisomeness. Those who being drowned in earthly cares come unto the word loathsomely ; those who being full of meat and

---

[1] " Spernendæ ac respuendæ," in spurning and rejecting.
[2] " Naturæ infirmitati," the infirmity of nature.

wine are thereby brought on [to] sleep; those who are vigilant enough in other matters, but hear the word as though they did not pass [care] for it, shall be justly condemned for drowsiness; but Luke doth in plain words acquit Eutychus, when he saith that he fell down, being overcome with deep sleep after midnight.

Moreover, the Lord meant not only by the sleep, but also by the death of this young man to awake and stir up the faith of his, that they might more joyfully receive Paul's doctrine, and might keep it deeply rooted in their minds. It was, indeed, at the first no small temptation, but such as might have shaken even a most constant man full sore; for who would have thought that Christ had been chief governor in that company wherein a miserable man through a fall became dead? Who would not rather have thought this to be a sign of God's curse? But the Lord, by applying a remedy, doth forthwith rid the minds of his of all perturbation.

10. *He lay down upon him.* We know that the apostles, in working miracles, did sometimes use certain external rites, whereby they might give the glory to God, the author. And now, whereas Paul doth stretch himself upon the young man, I think it was done to no other end, save only that he might more easily stir up himself unto prayer. It is all one as if he should mix himself with the dead man.[1] And, peradventure, this was done for the imitation of Elisha, of whom the sacred history doth report the same thing, (2 Kings iv. 34.) Yet the vehemency of his affection did more move him than the emulation of the prophet. For that stretching of himself upon him doth more provoke him to crave his life with all his heart at the hands of the Lord. So when he embraceth the body of the dead man, by this gesture he declared that he offered it to God to be quickened, and out of the text we may gather that he did not de-

---

[1] "Perinde agit, acsi se misceret cum mortuo," he acts just as if he were mixing himself up with the young man

part from embracing it until he knew that the life was restored again.

Be ye not troubled. We must note that Paul took great care principally for this cause, lest that sorrowful event should shake the faith of the godly, and should trouble their minds. Nevertheless, the Lord did, as it were, seal up and establish[1] that last sermon which Paul made at Troas. When he saith that his soul is in him, he doth not deny that he was dead, because by this means he should extinguish the glory of the miracle; but the meaning of these words is, that his life was restored through the grace of God. I do not restrain that which followeth, to wit, that they were greatly comforted through the joy which they had by reason of the young man which was restored to life; but I do also comprehend the confirmation of faith, seeing God gave them such an excellent testimony of his love.

13. *When we had taken ship.* It is uncertain why Paul did choose rather to go by land, whether it were because sailing might be to him troublesome, or that as he did pass by he might visit the brethren. I think that he did then eschew the sea for his health's sake. And his courtesy is greatly to be commended, in that he spared his companions. For to what end did he suffer them to depart, save only that he might ease them of the trouble? So that we see that they did strive among themselves in courtesy and good turns. They were ready and willing to do their duty; but Paul was so far from requiring things straitly[2] at their hands, that of his own accord and courtesy he did remit those duties which they were ready to do; yea, setting aside his own commodity, he commanded them to do that which was for their comfort. It is well known that the city Assos is by the describers of countries[3] attributed to Troas. The same, as Pliny doth witness, was called Appollonia. They say that it was a free city of the Ætolians.

---

[1] " Quasi insculpto sigillo apud eos sancivit," did sanction to them as with the impress of the seal   [2] " Rigidus exactor," from being a rigid exactor.   [3] " Geographis," geographers.

14. *And when we were come together at Assos, having received him we came to him.*
15. *And sailing thence the day following we came over against Chios; and on the morrow we arrived at Samos, and having tarried at Trogyllum, we came to Miletus.*
16. *For Paul purposed to sail beyond Ephesus, lest he should spend the time in Asia: for he made haste if it were possible for him to keep the day of Pentecost at Jerusalem.*
17. *And having sent messengers from Miletus to Ephesus, he called the elders of the church.*
18. *Who when they were come to him, he said unto them, Ye know from the first day wherein I entered into Asia, how I have been with you at all seasons,*
19. *Serving the Lord with all humility of mind, and with many tears, and temptations, which happened to me by the laying in wait of the Jews;*
20. *So that I have kept nothing back which might be for your profit, but did show to you and teach you publicly and through every house,*
21. *Testifying both to the Jews and Grecians the repentance which is towards God, and the faith which is toward our Lord Jesus Christ.*

16. *For Paul purposed.* It is not to be doubted but that he had great and weighty causes to make haste; not that he made so great account of the day, but because strangers did then use to come together to Jerusalem out of all quarters. Forasmuch as he did hope that he might do some good in such a great assembly, he would not foreslow [neglect] the opportunity. Therefore, let us know that the worship of the law[1] was not the cause that he made so great haste, but he set before his eyes the edifying of the Church; partly that he might show to the faithful that the kingdom of Christ was enlarged, partly that if there were any as yet strangers from Christ, he might gain them; partly that he might stop the mouths of the wicked.[2] Notwithstanding, we

---

[1] " Legalem cultum," legal worship.   [2] " Ut improborum hominum calumnias refelleret," that he might refute the calumnies of wicked men.

must note, that he did, in the mean season, provide for other churches. For, in sending for the elders of Ephesus to Miletus, he showeth that he did not neglect Asia. And whereas they come together when they be called, it is not only a token of concord, but also of modesty; for they were many; yet doth it not irk them to obey one apostle of Christ, whom they knew to be endued with singular gifts. Moreover, it appeareth more plainly by the text, [context,] that those are called elders, not which were grey-headed, but such as were rulers of the Church. And it is an usual thing almost in all tongues, that those be called elders and fathers who are appointed to govern others, though their age be not always accordingly.

18. *Ye know.* Paul, in this sermon, standeth principally upon this, that he may exhort those pastors of Ephesus,[1] by his own example, to do their duty faithfully. For that is the true kind of censure, and by this means is authority purchased to doctrine, when the teacher prescribeth nothing[2] which he himself hath not done indeed before. And it was no unseemly thing for Paul to speak of his virtues. There is nothing less tolerable in the servants of Christ than ambition and vanity; but forasmuch as all men knew full well what modesty and humility was in the holy man, he needed not to fear lest he should incur the suspicion of vain boasting; especially, seeing that benign information by necessity, he did declare his faithfulness and diligence, that others might take example thereby. He doth, indeed, greatly extol his labours, patience, fortitude, and other virtues, but to what end? Surely not that he may purchase commendation at the hands of his auditory, but that his holy exhortation may pierce more deeply, and may stick fast in their minds. He did also shoot at another mark, that his integrity and uprightness in dealing might serve afterward to commend his doctrine. And he citeth eye-witnesses, lest he seem to speak of things unknown. I call

---

[1] " Quos Ephesi creaverat pastores," those whom he had appointed pastors at Ephesus.   [2] " In verbis," verbally

those witnesses who did not only know all things, but had also a judgment which was pure, and corrupt with no affections.

19. *Serving the Lord.* He reckoneth up first not only in what straits he was, but most of all his humility, coupled with contempt of the world, and rebukes, and other afflictions; as if he should say, that he was not honourably received or with commendation; but he was conversant among them under the contemptible form of the cross. And this is no small trial,[1] when we faint not, though we see ourselves trodden under foot by the intolerable pride of the world.

Notwithstanding, we must note every thing more distinctly. To serve the Lord is taken in this place, not for to worship God in holiness and righteousness, which is common to all the godly; but it doth signify to execute a public function. Therefore, Paul doth not speak of [as] some one private man, but as one made a minister of the Church. And so he doth testify, that he fulfilled the apostleship to him committed with humility and modesty; both because, knowing his own infirmity, he did mistrust himself; and also, because, considering the excellency of his calling, he counted himself very unmeet;[2] and, lastly, because he did willingly submit himself to bear the reproach of the cross. For this humility is set both against vain confidence, and also haughtiness. Secondly, he toucheth[3] his tears, which strifes, divers assaults of Satan, the rage of wicked men, the inward diseases of the Church, and offences, had made him shed; at length, he addeth, that he led a fearful life,[4] amidst the layings in wait of the Jews; and he confesseth that he was tempted therewith, as he was not hardened, though he did not faint. For he is not ashamed to confess his infirmity.

---

[1] "Probatio," proof or test. [2] "Longe imparem," far from being equal to it [3] "Adjungit," he addeth. [4] "Trepidam vitam," a life of trembling.

His drift is, that those to whom he speaketh may not faint, through like tribulations; and that, being void of all ambition, they may do their duty carefully and reverently; and that they may not only with a patient mind suffer themselves to be despised of men, but that they may be cast down in themselves. Because, that man can never be rightly framed to obey Christ whose looks are lofty, and whose heart is proud. And (as men cannot long bear a show of virtue) to the end it may appear manifestly, that he behaved himself sincerely and from his heart, he maketh mention of his constancy which lasted three years, wherein he had still kept one course. Ye know (saith he) how I have behaved myself since the first day until this time. To conclude, this is the true trial of the servants of Christ, not to be changed as the times change; but to continue like to themselves, and always to keep a straight course.

20. *I have kept back nothing.* He commendeth his faithfulness and diligence in teaching in three respects, that he instructed his scholars thoroughly and perfectly, so that he omitted nothing which might make for their salvation; that being not content with general preaching, he did also endeavour to do every man good. Thirdly, he reciteth a brief sum of all his whole doctrine, that he exhorted them unto faith in Christ and repentance. Now, forasmuch as he depainteth out unto us a pattern of a faithful and good teacher, whosoever they be who are desirous to prove their industry to the Lord, they must set before their eyes the edifying of the Church, as he commandeth Timotheus in another place, to consider what things be profitable, that he may be instant in delivering those things, (1 Tim. iv. 7, 8.) And surely the Scripture (according to whose rule all manner of teaching must be examined, yea, which is the only method of teaching aright) doth not contain profound[1] speculations, to delight men when they have nothing else

---

[1] " Argutas," subtle.

to do;[1] but as the same Paul doth testify, it is all profitable to make the man of God perfect.

But Paul prescribeth such a desire to edify, that the pastor must omit nothing, so much as in him lieth, which is profitable to be known. For they be bad masters who do so keep their scholars in the first principles, that they do never come unto the knowledge of the truth, (2 Tim. iii. 7.) And surely the Lord doth not teach us in his word only to [by] halves, (as they say,) but he delivereth perfect wisdom, and such as is in all points absolute. Whereby it appeareth how impudently those men boast themselves to be ministers of the word, who do not only cloak and foster the ignorance of the people with their silence, but do also wink at gross errors and wicked superstitions; as at this day in Papistry, many send out some sparks of sound doctrine, but they[2] dare not drive away the darkness of ignorance, and whereas the wicked fear of the flesh doth hinder them, they pretend that the people is not capable of sound[3] doctrine.

Indeed, I confess that all things cannot be taught at one time, and that we must imitate Paul's wisdom, who did apply himself unto the capacity of the ignorant. But what moderation is this when they suffer the blind to fall into the ditch, when they leave miserable souls under the tyranny of antichrist, and whereas they see idolatry rage, the worship of God corrupt, his law broken, and, finally, all holy things profaned, they do either with silence pass over such filthy confusion, or else they show it underhand, sparingly and obscurely, like men that be afraid? Therefore, we must note Paul's word, when as he saith that he kept back nothing, but did show whatsoever things were profitable for the people; for by this we gather that the pure and free[4] profession of sound doctrine is required at the hands of the servants of Christ, wherein there must be no boughts nor crooks, and that nothing is more unseemly in them than

---

[1] " Sub umbra et in otio," when at ease under the shade the greater part [3] " Solidioris," more solid.

[2] " Plerique,"

[4] " Ingenuam," candid.

oblique insinuations, and such as are inwrapped in crafty dissimulation.

Publicly, and throughout every house. This is the second point, that he did not only teach all men in the congregation, but also every one privately, as every man's necessity did require. For Christ hath not appointed pastors upon this condition, that they may only teach the Church in general in the open pulpit; but that they may take charge of every particular sheep, that they may bring back to the sheepfold those which wander and go astray, that they may strengthen those which are discouraged and weak, that they may cure the sick, that they may lift up and set on foot the feeble,[1] (Ezek. xxxiv. 4;) for common doctrine will oftentimes wax cold, unless it be holpen with private admonitions.

Wherefore, the negligence of those men is inexcusable, who, having made one sermon, as if they had done their task, live all the rest of their time idly; as if their voice were shut up within the church walls, seeing that so soon as they be departed, thence they be dumb. Also, disciples and scholars are taught, that if they will be numbered in Christ's flock, they must give place to their pastors, so often as they come unto them; and that they must not refuse private admonitions. For they be rather bears than sheep, who do not vouchsafe to hear the voice of their pastor, unless he be in the pulpit; and cannot abide to be admonished and reproved at home, yea, do furiously refuse[2] that necessary duty.

21. *Testifying both to Jews.* Descending now unto the third point, he setteth down the sum of this doctrine in a few words, to wit, that he exhorted all men unto faith and repentance, as it was said before, that the gospel consisteth upon [of] these two points only. Whence we do also gather wherein the true edifying of the Church doth properly consist, the care and burden whereof doth lie upon the pastor's shoulders, and whereunto we must apply all

---

[1] "Debiles et infirmas," the feeble and infirm.   [2] "Ferociter repellunt," fiercely repel

our study, if we be desirous to profit profitably in God's school. We have already said that the word of God is profaned, when the readers of the same do occupy themselves in frivolous questions. But to the end we may not read the same wanderingly, we must note and aim at this double mark which the apostle setteth before us. For whosoever he be that turneth unto any other thing, in taking great pains, he shall do nothing else but walk in a circuit. By the word *testify* he expresseth great vehemency, as if he should have said that by testifying he did commend, that the excuse of ignorance might not remain. For he alludeth unto the custom used in courts, where testifying is used to take away all doubt. As men are not only to be taught, but also to be constrained to embrace salvation in Christ, and to addict themselves to God, to lead a new life. And though he affirm that he was wanting to none, yet doth he place the Jews in the first place; because, as the Lord hath preferred them in the degree of honour before the Gentiles, so it was meet that Christ and his grace should be offered them until they should quite fall away.

Repentance toward God. We must first note the distinction of faith and repentance, which some do falsely and unskilfully confound, saying, that repentance is a part of faith. I grant, indeed, that they cannot be separate; because God doth illuminate no man with the Spirit of faith whom he doth not also regenerate unto newness of life. Yet they must needs be distinguished, as Paul doth in this place. For repentance is a turning unto God, when we frame ourselves and all our life to obey him; but faith is a receiving of the grace offered us in Christ. For all religion tendeth to this end, that, embracing holiness and righteousness, we serve the Lord purely, also that we seek no part of our salvation anywhere else save only at his hands, and that we seek salvation in Christ alone. Therefore, the doctrine of repentance containeth a rule of good life; it requireth the denial of ourselves, the mortifying of our flesh, and meditating upon the heavenly life. But because we be all naturally corrupt, strangers from righteousness, and turned away from God himself. Again, because we fly from God, because we know that he is displeased with us, the means, as well to obtain free reconciliation as newness of life, must be set before us.

Therefore, unless faith be added, it is in vain to speak of repentance; yea, those teachers of repentance who, neglecting faith, stand only upon the framing of life, and precepts of good works, differ nothing, or very little, from profane philosophers. They teach how men must live; but, forasmuch as they leave men in their nature, there can no bettering be hoped for thence, until they invite those who are lost unto hope of salvation; until they quicken the dead, promising forgiveness of sins; until they show that God doth, by his free adoption, take those for his children who were before bond-slaves of Satan; until they teach that the Spirit of regeneration must be begged at the hands of the heavenly Father, that we must draw godliness, righteousness, and goodness, from him who is the fountain of all good things. And hereupon followeth calling upon God, which is the chiefest thing in the worship of God.

We see now how that repentance and faith are so linked together that they cannot be separate. For it is faith which reconcileth God to us, not only that he may be favourable unto us, by acquitting us of the guiltiness of death, by not imputing to us our sins, but also that by purging the filthiness of our flesh by his Spirit, he may fashion us again after his own image. He doth not, therefore, name repentance in the former place, as if it did wholly go before faith, forasmuch as a part thereof proceedeth from faith, and is an effect thereof; but because the beginning of repentance is a preparation unto faith. I call the displeasing of ourselves the beginning, which doth enforce us, after we be thoroughly touched with the fear of the wrath of God, to seek some remedy.

Faith toward Christ. It is not without cause that the Scripture doth everywhere make Christ the mark whereat our faith must aim, and as they say commonly, set him before us as the object. For the majesty of God is of itself higher than that men can climb thereunto. Therefore, unless Christ come between, all our senses do vanish away in seeking God. Again, inasmuch as he is the Judge of the world, it must needs be that the beholding of him without Christ shall make us afraid.[1] But God doth not only represent himself unto us in Christ's image, but also refresh us with his Fatherly favour, and by all means restore us to life. For there is no part of our salvation which may not be found in Christ. By the sacrifice of his death he hath purged our sins; he hath suffered the punishment that he might acquit us; he hath made us clean by his blood; by his obedience he hath appeased his Father's wrath; by his resurrection he hath purchased righteousness for us. No marvel, therefore, if we said, that faith must be fixed[2] in the beholding of Christ.

22. *And, behold, I go now bound in the spirit to Jerusalem, not knowing what things shall befall me there:*
23. *Save only that the Holy Ghost doth witness throughout every city, saying that bonds and afflictions are prepared for me.*
24. *But I care not, neither is my life dear to me, that I may finish my course with joy, and the ministry which I have received of the Lord Jesus, to testify the gospel of the grace of God.*
25. *And now, behold, I know that after this ye shall not see my face, all you through whom I have gone preaching the kingdom of God.*
26. *Wherefore I take you to record this day, that I am clean from the blood of all men.*
27. *For I have kept nothing back, but have showed you all the counsel of God.*

22. *And, behold.* He declareth now more fully to what end he intreated of his upright dealing; to wit, because they should never see him any more. And it was very expedient that the pattern which was set before them by God of them

---

[1] " Nos terrore exanimet," make us dead with terror.   [2] " Prorsus esse defixam," must be wholly fixed.

to be followed should be always before their eyes, and that they should remember him when he was dead. For we know how readily men degenerate from pure institution. But though he deny that he doth know what shall befall him at Jerusalem, yet because he was taught by many prophecies that bonds were prepared for him there, as if he were now ready to die, he cutteth off shortly after the hope of his return. And yet for all this he is not contrary to himself. He speaketh doubtfully at the first of set purpose, that he may soften that which was about to be more (hard and) bitter; and yet he doth truly affirm, that he knew not as yet the ends and events of things, because he had no certain and special revelation touching the whole process.

Bound in the spirit. Some expound this that he was bound to the churches, who had committed to him this function to carry alms. Notwithstanding, I do rather think that hereby is meant the inward force and motion of the Spirit, not as though he were so inspired,[1] that he was out of his wit, but because being certified of the will of God, he did meekly[2] follow the direction and instinct of the Spirit, even of his own accord. Therefore, this speech importeth as much as if he should have said, I cannot otherwise do, unless I would be stubborn and rebellious against God, who doth as it were draw me thither, being bound by his Spirit. For to the end he may excuse himself of rashness, he saith that the Spirit is the author and guide of his journey. But would to God those brain-sick men, who boast that the Spirit doth indite to them those things which proceed from their own fantasy, did know the Spirit as familiarly as did Paul, who doth, notwithstanding, not say that all his motions and instigations[3] are of the Spirit, but declareth that that fell out in one thing as a singular thing. For men do oftentimes foolishly and unadvisedly take in hand those things which they put in practice afterward stoutly, because they be ashamed of lightness and instability. And he doth not only

---

[1] " Non quod ενθουσιασμω correptus fuerit," not that he was so enraptured [2] " Sponte vel placide," calmly or spontaneously. [3] " Impulsus," impulses.

mean that he took in hand his journey for a good cause, which the Spirit of God showeth him, but that it is altogether necessary for him, because it is wickedness to resist. Furthermore, let us learn, by the example of the holy man, not to kick against the Spirit of the Lord, but obediently to give over ourselves by him to be governed, that he may rule us at his pleasure after we be as it were bound to him.[1] For if the reprobate, who are the bond-slaves of Satan, be carried not only willingly, but also greedily, through his motion,[2] how much more ought this voluntary bondage or service to be in the children of God?

23. *But that the Holy Ghost.* I do not understand this of secret oracles, but of those foretellings which he heard everywhere of the prophets. And this speech hath greater dignity to set forth the prophecies, than if the men themselves which spake were called and cited to be witnesses. For by this means the word of God hath his [its] authority, when we confess that the Spirit of God is the author thereof, though the ministers be men. Now, forasmuch as the same Spirit, which foretelleth Paul of bonds and tribulations, doth also hold him fast bound that he cannot refuse to submit himself unto him, by this we learn, that what dangers soever hang over our heads, we are not thereby acquitted, but that we must obey the commandments of God, and follow his calling. In vain, therefore, do those men flatter themselves, who will do good so long as they be free from molestation, and may make discommodities, damages, and dangers of death, sufficient excuses.

24. *I care not.* All the godly must be so framed in their minds, and chiefly the ministers of the Word, that, setting all things apart, they make haste to obey God. The life is, indeed, a more excellent gift than that it ought to be neglected; to wit, seeing we be therein created after the image of God, to the end we may think upon that blessed immor-

---

[1] " Nec tamen violenter trahamur," and yet be not violently dragged, omitted.   [2] " Ad ejus impulsum," as he impels them.

tality which is laid up for us in heaven, in which the Lord doth now by divers testimonies and tokens show himself to be our Father.

But because it is ordained to be unto us as a race, we must always hasten unto the mark, and overcome all hinderances, lest any thing hinder or stay us in our course. For it is a filthy thing for us to be so holden with a blind desire to live, that we lose the causes of life for life itself; and this do the words of Paul express. For he doth not simply set light by his life; but he doth forget the respect thereof, that he may finish his course; that he may fulfil the ministry which he hath received of Christ, as if he should say that he is not desirous to live, save only that he may satisfy the calling of God; and that, therefore, it shall be no grief to him to lose his life, so that he may come by death unto the goal of the function prescribed to him by God.

And we must note that which he saith, *with joy*, for his meaning is, that this is taken from the faithful by no sorrow or grief, but that they both live and die to the Lord. For the joy of a good conscience is more deeply and surely laid up, than that it can be taken away by any external trouble, or any sorrow of the flesh; it triumpheth more joyfully than that it can be oppressed. Also, we must note the definition of his course; to wit, that it is the ministry received of the Lord. Paul doth indeed speak of himself; yet, by his own example, he teacheth that all those go astray who have not God to be the governor of their course. Whereupon it followeth that his calling is unto every one of us a rule of good life. Neither can we be otherwise persuaded that the Lord alloweth that which we do, unless our life be framed and ordered according to his will, which certainly is required, especially in the ministers of the word, that they take nothing in hand unless they have Christ for their author. Neither is it to be doubted but that Paul, in giving his apostleship this mark, (as he useth to do very often,) doth confirm the credit thereof. He calleth it the gospel of the grace of God, of the effect or end, notwithstanding this is a title of rare commendation, that, by the gospel, salvation and the grace of God are brought unto us. For it is very expedient for us to know that God is found there to be merciful and favourable.

25. *And, behold, now I know.* He doth now utter that plainly which he had insinuated covertly. And we said that he did put them out of hope of his return, to the end he might more deeply imprint in their minds his exhortations. For we know what great force the words and speeches of men have which are uttered at their departure or death. Also, he would have them beware by this forewarning, that they do not depend upon his presence, and so their faith should faint through wearisomeness. The doctrine of the gospel is called the kingdom of God now again, which doth begin the kingdom of God in this world, by renewing men after the image of God, until it be made perfect at length in the last resurrection.

26. *Wherefore I take you to record.* It is all one as if he had said, I call you to witness, or I call you to bear witness before God and his angels. And this doth he not so much for his own cause, as that he may prescribe unto them their duty with greater authority. Furthermore, this place containeth a brief sum of teaching rightly and well, and it exhorteth the teachers themselves, vehemently and sharply, that they be diligent in their function. What order must pastors then keep in teaching? First, let them not esteem at their pleasure what is profitable to be uttered and what to be omitted; but let them leave that to God alone to be ordered at his pleasure. So shall it come to pass that the inventions of men shall have none entrance into the Church of God. Again, mortal man shall not be so bold as to mangle the Scripture and to pull it in pieces, that he may diminish[1] this or that at his pleasure, that he may obscure something and suppress many things; but shall deliver whatsoever is revealed in the Scripture, though

---

[1] " Delibet," sip at.

wisely and seasonably for the edifying of the people, yet plainly and without guile, as becometh a faithful and true interpreter of God. I said that wisdom must be used, because we must always have respect unto profit, so there be no subtilty used, wherein many take too great delight, when as they turn and wrest the word of God unto their methods, and forge to us a certain kind of philosophy mixed of the gospel and their own inventions; namely, because this mixture is more delectable. Thence have we free-will, thence the deserts of works, thence the denial of the providence and free election of God. And that which we said even now is to be noted, that the counsel of God, whereof Paul maketh mention, is included in his word, and that it is to be sought no where else.

For many things are kept from us in this life, the perfect and full manifestation whereof is deferred until that day, wherein we shall see God as he is, with new eyes, face to face, (1 Cor. xiii. 12.) Therefore, those do set forth the will of God who interpret the Scriptures faithfully, and out of them instruct the people in the faith, in the fear of God, and in all exercises of godliness. And, as we said of late, that those are condemned by this sentence, who, disputing philosophically, lest they should teach anything which is removed from the common sense of men, and therefore odious, do corrupt with their leaven the purity of the Scripture; so, both sharply and sore, doth Paul thunder against them, who, for fear of the cross and persecution, do speak only doubtfully and darkly.[1]

I am clean from the blood. I do not doubt but that he had respect unto the place of Ezekiel, where God denounceth that his prophet shall be guilty of the blood of the wicked unless he exhort them unto repentance, (Ezek. iii. 18, 20.) For upon this condition doth he appoint pastors over his Church, that if anything perish through their negligence, an account may be required at their hands; yea, that unless they show the way of salvation without guile

---

[1] " Ænigmatice," enigmatically.

and crooks, the destruction of those who go astray may be imputed unto them. Those men must needs be wonderful dull whom such a sharp threatening cannot awake. Wherefore the epicurish impiety of the Popish clergy doth the more bewray itself, where, though they craik and brag [1] of their honourable titles, yet they think no more upon giving of an account for so many souls which perish, than if there sat no Judge in heaven, neither is their ungodliness any whit less filthy before the whole world, in that being given only to devour sheep,[2] they usurp the name of pastors. Furthermore, the Lord showeth how dear souls be to him, seeing that he doth so sharply punish the pastor's sluggishness for their destruction; but we see what small account many men make of their own salvation, for which even God himself doth vouchsafe to be careful.

28. *Therefore, take heed to yourselves, and to all the flock, wherein the Holy Ghost hath made you overseers, to govern the Church of God, which he hath purchased with his blood.*
29. *For I know this, that after my departure grievous wolves will enter in among you, not sparing the flock.*
30. *And of your own selves shall arise men, speaking perverse things, that they may draw disciples after them.*
31. *For which cause watch ye, remembering that by the space of three years I ceased not night and day to warn every one of you with tears.*
32. *And now, brethren, I commend you to God, and to the word of his grace, who is able to build farther, and to give you an inheritance among all those who are sanctified.*

28. *Take heed, therefore.* He doth now apply his speech unto them, and by many reasons showeth that they must watch diligently, and that he is not so careful but because necessity doth so require. The first reason is, because they be bound to the flock over which they be set. The second, because they were called unto this function not by

---

[1] Make loud boast [2] " Quod deglutiendis tantum ovibus intenti," in that being only intent on devouring the sheep.

mortal man, but by the Holy Ghost. The third, because it is no small honour to govern the Church of God. The fourth, because the Lord did declare by an evident testimony what account he doth make of the Church, seeing that he hath redeemed it with his blood. As touching the first, he doth not only command them to take heed to the flock, but first to themselves. For that man will never be careful for the salvation of other men who will neglect his own. And in vain shall that man prick forward other to live godlily, who will himself show no desire of godliness. Yea, that man will not take pains with his flock who forgetteth himself, seeing he is a part of the flock. Therefore, to the end they may be careful for the flock to them committed, Paul commandeth and warneth that every one of them keep himself in the fear of God. For by this means it should come to pass, that every one should be as faithful towards his flock as he ought. For we said that Paul reasoneth from their calling, that they be bound to take pains in the Church of God, whereof they have the government. As if he should say, that they may not do whatsoever they like best, neither are they free after they be made pastors, but they be bound publicly to all the flock.

The Holy Ghost hath made you overseers. By the very word he putteth them in mind, that they be placed, as it were, in a watch-tower, that they may watch for the common safety of all men. But Paul standeth principally upon this, that they were not appointed by men, but the charge of the Church was committed unto them by God. For which cause they must be the more diligent and careful, because they must give a straight account before that high seat of judgment. For the more excellent the dignity of that Lord and Master whom we serve is, the more reverence do we give him naturally, and the reverence itself doth sharpen our study and diligence.

Moreover, though the Lord would have ministers of the word chosen from the beginning by the voices [suffrages] of men, yet doth he always challenge the government of the Church to himself, not only to the end we may acknowledge him to be the only governor thereof, but also know that the incomparable treasure of salvation doth come from him alone. For he is robbed of his glory if we think that the gospel is brought unto us, either by chance or by the will of men, or their industry. But this doth Paul attribute peculiarly to the Spirit, by whom God doth govern his Church, and who is to every man a secret witness of his calling in his own conscience.

Concerning the word *overseer* or *bishop*, we must briefly note this, that Paul calleth all the elders of Ephesus by this name, as well one as other.[1] Whence we gather, that according to the use of the Scripture bishops differ nothing from elders. But that it came to pass through vice and corruption, that those who were chief in every city began to be called bishops. I call it corruption, not because it is evil that some one man should be chief in every college or company; but because this boldness is intolerable, when men, by wresting the names of the Scripture unto their custom, doubt not to change the tongue of the Holy Ghost.

To govern the Church. The Greek word ποιμαινειν doth signify *to feed*. But by a fit similitude it is translated unto every kind of government. And we have said that this is the third argument drawn from the excellency of the function; as the same Paul telleth Timotheus elsewhere, that he take heed and see how he ought to behave himself in the house of God, which is the Church of the living God, the pillar and ground of truth. As if he should say, that there is no time to be idle in such a weighty calling, and that those are less excusable whom God hath made stewards of his family, the higher that degree of honour is, unless they be correspondent to so great dignity, that is, unless they do their duty diligently. Now, if bishops or overseers be made by the Holy Ghost, to the end they may feed the Church, the hierarchy of Papistry is ridiculous, wherein bishops being proud of their (painted sheath and)

---

[1] " Indifferenter," indifferently.

vain title, do not so much as once meddle with the function of teaching, no, not for fashion's sake.

Which he hath purchased. The four reasons, whereby Paul doth carefully prick forward the pastors to do their duty diligently, because the Lord hath given no small pledge of his love toward the Church in shedding his own blood for it. Whereby it appeareth how precious it is to him; and surely there is nothing which ought more vehemently to urge pastors to do their duty joyfully, than if they consider that the price of the blood of Christ is committed to them. For hereupon it followeth, that unless they take pains in the Church, the lost souls are not only imputed to them, but they be also guilty of sacrilege, because they have profaned the holy blood of the Son of God, and have made the redemption gotten by him to be of none effect, so much as in them lieth. And this is a most cruel offence, if, through our sluggishness, the death of Christ do not only become vile or base, but the fruit thereof be also abolished and perish; and it is said that God hath purchased the Church, to the end we may know that he would have it remain wholly to himself, because it is meet and right that he possess those whom he hath redeemed.

Notwithstanding, we must also remember, that all mankind are the bond-slaves of Satan until Christ set us free from his tyranny, gathering us into the inheritance of his Father.

But because the speech which Paul useth seemeth to be somewhat hard, we must see in what sense he saith that God purchased the Church with his blood. For nothing is more absurd than to feign or imagine God to be mortal or to have a body. But in this speech he commendeth the unity of person in Christ; for because there be distinct natures in Christ, the Scripture doth sometimes recite that apart by itself which is proper to either. But when it setteth God before us made manifest in the flesh, it doth not separate the human nature from the Godhead. Notwithstanding, because again two natures are so united in Christ, that they make one person, that is improperly translated sometimes unto the one, which doth truly and in deed belong to the other, as in this place Paul doth attribute blood to God; because the man Jesus Christ, who shed his blood for us, was also God. This manner of speaking is called, of the old writers, *communicatio idiomatum,* because the property of the one nature is applied to the other. And I said that by this means is manifestly expressed one person of Christ, lest we imagine him to be double, which Nestorius did in times past attempt; and yet for all this we must not imagine a confusion of the two natures which Eutychus went about to bring in, or which the Spanish dog, Servetus, hath at this time invented, who maketh the Godhead of Christ nothing else but a form or image of the human nature, which he dreameth to have always shined in God.

29. *For I know.* Paul doth now exhort the Ephesians to watch diligently, by the necessity, which is a most sharp prick. For he saith that " grievous wolves are ready to invade the sheepfold." This is a thing always incident to the Church to be hated of wolves. Wherefore, there is no time to sleep. But the more and the more hurtful those be who break in, the more watchful must the pastors be. For God doth sometimes release some part of trouble, that the flock may be fed quietly and peaceably; and as when the weather is fair and clear, the sheep are fed more safely in the fields, and there is more danger when the air is cloudy and dark; so the Church of God hath sometimes some fair weather granted to it. After that cometh a troublesome time, which is more fit for the subtilty[1] of wolves. Therefore, Paul doth mean, that it standeth them upon to be more watchful than they have been hitherto, because greater dangers hang over their heads. But the question is, how Paul knew this? First, we need not doubt of this, but that his presence was of great force to drive away wolves; and no marvel, if the power of the Spirit, which shineth in the ministers of Christ, do bridle the wicked so that they dare not utter their

---

[1] " Insidus," the snares.

poison; yea, if that heavenly light do drive away much darkness of Satan. Therefore, seeing that Paul did know that the malice of Satan was kept under for a time by his industry, he doth easily foretell what will happen after his departure, though it be likely he was certified by the Lord, through the spirit of prophecy, that others might be admonished by him, as we see it came to pass. Howsoever it be, so often as faithful pastors go away, let us learn that we must beware of wolves, whom they can hardly drive from the sheep-cots, though they watch most narrowly.

30. *Of your ownselves shall arise.* This amplifieth the grievousness of the evil, because there be some wolves within, and so hiding themselves under the title of pastors, [which] do wait for some opportunity wherein they may do hurt. Also, he declareth what danger these wolves do threaten, to wit, the scattering abroad of the flock, when the Church is drawn away from the unity of faith, and is divided into sects. Neither are all those wolves who do not their duty as they ought, but there be oftentimes hirelings, a kind of men not so hurtful as the other. But the corruption of doctrine is a most deadly plague to the sheep. Now, in the third place, the fountain and beginning of this evil is noted, because they will draw disciples after them. Therefore, ambition is the mother of all heresies. For the sincerity of the word of God doth then flourish when the pastors join hand in hand to bring disciples unto Christ, because this alone is the sound state of the Church, that he be heard alone;[1] wherefore, both the doctrine of salvation must needs be perverted, and also the safety of the flock must needs go to nought, where men be desirous of mastership. And as this place teacheth that almost all corruptions of doctrine flow from the pride of men, so we learn again out of the same that it cannot otherwise be, but that ambitious men will turn away from right purity, and corrupt the word of God. For seeing that the pure and sincere handling of the Scripture

---

[1] " Unus Magister," as the only Master.

tendeth to this end, that Christ alone may have the preeminence, and that men can challenge nothing to themselves, but they shall take so much from the glory of Christ, it followeth that those are corrupters of sound doctrine who are addicted to themselves, and study to advance their own glory, which doth only darken Christ. Which thing the Lord doth confirm in the seventh of John, (John vii. 18.) Furthermore, by the word *arise* which he useth, he signifieth that those wolves do nourish secret destruction until they may have some opportunity offered to break out.

And this place doth very well prevent an horrible stumbling-block and offence which Satan hath always cast in to trouble weak consciences. If external and professed enemies do resist the gospel, this doth not so much hurt to the Church,[1] as if inward enemies issue out of the bosom of the Church, which at a sudden blow to the field,[2] or which unfaithfully provoke the people to fall away; and yet God hath from the beginning exercised his Church with this temptation, and now doth exercise it. Wherefore, let our faith be fortified with this defence that it fail not, if at any time it so fall out that pastors begin to rage like wolves. He saith they shall be "grievous wolves," that he may the more terrify them; secondly, they shall be authors of wicked opinions, and that to the end they may draw disciples after them, because it cannot almost otherwise be but that ambition will corrupt the purity of the gospel.

By this it appeareth also how frivolous and vain the brag of the Papists is touching their continual succession. For seeing we can easily show that these horned beasts are nothing less than that which they will be thought to be, being always convicted, they fly unto this fortress, that they succeed the apostles by a continual course.[3] As if these did not also succeed them, of whom Paul willeth to take heed.[4] Therefore, seeing that God, either to prove the constancy of

---

[1] "Minus hoc consternat pias mentes," this does less alarm pious minds
[2] "Classicum canant," blow the trumpet
[3] "Continua serie," in an unbroken series
[4] "Cavendum . . . admonet,' admonishes us to beware.

his [people,] or in his just judgment doth oftentimes suffer wolves to rage under the person of pastors, the authority doth not consist in the name and place alone, neither is succession anything worth unless faith and integrity be joined therewithal. But and if the Papists object that they cannot be called wolves, one word of Paul shall be as a touchstone to prove whether this be so or no, that they may (saith he) draw disciples after them. And to what end tendeth all Popish religion, save only that men's lust and pleasure may reign instead of God's word? But Christ hath no disciples where he is not counted the only master.

31. *For which cause, watch.* Paul doth again exhort them unto diligence by his own example, though he doth join therewithal fear of danger, as if he should say that they have need of great attention to beware; and that it is an unseemly thing that they should be wearied who had seen his singular[1] patience by the space of three years. Also, he speaketh of his tears, which did add no small efficacy to his exhortations. Whereas he saith that he admonished every one, it may be referred as well unto the common people as unto the elders. For because he was determined to speak such things as should be common to the whole Church, he speaketh as if the whole body were present. Nevertheless, if any had rather restrain it unto the order of the pastors, the meaning shall be this, that their studies must be kindled, not only with this speech which he now maketh, but that it is meet that they remember those often exhortations which he did continually beat in[2] by the space of three years, and that with many tears. Yet it seemeth to me to be more likely that he speaketh of all in general.

32. *I commend you to God.* He useth a prayer which, in an oration serving to move the hearers greatly, ought not to be counted absurd. For he did not pass for dividing his sermon into parts as the Rhetoricians use to do, seeing no

[1] "Infractam," unbroken. [2] "Assidue inculcaverat," had assiduously inculcated.

words were sufficient to express the vehemency of the affections wherewith he was inflamed. He had intreated already of great matters and weighty, which did far exceed man's ability.

Therefore, he turneth himself unto prayer, and by little and little draweth toward an end of his speech, though it be rather an expressing of a desire than a direct prayer; as if he should have said, that they be unable to bear so great a burthen; but he doth wish to them new help from heaven, whereto they may trust and overcome all temptations. And it is not to be doubted, though he speak unto the pastors alone, but that he doth also comprehend the whole Church. First, he commendeth them to God; secondly, to the word of his grace. Notwithstanding, it is all one commendation; but Paul meant to express the means whereby the Lord doth defend the salvation of his, which (as Peter saith) is kept by faith, (1 Pet. i. 5;) and the means of this keeping dependeth upon the word, lest it come in hazard amidst so many dangers. And it is very expedient for us to know how God will keep us. For because his majesty is hid from us, until we come unto him by his word, we look to and fro, being in doubt.

Therefore, so soon as he receiveth us to be kept, he maketh his word the instrument to keep our salvation, in which sense, he addeth the adjunct "grace," (for the genitive case, after the manner of the Hebrews, doth signify an effect,) to the end the faithful might the more safely rest in the word, where God doth show forth his favour. This exposition is plain and apt; for whereas some understand it of Christ, it is too much racked.

Who is able to build farther. The participle, δυναμενος,[1] is to be referred unto God, not unto his word. And this consolation is added for this cause, lest they faint through the feeling of their infirmities. For so long as we be environed with the infirmities of the flesh, we be like to an house whose foundation is laid.[2] All the godly must be grounded

---

[1] " Quo utitur Paulus," which Paul uses. [2] " Inchoato ædificio," to a commenced building.

indeed in Christ, but their faith is far from being perfect. Yea, though the foundation continue stable and sure, yet some parts of the building be like to fall and quail.[1] Wherefore, there is great need both of continual building, and also now and then new props and stays be necessary. Nevertheless, Paul saith that "we must not faint," because the Lord will not leave his work unfinished; as he doth likewise teach in the first chapter to the Philippians, "He which hath begun a good work in you will perform it until the day of the Lord," (Philip. i. 6.) Whereto that of the Psalm (Psalm cxxxviii. 8) answereth, "Thou wilt not forsake the work of our [thy] hands."

That which is added immediately concerning the inheritance of life appertaineth unto the very enjoying of life. So soon as Christ hath appeared to us,[2] we pass indeed from death to life; and faith is an entrance into the kingdom of heaven; neither is the Spirit of adoption given to us in vain; but Paul promiseth in this place to the faithful a continual increase of grace until they see the possession of the inheritance whereunto they have been called, which is now laid up for them in heaven. He calleth it "the power of God," not as we use to imagine it, without effect, but which is commonly called actual. For the faithful must so lay hold upon it, that they may have it ready, like to a shield, or buckler, to hold up against all assaults of Satan. As the Scripture doth teach that we have aid enough in the power of God, so let us remember that none are strong in the Lord save those who, abandoning all hope and confidence of their own free will, trust and lean to him, who, as Paul saith very well, is able to build farther.

33. *I have desired no man's silver, or gold, or raiment*
34. *Yea, ye yourselves know how that these hands have ministered to my necessity, and to those which were with me.*
35. *I have showed you all things, that so labouring you must receive the weak, and remember the words of the Lord Jesus;*

---

[1] "Nutant," nod, totter.   [2] "Nobis affulsit," hath shone upon us.

because he said, It is a blessed thing rather to give than to take.
36. And when he had thus spoken, he kneeled down, and prayed with them all.
37. And there arose great weeping among them all ; and, falling upon Paul's neck, they kissed him,
38. Sorrowing most for the words which he spake, that they should see his face no more. And they brought him to the ship.

33. *I have not.* As he showed of late what an hurtful plague ambition is ; so now he showeth that they must beware of covetousness, [avarice;] and he maketh himself an example again, even in this point, that he did covet no man's goods; but did rather get his living with the work of his hands. Not that it was sufficient to find him without some help, but because in applying his handy-work, he spared the churches, that he might not be too chargeable to them, so much as in him lay. We must note, that he doth not only deny that he did take anything violently, as hungry fellows do importunately wring out preys oftentimes, but also he affirmeth that he was clean from all wicked desire. Whence we gather, that no man can be a good minister of the word, but he must also contemn money. And surely we see that nothing is more common, than that those corrupt the word of God, to win the favour of men, who are altogether filthily given to get gain. Which vice Paul doth sharply condemn in bishops elsewhere, (1 Tim. iii. 3.)

34. *Yea, ye know.* He doth not, in these words, precisely set down a law which all the ministers of the word must needs keep ; for he did not behave himself so loftily and lordlike, that he did take that away which the Lord had granted to his servants, but doth rather in many places maintain their right, which is, that they be maintained with that which is common, Matth. x. 10; 1 Cor. ix. 14; Gal. vi. 6; 1 Tim. v. 17; Phil. iv. 10, 16; 2 Cor. xi. 8.

Whereunto belongeth that, that he suffered many churches to minister unto him food and raiment. Neither did he only freely receive wages for the work which he did in any place of those who were there, but when he was in necessity at Corinth, he saith that he robbed other churches to relieve his poverty. Therefore, he doth not simply command pastors to maintain their life with their handy-work, but immediately after he declareth how far forth he exhorteth them to follow his example. Those men of Corinth did not deny him that which was due to him;[1] but seeing that the false apostles did boast that they did their work freely, and get thereby praise among the people; Paul would not be behind them in this point, nor give them any occasion to accuse him falsely; as he himself affirmeth, (1 Cor. ix. 15, and 2 Cor. xi. 10.) Therefore, he warneth that there be no stumbling-block laid in the way of the weak, and that their faith be not overthrown. For to receive the weak, importeth as much as somewhat to bear with their rudeness and simplicity, as it is, (Rom. xiv. 1.)

And to remember. We read this sentence in no place word for word; but the Evangelists have other not much unlike this, out of which Paul might gather this. Again, we know that all the sayings of Christ were not written; and he repeateth that general doctrine of the contempt of money; whereof this is a true token, when a man is more bent to give than to take. Neither did Christ speak only politicly,[2] as if those who are liberal are therefore blessed, because they bind other men unto them with their benefits, and it is a kind of bondage to owe anything; but he had respect unto an higher thing, because, he which giveth to the poor lendeth unto the Lord, (Prov. xix. 17;) that those be faithful and good stewards of God, who impart to their brethren some of that plenty which they have lent them; that men draw nearer unto God in nothing

---

[1] " Non negabant illi Corinthii debitam mercedem," those Corinthians did not deny that hire was due to him. [2] " Politice," of what was politic

than in liberality. We do also read these titles of liberality in profane authors; and a good part of the world confess that these things are true, but they consent (as it is in the proverb) with ass's ears. For the common life doth show how few be persuaded that nothing ought more to be wished, than that we bestow our goods to help our brethren. For which cause the disciples of Christ must more studiously think upon this felicity, that abstaining so much as in them lieth, from that which is another man's, they accustom themselves to give. And yet they must not do this with an haughty heart, as if it were a miserable thing for them to be in any man's danger;[1] either through ambition, that they may bind other men to them; but only that they may exercise themselves willingly in the duties of love, and by this means make known the grace of their adoption.

36. *And kneeling down.* The inward affection is indeed the chiefest thing in prayer; yet the external signs, as kneeling, uncovering of the head, lifting up of the hands, have a double use; the first is, that we exercise all our members to the glory and worship of God; secondly, that by this exercise our sluggishness may be awakened, as it were. There is also a third use in solemn and public prayer, because the children of God do by this means make profession of their godliness, and one of them doth provoke another unto the reverence of God. And, as the lifting up of the hands is a token of boldness[2] and of an earnest desire, so, to testify our humility, we fall down upon our knees. But he sealeth up and concludeth that sermon which he made before with prayer; because we can hope for no profit of our doctrine, save only from the blessing of God. Wherefore, if we be desirous to do any good by teaching, admonishing, and exhorting, let us always end after this sort; to wit, with prayer.

[1] "Ipsos cuiquam esse obnoxios," that they themselves should be subjected (under obligation) to any one.   [2] "Fiduciæ," confidence

37. *Great weeping.* No marvel if all the godly did entirely love this holy man. For it had been a point of too gross unthankfulness to despise him whom the Lord had so beautified with so many excellent gifts. And the chief cause of their weeping was, as Luke noteth, because they should see him no more. For they did bewail their own condition, and the condition of all the whole church of Asia, not in vain, which they saw to be deprived of an inestimable treasure. And when the Spirit commendeth their tears by the mouth of Luke, as witnesses of sincere godliness, he condemneth the rashness of those who require at the hands of the faithful hard and cruel constancy. For that is false whereof they dream that those affections proceed only of corruption, which we have naturally from God. Wherefore, the perfection of the faithful consisteth not in this, that they put off all affections; but that they be moved therewith only for just causes, and that they may moderate the same.

CHAPTER XXI.

1. *And when it came to pass that we had loosed, being pulled away from them, we came with a straight course to Coos, and the next day to the Rhodes, and thence to Patara;*
2. *And when we had gotten a ship, which sailed over to Phenicia, when we were entered into it, we launched.*
3. *And when Cyprus began to appear to us, leaving it on the left hand, we sailed into Syria, and came to Tyrus: for here the ship did unlade her burden.*
4. *And when we had found disciples, we stayed there seven days; who said to Paul by the Spirit, that he should not go up to Jerusalem.*
5. *And when the days were ended, we departed and went our way; and they all, with their wives and children, accom-*

panied us, until we were out of the city; and when we had kneeled down upon the shore, we prayed.

6. *And when we had taken our leave one of another, we went up into the ship; and they returned home.*

1. Luke reckoneth up briefly the course of his sailing; and that not only to win credit to the history, that we may know what was done in every place, but that the readers may weigh with themselves the invincible and heroic fortitude which was in Paul, who would rather be tossed and troubled with such long, unlevel,[1] and troublesome journeys, that he might serve Christ, than provide for his own quietness. Whereas he saith that they were drawn and pulled away, it is not simply referred unto the distance of places; but because the brethren stood on the shore, so long as they could see the ship wherein Paul and his companions were carried. He nameth the havens where the ship arrived,[2] for this cause that we may know that they sailed quietly without trouble of tempest. Let us search the describers of countries[3] touching the situation of the cities whereof he maketh mention; it is sufficient for me to show Luke's purpose.

4. *And when they had found disciples.* Though the number of the faithful was but small, yet there came some seed of the gospel thither, according to the prophecies of the prophets, (Isa. xxiii. 18,) lest Tyrus should be altogether void of the blessing of God. And here, as in other places going before, Luke calleth Christians disciples, that we may know that those alone are numbered in the flock of Christ who have embraced his doctrine by faith. For that is a vain[4] and false profession for a man to give his name to Christ, and not to understand what he teacheth or speaketh. And let the readers mark, that Paul stayed seven days at Tyrus, for no other cause, saving that he might strengthen them.

---

[1] " Ac flexuosis," and winding. [2] " Applicuit." touched [3] " Consulantur geographi," geographers may be consulted. [4] " Lusoria,' elusory.

So that we see, that whithersoever he came he foreslowed [neglected] no occasion to do good.

They said by the Spirit. Namely, with the approbation of speech, that Paul might know that they spake by the Spirit of prophecy. Surely this was no small temptation to cause him not to finish the journey which he had taken in hand, seeing the Holy Ghost did dissuade him from the same. And this was a very fair colour[1] to fly from the cross, if he had cared for his own safety, to be drawn back as it were with the hand of God. Notwithstanding, he ceaseth not to hold on thither whither he knew he was called by the Lord. Notwithstanding, here ariseth a question, how the brethren can dissuade him by the Spirit from doing that which Paul did testify he doth by the secret motion of the same Spirit? Is the Spirit contrary to himself, that he doth now loose Paul whom he held bound inwardly? I answer, that there be divers gifts of the Spirit; so that it is no marvel if those who excel in the gift of prophecy be sometimes destitute of judgment or strength.[2] The Lord showed to these brethren, of whom Luke maketh mention, what should come to pass; yet, nevertheless, they know not what is expedient, and what Paul's calling doth require, because the measure of their gift doth not reach so far. And the Lord would have his servant admonished of purpose, partly, that through long meditation, he might be better furnished and prepared to suffer whatsoever should come, partly that his constancy might more plainly appear, when as being certified by prophecies of the doleful event, he doth, notwithstanding, wittingly and willingly, make haste to endure whatsoever things shall befall him.

5. *With their wives and children.* This was no small testimony of love, in that they accompanied Paul out of the city with their wives and children, which thing Luke doth report, partly that he might commend their godliness according as it deserved; partly that he might declare that

---

[1] " Color apprime speciosus," a very specious pretext.   [2] " Fortitudine," fortitude.

Paul had that honour given him which was due to him. Whence we do also gather, that he meant nothing less than to provide for his own commodity, seeing that he was not kept back with so great good will, which was a pleasant bait to entice him to stay. And we must also note the solemn custom of praying in weightier affairs, and that being certified by God of the danger, they are more stirred up to pray.

> 7. *And when we had finished our course from Tyre, we came down to Ptolemais, and after that we had saluted the brethren, we abode with them one day.*
> 8. *And on the morrow, we which were with Paul departed, and came to Cesarea ; and, entering into the house of Philip the evangelist, which was one of the seven, we abode with him.*
> 9. *And this man had four daughters, virgins, which did prophesy*
> 10. *And when we abode many days, there came a certain prophet from Judea, named Agabus.*
> 11. *When he was come to us, he took Paul's girdle, and, binding his own feet and hands, he said, Thus saith the Holy Ghost, The man which owneth this girdle shall the Jews thus bind at Jerusalem, and shall deliver him into the hands of the Gentiles.*
> 12. *And when we had heard these things, both we, and also the rest which were of that place, requested him that he would not go up to Jerusalem.*
> 13. *Then Paul answered and said, What do you, weeping and afflicting my heart? I truly am ready not to be bound only, but also to die at Jerusalem, for the name of the Lord Jesus.*
> 14. *And when he would not be persuaded, we were quiet, saying, The will of the Lord be done.*

7. Luke doth briefly declare that Paul was also received at Ptolemais by the brethren. This is a city of Phenicia, standing upon the sea-coast, not far from the borders of Judea, from which Paul and his companions had no long journey to Cesarea. But if the readers be disposed to know

farther touching the situation of regions, let them resort unto the describers of places and countries, [geographers.] Furthermore, he saith, that when he came to Cesarea, they lodged with Philip, whom he calleth an Evangelist, though he were one of the seven deacons, as we may see in the sixth chapter, (Acts vi. 5.) By this we may easily gather, that that deaconship was an office which continued but for a time;[1] because it had not otherwise been lawful for Philip to forsake Jerusalem, and to go to Cesarea. And in this place he is set before us, not as a voluntary forsaker of his office, but as one to whom a greater and more excellent charge was committed. The evangelists, in my judgment, were in the midst between apostles and doctors. For it was a function next to the apostles to preach the gospel in all places, and not to have any certain place of abode;[2] only the degree of honour was inferior. For when Paul describeth the order of the Church, (Ephes. iv. 11,) he doth so put them after the apostles, that he showeth that they have more room given them where they may teach than the pastors, who are tied to certain places. Therefore, Philip did for a time exercise the office of a deacon at Jerusalem, whom the Church thought afterward to be a meet man to whom the treasure of the gospel should be committed.

9. *Four daughters.* This is added for the commendation of Philip, not only that we might know that his house was well ordered, but also that it was famous and excellent through the blessing of God. For, assuredly, it was no small gift to have four daughters all endowed with the spirit of prophecy.

By this means the Lord meant to beautify the first beginnings of the gospel, when he raised up men and women to foretel things to come. Prophecies had now almost ceased many years among the Jews, to the end they might be more attentive and desirous to hear the new voice of the gospel. Therefore, seeing that prophesying, which was in a manner

---

[1] " Temporale munus," a temporary office, (appointment)   [2] " Nec præficerentur certæ stationi," and yet not be appointed to a fixed station.

quite ceased, doth now after long time return again, it was a token of a more perfect state. Notwithstanding, it seemeth that the same was the reason why it ceased shortly after; for God did support the old people with divers foretellings, until Christ should make an end of all prophecies.[1] Therefore, it was meet that the new kingdom of Christ should be thus furnished and beautified with this furniture, that all men might know that that promised visitation of the Lord was present; and it was also expedient that it should last but for a short time, lest the faithful should always wait for some farther thing, or lest that curious wits might have occasion given to seek or invent some new thing ever now and then. For we know that when that ability and skill was taken away, there were, notwithstanding, many brain-sick fellows, who did boast that they were prophets; and also it may be that the frowardness of men did deprive the Church of this gift. But that one cause ought to be sufficient, in that God, by taking away prophecies, did testify that the end and perfection was present in Christ; and it is uncertain how these maids did execute the office of prophesying, saving that the Spirit of God did so guide and govern them, that he did not overthrow the order which he himself set down. And forasmuch as he doth not suffer women to bear any public office in the Church, it is to be thought that they did prophesy at home, or in some private place, without the common assembly.

10. *A certain prophet.* Though Luke doth not plainly express the same, yet do I conjecture that this Agabus was the same of whom mention is made in the eleventh chapter, (Acts xi. 28,) who foretold that there should be famine under the reign of Claudius Cæsar. And when as Luke calleth him a prophet, as of late he called the four daughters of Philip, he signifieth that it was not a common but a peculiar gift. Now, we must see to what end the persecution which was at hand was now again showed by Agabus. As con-

---

[1] "Adventu suo," by his advent.

cerning Paul, he was sufficiently told already.[1] Therefore, I do not doubt but that this confirmation was added for other men's sake; because the Lord meant every where to make known the bonds of his servant, partly that they might know that he entered the combat willingly, partly that they might perceive that he was appointed of God to be a champion to fight for the gospel. It was surely a profitable example of invincible constancy, seeing that he offered himself willingly and wittingly to the violence of the adversaries; and no less profitable is it for us at this day, that his apostleship should be confirmed with this voluntary and no less constant giving over of his life.

The man who owneth this girdle. It was an usual thing among the prophets to represent those things which they spake by signs; neither did they confirm their prophecies by using signs, through their own motion, but at the commandment of the Spirit, as when Isaias is commanded to go barefoot, (Isa. xx. 2;) Jeremiah to put a yoke upon his neck, to sell the possession and to buy it, (Jer. xxvii. 2, and xxxii. 7;) and Ezekiel to dig through the wall of his house privily, and in the same night to carry forth burthens, (Ezek. xii. 5.) These and such like might seem to the common sort to be toys;[2] but the same Spirit, who did apply signs to his words, did inwardly touch the hearts of the godly, as if they had been brought to the very thing itself. So this spectacle, mentioned by Luke, did no less move Paul's companions, than if they had seen him bound in deed. The false prophets did afterward essay to delude the simple by this policy, as Satan is in a manner God's ape, and his ministers do envy the servants of God. Zedekias made himself horns, wherewith he promised Syria should be pushed. Ananias, by breaking Jeremiah's yoke, put the people in a vain hope of deliverance. God hath suffered the reprobate to be deluded with such delusions, that he might punish their unbelief.

---

[1] " Jam satis superque admonitus fuerat," he had been more than sufficiently warned already. [2] " Ludicra," ludicrous.

But, forasmuch as there was in them no force of the Spirit, their vanity did no whit hurt the faithful. This is also worthy to be noted, that Agabus doth not set before their eyes a dumb spectacle, but he coupleth therewith the word, whereby he may show to the faithful the use and end of the ceremony.

12. *Both we.* Because they had not all one **revelation**, it is no marvel if their judgments were diverse. For seeing these holy men knew that there consisted much in the life or death of one man, they would not have him to come in danger rashly. And their desire is worthy [of] praise, in that they desired to provide for the common safety of the Church by keeping back Paul. But, on the other side, Paul's constancy deserveth so much the more praise, when as he continueth so stedfast[1] in the calling of God. For he was not ignorant what great trouble he should suffer by reason of his bands. But because he knoweth the will of God, which was his only rule in taking counsel, he maketh no account of all other things, that he may follow it. And, assuredly, we must be so subject to the will and pleasure of God, that no profit, no kind of reason may remove us from obeying him.[2] When Paul doth reprehend the brethren, because they afflict his heart with weeping, he doth sufficiently declare that he was not hardened,[3] but that he was brought unto some feeling and suffering together with them.[4] Therefore, the tears of the godly did wound his heart; but that softness did not turn him out of the way, but that he proceeded to follow God with a straight course. Therefore, we must use such courtesy toward our brethren, that the beck or will of God have always the upper hand. Now Paul doth again declare by his answer, that the servants of Christ cannot be prepared to do their duty, unless they despise death; and that none can ever be well encouraged to live to the Lord, but

---

[1] " Inflexibilis," inflexible   [2] " A simplici ejus obsequio," from simple obedience to him.   [3] " Ferreum," iron-hearted   [4] " Quin amore ad συμπαθειαν induceretur," but by love was induced to sympathy

those who will willingly lay down their lives for the testimony of the truth.

14. *We ceased saying.* If they had thought that he ran rashly unto death, they would not have ceased so. Therefore, they yield lest they resist the Holy Spirit, whereby they understand that Paul is governed. For that which they had heard before, by the mouth of Paul, that he was drawn, as it were, by the bands of the Spirit, was quite out of their heads by reason of the sorrow which they had conceived; but when they be taught again that it was the will of God that it should be so, they think it unlawful for them to resist any longer. And with this bridle must all our affections be kept in, that nothing be so bitter, or doleful, or hard, which the will of God may not mitigate and mollify. For so often as any thing which is hard or sharp doth fall out, we give God small honour, unless this cogitation prevail with us, that we must obey him.

15. *And after these days, having taken up our burdens, we went up to Jerusalem.*
16. *And there came together with us certain of the disciples from Cesarea, bringing with them one Mnason of Cyprus, an old disciple, with whom we should lodge.*
17. *And when we were come unto Jerusalem, the brethren received us gladly.*
18. *And on the morrow Paul went in with us unto James; and all the elders were present.*
19. *Whom after we had saluted, he told by order all things which God had done among the Gentiles by his ministry.*
20. *But when they had heard, they glorified the Lord, and said to him, Thou seest, brother, how many thousand Jews the be which believe; and they all are earnest followers of th law;*
21. *And it hath been told them concerning thee, that thou teachest all the Jews which are among the Gentiles to forsake Moses, saying that they must not circumcise their children, nor live according to the customs.*

22. *What is it then ? The multitude must needs come together; for they shall hear that thou art come.*
23. *Therefore, do this which we say to thee : We have four men which have a vow upon them ;*
24. *Them take, and purify thyself with them, and do cost on them, that they may shave their heads, and that all men may know that those things which they have heard concerning thee are nothing ; but that thou thyself also walkest and keepest the law.*
25. *And as concerning those which among the Gentiles have believed, we have written, decreeing that they observe no such thing, but that they keep themselves from things offered to idols, and from blood, and from that which is strangled, and from fornication.*

15. *When we had taken up our burdens.* Paul's companions declare, that when they went about to call back Paul from danger, they did rather care for the common safety of the Church, than every man for his own life. For after they had taken the repulse, they do not refuse to take part with him in the same danger; and yet this was a plausible excuse that they were bound by no law to be hauled to suffer death, through one man's stubbornness. And this is truly to bring our affections in subjection to God, when we are terrified with no fear, but every one of us endeavoureth, so much as he is able, to further that which we know doth please him. Also, it appeareth more plainly what great ferventness of godliness was in the rest, who of their own accord accompany him, and bring him an host; whereas, notwithstanding, they might well have feared many discommodities.

17. *They received us gladly.* Luke reciteth this, therefore, that he may set forth the equity of the brethren, who did not credit rumours[1] and false reports. Though many envious and wicked men did daily, one after another, endeavour to bring Paul in contempt, yet, because James and his fellows in office were well persuaded of his uprightness, they were

[1] " Sinistris rumoribus,' sinister rumours.

not estranged from him. Therefore, they receive him now courteously and brotherly as a servant of Christ, and declare that he is welcome. This moderation must we observe diligently, that we be not too hasty to believe wicked reports, especially when those who have given some testimony of their honesty, and whom we have tried[1] to serve God faithfully, are burdened with crimes unknown to us, or else doubtful, because Satan knoweth that nothing is more fit to lay waste the kingdom of Christ, than discord and disagreement among the faithful, he ceaseth not to spread abroad false[2] speeches, which may cause one to suspect another. Therefore, we must shut our ears against false reports, that we may believe nothing concerning the faithful ministers of the Word, but that which we know to be true.

18. *All the elders were present.* We may gather that out of this place which we had already in the fifteenth chapter. So often as any weighty business was to be handled, the elders were wont to come together, to the end the consultation might be more quiet without the multitude. We shall see anon, that the people were likewise admitted in their order, yet after that the elders had had their secret consultation[3] among themselves.

19. And now Paul showeth his modesty when he doth not make himself the author of those things which he had done, but giving the praise to God, doth call himself only the minister whose industry [agency] God had used. As we must grant, that whatsoever thing is excellent and worthy of praise, it is not done by our own power, but forasmuch as God doth work in us; and especially touching the edifying of the Church. Again, it appeareth how far off the elders were from envy, when they glorify God for the joyful success. But because mention is made of no other apostle besides James, we may conjecture that they

---

[1] " Experti sumus," experienced
[2] " Obliquos sermones," indirect speeches, insinuations.
[3] " Interius consilium," more private counsel.

were gone into divers places to spread abroad and preach the gospel as their calling did require; for the Lord had not appointed them to stay still at Jerusalem; but after they had made a beginning there, he commanded them to go into Judea and other parts of the world. Moreover, the error of those men, who think that James was one of the disciples whom Paul numbereth among the three pillars of the Church, is refuted before in the fifteenth chapter. And though the same commandment was given to him which was given to the rest of his fellows in office; yet I do not doubt but that they did so divide themselves, that James stood still at Jerusalem, whither many strangers were wont daily to resort. For that was all one as if he had preached the gospel far and wide in strange [1] places.

Thou seest, brother, how many thousands. This oration or speech hath two members. For, first, the elders say, that so many of the Jews as were converted, seeing they be earnest followers of the law, are evil affected towards Paul, because they think that he endeavoureth, with might and main, to abolish the law. Secondly, they exhort him that making a solemn vow he purge himself, that he may not be had in suspicion any longer. They object to Paul, the multitude of believers, that he may the more willingly yield to them. For if they had been a few stubborn fellows, he would not have been so much moved. But now he may not neglect both much people, and the whole body of the Church.

Undoubtedly, that zeal of the law, which was in them, was corrupt, and assuredly even the very elders declare sufficiently that they like it not. For though they do not condemn it openly, neither sharply complain of the same, yet because they separate themselves from their affection, they secretly confess that they err. If it had been a zeal according to knowledge, it ought to have begun at them [selves;] but they contend not for the law itself, neither do they pretend the due reverence thereof, neither do they

---

[1] "Remotis," remote.

subscribe to those who are earnest followers of it. Therefore, they both signify that they are of another mind, and also that they do not allow [approve] the superstition of the people.

Notwithstanding it is objected, that they say that Paul was burdened with a false report or slander; again, when they require at his hands satisfaction, they seem to nourish that zeal. I answer, that though that were a true report, in some respect, wherewith the Jews were offended, yet was it mixed with a slander. Paul did so teach the abrogating of the law, that notwithstanding by this means the authority thereof did not only continue sound and perfect, but it was more holy. For as we said, in the seventh chapter, the ceremonies should be vain, unless the effect thereof had been showed in Christ. Therefore, those who say that they were abolished by the coming of Christ, are so far from being blasphemous against the law, that they rather confirm the truth thereof. We must consider two things in ceremonies; the truth, whereto is annexed the efficacy; secondly, the external use. Furthermore, the abrogating of the external use, which Christ brought, dependeth hereupon, in that he is the sound body,[1] and that nothing was shadowed in times past which is not fulfilled in him. This differeth much from the falling away from the law, to show the true [2] end thereof, that the figures may have an end, and that the spiritual truth thereof may always be in force. Wherefore we see that they were malicious and unjust interpreters, who laid apostacy to Paul's charge, though he did call away the faithful from the external worship of the law. And whereas they command Paul to make a vow to that end, that he may prove himself to be a keeper of the law, it tendeth to no other end, saving that he may testify that he doth not detest the law like a wicked apostate, who did himself shake off the Lord's yoke, and move others unto the like rebellion.

---

[1] "Ipse est solidum corpus," he himself is the entire body.
[2] "Legitimum," legitimate.

That they ought not to circumcise. It was so indeed; for Paul taught that both Jews and Gentiles were set at liberty. For these sentences are general with him. Circumcision is nothing, (1 Cor. vii. 19.) Again, We be circumcised by baptism in Christ, not with circumcision made with hands; again, Let no man judge you in meat or drink, or in the choice of feasts, which are shadows of things to come; but the body is in Christ, (Col. ii. 11, 16.) Again, Whatsoever cometh into the shambles, and whatsoever is set before you, that eat, asking no question for conscience sake, (1 Cor. x. 25.) Again, Be not inwrapped again in the yoke of bondage, (Gal. v. 1.) Seeing that he spake thus everywhere without exception, he freed the Jews from the necessity of keeping the law.

And lest I stand too long upon this, one place shall be sufficient, where he compareth the law to a tutor, under which the old Church was, as in the childhood thereof; but now knowing the grace of Christ, it is grown up, that it may be free from ceremonies. In that place he speaketh undoubtedly both of the Jews and Gentiles. Also, when he saith that the hand-writing of the law, which did consist in decrees, (Col. ii. 14,) is blotted out and nailed to the cross by Christ, he setteth free the Jews, as well as the Gentiles, from the ceremonies, which he calleth in that place decrees. But seeing that he did not precisely reject ceremonies, in teaching that the coming of Christ did make an end of the observing thereof, that was no revolting, as the envious Jews thought it to be.

Neither were the elders ignorant of Paul's liberty. Therefore, seeing they understand the matter very well, their meaning is, to have this alone made known to the rude and unskilful, that Paul meant nothing less than to persuade the Jews to contemn the law. Therefore, they behold not the bare matter, but knowing what the common sort thought of Paul, by reason of the reports[1] which went about concerning him, they seek to cure the

---

[1] "Malignis rumoribus," malignant reports.

same. Though I wot not whether this were more importunate than equal, [just,] which they required at Paul's hands. And by this it appeareth how preposterous the cruelty [credulity] of men is in receiving false reports, and how fast a false opinion, once rashly received, doth stick. It is certain that James and his fellows in office did endeavour to maintain and defend Paul's good report, and to put away those lies which did hurt his estimation; yet let them do what they can, they will speak evil of Paul. Unless, peradventure, they were too slack in the beginning, that they might gratify their countrymen, so that they were not their own men [free] afterward.

22. *The multitude must needs come together.* The verb is a verb neuter, as if they should say, the multitude must of necessity come together. For it had been an absurd thing that an apostle, of such rare report, should not come before the whole multitude of the faithful. For if he had eschewed the light and sight of people, the sinister suspicion might have been increased. Nevertheless, we see how modestly the elders behaved themselves in nourishing concord, when as they prevent the offence of the people in time, saving that they bear too much[1] peradventure with their infirmity, in requiring a vow of Paul. But this moderation must be kept in the Church, that the pastors be in great authority, and yet that they rule not proudly as lords, neither despise the rest of the body. For the distinction of orders, which is the bond of peace, ought not to be any cause of dissension.

23. *Do that which we say to thee.* The elders seem (as I said even now) to be fallen unto a foolish pampering [indulgence] through too much love of their nation. But the manifest judgment of that thing[2] dependeth upon the circumstances which are hid from us at this day: yet they

---

[1] " Nimis indulgent," are too indulgent to judicium," a clear judgment on the case.

[2] " Liquidum ejus rei

knew them well. The whole body almost did consist upon [of] Jews, so that they needed not to fear the offending of the Gentiles. For in other regions this was the cause of departure,[1] because every man was wedded to his own custom, and would prescribe a law to others. Furthermore, they had at Jerusalem many things which might provoke them to keep the ceremonies of the law, so that they had a greater excuse if they did more slowly forsake them. And though their zeal were not void of fault, yet as it was an hard matter to reform it, so it could not be done at a sudden. We see how this superstition was scarce in long time pulled from the apostles; and because new disciples came daily unto the faith, the infirmity was nourished in all together. And yet, notwithstanding, we must not deny but that ignorance was coupled with obstinacy, which the elders did nevertheless tolerate, lest they should do more hurt by using violent remedies. I leave it indifferent whether they did pass measure or no.[2]

Having a vow upon them. Though these four be reckoned among the faithful, yet their vow was superstitious. Whereby it appeareth that the apostles had much trouble in that nation, which was not only hardened in the worship of the law through long use, but was also naturally malapert, and almost intractable. Though it may be that these men were as yet but novices, and therefore their faith was yet but slender, and scarce well framed; wherefore the doctors did suffer them to perform the vow which they had unadvisedly made. As touching Paul, because he made this vow not moved thereunto by his own conscience, but for their sakes, with whose error he did bear, the case stood otherwise with him. Notwithstanding, we must see whether this were one of the indifferent ceremonies, which the faithful might omit or keep at their pleasure. It seemeth, indeed, to have in it certain things which did not agree[3] with the profession of

---

[1] "Discessionis," schism or dissension
[2] "An votum excesserint in medio relinquo," whether or not they went farther than they wished, I do not take it upon me to determine
[3] "Parum consentanea," which ill accorded

faith. But because the end thereof was thanksgiving, (as we said before in the eighteenth chapter,) and there was nothing in the rite itself repugnant to the faith of Christ, Paul did not doubt to descend thus far to make his religion known. Therefore, Paul did that which he saith of himself elsewhere, because he made himself a companion of those which followed the law, as if he himself were in subjection to the law, (1 Cor. ix. 20.) Finally, he was made all things to all men, that he might win all; to wit, even unto the altars, so that he might pollute himself with no sacrilege under a colour of love.[1] It had not been so lawful for him to go unto the solemn sacrifice of satisfaction.[2] But as for this part of the worship of God, which consisted in a vow, he might do it indifferently, so it were not done for religion's sake, but only to support the weak. But it was neither his intent to worship God with this rite, neither was his conscience tied, but he did freely submit himself to his weak brethren.

24. *Which they have heard of thee are nothing.* They seem to persuade Paul to dissemble. For the rumour rose not upon nothing, that he did call away the Jews from the ceremonies, and that he did not walk in observing the law. But we must remember that which I said even now, that it was sufficient for Paul and the elders, if they could remove the slander which was unjustly raised, to wit, that he was a revolt [apostate] from the law, and there might a better opportunity be offered shortly, that in purging himself he might call them back by little and little from their error. Neither was it good or profitable that Paul should be counted an observer of the law any long time, as the disciples were then commonly; for by this means a thick[3] veil should have been put before their eyes to darken the light of Christ.

Wherefore, let us know that Paul did not dissemble, but

---

[1] "Sub prætextu charitatis," under a pretext of charity
[2] "Expiationis," expiation.
[3] "Crassius," a thicker.

sincerely professed that he did not hate the law, but that he did rather think reverently of it. They will him to bestow cost together with them, because they were wont to put their money together that they might offer sacrifice together.

25. *And as concerning those which have believed.* They add this lest they be thought to go about to take away or call back that liberty which they had granted to the Gentiles, so that they may be burdened with some prejudice. But, in the mean season, they seem to keep the Jews in bondage, from which they set free the Gentiles alone in plain words. I answer, forasmuch as the estate of all was alike, like liberty was granted to both. But there is mention made of the Jews, who were so addicted to their observations and ceremonies, that they would not take to themselves that liberty which they might well challenge. But the apostles did by name provide for the Gentiles, lest the Jews, after their wonted custom, should reject them as profane and unclean, because they were neither circumcised, neither nousled up [educated] in the worship of the law. Moreover, lest I load the paper with a superfluous repetition, let the readers repair unto the fifteenth chapter, (Acts xv. 20,) where they shall find those things which appertain unto the exposition of this decree.

26. *Then when Paul had taken the men, on the morrow, being purified with them, he entered into the temple, declaring the fulfilling of the days of purification until an offering might be offered for every one of them.*
27. *And when the seven days were now almost ended, certain Jews of Asia, when they saw him in the temple, moved the people, and laid hands on him,*
28. *Crying, Men of Israel, help: This is that man, which teacheth all men everywhere against the people, and the law, and this place. Moreover, he hath also brought Grecians into the temple, and hath defiled this holy place.*
29. *For they had seen Trophimus an Ephesian in the city with him, whom they thought Paul had brought into the temple.*

30. *And all the whole city was moved, and the people ran together: and when they had caught Paul, they drew him out of the temple: and by and by the doors were shut.*

26. Whereas some accuse Paul of subtilty,[1] as if he did play the hypocrite, I have before refuted this. Yet I do not deny but that he granted to do thus much at the request of the brethren, being thereunto in a manner enforced. Therefore, it hath more colour, and is (as they say) more disputable, that he was too easily entreated, and too ready to obey; and yet I do not admit that which some men say, that it went not well with Paul, because, taking upon him a new and unwonted person, he did not so constantly, as he was wont, maintain the liberty purchased by Christ. I confess, indeed, that God doth oftentimes punish foolish purposes with unhappy success; but I see not why this should be applied to Paul, who through voluntary subjection sought to win the favour of the rude, and such as were not thoroughly instructed, that he might do them good; being about to do that not willingly, but because he had rather yield to the brethren than stick to his own judgment. Furthermore, when he was once admitted, he might fitly have passed over to moderate that zeal. His courtesy doth rather deserve great praise, in that he doth not only gently abase himself for the unskilful people's sake, but doth also obey[2] their foolishness who did unworthily, and against reason, suspect him. He might well have reproved[3] them, because they had been so ready to believe reports contrary to his estimation, [reputation.] In that he abstaineth, he showeth great patience; in that he winneth their favour so carefully, it is singular modesty.

Moreover, he might have been more rough and round with[4] James and his fellows in office, because they had not been more diligent to root out errors from among the people. For though it be certain that they taught faithfully, yet it

---

[1] "Astutiæ," craftiness postulasset," expostulated with.
[2] "Morem gerit," defer to
[3] "Ex-
[4] "Durior," more severe on.

may be that the sight of the temple, and the very seat of the law, did hinder them in defending the use of liberty. But Paul, whether he went from his right of his own accord, or whether he think that they see better what is expedient than he, doth follow[1] their counsel. And whereas false Nicodemites, following this example of Paul, go about to colour their treacherous dissimulation, whilst they pollute themselves with all filthiness of Popery, it needeth no long refutation. They boast that they do this to win the weak brethren, (or that they follow their vein thus far,) as if Paul did yield to them in all things without choice. If, being Jews, they should take upon them according to the prescript of the law, to fulfil among the Jews a vow infected with no idolatry, then might they prove themselves to be like Paul. Now, forasmuch as they inwrap themselves in gross and altogether wicked superstitions, and that because they will escape the cross, what likelihood is that which they imagine?[2]

27. *The Jews which came from Asia.* It is certain that these men were enemies to the name of Christ and of Christians, so that whilst Paul is bent to pacify the faithful, he incurreth the rage of the enemies. Those of Asia are, indeed, the raisers of the tumult; but the minds of all the people were so corrupt with the hatred of him that they all became partners in the fury. But this place teacheth, that we must not take it impatiently if at any time our hope be frustrate, and our counsels, which we have taken with a right and holy affection, fall not out well, that our actions may have an happy end. We must attempt nothing but with a good conscience, and according to the Spirit of God. But and if things come not to pass as we would, even then, let that inward feeling uphold us, that we know that God alloweth [approveth] our desire, though it be laid open to the reproaches and mocks of men; neither

---

[1] "Acquiescit," acquiesces in
[2] "Qualis ista est quam fingunt similitudo," what resemblance is there in it to that which they feign.

let it repent us of our gentleness, if at any time the wicked reward us otherwise than we deserve.

28. *Men of Israel, help.* They cry out as if they were in extreme danger, and they call upon all men to help them, as if all religion were in hazard. Whereby we see with what furious hatred they were inflamed against Paul, only because in showing that the full and perfect truth is found in Christ, he taught that the figures of the law had an end. Now, whereas they conceive a false opinion, having seen Trophimus, they do more betray by this headlong lightness how venomous they be. They accuse Paul of sacrilege. Why? because he brought into the temple a man which was uncircumcised. But they laid a most cruel[1] crime to the charge of an innocent through a false opinion. Thus the boldness of those men useth commonly to be preposterous who are carried away with an opinion conceived before. But let us learn by such examples to beware of the distemperature of affections, and not to let light prejudices have the rein, lest we run headlong upon the innocent, being carried with blind force.

30. *And the city was moved.* We see in this place the vanity of the common people, which count Paul a condemned man before ever they hear him. Whereas the city is moved about godliness,[2] it is no marvel; but this is a point of perverse zeal and mad rashness, in that they set themselves against Paul before they know his matter. For in this corruption of nature frowardness is joined with foolishness, so that those will readily, of their own accord, make haste to maintain an evil cause who can hardly be moved with many exhortations to do well. This is a hard case, that the whole world should be armed against us at a sudden, through the persuasion of a few; but seeing it pleaseth the Lord it should be so, let every one of us prepare him-

---

[1] "Atrocissimum," most atrocious. [2] 'Quod tumultuatur civitas in negotio pietatis," that the city is in a tumult in a matter relating to godliness.

CHAP. XXI.   ACTS OF THE APOSTLES.   287

self by this, and such like examples, to suffer all manner [of] assaults, and to bear and abide all brunts.

31. *And as they sought to kill him, it was told the captain of the band, that all Jerusalem was in an uproar.*
32. *Who took with him straightway soldiers and under captains, and ran down unto them : but they, when they saw the chief captain and the soldiers, left smiting of Paul.*
33. *Then the chief captain drew near, and took him, and commanded him to be bound with two chains, and he asked what he was, and what he had done.*
34. *And some cried one thing, and some another, among the people : and when he could not know the truth, by reason of the tumult, he commanded him to be carried into the camp.*
35. *And when he came to the stairs, it happened that he was carried of* [by] *the soldiers, because of the violence of the multitude.*
36. *For the multitude of people followed, crying, Away with him*
37. *And when Paul began to be carried into the camp, he saith to the captain, May I speak to thee ? Who said, Canst thou speak Greek ?*
38. *Art not thou that Egyptian, which before these days madest an uproar, and leddest into the wilderness four thousand men which were murderers ?*
39. *And Paul said, I verily am a man which am a Jew, born in Tarsus, a citizen of no vile city of Cilicia : but I beseech thee suffer me to speak to the people.*
40. *And when he had given him leave, Paul, standing upon the stairs, beckoned with the hand unto the people. And when there was made great silence, he spake in the Hebrew tongue, saying.*

31. *As they sought to kill him.* Assuredly the force of Satan appeareth therein, in that he driveth the people headlong into such rage, that when they have shut the doors of the temple, being not content with mean punishment, they conspire to put Paul to death. We must thus think with ourselves that Satan doth prick forward the enemies of

godliness, lest their rage, how cruel and troublesome soever it be, trouble us. On the other side appeareth the wonderful goodness of God, when as he raiseth up the chief captain at a sudden, that he may deliver Paul from death. He himself thought upon no such thing, but he came to appease the tumult which was raised among the people; but the Lord showeth a more evident token of his providence, because Paul's life was delivered from such present danger without man's counsel. Thus doth he suffer the faithful not only to labour, but to be almost oppressed, that he may deliver them from death more wonderfully. Luke calleth him the chief captain [tribune] of the band[1] improperly, seeing every chief captain was set over a thousand, which doth also appear by the text, where he saith that the chief captain took with him under captains.[2]

32. *And when they saw the chief captain.* Those whose fury neither the majesty of God, nor yet the reverence of the temple, could once stay, begin to relent when they see a profane man. Whereby it appeareth that they were set on fire rather with barbarous cruelty than zeal. Now, whereas the chief captain bindeth Paul with chains, he declareth thereby sufficiently that he came not to ease him. The unbelievers would attribute this to fortune; but the Spirit hath depainted out unto us the providence of God as in a table [picture] reigning amidst the confused uproars of men. And though this be very hard that this holy minister of God is so shamefully handled, yet the equity of the chief captain is to be commended if he be compared with the Jews. He bindeth him with chains, as if he were some evil-doer, or some wicked person; yet doth he vouchsafe to hear him when he is bound, whom they did beat unmercifully; neither doth he determine to handle him hardly before he knew his cause. Yea, this was the best way to mitigate their cruelty, because they thought [hoped] that Paul should be punished immediately.

---

[1] "Tribunum cohortis," tribune of the cohort   [2] "Centuriones .. a tribuno assumptos," that the tribune took with him centurions.

34. *Some cried one thing, and some another.* The madness of the raging people doth betray itself on every side. They make horrible outcries, whereof one is contrary to another. Nevertheless, they desire with one consent to have him put to death who was convicted of no offence. In the mean season, we need not doubt but that they were blinded with a colour of holy zeal. But the truth of the cause well known maketh men truly zealous, as it maketh them true martyrs of God, but rage betrayeth devilish madness. Whereas mention is made in this place of the camp or fortress, we must know that the soldiers, which were placed to guard the city, had a place which was trenched and fortified on every side, which they might defend as if it were a castle, and from which they might beat back all assaults, if any sedition were raised. For it had not been good for them to have been dispersed here and there in divers inns,[1] seeing the people were treacherous, and the city troublesome. And we gather by this that the place was high, because Luke saith, that when they came to the steps, Paul was carried of [by] the soldiers. And whether the soldiers did lift Paul up on high that they might bring him safe to the station or camp, or he was thus tossed with the violence of the crowd, this was no duty [office] of favour. But the greater the cruelty of those which followed him was, God did more plainly declare that he was favourable to his servant in sparing his life, lest if he should have been murdered in the tumult, his death should have wanted due fruit.

37. *May I speak unto thee?* Paul offered himself to defend his cause, which all the servants of God must do. For we must do our endeavour to make our integrity known to all men, lest through our infamy the name of God be blasphemed. But when the chief captain demandeth whether Paul be not that Egyptian which was a murderer, which a little before had led away a company of men,[2] let us learn

---

[1] "Neque enim.... tutum fuisset in varia hospitia passim distribui," for it had not been safe for them to have been quartered up and down in various places.   [2] "Hominum turbam ad defectionem impulerat," had induced a body of men to revolt.

that how modestly and quietly soever the ministers of Christ behave themselves, and howsoever they be void of all fault, yet cannot they escape the reproaches and slanders of the world. Which thing we must note for this cause, that we may acquaint ourselves with rebukes;[1] and that in well-doing we may be prepared to be evil-spoken of. When he asketh him concerning the Egyptian, he meaneth not Theudas the sorcerer, as some men falsely suppose; of whom Gamaliel made mention before in the fifth chapter, (Acts v. 36,) and of whom Josephus speaketh more in his twentieth of Antiquities. For, besides that we read there that Theudas carried away only four hundred men, and the chief captain reckoneth up in this place four thousand, and saith that they were all murderers, that is more, in that Theudas raised that faction during the reign of Tiberius or Augustus Cæsar; whereof remained only an obscure report, because, so soon as a troop of horsemen was sent after them, they were forthwith destroyed.

Notwithstanding, it seemeth to me that Josephus is deceived in that where he saith, first, that Cuspius Fadus was sent by Claudius, and then he addeth, that Theudas was of him overcome, seeing I have before showed that that former insurrection was made at such time as Claudius was but a private man. Though he disagree much with Luke's narration, even in the number, seeing he saith that there were about thirty thousand made partners in the sedition, unless happily we expound it thus, that, after he was put to flight by Felix, he fled into the wilderness with four thousand. And it had been an absurd thing that the number should be made ten times greater, as also, that a troop, having no skill in war, or being altogether without courage, should have been defamed with the name of murderers. For as Josephus doth witness, that seducer had deceived the simple and credulous common people with false promises, boasting that he was a prophet of God, which would lead the people dry foot through the midst of Jordan.

[1] " Ut ad contumelias assuescamus," that we may accustom ourselves to contumely.

But the same Josephus putteth the matter out of doubt when he saith, that an Egyptian, a prophet, did gather together a band of men under Felix the president, and did carry them into Mount Olivet, whereof four hundred were slain, two hundred taken, and the residue dispersed. The history was fresh in memory. Again, forasmuch as the author of the sedition was escaped, and the region filled with murderers,[1] it is not without cause that the chief captain demandeth of Paul, when he seeth all men so hate him, whether he were that Egyptian. Luke recordeth no longer conference had between the chief captain and Paul; yet it is likely, forasmuch as both of them understood the Greek tongue, that they had farther talk. Whereby it came to pass, that so soon as Paul had well purged himself, he had licence granted him to speak to the people. For the chief captain would never have suffered a wicked man to make any public speech in a city which was so sore suspected.

CHAPTER XXII.

1. *Men, brethren, and fathers, hear mine excuse which I make now before you.*
2. *And when they heard that he spake to them in the Hebrew tongue, they kept the more silence : And he said,*
3. *I truly am a man, a Jew, born in Tarsus, a city of Cilicia, and brought up in this city at the feet of Gamaliel, and taught according to the perfect manner of the law of the fathers, and was zealous toward God, as ye all are this day*
4. *And I persecuted this way unto death, binding and delivering into prison both men and women.*
5. *As the chief priest doth bear me witness, and all the order of elders, of whom also I received letters unto the brethren,*

---

[1] " Latronibus infesta," infested with robbers.

and went to Damascus, to bring them which were there bound to Jerusalem, that they might be punished.

Though we may guess by the beginning of this speech what was Paul's drift, yet because he was interrupted, we know not certainly what he was about to say. The sum of that part which is refitted is this, that forasmuch as he was well and faithfully instructed in the doctrine of the law, he was a godly and religious worshipper of God in the sight of the world. Secondly, that he was an enemy to the gospel of Christ, so that he was counted among the priests one of the principal maintainers and defenders of the law. Thirdly, that he did not change his sect unadvisedly; but that being tamed and convict by an oracle from heaven, he gave his name to Christ. Fourthly, that he did not embrace unknown things, but that God appointed him a faithful teacher, of whom he learned all things perfectly. Lastly, that when he was returned to Jerusalem, and sought to do good to his countrymen, God did not permit him. So that he brought not the doctrine of salvation unto foreign nations without good consideration, or because he hated his own nation, but being commanded by God so to do.

1. *Men, brethren, and fathers.* It is a wonder that he giveth so great honour yet to the desperate enemies of the gospel, for they had broken all bond of brotherly fellowship, and by oppressing the glory of God, had spoiled themselves of all titles of dignity. But because Paul speaketh in this place as some one of the people, he speaketh so lovingly unto the body itself, and useth towards the heads words honourable without dissembling. And surely because their casting off was not made known as yet, though they were unworthy of any honour, yet it was meet that Paul should reverently acknowledge in them the grace of God's adoption. Therefore, in that he calleth them brethren and fathers, he doth not so much regard what they have deserved, as into what degree of honour God had exalted them. And all his oration is so framed that he goeth about to satisfy them,

freely indeed, and without flattering, yet humbly and meekly. Therefore, let us learn so to reverence and honour men that we impair not God's right. For which cause the pope's pride is the more detestable, who, seeing he hath made himself an high priest without the commandment of God and the consent of the Church, doth not only challenge to himself all titles of honour, but also such tyranny, that he goeth about to bring Christ in subjection; as if when God doth exalt men he did resign up his right and authority to them, and did stoop down to them.

2. *That he spake Hebrew.* This is indeed an usual thing, that when men which speak divers languages are together, we hear those more willingly who speak our own language; but the Jews were moved with another peculiar cause, because they imagined that Paul was offended[1] with his own kindred, so that he did even hate their tongue, or that he was some rogue which had not so much as learned the speech of that nation whereof he said he came. Now, so soon as they heard their own language, they began to have some better hope. Furthermore, it is uncertain whether Paul spake in the Hebrew or in the Syrian tongue; for we know that the speech of the Jews was corrupt and degenerate after their exile, forasmuch as they had much from the Chaldeans and Syrians. For mine own part, I think, that because he spake as well to the common sort as unto the elders, he used the common speech which was at that day usual.

3. *I am a Jew.* As all things were out of order at that day among the Jews, many rogues and vagabonds, to the end they might have some shroud for their wickedness, did falsely boast that they were Jews. Therefore, to the end Paul may acquit himself of this suspicion, he beginneth at his birth; that done, he declareth that he was known in Jerusalem, because he was brought up there of [from] a child;

---

[1] " Ex professo infensum," professedly hostile to.

though this latter thing seemeth to be spoken not only for certainty's sake, but because it skilled much that this should also be known how well he had been instructed.

There is nothing more bold to cause trouble than unlearned men. And at that day the government of the Church was so decayed, that religion was not only subject to sects, but also miserably mangled and torn in pieces. Therefore, Paul nameth his master, lest any man may think that he had not been nousled up in learning,[1] and therefore had he forsaken the worship of the fathers; as many men, who are not trained up in learning, forget their nature and grow out of kind.[2] But Paul saith chiefly that he was well taught in the law, that the Jews may understand that it was not through ignorance (as it falleth out oftentimes) that he causeth such ado, and doth counterfeit their monsters.

It is to be doubted whether this be that Gamaliel of whom mention is made before, (Acts v. 34.) Scholars are said to sit at their masters' feet, because forasmuch as they be not as yet of strong and sound judgment, they must bring such modesty and aptness to be taught, that they must make all their senses subject to their masters, and must depend upon their mouth. So Mary is said to sit at Jesus' feet (Luke x. 39) when she giveth ear to his doctrine. But and if such reverence be due to earthly masters, how much more ought we to prostrate ourselves before the feet of Christ, that we may give ear to him when he teacheth us out of his heavenly throne? This speech doth also put boys and young men in remembrance of their duty, that they be not stout nor stubborn, or that they be not puffed nor lifted up against their masters through some foolish confidence, but that they suffer themselves quietly and gently to be framed by them.

Taught in the law of the fathers. The old interpreter doth translate it word for word, taught *according to the truth of the fathers' law*, saving that ἀκρίβεια is rather a *perfect way*[3] than *truth*. Notwithstanding the question is, What he

---

[1] "Nulla disciplina imbutum," not imbued with any discipline.
[2] "Fiunt degeneres," become degenerate.   [3] "Exacta ratio," an exact method.

meaneth by this perfect way, seeing all of them had one and the same form of the law? He seemeth to me to distinguish that purer form of knowledge wherein he had been trained up from the common instruction, which did more disagree with the true and natural meaning of the law. And although the law of the Lord was then corrupt by many additions, even among the best doctors, yet because religion was altogether there corrupt among many, Paul doth for good causes boast, that he was both well and also diligently instructed in the law of the fathers; or (which is all one) exactly or perfectly, lest any man should think that he had gotten only some small smattering, as if he were one of the common sort.

But because many who are well taught are, notwithstanding, full stuffed with Epicurish contempt of God, he declareth that he was zealous toward God; as if he should say, that the serious study of godliness was annexed to doctrine, so that he meant not to dally in holy things, as profane men do of set purpose confound all things.

But because this his zeal was altogether rash, he maketh himself like to the other Jews for that time. Notwithstanding, this may be taken in good part, that he did long ago no less worship God from his heart than they did then.

4. *I persecuted this way.* This is the second point, that he was an enemy to Christ's doctrine, and that he was more fervent in resisting the same than all the rest, until he was pulled back by the hand of God; which thing he saith the chief priests and elders can testify. Therefore, there can be no suspicion in such a sudden change. Whereas he saith, that he had letters given him to deliver to the brethren, it must be referred unto the Jews, as if he had called them his countrymen; but he meant to appease them with a more honourable title. For this is Paul's drift, that he may declare his natural and lawful beginning which he took of that nation;[1] and also how desirous he was to be linked with them in friendship.

---

[1] " Ab illa genta . . . originem," origin from that nation

6. *And it happened that as I journeyed and drew near to Damascus about noon, that suddenly a great light shone round about me from heaven.*
7. *And I fell to the ground, and heard a voice saying to me, Saul, Saul, why persecutest thou me?*
8. *And I answered, Who art thou, Lord? And he said to me, I am Jesus of Nazareth, whom thou persecutest.*
9. *And they which were with me saw indeed the light, and were afraid: but they heard not the voice of him which talked with me.*
10. *Then I said, What shall I do, Lord? And the Lord said to me, Arise, and go to Damascus; and there it shall be told thee what things be ordained for thee to do.*
11. *And when I saw not by reason of the glory of the light, being led by the hand by those companions which were with me, I came to Damascus.*

6. *And it happened.* Because this history was expounded more at large in the ninth chapter, I will only briefly touch those things which were there spoken. But this is peculiar to this present place, that Paul reckoneth up his circumstances, that by them he may prove that he was converted by God. And this is the third member of the sermon; otherwise this change should have been thought to have proceeded of inconstancy, or rashness, or else it should not have been void of some infamy. For nothing is more intolerable than to start aside from the course of godliness which men have once entered; and also not to do that which they are commanded to do. Therefore, lest any man might suspect Paul's conversion, he proveth by many miracles which he bringeth to light, that God was the author thereof. In the night-season there appear oftentimes lightnings, which come of the hot exhalations of the earth; but this was more strange, that about noon a sudden light did not only appear, but did also compass him about like a lightning, so that through fear thereof he fell from his horse, and lay prostrate upon the ground. Another miracle, in that he heard a voice from heaven; another, in that his companions heard it not as well as he. Also, there follow other things, that, after that he was sent to Damascus, the event is cor-

respondent to the oracle; because Ananias cometh to meet him. Also, in that his sight is restored to him in a moment.

I fell to the earth. As Paul was puffed up with Pharisaical pride, it was meet that he should be afflicted and thrown down, that he might hear Christ's voice. He would not have despised God openly, neither durst he refuse the heavenly oracle; yet his mind should never have been framed unto the obedience of faith, if he had continued in his former state; therefore, he is thrown down by violence, that he may learn to humble himself willingly. Furthermore, there is in Christ's words only a brief reprehension, which serveth to appease the rage of Paul being so cruelly bent. Nevertheless, we have thence an excellent consolation, in that Christ taking upon him the person of all the godly, doth complain that whatsoever injury was done to them was done to him. And as there can no sweeter thing be imagined to lenify the bitterness of persecution, than when we hear that the Son of God doth suffer not only with us, but also in us, so again, the bloody enemies of the gospel, who being now besotted with pride, do mock the miserable Church, shall perceive whom they have wounded.

9. *They which were with me.* I showed in the other place, that there is no such disagreement in the words of Luke as there seemeth to be. Luke said there, that though Paul's companions stood amazed, yet heard they a voice.[1] But in this place he saith, they heard not the voice of him which spake to Paul though they saw the light. Surely it is no absurd thing to say that they heard some obscure voice; yet so that they did not discern it as Paul himself, whom alone Christ meant to stay and tame with the reprehension. Therefore, they hear a voice, because a sound doth enter into their ears, so that they know that some speaketh from heaven; they hear not the voice of him that spake to Paul, because they understand not what Christ saith. Moreover,

---

[1] "Vocem audisse, neminem vidisse," heard a voice, and saw no one.

they see Paul compassed about with the light, but they see none which speaketh from heaven.

10. *What shall I do, Lord?* This is the voice of a tamed man, and this is the true turning unto the Lord; when laying away all fierceness and fury, we bow down our necks willingly to bear his yoke, and are ready to do whatsoever he commandeth us. Moreover, this is the beginning of well-doing, to ask the mouth of God; for their labour is lost who think upon repentance without his word. Furthermore, in that Christ appointeth Ananias to be Paul's master, he doth it not for any reproach, or because he refuseth to teach him; but by this means he meaneth to set forth, and also to beautify the outward ministry of the Church.

And even in the person of one man, he teacheth us[1] that we must not grudge to hear him speak with the tongue of men. To the same end tendeth that which followeth immediately, that he was blind, until offering himself to become a scholar, he had declared[2] the humility of his faith. God doth not indeed make blind all those whom he will lighten; but there is a general rule prescribed to all men, that those become foolish with themselves who will be wise to him.

12. *And one Ananias, a godly man according to the law, approved by the testimony of all the Jews which dwelt there,*
13. *Coming unto me, and standing by me, said to me, Brother Saul, receive thy sight. And I receiving my sight, the same hour saw him.*
14. *But he said to me, The God of our fathers hath prepared thee that thou mightest know his will, and see the Just, and hear a voice from his mouth.*
15. *Because thou shalt be his witness before all men of those things which thou hast seen and heard.*
16. *And now why stayest thou? Arise, and be baptized, and wash away thy sins, in calling upon the name of the Lord.*

---

[1] "Commune documentum nobis præbuit," he hath given us a common proof. [2] "Probasset," he had proved

12. *One Ananias.* Paul proceedeth now unto the fourth point, to wit, that he did not only give his name to Christ, being astonished with miracles, but that he was also well and thoroughly instructed in the doctrine of the gospel. I have already said that Ananias met Paul, not by chance, but through the direction of Christ. And whereas he giveth him the title of godliness as concerning the law, and saith that he was well reported of by the whole nation, in these words he preventeth the wrong[1] opinion which they might conceive. As they loathed the Gentiles, so they would never have allowed any teacher coming from them; and one that had revolted from the law should have been most detestable. Therefore, he witnesseth that he worshipped God according to the law, and that his godliness was known and commended among all the Jews, so that they ought not to suspect him. These words, according to the law, are ignorantly, by some, coupled with the text following, that he was approved according to the law. For Ananias' religion is rather distinguished by this mark from the superstitions of the Gentiles. Though we must note, that the law is not mentioned to establish the merits of works, that they may be set against the grace of God; but Ananias' godliness is clearly acquitted of all evil suspicion which might have risen among the Jews. And seeing that he restoreth sight to Paul with one word, it appeareth thereby that he was sent of God, as I have said before.

14. *The God of our fathers.* As nothing is more fit to provoke us joyfully to go forward toward God, than when we know that God doth prevent us with his free goodness, that he may call us back from destruction to life; so Ananias beginneth here. God, saith he, hath ordained thee to know his will. For by this means Paul is taught that God had respect unto him at such time as he went astray, and was altogether an enemy to his own salvation; and so God's predestination doth abolish all preparations which sophisters

---

[1] "Sinistram," sinister

imagine, as if man did prevent God's grace by his own free will. In calling him the God of the fathers, he reneweth the remembrance of the promises, that the Jews may know that the new calling of Paul is joined with them, and that those fall not away from the law who pass over unto Christ. Therefore Paul confirmeth that by these words which he avouched before in his own person, that he had not made any departure from the God of Abraham, whom the Jews had in times past worshipped, but that he continueth in the ancient worship which the fathers did use, which he had learned out of the law.

Wherefore, when the question is about religion, let us learn by the example of Paul, not to imagine any new God, (as the Papists and Mahometans have done, and as all heretics use to do,) but let us retain that God who hath revealed himself in times past to the fathers, both by the law, and also by divers oracles. This is that antiquity wherein we must remain, and not in that whereof the Papists boast in vain, who have invented to themselves a strange God, seeing they have forsaken the lawful fathers.

The same is to be said at this day of the Jews, whose religion, seeing it disagreeth with the law and the prophets, their God must also be degenerate and feigned. For he who would in times past be called the God of Abraham and of the fathers, appeared at length in the person of his Son, that he may now be called by his own name,[1] or title, the Father of Christ. Therefore, he which rejecteth the Son hath not the Father, who cannot be separated from him. And Ananias saith, that it cometh to pass, through the free election of God, that the truth of the gospel doth now appear to Paul; whereupon it followeth, that he did not attain unto this by his own industry, which the experience of the thing did also declare. For nothing was more stubborn than Paul until Christ did tame him. And if we desire to know the cause and beginning, Ananias calleth us back unto the counsel of God, whereby he was appointed and ordained;

---

[1] "Proprio elogio," by the proper title.

and assuredly it is a more precious thing to know the will of God, than that men can attain unto it by their own industry.[1] That which Ananias affirmeth of Paul ought to be translated unto all, that the treasure of faith is not common to all;[2] but it is offered peculiarly to the elect. Furthermore, it appeareth more plainly by the next member what this will of God is. For God spake at sundry times and many ways by his prophets, but last of all, he revealed and made known his will and himself wholly in his Son, (Heb. i. 1.)

To see the Just. Seeing all the Greek books[3] in a manner agree together in the masculine gender, I wonder why Erasmus would rather translate it in the neuter, *Which is Just;* which sense the readers see to be cold and far fet, [fetched.] Therefore, I do not doubt but that *Just* is taken in this place for Christ; and the text runneth very finely[4] thus, because it followeth immediately after, *and hear a voice from his mouth.* And it is certain that all the godly and holy men did most of all desire that they might see Christ. Thence flowed that confession of Simeon, " Lord, now lettest thou thy servant depart in peace ; because mine eyes have seen thy salvation," (Luke ii. 29.) Therefore this seeing, which godly kings and prophets did most earnestly desire, as Christ himself doth witness, (Luke x. 24,) is not without cause extolled as a singular benefit of God. But because the sight of the eyes should profit little or nothing, which we know was to many deadly, he adjoineth the hearing of the voice. Ananias setteth down the cause why God did vouchsafe Paul of so great honour, to wit, that he might be to his Son a public witness ; and he doth so prepare him, that he may learn not only for himself alone,[5] but that he may have so much the more care to profit, because he shall be the teacher of all the whole Church.

---

[1] " Suo marte," by their own strength [2] " Non esse omnibus promiscue expositum," is not set before all promiscuously. [3] " Græci codices," the Greek manuscripts. [4] " Concinne," elegantly, appositely. [5] " Privatim," privately.

16. *And now, why tarriest thou?* It is not to be doubted but that Ananias did faithfully instruct Paul in the principles of godliness; for he would not have baptized him if he had been void of true faith. But Luke passeth over many things, and doth briefly gather the sum. Therefore, seeing Paul doth understand that the promised redemption is now given in Christ, Ananias saith, for good causes, that nothing ought to stay him from being baptized. But when he saith, Why tarriest thou? he doth not chide Paul, neither doth he accuse him of slackness, but he doth rather amplify the grace of God by adding baptism. The like sentence had we in the tenth chapter, (Acts x. 47,) " Can any man let [hinder] those from being baptized with water who have the Holy Ghost given them even as we?" But when he saith, Wash away thy sins, by this speech he expresseth the force and fruit of baptism, as if he had said, Wash away thy sins by baptism. But because it may seem that by this means more is attributed to the outward and corruptible element than is meet, the question is, whether baptism be the cause of our purging. Surely, forasmuch as the blood of Christ is the only means whereby our sins are washed away, and as it was once shed to this end, so the Holy Ghost, by the sprinkling thereof through faith, doth make us clean continually. This honour cannot be translated unto the sign of water, without doing open injury to Christ and the Holy Ghost; and experience doth teach how earnestly men be bent upon this superstition. Therefore, many godly men, lest they put confidence in the outward sign, do overmuch extenuate the force of baptism. But they must keep a measure, that the sacraments may be kept within their bounds, lest they darken the glory of Christ; and yet they may not want their force and use.

Wherefore, we must hold this, first, that it is God alone who washeth us from our sins by the blood of his Son; and to the end this washing may be effectual in us, he worketh by the hidden power of his Spirit. Therefore, when the question is concerning remission of sins, we must seek no other author thereof but the heavenly Father, we must imagine no other material cause but the blood of Christ; and when we be come to the formal cause, the Holy Ghost is the chief. But there is an inferior instrument, and that is the preaching of the word and baptism itself. But though God alone doth work by the inward power of his Spirit, yet that doth not hinder but that he may use, at his pleasure, such instruments and means as he knoweth to be convenient; not that he includeth in the element anything which he taketh either from his Spirit or from the blood of Christ, but because he will have the sign itself to be an help for our infirmity.

Therefore, forasmuch as baptism doth help our faith, that it may reap forgiveness of sins by the blood of Christ alone, it is called the washing of the soul. So that the washing, spoken of by Luke, doth not note out the cause; but is referred unto the understanding of Paul, who, having received the sign, knew better that his sins were done away.[1] Though we must also note this, that there is no bare figure set before us in baptism, but that the giving of the thing is thereto annexed; because God promised nothing deceitfully, but doth, indeed, fulfil that which under the signs he doth signify. Notwithstanding, we must again beware that we tie not the grace of God to the sacraments; for the external administration of baptism profiteth nothing, save only where it pleaseth God it shall. By this there is also another question answered which may be moved. For seeing Paul had the testimony of the grace of God, his sins were already forgiven him. Therefore, he was not washed only by baptism, but he received a new confirmation of the grace which he had gotten.

In calling upon the name of the Lord. It is out of question that he meaneth Christ, not because the name of Christ alone is called upon in baptism, but because the Father commandeth us to ask of him whatsoever is figured in baptism; neither doth the operation of the Spirit tend to any other end, saving that it may make us partakers of his

---

[1] "Expiata esse," were expiated

death and resurrection. Therefore, Christ is appointed to excel in baptism, yet inasmuch as he is given us of the Father, and inasmuch as he poureth out his graces upon us by the Holy Ghost. Whereby it cometh to pass that the calling upon the name of Christ containeth both the Father and the Son.

Wherefore, Ananias doth not mean, that the name of Christ must only be named, but he speaketh of prayer, whereby the faithful do testify, that the effect of the outward sign is in the power of Christ alone. For the sacraments have neither any power of salvation included in them, neither are they anything worth of themselves. Wherefore, this member is, as it were, a correction of the former saying, because Ananias doth, in plain words, send Paul from reposing confidence in the external sign unto Christ.

It is well known how much the Papists differ from this rule, who tie the cause of grace to their exorcisms and enchantments; and they are so far from studying to direct the miserable people unto Christ, that they rather drown Christ in baptism, and pollute his sacred name by their enchantments.

17. *And it came to pass, that, when I was returned to Jerusalem, and prayed in the temple, I was in a trance ;*
18. *And saw him say to me, Make haste, and get thee quickly out of Jerusalem : because they will not receive thy testimony concerning me.*
19. *Then I said, Lord, they know that I did cast into prison, and did beat in every synagogue those which did believe in thee :*
20. *And when the blood of thy witness, Stephen, was shed, I did also stand by and consented to his death, and kept the raiment of those which slew him.*
21. *And he said unto me, Go : because I will send thee far hence unto the Gentiles.*
22. *And they heard him unto this word, then they lifted up their voice, saying, Away with such a fellow from off the earth : for it is not meet that he should live.*

17. *And it came to pass.* This had not been the last conclusion,[1] if Paul had not been cut off [stopped short] with their outrageous outcries. Notwithstanding, his drift and purpose doth plainly appear by the former text, [context;] for he beginneth to intreat of his ministry, that he may show that he departed not from the Jews of his own accord, as if he withdrew him of malice from taking pains with them; but he was drawn unto the Gentiles contrary to his expectation and purpose. For he came purposely to Jerusalem, that he might impart with his own nation that grace which was committed to him. But when the Lord cutteth off his hope which he had to do good, he driveth him thence. But there was a double offence which Paul goeth about to cure. For they both thought that the covenant of God was profaned if the Gentiles should be admitted into the Church together with them, and nothing did grieve the proud nation so much as that others should be preferred before them, or so much as made equal with them. Therefore Paul's defence consisteth in this, that he was ready, so much as in him lay, to do them the best service he could; but he was afterward enforced by the commandment of God to go to the Gentiles, because he would not have him to be idle at Jerusalem. Whereas Erasmus translateth it, That I was carried without myself, is in Greek word for word, That I was in a trance; whereby he meant to purchase credit to the oracle. Also the circumstance of the time and place doth confirm the same, in that the Lord appeared to him as he prayed in the temple; which was an excellent preparation to hear the voice of God. Concerning the manner of seeing,[2] read that which we touched about the end of the seventh chapter.

18. *Because they will not.* Though the commandment of God alone ought to be sufficient enough to bind us to obey, yet to the end Paul might be the more willing to

---

[1] " Clausula," clause or sentence the manner of the vision

[2] " De modo visionis," as to

follow, Christ showeth him a reason why he will have him depart out of Jerusalem; to wit, because he should lose his labour there; but he was not chosen to that end that he might be idle, or do no good by teaching; though this were a sore trial, and such as we may think did sore shake him.[1] Not long before the function of preaching the gospel was enjoined him, that his voice might sound throughout the whole world; now even at the first entrance he is inhibited; yea, his labour seemeth to be condemned of peculiar reproach when his witness [testimony] is rejected, because his person is hated. But it was meet that the holy servant of the Lord should be thus humbled, that all the preachers of the gospel might learn to give over themselves wholly to obey Christ, that when they be excluded from one place, they may be ready immediately to go to another, and that they may not be discouraged, nor cease off from doing their duty, though they be undeservedly loathed.

19. *Lord, they know.* By this speech Paul doth testify that he was not beside himself, or brought into perplexity,[2] but that he did assuredly believe the oracle. For without doubt he knew Christ, whom he calleth Lord. And Paul objecteth, that it cannot almost be, but that when they see him so suddenly changed, such a spectacle will move them. Whence he gathereth that he shall not be unfruitful. He thought so indeed; but Christ answereth flatly, that he hath appointed him another charge, and he taketh from him the hope which he had in vain conceived touching the Jews. The question is, whether it were lawful for Paul to object these reasons to Christ; for it is as much as if he did avouch that that is probable, which Christ said could not be. I answer, that God giveth his saints leave, familiarly, to utter their affections before him;[3] especially when they seek no other thing but the confirmation of their faith.

---

[1] " Sancti hominis pectus," the holy man's bieast.   [2] ' Mente aliena-
tum vel perplexum," alienated or perplexed in mind   [3] " Ut familiariter in ejus sinum exonerent suos affectus," to unburden their feelings familiarly into his breast

If any man stand in his own conceit, or stubbornly refuse that which God commandeth, his arrogancy shall be worthily condemned ; but God vouchsafeth his faithful servants of a singular privilege, that they may modestly object those things which may call them back from the desire to obey; to the end that being free from lets, they may wholly addict themselves to serve God ; as Paul, after that he was taught that it pleased the Lord that it should be so, he doth not gainsay nor contend any longer, but being content with that one exception, and making an end there, he maketh himself ready to take his journey, which he seemed to be loath to take. In the mean season, whereas the Jews are not touched with so many miracles, their stubbornness and pride, which cannot be tamed, is discovered. Which upbraiding did undoubtedly cause them to rage.

22. *Away with such a fellow.* Luke showeth here how outrageously Paul's sermon was interrupted. For they do not only oppress him with their crying, but they desire to have him put to death; where it doth also plainly appear how frenzy [frenzied] pride is. The Jews conceived so great good liking of themselves, that they did not only despise all the whole world in comparison of themselves, but they stood also more stoutly in defence of their own dignity than of the law itself, as if all religion did consist in this, that Abraham's stock might excel all other mortal men. So now they rage against and rail upon Paul, because he said that he was sent to be the apostle of the Gentiles; as if God were bound by his own liberality to suffer the contempt of his power[1] in the wicked and unthankful, on whom he bestowed excellent graces above all other. And it is no marvel if there were such fierceness and fury at that day among the Jews, seeing that being by all means wasted,[2] and accustomed to suffer extreme reproaches at this day, they cease not, notwithstanding, to swell with servile pride. But these

---

[1] " Numinis sui," of his Deity. [2] ' Attriti," trampled upon.

be fruits of reprobation, until God gather together the remnant according to Paul's prophecy, (Rom. xi. 5.)

23. *And as they cried, and cast off their garments, and threw dust into the air,*
24. *The chief captain commanded him to be led into the camp; and he commanded that he should be scourged and examined, that he might know for what cause they cried so on him.*
25. *And when they had bound him with thongs, Paul said to the centurion that stood by, Is it lawful for you to scourge a man that is a Roman, and uncondemned?*
26. *When the centurion heard that, he went to the chief captain, and told him, saying, What wilt thou do? for this man is a Roman*
27. *And when the chief captain came, he said to him, Tell me, art thou a Roman? And he said, Yea.*
28. *And the chief captain answered, With a great sum I purchased this freedom. And Paul said, I was so born.*
29. *Then those who were about to examine him departed from him immediately: and the chief captain also was afraid, after that he knew that he was a Roman, and that he had bound him.*
30. *And on the next day, when he would know the truth,[1] he loosed him from his bonds, and commanded the high priests and all the council to come together, and he brought Paul and set him before them.*

24. *The chief captain.* It was well and wisely done of the chief captain thus to withdraw Paul from the sight of the people, forasmuch as his presence did move and more provoke them who were already too much moved. For by this means he provideth for the life of the holy man, and partly appeaseth the madness of the people. But when he commandeth him to be scourged, to whose charge he heard no certain crime laid, he seemeth to deal unjustly. And yet this injury [injustice] was not without colour, because it was likely that it was, not without cause, that all the people

---

[1] " Certum qua ex causa accusaretur a Judæis," certainly for what cause he was accused by the Jews

had conspired to put one man to death. Therefore, a vehement presumption was the cause of so strait examination. But we must note that this is a common custom among politic men, that they be just judges, so far as is expedient for them; but if they be called away by profit, then they go out of the way. Nevertheless, it is sufficient for them to colour this their wickedness with the title of wisdom, because they hold that general principle, that the world cannot be governed without some show or colour of justice; but in all actions that subtilty whereof I spake doth prevail, that they consider rather what is profitable than what is equal and right.

25. *Is it lawful?* He allegeth first the privilege of the city, then he defendeth himself by common law. And though there were more weight in the second point, (to wit, that it is not lawful to scourge a man before his cause is heard,) yet should he have prevailed nothing, unless the centurion had been more moved with the honour of the Roman empire. For nothing was then more heinous than to do any thing which was contrary to the liberty of the people of Rome. Valerius' law, the law of Porcius, and of Sempronius, and such like, did forbid that no man should do any violence to the body of the city of Rome[1] without the commandment of the people. The privilege was so (sure and) holy, that they thought it to be not only a deadly offence, but also such an offence as could not be purged, that a citizen of Rome should be beaten.

Therefore, Paul escaped rather by the privilege than by common equity, yet did he not doubt in a good cause to bear off the injury which was prepared for him, with this buckler of the city. But we must know that he did so allege the right and privilege of the city, that the chief captain was brought to believe him, because his words should not have been credited unless he had used some proof. Moreover, it was no hard matter for a man, who was well

---

[1] "Civis Romani," a Roman citizen

known, to bring forth witnesses. We alleged a cause in the sixteenth chapter, why he suffered himself to be scourged at Philippos, [Philippi,] which he now preventeth by his own declaration; to wit, because he should not have been heard in a tumult raised among the common people, (Acts xvi. 37.) But because he hath now to deal with the soldiers of Rome, who did behave themselves more moderately and gravely, he useth the opportunity.

26. *This man is a Roman.* Some man may marvel that he was so credulous, who was appointed to be chief in examining Paul, that he doth affirm the thing, as if he knew it to be so. For if he ought to believe Paul's words, every malefactor might, by this shift, have escaped punishment. But this was their manner of dealing, he which did say that he was a citizen of Rome, unless he could bring in some which knew him, or prove it lawfully, he was punished; for it was death for any man to pretend the freedom of the city falsely. Wherefore, the centurion referreth the matter unto the chief captain, as doubting thereof; and he (as we have said) doth straightway examine the matter more thoroughly. And though Luke doth not express by what testimonies Paul did prove himself to be a citizen of Rome, yet, undoubtedly, the chief captain knew the truth of the matter before he loosed him.

28. *With a great sum.* The chief captain objecteth this to refute him, as if he should say, that the freedom of the city is not so common, and easily to be obtained. How can it be that thou, being some base fellow of the country of the Cilicians, shouldst obtain this honour, for which I paid sweetly? Whereas Paul maketh answer, that he was free born, who never saw the city, yea, whose father it may be was never there, there is no cause why this should trouble any man. For those who are skilful in the Roman history know that certain were made free of the city who dwelt in the provinces, if, having deserved well of the commonwealth, or in war, or in other weighty affairs, they did desire and

crave this reward of the deputies, [proconsuls;] so that it is no absurdity to say that he was born a citizen of Rome, who, descending by his ancestors of some province far distant from Rome, did never set foot in Italy. Notwithstanding, the question is, how this can hang together, that the chief captain was afraid, because he had bound a citizen of Rome, and yet he did not loose him from his bonds until the morrow? It may be that he deferred it till the next day, lest he should show some token of fear. Notwithstanding, I think that the chief captain was afraid, because Paul was bound at his commandment, that he might be scourged, because this was to do injury to the body of a citizen of Rome, and to break the common liberty, and that [although] it was lawful to put a Roman in prison.

CHAPTER XXIII.

1. *And Paul beheld the council stedfastly, and said, Men and brethren, I have served God until this day in all good conscience.*
2. *And the high priest Ananias commanded those that stood by him to smite him on the face.*
3. *Then Paul said to him, God will smite thee, thou painted wall; and thou sittest judging according to law, and transgressing the law, commandest thou me to be smitten?*
4. *And those which stood by said, Railest thou on God's high priest?*
5. *And Paul said, I wist not, brethren, that he was the high priest; for it is written, Thou shalt not speak evil of the ruler of thy people.*

1. *Looking earnestly.* Paul beginneth with the testimony of a good conscience, that all the whole multitude may understand that he is unjustly charged with such an heinous offence, as if he had gone about to overthrow the worship of

God. It may be, indeed, that a man may offend of ignorance, who will not otherwise be a contemner either of God or of religion; but Paul meant at the first, only with this excuse, to mollify their nettled minds, that he might the better be heard; for it had been in vain for him to have defended himself, so long as that opinion did stick in the minds of the priests, that he was a wicked revolt, [apostate.] Therefore, before he enter the cause, he excuseth himself of that crime, not only that he may purchase favour by that desire which he had to live godlily, but also that he may prevent false accusations, or at least that he may refute unjust prejudices which might have made against him, wherewith he saw the whole multitude infected and corrupted. We know not what he meant to say besides. Notwithstanding, this preface teacheth that no man can rightly handle the doctrine of godliness, unless the fear of God reign and bear the chief sway in him. And now, though he give not the priests so honourable a title here as he did a little before, when he stood upon the steps of the fortress, yet he calleth them brethren, giving them that honour, not because they deserve it, but that he may testify that he is not the cause of the breach of friendship.

2. *And the chief priest.* Luke's narration seemeth not to agree with the usual history; for Josephus writeth thus concerning the high priests of that time, that Quadratus, deputy [proconsul] of Syria, deposing Cumanus from the government of Judea, commanded him to answer for himself before Cæsar, and sent Ananias, the highest priest, bound with him, into whose place who was chosen he maketh no mention, saving that it is likely that Jonathas had the honour given him, who, as he reporteth, was afterward slain by the subtilty and treachery of Felix, deputy [prefect] of Judea, who succeeded Cumanus; for when he had oftentimes told Felix part of his mind, and he could not away with the constancy of the man, he made a compact with one Doras, that he should privily convey in murderers to slay him. Then, as the same Josephus doth witness, king

Agrippa made Ismael, the son of Phebeus, priest. But when he was sent by the people to Rome about a certain suit, and was kept there by Popea, wife to Nero, Agrippa putteth in his place one Josephus, whose name was Chabus, the son of Simon. But immediately being also weary of him, he appointeth Ananus, the son of Ananus, to be high priest.

Furthermore, he saith that this last thing happened at such time as, after the death of Festus, Albinus did succeed him. And I see not why some call this Ananus Ananias. That hath indeed some colour, in that he is called a Pharisee; also in that it is said that he was bold and stout, who, without any lawful authority, caused James, the Lord's brother, to be stoned. But if we give credence to Josephus, he could not be that Ananias of whom mention is made in this place by Luke, who was then made priest, when many years were past and gone, after that Felix departed out of the province.

I have another conjecture in my head. For there flourished during all that time one Ananias, an high priest, who, excepting the title of honour, was almost chief in the order. And because Josephus leaveth some void time between Ananias and Ismael, it may be that this man had the room of the highest priest in the mean time.[1] But though this were not so, it appeareth out of Josephus, that Ananias, who died when the city was besieged, was, in the reign of Claudius Cæsar and Nero, equal in dignity with the chief priests which were then.

Yea, his authority is so highly extolled, as if he had the chief government, howsoever other men did bear the ensigns of honour. Again, he is called ἀρχιερεὺς confusedly,[2] as those who were the highest priests. Now, let the readers ponder and consider, whether the word ἀρχιερεὺς doth not rather signify in this place *chief* than *highest*, as it doth in many other places. For the Evangelists do every-

---

[1] " Intermedio illo tempore," during the intermediate time.
[2] " Promiscue," indiscriminately.

where call the priests who were of the course of Aaron αρχιερεις, that they may distinguish them from the Levites, who had a more inferior degree of priesthood. Moreover, it may be that that Ananias, who was counted stout and courageous, did supply the high priest's room in his absence. Those things which we have recited out of Josephus are recorded partly in the Twentieth Book of Antiquities, from the third chapter until the eight, partly in the Second Book of the Wars of the Jews.

He commanded him to be smitten. We see that there was in this assembly great distemperature. For whereas the high priest was in such rage, that he commanded Paul to be smitten for nothing, he did it undoubtedly with the consent of all the rest; yea, to the end he might win the favour of mad men. The Lord doth suffer the wicked to be so carried away by Satan, that they fall from all show of equity and temperance. For hypocrites would fain bear some show of moderation; and undoubtedly this high priest went about to pretend such gravity as did beseem his person. But the Lord did pluck this visure [mask] from his face, so that there was not found in him so much as the modesty of a mean man, but he poured out his furious force like a beast.

In the mean season, we see what horrible and filthy disorder there was at that day in the Church. Ananias, who was the chief of the council, whereas he ought to have stayed others by his gravity, forgetting all modesty, he enforceth them unto violence and savageness. Therefore they had at that day no regard of discipline, but there remained among them confused barbarism. And no marvel, for they had estranged themselves from God; they had most reproachfully rejected Christ; all their religion was set to sale. Therefore it was meet that they should run headlong into furious madness, which might be loathsome even among profane men, that they might be punished in their own shame for their ungodliness.

3. *God shall smite thee.* Paul cannot put up that injury,

but he must, at least, with sharp words reprehend the high priest,[1] and denounce God's vengeance unto him. For it is no curse, as appeareth sufficiently by the Greek text, but rather a reprehension, joined with the denouncing of a punishment. If any man object, that Paul did not use that modesty which Christ commandeth his to use, when he commandeth them after they have received a blow on the left cheek to turn the right cheek also, (Matth. v. 39;) we may readily answer, that Christ doth not in these words require silence, whereby the wickedness and frowardness of the wicked may be nourished; but he doth only bridle their minds, that they may not take that injury, which they have already received, impatiently. Christ will have those that be his to be ready to suffer another injury after that they have already received one; and by this means he represseth all desire of revenge. This is a brief and true definition of patience which beseemeth all the faithful, that they break not out into wrathfulness, that they do not one evil turn for another; but that they overcome evil with goodness. But this is no let but that they may complain of those injuries which they have suffered, but that they may reprove the wicked, and cite them to the judgment-seat of God; so they do this with quiet and calm minds; and, secondly, without evil will and hatred; as Paul appealeth, in this place, unto God's judgment-seat, that the high priest may not flatter himself in his tyranny. Therefore he accuseth him, because he breaketh the law, from which (as he pretendeth) he hath his authority; whence he gathereth, that he shall not escape unpunished.

If any man, being overcome with impatience, do but murmur, he shall not be blameless. But a manifest and sharp accusation, if it proceed from a quiet mind, doth not pass the bounds set down by Christ. If any man say that it is mixed with railing, I answer, that we must always mark with what affection the words be uttered. Christ pronounceth that man to be worthy to be punished

---

[1] " Silentio . quin saltem expostulet graviter verbis cum pontifice,' in silence, without at least sharply expostulating with the high priest.

by the council who shall only say to his brother *raca;* and as for him who shall say *thou fool,* he maketh him subject to a more heavy judgment, (Matth. v. 22.) But if opportunity be offered to reprove, we must oftentimes reprehend sharply. Whereby it appeareth, that this only was Christ's drift to keep back his, first, from all indignation, secondly, from speaking anything in despite[1] of any man. Therefore, let us beware of railing, and then we may not only note in our brethren foolishness, but also it shall be lawful for us to express their offences by their names when need shall be. So Paul did not speak for his own sake, that he might, with sharp words, requite the injury done to him by the high priest; but because he was a minister of the word of God, he would not wink at an offence which did deserve sharp and serious reprehension; especially seeing it was profitable to bring to light the gross hypocrisy of Ananias. Therefore, so often as we have any dealings with the wicked, if we be desirous to handle a good cause well, we must beware that there break out in us no motion of anger, that no desire of revenge provoke us to break out into railing. But if the spirit of meekness reign in us, we may handle the wicked according to their deserts, as it were out of the mouth of God; yet so that it may appear that we be rather prophets, than that we blunder out anything rashly through immoderate heat.

4. *Those which stood by said.* By this it appeareth that they were all sick of one disease.[2] For why do they not rather blame Ananias, when they saw that he had quite forgotten all modesty, and that he brake out into violence and stripes after a barbarous manner? for even this did turn to the reproach of them all.[3] But this is a solemn [marked] thing among hypocrites, they look narrowly into other men's faults and wink at their own. Again, this pride is coupled with tyranny, so that their subjects, and those who

---

[1] " Contumelia," with contumely.   [2] " Eadem omnes intemperie laborasse," that they all laboured under the same intemperance.   [3] " In commune illorum dedecus," to their common disgrace.

are under them, may do nothing, but as for themselves, they may do whatsoever they will. So fareth it at this day in Popery, the more liberty that impure clergy doth grant to itself, and the more carelessly it waxeth wanton, and polluteth the whole world with the sins which flow thence, the more straitly do they rule and stay the tongues of the people. Therefore, if any man dare be so bold as once to whisper, a little liberty doth cause them to make outrageous outcries as it were heinous sacrilege.

5. *I knew not, brethren.* Those who think that this excuse of Paul hath in it no figure, do not well mark the contrary objections wherewith their error is refuted. They say that Paul knew not the high priest, because he had been absent long time; as if he were ignorant that he was chief priest, who is the chief in the council, and hath the uppermost room. Neither was Ananias so base and obscure that Paul was ignorant of his degree. But his words cut off all occasion of disputation, when as he chideth him, because, occupying the place of a judge, under colour of the law, he doth, in his rage, that which is contrary to law. Therefore Paul knew what place he had, when he said that he abused his power. Other some invent a more subtle answer, that he spake not here of the man, but of the office and public person. But, first, the exposition is far fet, [fetched,] because, if Paul did reverence the priesthood, he must needs have given some honour to the man which had the same. And now it is not to be thought (forasmuch as the majesty of the priesthood was abolished by the coming of Christ, and that there followed such filthy profanation) that Paul did honour those as he was wont, (as if their perfect and lawful authority did continue,) who, under the title of the high priests, did reign as lords without any law or right.

Therefore, subscribing to Augustine, I do not doubt but that this is a taunting excuse. Neither doth that any whit hinder, because plain speech becometh the ministers of the word. For seeing there be two sorts of ironies, one which is covered with subtilty and means to deceive, another which doth so figuratively note out the thing which is in hand, that it doth prick sorer; in this second, there is nothing which doth not well beseem the servants of Christ. Therefore, this is the meaning of the words, Brethren, I acknowledge nothing in this man which belongeth to the priest. Also, he added a testimony of the 22d chapter of Exodus, (Exod. xxii. 28,) in which place, though Moses speak of judges, yet the sentence is extended properly unto any lawful order. Therefore all dignity, which is appointed for maintenance of civil government, ought to be reverenced and had in honour. For whosoever he be that rebelleth against or resisteth the magistrate, or those who are appointed to rule, and are promoted unto honour, he would have no government.[1] And such desire tendeth to the disturbing of order. Yea, it shaketh and overthroweth all humanity. Therefore Paul purgeth himself of this crime; yet so, that he denieth that Ananias is to be counted a priest of God, who hath corrupted and perverted all the order of the Church.

But here riseth a question, whether we ought not to obey a ruler, though he exercise tyranny? For if that man be not to be deprived of honour which executeth his office amiss, Paul offended in robbing the high priest of his honour. Therefore I answer, that there is some difference between civil magistrates and the prelates of the Church. For though the exploiting [administration] of earthly or civil rule be confused or perverse, yet the Lord will have men to continue still in subjection. But when the spiritual government doth degenerate, the consciences of the godly are at liberty, and set free from obeying unjust authority; especially if the wicked and profane enemies of holiness do falsely pretend the title of priesthood to overthrow the doctrine of salvation, and challenge to themselves such authority, as that they will be thereby equal with God. So it is not only lawful for the faithful at this day to shake off

---

[1] " Anarchiam appetit," he longs for anarchy

from their shoulders the Pope's yoke, but they must do it of necessity, seeing they cannot obey his laws unless they forsake God.

> 6. *And when Paul knew that the one part were of the Sadducees, and the other of the Pharisees, he cried out in the council, Men and brethren, I am a Pharisee, the son of a Pharisee : I am judged of the hope and resurrection of the dead.*
> 7. *And when he had thus said, there was a dissension among the Pharisees and Sadducees : and the multitude was divided.*
> 8. *For the Sadducees say there is no resurrection, neither angel, neither spirit : but the Pharisees confess both.*
> 9. *And there was a great cry : and the scribes of the Pharisees' sect arose, and strove, saying, We find no evil in this man : but if the spirit or an angel have spoken to him, let us not fight against God.*

6. *And when Paul knew.* The policy[1] of Paul, whereof Luke maketh mention, doth seem not to beseem the servant of Christ. For the subtilty which he used was inwrapped in dissimulation, which was not far from a lie. He saith that the state of his cause did consist in the resurrection of the dead: but we know that the strife arose about other matters: because he disannulled the ceremonies, because he admitted the Gentiles into the covenant of salvation. I answer, that though these things be true, yet did not he lie. For he doth neither deny that he was accused of other matters, neither doth this make the whole controversy to consist in one point; but he saith truly that the Sadducees were therefore offended with him, because he did hold the resurrection of the dead. He knew that those who had conspired together against him were enemies also one to another.[2] He knew that his own conscience was clear; and it had been an easy matter for him to prove his cause good before just judges. Yet because he seeth them cry out on him clamorously, and that he had

---

[1] "Stratagema," stratagem

[2] "Intestinis dissidiis laborare," were involved in intestine dissensions.

no place granted to defend himself, he setteth his enemies together by the ears. Whereby it doth also appear, that they were carried away through ignorance and blind zeal. Therefore we must note that Paul did so begin, as that he was desirous truly and plainly to unfold the whole matter; and that he did not craftily refuse to make a pure and sound confession, such as the servants of Christ ought to make; but because the way was stopt before him, neither could he be heard, he used the last remedy,[1] to declare that his adversaries were carried headlong with blind hatred. For the end doth show, that those are not guided with reason or judgment, who are carried out of the way by mutual discord.

Now, if any man, which darkeneth the light of doctrine, excuse his craft, by the example of Paul, he is easily refuted. For it is one thing for a man to provide for himself alone with the loss of truth, and another to lead the professed enemies of Christ from resisting him, that they may strive among themselves.

Furthermore, we see the nature of the wicked, though they disagree among themselves like enemies, yet when they are to make war against the gospel, they forget their own garboils, [strifes.] For Satan, the father of discord, doth procure this one consent only among his, that they may be of one mind and of one affection, to extinguish godliness. So we see that the factions which are in Popery hot,[2] are quiet only so long as they join hand in hand to oppress the gospel. For which cause, the disciples of Christ must be more courageous to foster and nourish truth, that, being joined together, they may the better resist. Also, we gather by this what manner of peace the Scripture commendeth unto us. Christ saith that the peace-makers are the children of God, (Matth. v. 9,) and this is true, that they must do what they can to bring all men that they may grow together[3] under the Lord. Yet this doth not hinder but that we may, (fight-

---

[1] "Extremo remedio," an extreme remedy
[2] "Fervent," prevail.
[3] "Fraterne," like brothers, omitted

ing under the banner of the same Lord,) as it were, with the sound of the trumpet, stir up the wicked, that they may, like Midianites, one slay another, (Judges vii. 22;) so that both simplicity of zeal, and the wisdom of the Spirit, direct us hither.

One part were Sadducees. We see here again, as in a glass, how deformed and confused the ruin of the Church was at that day. Faith is the soul of the Church; nothing is more proper to faith than agreement, nothing more contrary than sects. And this thing must needs follow, when every man (setting aside the word of God) did draw his disciples unto his own inventions. For there is no other holy bond of unity than the natural and plain[1] truth of God. So soon as men depart from that, no marvel if they be dispersed and drawn hither and thither like members pulled asunder.

Therefore, the beginning of sects among the Jews was the corruption of the law; like as the Lord did revenge the profanation of his word, which was corrupt with divers inventions of men, with like punishment in Popery. Wherefore, we must the more fear, lest horrible and more lamentable scatterings hang over our heads than was that which was in time of Popery, whereof there appear some tokens. And no marvel, seeing we provoke the Lord to wrath so many ways with our unthankfulness. But though the face of the Church be blotted and blurred with many spots and blots; and what manner of deformity soever fall out hereafter, let us comfort ourselves with this, that as God was careful then to deliver the Church wonderfully from destruction, so through his grace there shall always some seed continue. It cannot be, indeed, but that godly minds will somewhat despair, when they see things so far out of order; but let us learn straightway to hold up that buckler, that the Lord, who, in such a thick mist of errors, in such a heap of superstitions, in the unbridled licentiousness of sects, did preserve his Church among the Jews, will never suffer the same to be quite put out wholly in the world.

The same thing did likewise happen in Popery. For when as the worship of God was overthrown there, the

---

[1] " Simplex et genuina," simple and genuine.

doctrine of salvation was oppressed, the kingdom of Christ was thrown down, and ungodliness did openly reign, yet God did save certain hidden remnants, and there was always some wheat in the chaff. It is very profitable to confer these examples together. When as we inveigh at this day against Popery, the hired patrons thereof cry out on the other side, that nothing is more absurd than that we should imagine that the Church of God was extinguished during many ages, as if we did imagine that God had no people left, when those had forsaken him who ought to have maintained his pure worship. Yea, we complain that those tyrants did corrupt the Church, that the temple was by them profaned, so that it did not greatly differ from an hog's-sty, that the flock of Christ was scattered abroad, and his sheepfold broken down. Finally, that the Church was hidden from the eyes of men, yet so that the Lord knew his elect, though they were dispersed, and did brood them under his wings. And by this it appeareth how foolishly the Papists brag and boast of the titles of honour, in that not the common sort, or any private men, but the priests themselves did in times past divide the Jewish church by deadly dissension.

Wherefore, there is no cause why we should be afraid stoutly to resist the pride of the Pope and of all his adherents, with whom we have the same combat which the prophets and apostles had with the priests of their time. And as the reverence of the Church did not keep back holy men, but that they did molest the tyranny of the wicked priests, so we must not be terrified with vain visures, [masks,] under which the Papists do vainly boast, seeing they have, notwithstanding, cast from them the doctrine of godliness. It is certain that the people were then divided into three sects; but Luke doth only make mention of the Pharisees and Sadducees, omitting the Essenes, because it was most fit for his purpose thus to do. And though this be the common opinion concerning their names, that the former took their name of separating, because they withdrew themselves from the company of other men, by reason of their feigned holiness; and that the second sort took their name of righteousness, as if they were called *zeduchim;* notwithstanding, for mine own part, as I have said elsewhere, I am rather of their mind who say that the Pharisees took their name of interpreting. For *phrus* signifieth exposition, whereupon also interpreters are called *phruschim;* and we know that the Pharisees, being not content with the natural doctrine of the law and prophets, did put in many inventions which they said they received[1] of the fathers.

8. *The Sadducees say.* Though Luke maketh mention of three points wherein these sects did dissent, yet shortly after he bringeth[2] them to two, because there is like respect to be had of spirits and of angels. Therefore, he saith that the Pharisees did confess both; to wit, that the dead shall rise again, and that human and angelical spirits are immortal. And here Luke declareth in what sense the apostle professed himself to be a Pharisee, not because he did subscribe to all their inventions, but only in the resurrection of the dead. We know how sharply Christ reproveth their errors, (Matth. xxii. 29,) therefore, it had been good that some exception had been added,[3] lest any man might think that Paul was one with them in all things. Now, though the Sadducees did deny the resurrection, yet may we not think that they were altogether like to the Epicures, [Epicureans.] For they did confess that the world is governed by the providence of God, and that every man is rewarded for his works. In this point they were sounder than the Epicures, [Epicureans.] But they did dote too grossly, when they included the rewards of righteousness and the punishments of wickedness in this life. For that I may omit the Scripture, experience doth teach, that as well the godly as the ungodly are either punished with many miseries, or else gently[4] dealt withal; and that the wicked do oftentimes live in wealth and pleasures, when as the worshippers of God are

---

[1] " Per manus tradita jactabant," boasted, had been handed down
[2] " Restringit," restricts   [3] " Itaque addenda fuit exceptio," therefore, it was necessary to add the exception   [4] " Benigne et indulgenter," kindly and indulgently.

oftentimes miserably tormented, as it is Psalm lxxiii. 4. Therefore, whosoever esteemeth the judgment of God by the present estate of men, whether it be good or bad, he must needs fall away from faith at length unto Epicurish contempt of God.

Now, this is beastly blockishness to rest in an uncertain and transitory life, and not to be wise above[1] the earth. For which cause we must flee from that error as from a detestable monster. For though godliness have the promises of the earthly life also, yet because we be most miserable if our hope stay still in this world, the children of God must begin with this, that they may lift up their eyes toward heaven, and think continually upon the glory of the last resurrection.

Neither angel nor spirit. This place is expounded two manner of ways.[2] Many refer it unto the Holy Ghost, which seemeth to be unlikely. For howsoever the Sadducees be to be holden excused in other errors, yet because the Scripture doth so often repeat the name of the Spirit, I will scarce believe that they denied that which the Pharisees believed only lightly and obscurely. For even these men had no distinct faith concerning the Holy Spirit, that they did acknowledge the proper person of the Spirit in the substance of God.[3] Some will have angel and spirit to signify one thing,[4] as if one thing were spoken twice. But to what end was it to repeat a thing which was plain enough? I warrant you, that member which followeth did deceive them, where Luke seemeth to make no distinction. But we showed the reason before; because, seeing the souls of men and angels are of one and the same nature and substance, they be both placed in one order. Therefore, I do not doubt but that this is Luke's true meaning, that the Sadducees did deny angels, and also all manner of spirits.

Now, forasmuch as Paul crieth that he is a Pharisee in

---

[1] "Nec sapere," and not have a feeling or relish   [2] "Tribus modis," in three ways.   [3] "Propriam Spiritus hypostasin . . in Dei essentia," the proper personality of the Spirit in the divine essence.
[4] "Synonyma esse," to be synonymous

this point of doctrine, he doth flatly condemn all brain-sick fellows, who at this day are in the same error. For there be certain profane and unlearned men who dream that angels and devils are nothing else but good and evil inspirations; and lest they want some colour, they say that all that came from the heathen which the Scripture hath concerning good and evil angels, whereas that opinion which was common in the world had his [its] beginning from the heavenly doctrine. But the heathen did with their lies pollute that doctrine which they had from the Fathers. As touching men's souls, because even at this day certain miscreants do feign that the souls do vanish away in death until the day of the resurrection, their madness is likewise refuted by the testimony of Luke.

9. *There was a great cry.* That sedition whereof Luke spake a little before is more plainly expressed in this place; to wit, that they were not only of divers opinions, but did strive clamorously with outcries. Wherefore, ςασις doth signify somewhat more than dissension. Furthermore, this place doth teach what mischief disagreements bring with them. For because they take their beginning for the most part of ambition, men proceed thence unto contention, and straightway stubbornness breaketh out. When they be come thither, because there is no place left either for judgment or moderation, they can no longer judge of the cause. Those who did detest Paul begin at a sudden to defend him. It was well done, if they had done it with judgment. But because they inveigh against the Sadducees, they are so inflamed with hatred against them, that they be blind in Paul's matter. For which cause we must beware of heat of contention, which disturbeth all things.

If the Spirit. This ought undoubtedly to be expounded of the Holy Ghost. And nothing could be spoken either more godly or modestly. For so soon as it is apparent that any doctrine is revealed from heaven, those do wickedly resist God who do not receive the same. But how is it that the scribes do so suddenly count Paul a prophet of God whom they were once ready to have murdered—whom they had condemned with their prejudice until the contention arose?[1] Furthermore, as they did cut their own throats with these words as with a sword, so God would have them to be to us teachers to instruct us, that we despise not the oracles which come from heaven. Notwithstanding, we see again that those stand in doubt who take not good heed, and are not careful to mark the word of God; and that they waver so often as any thing is brought to light, because they be unworthy to understand the certain truth. Wherefore, if we be desirous to have our studies governed by the spirit of discretion, let us apply ourselves to learn.

10. *And when there arose a sore dissension among them, the chief captain feared lest Paul should have been pulled in pieces by them, and he commanded the soldiers to go down, and to take him from them, and to bring him into the camp.*
11. *And the night following the Lord stood by him, and said, Be of good courage, Paul: for as thou hast borne witness of me at Jerusalem, so must thou bear witness of me at Rome also.*
12. *And when it was day, certain of the Jews gathered themselves together, and bound themselves with a curse, saying that they would neither eat nor drink until they had killed Paul.*
13. *And there were more than forty men which had made this conspiracy.*
14. *And they came to the chief priests and elders, and said, We have bound ourselves with a curse, that we will eat nothing until we have killed Paul.*
15. *Now therefore signify ye to the chief captain and council that he bring him forth to you to-morrow, as if ye would know somewhat more certainly of him: and we, before he come near, are ready to kill him.*
16. *But when Paul's sister's son heard of the lying in wait, he came and entered into the camp, and told Paul.*

10. We see again what a cruel mischief contention is,

---

[1] "Cum Pharisæis," with the Pharisees.

which so soon as it doth once wax hot, hath such violent motions, that even most wise men are not well in their wits. Therefore, so soon as any beginning shall show itself, let us study to prevent it in time, lest the remedy be too late in bridling it when it is in the middle, because no fire is so swift as it. As for the chief captain, as he was appointed to be the minister of God's providence to save Paul's life, so he delivereth him now the second time by his soldiers from death. For though the chief captain defend[1] him so diligently, for no other purpose save only that he may prevent uproars and murder; yet the Lord, who from heaven provided and appointed help for his servant, doth direct his blind hands thither.

11. *And the night following.* Luke declareth that Paul was strengthened with an oracle, that he might stand courageously against terrible assaults when things were so far out of order. Surely it could not be but that he was sore afraid, and that he was sore troubled with the remembrance of things to come. Wherefore, the oracle was not superfluous. Those former things whereby he was taught that God cared for him, ought to have sufficed to nourish his hope, and to have kept him from fainting; but because in great dangers Satan doth oftentimes procure new fears, that he may thereby (if he cannot altogether overwhelm God's promises in the hearts of the godly) at least darken the same with clouds, it is needful that the remembrance of them be renewed, that faith, being holpen with new props and stays, may stand more stedfastly. But the sum is, that Paul may behave himself boldly, because he must be Christ's witness at Rome also. But this seemeth to be but a cold and vain consolation, as if he should say, Fear not, because thou must abide a sorer brunt; for it had been better, according to the flesh, once to die, and with speed to end his days, than to pine away in bands, and long time to lie in prison. The Lord doth not promise to deliver him; no, he

---

[1] "Succurrit," succour.

saith not so much as that he shall have a joyful end; only he saith, that those troubles and afflictions, wherewith he was too sore oppressed already, shall continue long. But by this we gather better of what great importance this confidence is, that the Lord hath respect unto us in our miseries, though he stretch not forth his hand by and by to help us.

Therefore, let us learn, even in most extreme afflictions, to stay ourselves upon the word of God alone; and let us never faint so long as he quickeneth us with the testimony of his fatherly love. And because oracles are not now sent from heaven, neither doth the Lord himself appear by visions, we must meditate upon his innumerable promises, whereby he doth testify that he will be nigh unto us continually. If it be expedient that an angel come down unto us, the Lord will not deny even this kind of confirmation. Nevertheless, we must give this honour to the word, that being content with it alone we wait patiently for that help which it promiseth us.

Moreover, it did profit some nothing to hear angels which were sent down from heaven; but the Lord doth not in vain seal up in the hearts of the faithful by his Spirit those promises which are made by him. And as he doth not in vain beat them in and often repeat them,[1] so let our faith exercise itself diligently in the continual remembrance of them. For if it were necessary that Paul's faith should be oftentimes set and stored up with a new help, there is none of us which needeth not many more helps. Also, our minds must be armed with patience, that they may pass through the long and troublesome circuits of troubles and afflictions.

12. *And when it was day.* By this circumstance, Luke showeth how necessary it was for Paul to gather new and fresh strength of faith, that he might not quake in most great and sudden danger. For being told of this so desperate madness of his enemies, he could not otherwise

---

[1] "Inculcat," inculcates.

think but that he should lose his life. This vow whereof Luke speaketh was a kind of curse. The cause of the vow was, that it might not be lawful for them to change their purpose, nor to call back that which they had promised. There is always, indeed, in an oath a secret curse,[1] if any man deceive or forswear, but sometimes to the end men may the more bind themselves, they use certain forms of cursing;[2] and they make themselves subject to cruel torments, to the end they may be the more afraid. This history doth teach that zeal is so bloody in hypocrites, that they weigh not what is lawful for them, but they run carelessly whithersoever their lust doth carry them. Admit we grant that Paul was a wicked man, and worthy to die, yet who had given private men leave to put him to death? Now, if any man had asked why they did so hate Paul, they would quickly have answered, because he was a revolt [apostate] and schismatic; but it was but a foolish opinion, and an opinion conceived of an uncertain report concerning this matter which had rashly possessed their minds.

The same blindness and blockishness doth at this day prick forward the Papists, so that they think nothing unlawful for them in destroying us. Hypocrisy doth so blind their ears, that as men freed from the laws of God and men, they are carried by their zeal sometimes unto treachery, sometimes unto guile, sometimes unto intolerable cruelty, and, finally, to attempt whatsoever they will. Moreover, we see in this history how great the rashness of the wicked is. They bind themselves with a curse that they will eat no meat till they have slain Paul, as if his life were in their hands. Therefore, these brain-sick men take to themselves that which the Lord doth so often in Scripture say is his, to wit, " To have the life and death of those men whom he hath created in his hand," (Deut. xxxii. 39.) Moreover, there be not only two or three who are partners in this madness, but more than forty. Whence we do also gather how

---

[1] " Tacita execratio," a tacit execration.

[2] " Anathematis," of anathema.

willing and bent men are to do mischief, seeing they run together thus on heaps.[1]

Furthermore, seeing Satan doth drive them headlong into their own destruction, how shameful is then our sluggishness, when as we scarce move one finger in maintaining the glory of God? We must use moderation, that we attempt nothing without the commandment of God; but when God calleth us expressly, our loitering is without excuse

14. *They came to the chief priests.* Seeing that the priests agree to such a wicked and ungodly conspiracy, by this they prove that there was in them neither any fear of God, neither yet any humanity. They do not only allow [approve] that which is brought before them concerning the murdering of the man by laying wait, but also they are ready to be partners in the murder, that they may deliver him into the hands of the murderers, whom they would have made away some way, they pass not how. For what other thing was it to take a man out of the hands of the judge and to slay him, than like murderers to rage even in the very place of judgment? The priests surely would never have allowed [approved] such a wicked purpose if there had been in them any drop of godly and right affection, or of humane feeling. Moreover, they did what they could to bring destruction upon all the people and themselves also. But the Lord did by this means disclose their wicked impiety, which lay hid under a colour of honour.

16. *Paul's sister's son.* We see in this place how the Lord doth cross the purposes of the ungodly. He permitteth them to attempt many things, and he suffereth their wicked endeavours, but at length he showeth even in the twinkling of an eye[2] that he doth from heaven deride whatsoever men go about upon earth. "There is no wisdom," saith Solomon, "there is no counsel against the Lord,"

---

[1] " Turmatim," in crowds.   [2] " Ipso articulo," at the very nick of time.

(Prov. xxi. 30.) Whereto that of Isaiah doth answer, "Take counsel together, and it shall come to nought: speak the word, and it shall not stand," (Isaiah viii. 10.) This is set before our eyes to be considered, in this present history, as in a glass. The matter was almost dispatched, that Paul should come out on the morrow to be slain as an avowed sacrifice.[1] But the Lord doth show that his life is most safely kept, so that whatsoever men go about all is in vain. As for us, let us not fear but that his providence, whereof he showed some token then, reacheth even unto the defending of us, because this promise continueth sure, "There shall not an hair fall from your heads," &c., (Luke xxi. 18.) Moreover, it is worth the noting, that he worketh sometimes by means unlooked for to save those that be his, that he may the better exercise our faith. Who would have thought that a boy would have disclosed their lying in wait, which those who were partners in the conspiracy thought was known to none but to themselves? Therefore, let us learn to lean unto and stay ourselves upon the Lord, though we see no ordinary way to save ourselves, who shall find a way even through places where nothing can pass.

17. *And when Paul had called unto him one of the centurions, he saith, Bring this young man unto the chief captain: for he hath a certain thing to show him.*
18. *And he took him, and led him unto the chief captain, and said, Paul the prisoner called me unto him, and desired me to bring this young man unto thee, who hath somewhat to say to thee.*
19. *And the chief captain took him by the hand, and went aside with him, and asked him, What is it that thou hast to say to me?*
20. *And he said, The Jews have conspired together to desire thee that thou bring forth Paul into the council to-morrow, as if they would know somewhat more certainly of him.*
21. *But do not thou obey them :[2] for more than forty of them lie in wait for him, who have bound themselves with a curse,*

---

[1] "Devota victima," a devoted victim.
[2] "Tu vero ne morem gesseris illis," but do not thou grant their request

that they will neither eat nor drink until they have slain him : and now they be ready waiting that thou shouldst promise.

22. *Therefore the chief captain let the young man go, and commanded him, Tell no man that thou hast told me these things.*

23. *And when he had called unto him two under captains, he said, Make ready two hundred soldiers that they may go to Cesarea, and horsemen seventy, and two hundred with darts,*[1] [*or javelins,*] *at the third hour of the night.*

24. *And make ready beasts, that they may set Paul thereon, and bring him safe to Felix the governor.*

17. *Calling unto him.* Paul was not so desirous of life, but he would have made haste to die, if the Lord had thought it good so to be; but because he knoweth that he serveth Christ upon that condition, that he may no less live than die to him, he doth not neglect to avoid the danger which was revealed to him. And though he be fully persuaded that God is the keeper of his life, yet he doth not wait until God put forth his hand out of heaven to work a miracle, but doth rather use the remedy which is offered him; nothing doubting but that it is appointed by God.

Thus must all the ministers of Christ deal, that being furnished with invincible constancy, so far as their calling requireth, they fear not danger, and yet that they cast not away themselves through rashness. Let them call upon the name of the Lord cheerfully, even amidst the pikes;[2] and yet let them not contemn those helps which are offered; otherwise they shall be injurious to God, in that they are not only not moved with his promises,[3] but also despise the means which he hath appointed for their deliverance.

19. *Taking him by the hand.* In that the chief captain

---

[1] "Lanceros," lancers.   [2] "In mediis augustiis," in the midst of straits.   [3] "Ad ejus promissiones surdi," deaf to his promises.

did show himself so courteous to the young man, in that he led him by the hand into a secret place, in that he vouchsafeth to hear him so gently, all this must be attributed to the grace of God, who promised to give his people favour in the sight of the Egyptians, (Exod. iii. 21,) who useth to mollify hard hearts, to tame fierce spirits, and to fashion those unto all humanity, whom he hath determined to use as means to help those that be his. A man trained up in the wars might no less have given this young man the repulse, whom he knew not, than have despised Paul's suit. Therefore, the Lord, who hath in his hand the hearts of men, did frame the profane man to give ear unto him. Also, it was well that he knew before how furiously they raged against Paul, that he might the more willingly succour a miserable and forsaken man. Those who are in authority are taught by this example what a great virtue courtesy is. If it had been a hard matter to come to him,[1] he might, through ignorance, have delivered Paul to the Jews to be put to death. So oftentimes magistrates do fall into many and great offences through their own pride, because they will not admit those who would give them good counsel.

Calling unto him. And here we see the providence of God yet more manifestly; for though this be the drift of the chief captain, to prevent a public uproar, whereof he should have given an account before the governor, yet he executeth the counsel of God in delivering Paul. For he was to gather soldiers together; also, the city must needs be stripped of the garrison, and the voyage required some cost. Therefore, we must so consider the wisdom of the chief captain, that our faith lift up her eyes into heaven, and understand that God doth guide the heart of a profane man by a secret instinct, and that he is at length a guide to Paul and the soldiers, that he may come safe to Cesarea. The third hour of the night was the end of the first watch.

---

[1] " Si difficilis ad eum fuisset accessus," if he had been of difficult access.

Therefore, it is all one as if the chief captain did command that the soldiers be in readiness at the second watch. Luke calleth those who carried darts *lancearios*, who being more lightly weaponed, were placed in the wings, when as the soldiers which pertained unto the legions were more fit for set war.[1]

25. *And he wrote a letter after this sort :*
26. *Claudius Lysias to the most mighty ruler,* [prefect,] *Felix, sendeth greeting.*
27. *This man being taken of the Jews, and almost killed of them, did I rescue, coming upon them with soldiers, after that I knew that he was a Roman.*
28. *And being desirous to know the cause for which they did accuse him, I brought him into their council :*
29. *Whom I perceived they accused of questions of their law, having in him no crime worthy of death or of bonds.*
30. *And when I was certified of the laying await of the Jews. I sent him straightway unto thee, and gave commandment to his accusers, that they should tell those things before thee what they have against him. Farewell.*
31. *And the soldiers, as they were commanded, took Paul, and brought him by night unto Antipatris.*
32. *And on the morrow when they had sent away the horsemen that they might go with him, they returned to the camp.*
33. *When they were come to Cæsarea, and had delivered the epistle to the governor, they presented Paul also before him.*
34. *And when the governor had read it, and had asked of what province he was, and had known that he was of Cilicia ;*
35. *I will hear thee, saith he, when thine accusers are come. And he commanded him to be kept in Herod's judgment-hall.*

25. *And he wrote a letter.* First, we must briefly admonish the readers who have not been conversant in his-

---

[1] "Statariæ militiæ," stationary warfare.

tories, that this Felix was brother to Pallas, who being Cæsar's freeman, became equal with the chief of the city in wealth and power. Yea, moreover, the senate gave him the ornaments of the prætor, not without titles of filthy and shameful flattery. Therefore, seeing the servants of Claudius abusing his folly, did rule the Roman empire at their pleasure, and chiefly Narcissus and Pallas, no marvel if this latter did appoint his brother to be governor of Judea. The sum of the epistle tendeth to this end, that the chief captain may help Paul with his prejudice;[1] and may admonish Felix of the injuries of his adversaries, and may so discredit them, that they may not be able to do him any hurt.

27. *This man being taken.* This was spoken odiously concerning the Jews, that he might purchase more favour for Paul, that a man, being a Roman, was by them sore beaten, and almost slain; also, he commendeth him for the right and privilege of his freedom, that he may be the more courteously handled. Furthermore, this commendation was not purchased by prayer or flattery, neither was it bought with money. How came it to pass, then, that the chief captain did show himself so courteous freely to an obscure man, and whom all men did hate, save only because the Lord had appointed him to be his servant's patron? Therefore, we see how he governeth the tongues and hands of the infidels to the profit of those that be his.

29. *Whom I perceived.* In this place he acquitteth Paul, so far as his judgment could reach. But let us note that a profane man speaketh. For among the people of God it is an offence worthy of no less punishment, to corrupt the doctrine of godliness with wicked and false opinions, than to do injury to, or commit wickedness among men. The Romans would not have suffered their superstitions, or feigned worshippings of their gods, to be freedom;[2] but for-

[1] " Suo præjudicio," by bearing previous testimony in his favour.
[2] " Convelli," to be plucked up, eradicated.

asmuch as they made no account of the law of God, yea, seeing they were desirous to have the same quite put out, it was among them no fault to believe Moses and the prophets no more, or to trouble the Church with false opinions. Therefore, there was a law, that the governors should not meddle with such matters; but that those who were abiding in the provinces should so retain their religion, that if anything were done contrary to the same, the Roman magistrates should not meddle with the punishing thereof. This is the reason why the chief captain thinketh it no offence to have moved questions concerning the law. And under colour hereof, unlearned men will have leave granted to themselves and others amiss to cause trouble. The Lord saith far otherwise, who doth more sharply punish the violating of his worship, than any injuries done to men. And surely nothing is more absurd than to let those who rob God of his honour escape scot free,[1] seeing theft is punished. But as the chief captain careth not for the Jewish religion, so the false accusations and slanders of the Jews are refuted, wherewith they would gladly have burdened Paul.

30. *When it was showed to me.* The second part of the epistle where the chief captain doth bring the adversaries into contempt,[2] because they went about to kill Paul treacherously. Whence it is also gathered, that they trouble Paul unjustly, and that they sought so sore against his life without any cause. For if they had persecuted him lawfully, they would have trusted to the goodness of their cause, and not have suffered him to be judged according to law. Now, when as they seek to kill him, it appeareth that they have no reason.

32. *And the next day.* Though Luke did not express before that the soldiers were commanded to return before

---

[1] " Quam sacrilegus impunitatem dare," than to let blasphemers escape without punishment   [2] " Odium in adversarios retorquet," retorts upon his adversaries their hatred.

they came at their way's end, yet it is certain, that they were appointed to accompany him only unto that place where the chief captain thought Paul would be safe; for he went out privily in the night. And the chief captain knew that so soon as they had finished some part of their journey, there was no farther danger, because the adversaries could have no hope to overtake him; and that it was no point of wisdom[1] to send part of the garrison far away.

CHAPTER XXIV.

1. *And after five days the chief priest Ananias came down with the elders, and one Tertullus, a rhetorician, who came before the governor against Paul.*
2. *And when Paul was called forth, Tertullus began to accuse him, saying, Seeing that we live in great peace by means of thee, and seeing many things are restored in this nation by thy providence,*
3. *That allow we ever, and in all places, most noble Felix, with all thanks.*
4. *But lest I become tedious unto thee, I pray thee hear us a little of thy courtesy.*
5. *For we have found this man a pestilent fellow, and a mover of debate unto all the Jews throughout the whole world, and an author of the sect of the Nazarites:*
6. *Who did also go about to pollute the temple; whom when we had taken, we would have judged him according to our law.*
7. *But the chief captain Lysias came upon us, and with great violence took him from us,*
8. *Commanding his accusers to come down unto thee: of whom*

---

[1] " Tutum . non esse," it was not safe.

thou mayest, if thou wilt inquire, know the certainty of all these things whereof we accuse him.

9. And the Jews added, saying that these things were so.

1. Seeing Ananias goeth down to Cesarea to accuse Paul, it maketh the conjecture more probable, which I brought before touching his priesthood. For it was not meet for the highest priest to take such a journey. Therefore some other man was highest priest at that time; and Ananias being one of the chief priests, forasmuch as he was in great authority, and was withal a stout[1] man, did take this embassage upon him. He bringeth with him a train, and that of the worshipful company of elders, that the governor might be moved with their very pomp to condemn Paul. But forasmuch as Paul did use no eloquence, they had no need to hire a rhetorician to contend with him in eloquence. Moreover, they did exceed both in dignity and also in multitude, so that it was an easy matter for them to oppress a poor man, and such a one as was destitute of man's help. Therefore it was a sign of an evil conscience, in that seeing they were men of great experience, exercised in public affairs, and skilful in matters pertaining to courts, they hire a rhetorician. Eloquence is, I confess, the gift of God; but in this matter they went about nothing else but to deceive the judge therewith. And Luke declareth this, therefore, that we may know that the Jews did omit nothing whereby they might oppress Paul; and that they might not only prove him guilty,[2] but so dash him out of countenance, that he might not be able to defend himself; and so let us consider that it came to pass by the wonderful providence of God, that Paul did so stoutly endure such sore assaults. Wherefore, if it so fall out at any time that a godly man being alone be beset with a great number of enemies, let him call to mind this history, and let him be of good courage. As David doth likewise exhort us by his own example, " If

[1] " Strenuus," active [2] " Perverterent ejus innocentiam," perver his innocence.

tents were pitched about me, I will not fear, because thou art with me," (Psalm xxvii. 3.)

2. *Seeing we live in great peace.* Tertullus useth a preface nothing appertinent to the matter; because he commendeth Felix's wisdom and virtues that he may purchase favour. Therefore it is a filthy and flattering *exordium*. Not that I am of their mind who reprehend Tertullus for speaking the judge fair, and for seeking to win his favour. For it is not always disagreeing with the right and lawful form of pleading to commend the judge; and there may reasons be brought on both sides (as they say) touching this matter. But I mislike nothing but this which is altogether corrupt. For the rhetorician doth insinuate himself under false praises, that he may darken the matter which is called in question. For to what end doth he speak of peace and a well ordered state, save only that Felix may think that the safety of Judea consisteth in condemning Paul, and that he may examine the matter no further? Moreover, it appeareth by Josephus, how covetously, cruelly, and voluptuously, Felix behaved himself in that province. The unworthy and tragical murdering of the highest priest, Jonathas, because he set himself against his dissolute tyranny, was already past;[1] and, finally, almost at the very same time, Claudius Cæsar was enforced with the complaints of the whole nation, to put Festus in his place, and to call him to answer for himself.

Therefore we see how shamefully this orator did lie. And seeing all Paul's adversaries sing the same song, we see that they be blinded with hatred and malice, and that they treacherously betray the state of their country; neither do they pass what befall them so Paul may die the death.

Where Erasmus translateth it, *Many things are well done*, the old interpreter seemeth to come nearer unto Paul's meaning, who saith, that κατορθωματα are wrought, which signifieth as much as *reformations* or *dressings*. Therefore Tertullus commendeth the industry of Felix, because he had

---

[1] "Jam præcesserat," had already been committed.

cleansed Judea from many corruptions, and he restored many things which would otherwise have decayed;[1] to wit, to the end he may the more greedily seek to purchase the favour of the nation (which he knew was otherwise offended with him) by the death of one man.

5. *For we found this man.* Tertullus doth aim at a double mark. The first is this, that Paul may be delivered to the Jews, because they be very skilful in matters which concern the worship of God and the law of Moses. But and if he deny this, he layeth to his charge a crime worthy of death, because he procured contention[2] among the people. They knew that the Romans did hate nothing more, therefore they urge that the sorest against Paul. This doth Tertullus amplify when he saith, that Paul had moved the Jews throughout the whole world. But I wonder why he addeth that he is the author or chief of the sect of the Nazarites, which we know was rather a praise than a dispraise among the Jews. I think that they mean not those who, according to the old and lawful custom of the law, did consecrate themselves to God, but those troublesome murderers who did also vaunt and boast that they were zealous men.[3] Some[4] think that Nazarites are here put for Christians, which may very well be. But if we like the former exposition better, he doth craftily lay to Paul's charge that he was one of that sect which the Romans did hate. For whereas these zealous men would above all other have been counted for notable observers of the law, they advanced a colour of zeal as a banner to stir up the minds of the common people. Nevertheless, these good men, who are so zealous over their liberty, do not spare the chiefest maintainers

---

[1] "Quæ alioqui pessum ibant," which were otherwise becoming worse.
[2] "Seditionem ... concitaverit," stirred up sedition.   [3] "Tumultuosos illos sicarios qui se etiam plausibili nomine vociferabant zelotas," those tumultuary assassins who, assuming a specious name, boasted of being zelotæ, (zealous.)   [4] "Quæ factio circiter illud tempus emerserit; imo ex Josephi historia colligitur jam tunc fuisse grassatos," about this time that faction had broken out, nay, it appears from Josephus that it had even then made considerable progress, omitted

thereof, so they may cause Paul to be hated by means of them. They would have commended the Nazarites as courageous defenders of the law, if it had not been in this matter, but now, as if they did infect the whole world, they seek to bring upon Paul great reproach by saying that he is one of them. Moreover, they slander Paul impudently, for no man did think that he was guilty of that crime. Therefore they lay to his charge, no less wickedly than maliciously, a crime which they take up at their foot,[1] and invent without all colour. But such is the careless security of hypocrites, that they think they may do whatsoever they will, so they colour their doings with zeal.

6. *Who went about to pollute the temple.* It was a light and almost a frivolous accusation to lay this to his charge before the Roman governor, who could have wished that the temple had been turned topsy-turvy. But because nothing was more fit for procuring uproars than the polluting of the temple, he doth craftily accuse Paul thereof, as if he should say, that it was no thanks to him that Jerusalem was not on an uproar; and that he carried such a firebrand as might have procured sore hurt if he had not been prevented. Also he includeth that other thing, that because Paul had offended in matters of religion, it did belong properly to the Jews to give judgment in that matter. And here he complaineth also of the chief captain Lysias, because he robbed them of their right. Therefore his drift is, to obtain at the hands of the ruler that he will restore to them that which Lysias had taken from them. This is also not void of subtilty, in that Tertullus doth discredit the chief captain, because he dealt more courteously towards Paul than the priests would he should; and glancingly he bringeth him in suspicion, because he dare not openly accuse him. But the question is, whether they could hope that the governor would grant them so much, seeing the Roman magistrates alone were to sit upon life and death? I answer, that he maketh in this

---

[1] " Crimen velut ex trivio arreptum," some charge, picked up, as it were, in the streets.

place some semblance of equity, as if they were purposed to handle him more gently than he deserved. For though they might not condemn any man to death, yet they might use some light chastisement as was scourging. Nevertheless, Tertullus doth not cease to desire before the president to have him put to death.

8. *Having made inquiry.* A good[1] request, that the governor do not give sentence before he thoroughly examine and know the matter; and that he do not condemn Paul before he be lawfully convict. But how dare they put in these conditions, seeing their own consciences do accuse them of unjust dealing? I answer, that they had witnesses in readiness; and that they do not offer themselves to prove the matter until they do call them;[2] though there were another end. For they did hope that Felix would be so persuaded with such glorious words,[3] that he would turn over unto them the man whom they did accuse for a condemned man, whom they might handle at their pleasure. In sum, the more fierce they be upon him, and the more they were puffed up with some affiance they had in themselves, they think they shall get the upper hand by this means, because the party arraigned shall have no license granted to defend himself. Thus do false accusers boldly boast that their matter is plain, that they may blind the eyes of the judges.

> 10. *And Paul answered, after that the governor had beckoned to him that he should speak, With a better mind do I speak for myself, forasmuch as I know that thou hast judged this nation this many years:*
> 11. *Seeing that thou mayest know that there are yet but twelve days since that I came up to Jerusalem to worship.*
> 12. *And they neither found me in the temple disputing with any man, or causing any concourse of people, neither in the synagogues, neither in the city:*

---

[1] "Æqua," just, equitable. [2] "Nec se ad probandum offerre nisi suo arbitrio," and that they do not offer proof unless he decide that it shall be taken [3] "Ampullis," bombast

13. *Neither can they prove those things whereof they accuse me.*
14. *But this I confess to thee, that according to the way which they call heresy, so worship I the God of my fathers, believing all things which are written in the law and the prophets ;*
15. *And have hope toward God, that the same resurrection of the dead which they wait for, shall be both of the just and unjust.*
16. *And herein I study always to have a clear conscience toward God and toward men.*
17. *And after many years I came and brought alms to my nation, and offerings.*
18. *Wherein they found me purified in the temple, neither with multitude, neither with unquietness,* [tumult.]
19. *And certain Jews out of Asia, who ought to have been present here, and to accuse if they had any thing against me.*
20. *Or else let these same here say if they have found any iniquity in me when I stood (or seeing I stand) in the council;*
21. *Except it be for this one voice, that I cried standing among them, I am judged of you this day of the resurrection of the dead.*

10. *And Paul.* The state of Paul's defence is not conversant in the quality; but he denieth the crime that was laid to his charge; not that he was ashamed of the gospel, or afraid of the cross, but because that was no place to make any full confession of faith in. Therefore, omitting the cause of the gospel, which his accuser had not touched, he answereth simply unto the crimes whereof he was accused. But before he come thither, he saith that he doth the more willingly answer for himself before Felix, because he had long time been governor of Judea; because, peradventure, some new governor[1] would have been sore moved hearing such things laid to his charge. He doth not commend the virtues of the governor, but he saith that he is glad, because he is of great experience, that he may judge more justly.[2] This is surely a sincere and free manner of defending, to set mat-

---

[1] " Propter inscitiam," through ignorance, omitted calmly.
[2] " Composito,"

ter against words. Yet Paul seemeth to gather amiss, that Felix can know the time of his coming, because he had been governor many years. I answer, that this is said therefore, because it is likely that he will deal more moderately; as if he should say, Because thou hast been acquainted with their conditions long time, I have the better hope that they shall not deceive thee. For want of skill doth make judges too credulous, and doth enforce them to make too much haste.

11. *To worship.* First, it is certain that he came for other causes, and he will afterward confess that this was the chief, that he might bring alms for the sustentation of the brethren. But we may well excuse him, because it was not of necessity that he should give an account of his coming; only he meant, by the way, to excuse himself of corrupt religion. Wherefore, though he came to Jerusalem for some other cause, yet this is always true, that he came with no other mind, but to profess himself to be a worshipper of God, and to approve the holiness of the temple by his worshipping. The other question is more hard, how he saith that he came to worship, seeing the religion of the temple was already abolished, and all difference of the temple [1] taken away? I answer in this place likewise, that though he do not make his purpose known, yet he doth not lie or dissemble. For the faithful servants of Christ were not forbidden to worship in the temple, so they did not tie holiness to the place, but did lift up pure hands freely without making choice of places, (1 Tim. ii. 8.) It was lawful for Paul to enter into the temple after he was come to Jerusalem, that he might make his godliness known, and there to use the solemn rites of the worship of God, because he was void of superstition; so he did not offer any propitiatory sacrifices which were contrary to the gospel. Therefore religion did not compel him to come to Jerusalem according to the appointment of the law, as if the sanctuary were the face of God as in times past; yet he

---

[1] " Omne templi discrimen," all distinction of temple.

doth not abhor the external worship which was unto men a testimony of godliness.

12. *Disputing with any man.* Paul had no need to deny any of these things if he had done them; because he might have answered for himself that it was well done. He had been one of the scribes which disputed daily; neither were they forbidden either by the law or by custom, but that they might assemble themselves together [1] to be taught. Yea, to this end there were in divers places of the city synagogues, wherein they met together. Moreover, he knew that both Christ and also his apostles had done the same thing. Also he might easily have turned [retorted] back upon his adversaries the crime which they did object to him, who did daily use the very same things. But because he aimeth at no other thing at this present, but to refute the false accusations of his adversaries, and to prove that importunate men had unadvisedly molested him for no cause; he intreateth not of the lawfulness of the fact, (as they say,) but only of the fact. And he standeth chiefly upon this point to refute that slander, because he was burdened to be [2] a raiser of tumults. Therefore he concludeth that he was falsely and unjustly accused; because the adversaries had never proved those things which they had alleged. This ought to have been sufficient to discharge him, seeing he was thus burdened with wicked lies, whereas there rested in him not the very least suspicion that could be devised.

14. *But I confess.* Because they had laid to Paul's charge impiety and the polluting of the temple, he purgeth himself of both now, that Felix may understand that his adversaries were moved with evil will.[3] For though the religion, which is pretended, be false and preposterous, yet the study thereof did oftentimes find favour with men, who

---

[1] " Turmatim," in crowds.   [2] " Delatus fuerat tanquam," was charged with being   [3] " Sola malevolentia impelli," were instigated by sheer malevolence.

took no great heed. Wherefore it was to be feared lest Felix, if he had conceived any sinister suspicion of Paul, should not only have pardoned the zeal of the priests, but also have granted their requests. Wherefore Paul doth also refute this point of the accusation; and that so, that he doth not touch the faith of the gospel, because (as we have said) that was no fit place for making confession thereof. But what is this that he saith, that he worshippeth God according to the way which they call heresy? Some think that this is added like to a concession; because the enemies take that in evil part which ought to be attributed to judgment and right election; as if Paul had said, that that form of religion which he had followed is, indeed, called heresy, but unworthily. But seeing that name was not infamous either among the Jews or Gentiles, it is unlikely that he maketh answer before a profane man, touching that which they counted everywhere rather a commendation than any vice. When Christians have conference together, the Spirit of God commandeth that heretics be counted detestable; and he teacheth us to beware of heresies, because they bring upon the Church plague, dissension, and wasteness. Therefore, it is a thing not to be suffered among the people of God, whose safety consisteth in the unity of faith. But because the Jews did then openly boast of their sects, that excuse, whereof we spake of late, was superfluous. Therefore, it remaineth that he do either mean that he is a Pharisee, or that he call the Jewish religion or the profession of the gospel (without infamy) heresy; because they were distinguished from the use and custom of all nations. Seeing he did before confess himself to be a Pharisee, there shall no inconvenience ensue, if we say that he doth repeat the same now; especially seeing he speaketh shortly after of the resurrection of the dead. But because this first point doth only contain a confession concerning the worship of the God of the fathers, I think that he doth rather speak generally of the Jewish religion, or of the Christian faith which did flow thence. Paul was a citizen of Rome, notwithstanding as he came of the Jews by his ancestry, he confesseth that he continueth in the religion which he had learned of the fathers. And to this end doth the adverb of likeness tend; for it showeth a known thing, namely, the manner of worship whereunto the Jews were addicted. He maketh express mention of the God of his fathers, because it was not lawful for a man that was a Roman to receive the doctrine of the law unless he had come of the Jews. Also he toucheth his adversaries, which handle him so cruelly; whereas, notwithstanding, they both worship one God. I (saith he) worship the same God (according to the manner delivered by mine ancestors) which they themselves worship, and even as they worship him. Neither doth that hinder because he was fallen from the ceremonies of the law, and was content with the spiritual worship of God. For Paul thinketh it sufficient for him to wipe away that blot of impiety which his adversaries had falsely cast upon him. Therefore the Papists are ridiculous, who feign that Paul alloweth [approveth] all manner [of] antiquity. We, say they, worship the God of our fathers with Paul, as the custom was delivered to us from hand to hand; as if (even they themselves being judges) it were sufficient for the Jews or Turks to hold up the same buckler against the faith of Christ. But the apostle meant nothing less than simply to ground religion in the authority of ancestors, and to defend his godliness with that defence, which might have been common to all the superstitions of the Gentiles; he meant only to stop the mouth of his adversaries. Nevertheless, he taketh this for a plain matter, that the fathers, from whom the Jewish religion came, were good and sincere worshippers of God; so that the Jews, which were not degenerate, might well boast, that the God of their fathers whom they worshipped was the only Creator of heaven and earth; and that the country gods[1] of all the rest of the world were mere and vain inventions.

Believing all things. A short exposition of the sentence

---

[1] " Gentiles," the Gentile.

next going before. For, because he had not simply affirmed that he worshipped God, but did add this word ουτως, or so: he doth now set down how he worshippeth God. Whereby it appeareth what great heed he taketh for fear he entangle himself in those accidental [1] superstitions which reigned among the Jews. As if any of us do at this day answer the Papists, that he worshippeth the God whom they profess, as we be taught out of the law and out of the gospel. By this let us learn that God is not rightly worshipped, so that our obedience can please him, unless it be of faith, which is the only ground-work of godliness. For he (to the end he may prove himself to be the servant of God) doth not thrust upon them bare ceremonies; but he saith flatly that he believeth. Furthermore, this place containeth a profitable doctrine, that this is the only foundation of right and true [2] faith, for a man to submit himself to the Scripture, and reverently to embrace the doctrine thereof. Furthermore, Paul doth in this place divide the Scripture into the law and the prophets, that he may the more plainly prove that he doth not dissent from the universal consent of the Church.

15. *Hoping in God.* We must note the course of his speech. For after that he hath professed that he believeth the Scripture, he doth now add the hope of the resurrection to come, that it may appear that it cometh not from the understanding of the flesh,[3] or from the decrees of men, but it is conceived out of the word of God. Thus doth the reverence of the Scripture go before,[4] that it [5] may hold us fast bound, and it is the beginning of faith. After that the knowledge of those things which God hath revealed there doth follow, being coupled and linked with sure hope. And whereas he maketh them his fellows, it is referred unto the sounder sort. Though it be not to be doubted, but that he seeketh, by this means and policy, to bring

---

[1] "Adventitiis," adventitious.
[2] "Orthodoxæ," orthodox.
[3] "Carnis sensu," from carnal sense.
[4] "Præcedit," take precedence
[5] "Ejus auctoritas," its authority.

them out of their lurking places into the clear light, and that before Felix; as it shall again appear by the conclusion of the defence. But in this place, the general resurrection is defended [asserted] against certain brain-sick fellows, who restrain the same unto the members of Christ. But as Paul doth in this place say that all men shall rise again, so by the plain voice of Christ all are cited;[1] some unto judgment, some unto life, (John v. 29.)

16. *And herein do I study.* There is no sharper prick to prick men forward, with all desire to lead a godly and holy life, than the hope of the last resurrection, as the Scripture teacheth in many places. Therefore, when Paul will effectually exhort the people anywhere, he calleth them back to remember the same, (Philip. iii. 20.) Wherefore, it is not without cause that he saith in this place, that staying himself upon this faith, he hath endeavoured to live purely before God, and righteously among men. And surely an evil conscience is as good as a thousand witnesses to accuse[2] men of blockishness, that they may gather for a certainty that they do not earnestly and thoroughly believe eternal life, after which they never long. He calleth it a conscience, απροσκοπον, that is, without offence, where the servants of God labour to remove all lets which hinder their course. And he putteth two parts of the conscience. For there is a certain inward sense or feeling which beholdeth[3] God alone, and thence cometh faithfulness and integrity which we use towards men. At length, when he saith that he hath constantly followed as well godliness in worshipping God, as just dealing among men, he signifieth unto us that those do indeed hope for the last resurrection who are never weary of well-doing. For this word always doth signify perseverance in a straight course.

17. *And after many years.* His meaning is, that he had not of long time been at Jerusalem, but was conversant in

---

[1] " Promiscue," promiscuously
[2] " Ad coarguendos," to convict.
[3] " Respicit," has respect to.

other countries far distant, and that after long time he came now to bring alms, and to offer to God the sacrifice of thanks. Whereby doth also appear their want of good nature and their unthankfulness, because, seeing he had by all means deserved the good-will of all the whole nation, they recompense him so evil. This place doth expound the former, where mention was made of worshipping. For it is certain that Paul came not purposely to offer in the temple, because he purposed to do that after he was come. But he doth only recite what the Jews found in him, which was of greatest weight for the matter which was now in hand. At length, when he saith that he was found in the temple doing this, and that having used first solemn purging, and, secondly, quietly without raising any tumult, he cleareth himself again of both crimes. For his purifying did witness that he did not pollute the temple; and, secondly, forasmuch as he did it quietly without any multitude, there was no suspicion of tumult.

19. *Certain Jews.* This is an imperfect speech; yet the sense is plain, that these men of Asia, as it should seem, had caused a tumult without cause, of whose absence he complaineth; as if he should say, Ye which lay so many things to my charge, cannot tell how the matter standeth; but you bring before the judgment-seat of the governor a tale which was rashly believed. But those who are to be blamed for the matter, and who were as fans to set all on fire, appear not. After that Paul hath turned back [retorted] the crime upon others, taking to himself a good courage, he doth now appeal unto the adversaries which are present, willing them if they know anything by him freely to utter it; though I dissent from Erasmus and the old interpreter in the participle σταντος, for they translate it in the present tense; and they expound the word συνεδριον, or *council*, of the sitting of the governor, which I think is far from Paul's meaning. For his meaning is, in my judgment, that he was ready to give an account of all things in their council. And that they knew nothing then which they can lay to his

charge, because they began to stir only for this one voice, when he said that he was judged of the resurrection of the dead; that is, that he suffered all this trouble for no other cause, save only because he did hope for the resurrection of the dead. Whereby it appeareth that they now coin a new accusation for no cause, because, if there had been in him any fault, they would not have concealed it then. It is likely that they had farther talk, and that they came nearer together,[1] because we shall see elsewhere that they did contend about Christ; but it was Luke's drift only to declare how well Paul had cleared himself of the false accusations of his accusers.

> 22. *And when Felix heard these things, he deferred them, certainly knowing those things which did appertain unto that way, and said, When the chief captain Lysias shall come, I will thoroughly know your matter.*
> 23. *And he commanded a centurion to keep Paul, and that he should suffer him to have ease, and that he should forbid none of his acquaintance to minister to him, or to come to him.*
> 24. *And after certain days came Felix, with his wife Drusilla, which was a Jewess, and he called Paul, and heard him concerning the faith which is in Christ.*
> 25. *And as he disputed of righteousness and temperance, and of judgment to come, Felix trembled, and answered, For this time go thy way; and when I have convenient time, I will send for thee.*
> 26. *He hoped also that Paul would have given him money to loose him: wherefore he sent for him the oftener, and communed with him.*
> 27. *And when two years were expired, Porcius Festus came into Felix' room: and because Felix would do the Jews a pleasure, he left Paul bound.*

22. *When Felix.* It appeareth that Felix (though he pronounced nothing concerning the matter) did perceive that Paul was burdened with no fault of his own, but with

[1] "Et proprius quasi manu conserta congressos esse," and came, as it were, to close quarters.

the malice of the priests. For when Luke saith that the matter was deferred until the coming of Lysias, he putteth in this instead of a reason, that the ruler did perfectly know those things which did appertain unto the way, by which words, I think, is signified, either that through long experience he had been acquainted with the conditions of the priests, and knew full well how they were wont to behave themselves; or else that he saw by these things which had been spoken on both sides how frivolous the accusation was, which is confirmed by the courteous and remiss[1] usage of Paul; for he putteth a centurion in trust with him, that he may have the more liberty. Others had rather read it in one text in the person of Felix: when Lysias, who doth better know the truth of this matter, is come, I will then give judgment. But they fet [draw] and gather this racked sense from a reason which is scarce firm. They say that this word *way* is no where taken for the doctrine of the law without some addition. But I do not interpret it of the law, but of those sects whereof no strangers were ignorant. No man did doubt but that the Pharisees did hold the immortality of the soul. Therefore, seeing it was a thing so common, no marvel if Felix do acquit Paul. Furthermore, it were hard to take *way* for the knowledge of the fact. And I see not how this can hang together, that the governor doth confess that Lysias was more expert in the law than he. But his innocency is made more famous and evident by this, because a profane man did straightway give such a prejudice[2] thereof that he did suffer him to be visited and holpen by his friends, being, as it were, exempted from the order of prisoners. Also, we gather by this that Paul's companions and the residue of the Church had not forsaken him. For to what end had it been to grant liberty to his friends and acquaintance to have access unto him unless they had been present, had showed themselves to be careful for him, and had been desirous to do their duty?[3] There-

---

[1] "Magis remissa . . . tractatio," more indulgent treatment.
[2] "Tale præjudicium tulit," did so favourably prejudge it
[3] "Officio defungi," to do offices of kindness to him

fore, let us learn by this example, that so long as we may, and are able, we must not defraud the martyrs of Christ of any manner of comfort whilst they labour for the gospel.

24. *Felix, with his wife Drusilla.* We said somewhat already concerning the covetousness and corruptions of Felix. Now, as touching his wife Drusilla, the readers must understand that she was daughter to Agrippa the elder, of whose filthy death Luke spake before, chapter 12, (Acts xii. 23.) She was betrothed to Epiphanis, the son of Antiochus. But forasmuch as the young man would not take on him the rites which the Jews did use, which he promised to do, her brother, Agrippa the younger, (of whom mention shall be made in the next chapter,) after the death of his father, gave her to wife to Azizus, king of the Emesenes; from whose company she was enticed by the flattery of Felix. For Felix being taken with her singular beauty, did persuade one Simon, a Jew, born in Cyprus, to persuade and allure her to make a new match. Therefore, it came to pass, that this voluptuous woman, having broken promise with her former husband, did marry with an uncircumcised man contrary to the law. But though she had polluted herself with profane wedlock, yet we may easily conjecture by this place that she had not quite abandoned that feeling of religion which she had of [from] a child.

For Felix would neither have desired to hear Paul, neither would he have vouchsafed to speak to him, unless it had been for his wife's sake. Luke doth not express thus much, but in that he nameth Drusilla, we may well gather that Paul was called for her sake, that he might dispute of the gospel; though such revolts [apostates] be rather tickled with curiosity, than moved with a sincere desire to learn.

He heard him touching the faith. This confession of Paul doth witness, that he did not spare to speak of Christ before, because he was afraid, or because he would escape the trouble of the cross;[1] but because it was not yet time to speak.

---

[1] "Vel ut se subtraheret a crucis molestia," or that he might escape from bearing the cross.

Seeing he was cited unto the judgment-seat to answer for himself, it stood him upon to answer concerning the crimes which were objected to him, that he might afterward frankly and freely profess the faith of Christ. Therefore, when he now seeth the gate set open, and opportunity offered for speaking, he is not afraid to offend the governor, neither is he terrified with danger, that he doth craftily make as if he were not a Christian. Therefore, we see that he was as well furnished with invincible constancy as with wisdom and judgment; neither did he ever of set purpose suppress the light of the gospel, but did only make choice of the time.

Now, the wonderful counsel of God is worth the noting in this place, who will have the gospel offered sometimes to the reprobate; not that they may profit thereby, but rather that they may be made inexcusable. It had been better for Felix and Drusilla never to have heard anything concerning Christ; because they did not escape without punishment for refusing the grace of salvation which was offered to them, or for neglecting the same with loathsomeness. Furthermore, we must note this, that certain, by reason of that seed of godliness which is in them engendered, do desire to hear the gospel preached, which, so soon as they have heard, they do by and by either loathe, or else they cannot suffer it. Nevertheless, the preaching of the gospel (what success soever it have) is a good and sweet savour to God; whether it quicken or kill men, (2 Cor. ii. 15.)

25. *And as he disputed.* Felix hoped that he should take some delight in Paul's sermon; as men who are desirous of new things do willingly feed their ears with subtle disputations; also he meant to satisfy his wife's desire without his own trouble; now, he is enforced to feel that force of the Word of God, whereof he never thought, which driveth away all his delights. Paul, out of bonds, disputeth of the judgment of God; he which had power to put him to death, or to save his life, is afraid and quaketh as if he stood before his own judge; neither doth he find any other comfort, but

to send him away out of his sight. Let us first learn by this, what great force of the Spirit of God there was both in the heart and also in the tongue of Paul, because he seeth that he must speak in the name of Christ, he doth not behave himself like an underling;[1] but he declareth the embassage which was enjoined him, with a grace, as from on high, and having forgotten that he was in bonds, he denounceth the heavenly judgment in the person of Christ. And now, seeing Felix' heart is so pricked with the voice of a prisoner, the majesty of the Spirit doth show itself in that also, which Christ extolleth; when the Spirit shall come he shall judge the world, &c., and that force of prophesying, which the same Paul setteth forth elsewhere, (1 Cor. xiv. 24.) Also, that is fulfilled which he saith in another place, that the word of God was not bound with him; which he did not only stoutly maintain and affirm to be true, but which did effectually pierce into the hearts of men, (and that of such as were proud of their greatness,) as if it did lighten from heaven.

Again, we must note, that although the reprobate be stricken with the judgment of God, yet are they not renewed unto repentance by that terror alone. Felix is touched indeed, when he heareth that God shall be the Judge of the world; yet he fleeth therewithal from his judgment-seat, (whereof he is afraid,) so that this is feigned sorrow, which doth not work salvation. Therefore, repentance requireth such fear as may both engender a voluntary hatred of sin, and may also present a man before God, that he may willingly suffer himself to be judged by his word. And this is a token of true profiting when the sinner seeketh for medicine there, from whence he received his wound. Furthermore, this place doth teach that men are then examined and tried to the quick, when their vices, wherewith they are infected, are brought to light, and their consciences are called back unto the judgment to come. For when Paul disputeth of righteousness and temperance, he did rub

---

[1] " Non submisse agit," he does not act crouchingly.

Felix sore upon the gall; forasmuch as he was both a man given to filthy pleasure, and also to dissolute riot, and given over unto iniquity.

26. *Hoping that money.* Though Felix had thoroughly tried Paul's integrity, so that he was ashamed to take money of the Jews for condemning him; yet forasmuch as he was a covetous man, and a man given to corruptions, he would not acquit him for nothing; for this cause he doth often call Paul, that he may with fair words put him in some hope of deliverance.[1] For judges which gape after money do insinuate themselves thus, when as they will make way for corruptions. Whence we gather, that it was but a vain and transitory fear wherewith Felix was taken when he heard Paul dispute, seeing hope of gain doth compel him to call for him whom he was enforced with fear to send away. How did Felix hope for some reward at the hands of a poor man, and one that was destitute? for that goulf would not have been content with a small prey. I do not doubt but that (as those who have the law and right to sell are witty and can perceive things[2]) when he saw the Jews did make such earnest suit to have Paul put to death, he smelled somewhat afar off touching him;[3] to wit, that he was none of the common sort; but such a man as was in great favour with many. Wherefore, he did not doubt but that many of his friends would willingly bestow cost to redeem him.

27. *And when two years were expired.* Seeing Paul knew that the judge who did gape for gain would be favourable to him so soon as he should offer him money, and seeing he had sufficient time to gather the same; it is likely that he did not only bear with the brethren,[4] but also detest

---

[1] " Liberationes redimendæ," of purchasing deliverance. [2] " Ut sagaces sunt et acuti qui jus habent venale," as those judges who act venally are sagacious and acute   [3] " Aliquid procul de ipso subodoratum esse," he had some distant idea of what kind of a person he was.
[4] " Pepercisse fratribus," spare the brethren.

such bribery, wherewith the holiness of civil order is shamefully polluted. Now, whereas governors use to let loose such prisoners as they know are not guilty when they go from the province, Felix took the contrary way to win favour. The Jews had often complained of his filthy gain, of his extortion, cruelty, and unruly government. Claudius Cæsar being wearied with so many complaints, did call him out of Judea; to the end the Jews may not spite him so sore, he leaveth Paul bound; so that he maketh the guiltless servant of God, as it were, an offering for his evil deeds, that he may therewithal appease the priests.

CHAPTER XXV.

1. *Then when Festus was come into the province, after three days he went up to Jerusalem from the city of Cesarea.*
2. *And the high priests and chief Jews informed him of Paul, and besought him,*
3. *Desiring favour against him, that he would send for him to Jerusalem, laying await to kill him by the way.*
4. *But Festus answered, that Paul should be kept at Cesarea, and that he himself would go thither shortly.*
5. *Therefore, let them, saith he, which are able among you, go down with me, and if there be any fault in this man, let them accuse him.*
6. *And after that he had staid more than ten days among them, he went down to Cesarea; and on the morrow he sat down in the judgment-seat, and commanded Paul to be brought.*
7. *Who being come, those Jews which came from Jerusalem stood about him, laying many and great crimes to Paul's charge, which they could not prove.*
8. *Forasmuch as he answered, That he had neither offended any thing against the law of the Jews, neither against the temple, neither against Cæsar.*

1. *Then when Festus.* The second action is described in

this place, wherein Paul hath as hard a combat, and is in no less danger than in the first. Seeing he was left in bonds, Festus might suspect that the cause was doubtful, and so gather an unjust prejudice. But there was another thing which was cause of great danger. We know that new rulers, because they will win the favour of those who are in the provinces, use to grant them many things at their first coming; so that it was to be thought that the death of Paul should be to Festus a fine means to win favour with all. Therefore, the faith of the holy man is assailed afresh with a new trial, as if the promise had been vain whereto he had hitherto trusted; but the grace of God doth so much the more plainly show itself in delivering him, because, contrary to all hope, he is delivered out of the jaws of death. The Jews prevent the governor with their false accusations, yet they do not as yet seek to have him punished, but they do only desire that he may not be brought into any foreign court to plead his cause. They desire that ambitiously as a great benefit, which was to look to equal. How is it then that they do not obtain, save only because God doth hold the mind of Festus, so that he doth stoutly deny that which he was afterward ready to grant? And as the Lord did then hold his mind bound with the secret bridle of his providence, so when he granted him freedom of will he bound his hands, that he could not execute that which he would. Let this confidence support us in dangers, and let it also stir us up to call upon God; and let this make our minds quiet and calm, in that the Lord, in stretching forth his hand, and breaking such a strong conspiracy, did show an eternal example of his power in defending his.

5. *Those, therefore.* It is in the Greek word for word, [literally,] Those who are mighty or able; yet he meaneth those who can conveniently. Also, we may easily conjecture, that they did object the trouble and charges, and besought the governor that he would not make weary with a superfluous journey so many of their chief men, and also certain which were very aged; but would rather (which he might

easily do) command Paul to be brought by a few keepers, [guards.] Therefore, lest they complain that he is burdenous unto them, he unloadeth them of this necessity, and giveth them leave to choose out from among themselves such as they will. In the mean season, he doth sufficiently declare that he doth not believe their false reports; and he professeth that he will be an upright judge, and will do nothing but according to the truth of the matter. The next sentence also is diversely read among the Grecians. For some books [manuscripts] have the same which is in the old interpreter but eight or ten days. If this reading like us, the sense shall be, that the governor came shortly after to Cesarea, lest the Jews should be importunate upon him under colour of his long tarriance. The other reading, which is more usual among the Grecians, shall have another meaning; though he stayed long enough at Jerusalem to hear the matter, yet did he not hearken to their requests, who would have Paul brought thither; whence we may gather a probable conjecture, that he already knew of their laying await.

7. *Many and grievous crimes.* So long as Paul lived under the law, his integrity was well known and famous. Again, when he was converted to Christ, he was a singular pattern of innocence. Yet we see how he is subject to many slanders, cruel and false accusations. And this is almost always the estate of the servants of Christ, wherefore they must be the more courageous, to pass valiantly through evil report and good report; neither let them think it strange to be evil reported of where they have done good.

In the mean season, they must do their endeavour, that they may not only have a clear conscience before God, but that they may be very well able to defend themselves before men, when they have time and place. For Paul doth not fail in his cause, but courageously setteth the defence of his innocency against their false crimes. Furthermore, let us note that the wicked can never be bridled, but they will speak evil of good men, and will impudently slander them; for they resemble the nature of Satan, by whose spirit they are led. Therefore, whereas we be commanded to stop the mouth of the wicked, it must not be so taken as if he shall be free from all backbiting,[1] whosoever shall behave himself uprightly, but that our life may answer for us, and may wipe away all blots of false infamy. So we see the adversaries of Paul, though they had a favourable judge, yet their slanders were all in vain, seeing he did defend and avouch his innocency by his deeds. And yet it is likely that they wanted not false witnesses, neither were they slack in suborning them; but because the Lord giveth his servants invincible strength, so that the brightness of honesty doth drive away their vain clouds; they are ashamed, and at length they depart from the judgment-seat with this infamy, that they were false accusers. But the defence of Paul doth show what things the Jews laid principally to his charge. The first crime was ungodliness against God, that he overthrew the law and polluted the temple; the other, rebellion against Cæsar and the Roman empire, because he raised tumults everywhere. He was helped by the singular grace of God to answer and refute both, who maketh the innocence of his as bright as the morning.

> 9. *And Festus, being willing to do the Jews a pleasure, answered Paul, and said, Wilt thou go up to Jerusalem, and there be judged of these things before me?*
> 10. *But Paul said, I stand before Cæsar's judgment-seat, where I must be judged: to the Jews have I done no wrong, as thou thyself knowest full well.*
> 11. *And if I do injury, or have committed any thing worthy of death, I refuse not to die; but if there be nothing of these things whereof they accuse me, no man can deliver me to them. I appeal to Cæsar.*
> 12. *Then spake Festus with the council, and said, Hast thou appealed to Cæsar? to Cæsar shalt thou go.*

9. *And Festus.* Whether Festus knew somewhat of their

---

[1] "Ab omni falsa obtrectatione," from all groundless detraction.

laying await, (which we may well conjecture,) or whether he were altogether ignorant thereof, he dealeth unjustly with Paul; and we see how soon those are drawn unto all corruption which are not guided by the Spirit of God. For Festus doth not openly contemn or hate Paul; but ambition, and peradventure also desire of gain, got the upper hand, so that, for pleasing the other part, he doth unjustly bring him in danger of death; also, it is likely that he was enticed with the smell [hope] of some reward to hearken so courteously to the priests. Notwithstanding, I marvel that he giveth Paul leave to choose, and doth not rather, according to this authority, command them to carry him whether he would or no. Surely we gather that he was kept back with fear, lest he should infringe the privilege of the city of Rome,[1] which was a very odious crime. Notwithstanding, he studied craftily to persuade Paul not to refuse to be judged at Jerusalem. For he was not ignorant of that which indeed came to pass, that a citizen of Rome might lawfully appeal, so that he could then go no farther. Nevertheless, it was no thank to him that he was not delivered into the hands of murderers.[2]

10. *I stand at Cæsar's judgment-seat.* Because Paul seeth that he is betrayed into the hands of the Jews through the ambition of the governor, he objecteth the privilege of the city of Rome. He had submitted himself modestly, if he had commanded him to do[3] that which was just and equal. Now, because the governor doth not his duty willingly, necessity compelleth the holy man to defend himself by law; and by this means the Lord delivereth him now again, even when he was almost given over into the hands of the enemies. And whereas he desireth to have his matter handled before Cæsar's judgment-seat, he doth not, therefore, make the doctrine of the gospel subject to the judgment of a pro-

---

[1] "Jus Romanæ civitatis," the privilege of a Roman citizen. [2] "Quominus sceleratis latronibus mactandum objiceret," that he did not expose himself to be murdered by nefarious assassins. [3] "Si impetrasset," if he had obtained

fane and wicked man; but being ready to give an account of his faith everywhere, he appealeth from that court where he could no longer hope for equity. Furthermore, though the citizens of Rome did retain their privilege, yet the order was then altered, because the Cæsars had taken into their own hands the judging of the people,[1] as if they would be good maintainers and patrons of common liberty.

To the Jews have I done. Because those whose consciences do accuse them, and which mistrust their matter, fly unto certain odd excuses and exceptions, Paul turneth away from himself this opinion. And surely the ministers of Christ ought to have no less care to make their innocency known than to save their life. If Paul had flatly denied to answer for himself, the enemies would have triumphed, and the doubtfulness of an evil conscience should have been objected to him to the reproach of the gospel. But now when he citeth the governor himself to be a witness of his integrity, and doth refuse no punishment if he should be found guilty, he cutteth off all occasion of slanderous reports. Therefore, he showeth that he doth not seek to save himself by turning his back,[2] but flyeth unto the fortress of a just defence, that he may there save himself from injury, seeing his adversaries have hitherto handled him unjustly; and now refusing to deal with him any longer by law, they go about to have him murdered. Neither doth Paul go behind the president's back to tell him that he doth unjustly, in that he doth so dally with his accusers; and therewithal he doth, as it were, bridle his lust, so that he dare go no farther.

11. *I appeal unto Cæsar.* After that he hath professed that he doth not refuse to die if he be found guilty, he freely useth such helps as he could find at the hands of men. Wherefore, if we be at any time brought into like straits, we must not be superstitious, but we may crave help of the laws and politic order. Because it is written, that magistrates are made and appointed by God to the praise of the

---

[1] "Judicium populi," the right of judging (formerly) in the people.
[2] "Tergiversandi," by tergiversation.

godly, (Rom. xiii. 3; and 1 Pet. ii. 13.) Neither was Paul afraid to go to law under an unbelieving judge; for he which appealeth commenceth a new action.

Therefore, let us know that God, who hath appointed judgment-seats, doth also grant liberty to his to use the same lawfully. Therefore, those mistake Paul who think that he doth flatly condemn the Corinthians, (1 Cor. vi. 1,) because they require help of the magistrate for defence of their right, seeing he reproveth in that place a manifest fault, to wit, because they could suffer no wrong, and because they were too much set upon suing one another, whereby they caused the gospel to be evil spoken of.

12. *Festus having talked with the council.* The governors did use to have certain of the chief citizens which did attend upon them, and sat with them in judgment, that they might decree nothing without the consent of the council. Furthermore, it doth seem that Festus pronounced this with indignation, when he said interrogatively, Hast thou appealed to Cæsar? to wit, because it grieved him that he could not do the Jews such a pleasure as he desired; though I leave that indifferent, because it is neither of any great importance, and it leaneth only to a conjecture.

13. *And after certain days, king Agrippa and Bernice came to Cesarea to salute Festus.*
14. *And when they had stayed there many days, Festus rehearsed Paul's cause to the king, saying, There is a certain man left in bonds of Felix:*
15. *About whom, when I came to Jerusalem, the high priests and elders of the Jews informed me, requiring judgment against him.*
16. *To whom I answered, It is not the custom of the Romans for favour to deliver any man that he should perish, before he that is accused have his accusers face to face, and have licence to answer for himself, concerning the crime laid against him.*
17. *Therefore, when they were come hither without delay, on the*

morrow I sat on the judgment-seat, and commanded the man to be brought.

18. *Against whom when the accusers stood up, they brought none accusation concerning such things as I supposed :*
19. *But they had certain questions concerning their superstition (or religion) against him, and concerning one Jesus which was dead, whom Paul affirmed to be alive.*
20. *And because I doubted of this question, I asked him if he would go to Jerusalem, and there be judged of these things.*
21. *And when Paul had appealed, that he might be kept unto the knowledge of Augustus, I commanded him to be kept until I might send him to Cæsar.*

13. *And after certain days.* This long narration tendeth to this end, that we may know that though the handling of the cause were broken off, yet were Paul's bands famous; and that he was nevertheless brought out of prison, that he might make profession of his faith, and dispute touching the gospel before a famous auditory; and again, that though he were contemned, yet was he not counted a wicked person, lest the glory of Christ should be abased by his slander and reproach, yea, that he had more liberty to preach the gospel being in prison, than if he had lived free in a private house.

King Agrippa and Bernice. It is certain that this Agrippa was son to Agrippa the elder, whose filthy and detestable death was set down in the twelfth chapter. When this man was made king of Chalcis, in his uncle's stead, after the decease of his father, he did afterward obtain a more large dominion.[1] Bernice, of whom mention is made in this place, was his own natural sister, which was first married to Herod, king of Chalcis, her uncle, and did keep herself widow a certain season after his death, yet she did not live honestly and chastely during that time; for her great familiarity with her brother Agrippa was suspected. And to the end she might not be counted an incestuous person, she married with Polemon, king of Cilicia. Notwithstand-

---

[1] "Tetrarchiam," tetrarchy.

ing, because she gave herself more to lust than to chastity, she forsook him. The historiographers do nowhere say that she was her brother's wife; and Josephus, in his Life, assigned her a dominion of her own in part of Galilee. Therefore, it is to be thought that forasmuch as they were hardened in their wickedness, they dwelt together, not regarding what men did say; yet did they abstain from marriage, lest their incestuous marriage should betray and also augment their crime. Neither is it any marvel that he came for honour's sake to salute the governor, who did reign only at the will and pleasure of another, and did depend upon the beck and favour of the Emperor of Rome, which he was to retain and nourish by means of the governor.

14. *When many days.* Therefore, when (after some time was spent) they wanted matter of talk, as idle men use to invent somewhat whereon they may talk, mention was made of Paul; for Luke meant to note that, when he said that after many days were idly spent, Festus told the king of a certain man which lay bound. And although he doth here both touch the malice of the priests, and also make a show of wonderful equity on his part, yet in that he shortly after cleareth the party which was accused, he condemneth himself unawares, when as he confesseth that he was enforced to appeal that he might not be carried to Jerusalem.

But when Festus commendeth the Romans, he showeth what doth beseem judges. And if nature did tell profane men thus much, that they must admit no such favour as may oppress the guiltless, how much more must judges (who have the light of the word of God) be careful to avoid all corruption.

18. *They laid no such crime to his charge.* I marvel why Festus doth say, that there was no such crime objected to Paul as he supposed, seeing he was accused of sedition; but we may again conjecture by this, yea, plainly know,

that their accusations were so vain, that they ought not to have been brought before the judgment-seat; as if a man did utter a slanderous speech unadvisedly. For which cause he saith, that the state of the cause did consist in questions of the law. Therefore, we see that he putteth a difference between those offences which were wont to be punished by man's laws, and the controversy which was between Paul and the Jews; not that the religion ought to be corrupted freely,[1] or that their malapertness is tolerable, who overthrow the worship of God with their own inventions; but because the man being a Roman, cared not for Moses' law; therefore he speaketh so disdainfully when he saith, that they did strive about their superstition; though this word δεισιδαιμονια be taken of the Grecians, as well in good as evil part; to wit, because the worshipping of false gods was common in all places. Notwithstanding, his meaning is, that he careth not what manner of religion the Jews have. And no marvel if a man which was an ethnic, [heathen,] and had not learned that the rule of godliness must be fet [sought] from the mouth of God, know not how to distinguish between the pure worship of God and superstitions.

Wherefore, we must hold fast that mark whereby we may discern the one from the other, that there is no godliness but that which is grounded in the knowledge of faith, lest we grabble [grope] in darkness. Moreover, the Romans were so drunken with prosperous success, that they thought that they were more acceptable to God than any other; as at this day the Turks, by reason of their manifold victories, deride the doctrine of Christ. This was a lamentable case, that a man being an unbeliever and idolater, sitteth as judge amidst the Jews, to give judgment of the sacred oracles of God according to his ignorance, but all the fault was in Paul's adversaries, who did not care for the majesty of God, so they might satisfy and obey their own madness. Notwithstanding, there rested nothing for Paul to do, but

---

[1] " Impune violari," be violated with impunity.

to clear himself of those crimes which were laid against him. So at this day, though inward brawls, which are among Christians, do defame the name of Christ and his gospel among the Turks and Jews, yet the defenders of holy doctrine are unworthily blamed, which are enforced to enter the combat.

Of one Jesus. It is not to be doubted but that Paul intreated, both gravely and with such vehemency as became him, of the resurrection of Christ; but Festus, by reason of his pride, thought it no meet matter for him to occupy his head about. He doth not, indeed, openly deride Paul, but he showeth plainly how negligently he heard him when he disputed of Christ. Whereby we see how little preaching availeth, yea, that it availeth nothing at all, unless the Spirit of God do inwardly touch the hearts of men. For the wicked do lightly pass over whatsoever is spoken, as if a man should tell them a tale of Robin Hood.[1] Wherefore, there is no cause why the carelessness of many should trouble us at this day, seeing Paul prevailed nothing with Festus. But this place doth witness that many speeches did pass in the handling of the matter, whereof Luke maketh no mention. For he had spoken nothing as yet of Christ, and yet this latter narration doth show that Paul intreated seriously before the Jews of his death and resurrection. Which could not be, but he must needs intreat of the principal points of the gospel. Therefore, I guess tha Paul did so handle the matter, that when he had refuted the false accusations of the Jews, wherewith they went about to burden him before the governor, having gotten a fit occasion, he began afterward to speak freely of Christ.

22. *And Agrippa said unto Festus, I would also myself hear the man. To-morrow, saith he, thou shalt hear him.*
23. *And on the morrow, when Agrippa was come, and Bernice, with great pomp, and was entered into the common hall with the chief captains, and the principal men of the city, at Festus' commandment Paul was brought.*

[1] " Acsi quis fabulas narraret," as if one were telling them fables.

24. *And Festus saith, King Agrippa, and all men which are present with us, ye see this man, about whom all the multitude of the Jews hath called upon me, both at Jerusalem and here, crying that he ought not to live any longer.*
25. *Yet have I found that he hath committed nothing worthy of death, and because he hath appealed unto Augustus, I have determined to send him.*
26. *Of whom I have no certain thing to write unto my lord. Wherefore I have brought him forth unto you, and chiefly unto thee, O king Agrippa, that, after examination had, I may have somewhat to write.*
27. *For it seemeth to me an unmeet thing to send a prisoner, and not to show the crimes whereof he is accused.*

22. *I would also.* By this we may gather that Agrippa did so desire to hear Paul, that he was ashamed to make his desire known, lest Festus should think that he came for some other end than to salute him. And it may be that not only curiosity did move him to be desirous to hear Paul, but because he did hope to profit by hearing him. Notwithstanding, we may easily gather by this how cold his desire was, because he suffered many days to pass before he showeth any sign of his desire, because he was more in love with earthly commodities, which he counted better. Neither durst he make any words; neither did he pass for uttering any speech until such time as Festus did of his own accord will him so to do. So that the holy minister of Christ is brought forth as on a stage, that a profane man may cheer up his guest, save only that Festus will be holpen with the advice of Agrippa and his company, that he may let Cæsar understand how diligent he is. But the matter was turned to another end by the secret providence of God. Neither need we doubt but that such report went abroad as made much for the confirmation of the godly; and it may be also that some of the hearers were touched, and did conceive seed of faith, which did afterward bring forth fruit in due time. But admit none of them did embrace Christ sincerely and from his heart, this was no small profit, that the unskil-

ful were appeased after that the malice of the enemies was discovered, that they might not be inflamed with such hatred against the gospel. Impiety was made ashamed, and the faithful did gather new strength, so that they were confirmed more and more in the gospel.

23. *And on the morrow.* Agrippa and his sister do not come like humble disciples of Christ, but they bring with them such pomp and gorgeousness as may stop their ears and blind their eyes; and it is to be thought that like haughtiness of mind was joined with that gorgeous and great pomp. No marvel, therefore, if they were not brought to obey Christ. Notwithstanding, it seemeth that Luke maketh mention of the pomp, that we might know that, in a great assembly, and before choice witnesses, whose authority was great, Paul had leave granted not only to plead his matter as a party defendant, but also to preach the gospel. For he cometh forth as in the person of a teacher, that he may set forth the name of Christ. So that the truth of God brake out of his bands, which was forthwith spread abroad everywhere with a free course; yea, it came even unto us. By this word $\varphi a \nu \tau a \sigma \iota a$, Luke understandeth that which we call commonly preparation or pomp.[1] But there must other furniture be brought unto the spiritual marriage of Jesus Christ.

26. *That after examination had.* We cannot tell whether the governor, in acquitting Paul before them, doth seek by this policy to entice him to let his appeal fall. For it was a thing credible that he might easily be persuaded to lay away fear, and to submit himself to the judgment and discretion of a just judge, especially if Agrippa should give his friendly consent. To what end soever he did it, he condemneth himself of iniquity by his own mouth, in that he did not let a guiltless man go free whom he is now ashamed to send unto Cæsar, having nothing to lay against him. This did

[1] "Apparentiam," show.

also come to pass by the wonderful providence of God, that the Jews themselves should give a former judgment on Paul's side. Peradventure, the governor goeth subtilely to work, that he may pick out what the king and the chief men of Cesarea do think, that if it so fall out that Paul be set at liberty, he may lay the blame on their necks. For he would not have the priests to be his enemies for nothing, upon whom a good part of Jerusalem did depend, and that was the best way that he could take in writing to Cæsar to intermingle the authority of Agrippa. But the Lord (to whom it belongeth to govern events contrary to man's expectation) had respect unto another thing, to wit, that when the clouds of false accusations were driven away, Paul might more freely avouch sound doctrine.

CHAPTER XXVI.

1. *And Agrippa said unto Paul, Thou art permitted to answer for thyself. Then Paul stretched forth his hand, and answered for himself:*
2. *I think myself happy, O king Agrippa, because I shall answer this day before thee of all the things whereof I am accused of the Jews;*
3. *Seeing thou art most expert in all those customs and questions which are among the Jews: wherefore I beseech thee hear me patiently.*
4. *My life which I have led from my youth, which was at the first in mine own nation at Jerusalem, know all the Jews;*
5. *Who knew me before since the beginning, if they would testify, that after the most strait sect of our religion I lived a Pharisee.*
6. *And now I stand subject to judgment for the hope of the promise which God made to our fathers:*

7. *Whereunto our twelve tribes, serving God instantly day and night, hope to come. For which hope, O king Agrippa, I am accused of the Jews.*
8. *Why doth it seem to you a thing incredible, if God raise the dead?*

2. We have declared to what end Paul was brought before that assembly, to wit, that Festus might write unto Cæsar as he should be counselled by Agrippa and the rest. Therefore, he doth not use any plain or usual form of defence, but doth rather apply his speech unto doctrine. Luke useth indeed a word of excusing; yet such a one as is nothing inconvenient whensoever there is any account given of doctrine. Furthermore, because Paul knew well that Festus did set light by all that which should be taken out of the law and prophets, he turneth himself unto the king, who he hoped would be more attentive, seeing he was no stranger to the Jewish religion. And because he had hitherto spoken to deaf men, he rejoiceth now that he hath gotten a man who, for his skill and experience, can judge aright. But as he commendeth the skill and knowledge which is in Agrippa, because he is a lawful judge in those matters whereof he is to speak, so he desireth him on the other side to hear him patiently; for otherwise contempt and loathsomeness should have been less excusable in him. He calleth those points of doctrine, which were handled among the scribes, questions, who were wont to discuss religion more subtilely. By the word *customs*, he meaneth those rites which were common to the whole nation. Therefore, the sum is this, that king Agrippa was not ignorant either in doctrine, either in the ceremonies of the law. That which he bringeth in or concludeth,[1] wherefore I pray thee hear me patiently, (as I said even now,) doth signify that the more expert a man is in the Scripture, the more attentive must he be when the question is about religion. For that which we understand doth not trouble us so much.

---

[1] "Illatio ista," the inference.

And it is meet that we be so careful for the worship of God, that it do not grieve us to hear those things which belong to the defining thereof, and chiefly when we have learned the principle,[1] so that we may readily judge, if we list to take heed.

4. *My life which I have led.* He doth not as yet enter into the state of the cause; but because he was wrongfully accused and burdened with many crimes, lest king Agrippa should envy the cause[2] through hatred of the person, he doth first avouch his innocency. For we know that when a sinister suspicion hath once possessed the minds of men, all their senses are so shut up that they can admit nothing. Therefore, Paul doth first drive away the clouds of an evil opinion which were gathered of false reports, that he may be heard of pure and well purged ears. By this we see that Paul was enforced by the necessity of the cause to commend his life which he had led before. But he standeth not long upon that point, but passeth over straightway unto the resurrection of the dead, when he saith that he is a Pharisee. And I think that that is called the most strait sect, not in respect of holiness of life, but because there was in it more natural sincerity of doctrine, and greater learning. For they did boast that they knew the secret meaning of the Scripture. And surely forasmuch as the Sadducees did vaunt that they did stick to the letter, they fell into filthy and gross ignorance after they had darkened the light of the Scripture. The Essenes, contenting themselves with an austere and strait kind of life, did not greatly care for doctrine. Neither doth that any whit hinder, because Christ inveigheth principally against the Pharisees, as being the worst corrupters of the Scripture, (Matth. xxiii. 13.) For seeing they did challenge to themselves authority to interpret the Scripture according to the hidden and secret meaning, hence came that boldness to change and innovate,

---

[1] "Ne præsertim ubi jam principiis imbuti sumus," and especially when we have already been imbued with the principles.   [2] "Causæ sit infensus," be prejudiced against the cause.

wherewith the Lord is displeased. But Paul doth not touch those inventions which they had rashly invented, and which they urged with tyrannous rigour. For it was his purpose to speak only of the resurrection of the dead. For though they had corrupted the law in many points, yet it was meet that the authority of that sect should be of more estimation in defending the sound and true faith, than of the other, which were departed farther from natural purity. Moreover, Paul speaketh only of the common judgment, which did respect the colour of more subtile knowledge.

6. *For the hope of the promise.* He doth now descend into the cause, to wit, that he laboureth for the principal point of faith. And though he seem to have spoken generally of the resurrection, yet we may gather out of the text, that he beginneth with a farther point, and that he did comprehend those circumstances which did properly appertain unto the faith of the gospel. He complaineth that the Jews did accuse him, because he maintained the hope of the promise made to the fathers. Therefore, this was the beginning and also the issue of the matter, that the covenant which God had made with the fathers is referred unto eternal salvation. Wherefore this was the sum of the disputation, that the Jewish religion was nothing worth unless they took heed to the heavens, and did also lift up their eyes unto Christ, the author of the new life. They did boast that they were chosen from among all people of the world. But their adoption did profit them nothing, unless they did trust to the promised Mediator, and look unto the inheritance of the kingdom of God. Therefore, we must conceive much more than Luke doth plainly express. And surely his narration tendeth to no other end, save only that we may know of what things Paul intreated. But what this was, and in what words he uttered it, we cannot tell. Nevertheless, it behoveth us to gather out of a brief sum those things which appertain unto this disputation, which was freely handled before Agrippa, when Paul had free liberty granted to him to plead his own cause.

7. *Whereunto our twelve tribes.* Paul complaineth before Agrippa, that the state of the Church is come to that pass, that the priests set themselves against the common hope of all the faithful; as if he should say, To what end do those of our nation, who worship God carefully, and spend both days and nights in the duties of godliness, sigh in their prayers, save only that they may at length come unto eternal life? But the same is the mark whereat I aim in all my doctrine; because, when the grace of redemption is set before men, the gate of the kingdom of heaven is set open therewithal. And when I preach the author of salvation raised up from the dead, I offer the first-fruits of immortality in his person; so that the former confirmation of his doctrine was taken out of the Word of God, when he cited the promise made to the fathers. Now, in the second place, he addeth the consent of the Church. And this is the best way to maintain and avouch the opinions of faith, that the authority of God go foremost; and that then the consent of the Church come next. Though we ought therewithal wisely to make choice of the true Church, as Paul doth teach us in this place by his own example; for though he knew that the priests did pretend the visor [mask] of the Church against him, yet he doth boldly affirm, that the sincere worshippers of God are on his side, and he is content with their defence. For when he meaneth [nameth] the twelve tribes, he doth not speak generally of all those which came of Jacob according to the flesh; but he meaneth those only which did retain the true study of godliness. For it had been an unmeet thing to commend the nation generally for the fear of God, which was only in a few.

The Papists deal very disorderly in both; who, by the voices and consents of men, oppress the Word of God, and give also the name and title of the Catholic Church to a filthy rabblement of unlearned and impure men, without any colour or shame. But if we will prove that we think as the true Church thinketh, we must begin with the prophets and apostles; then those must be gathered unto them whose godliness is known and manifest. If the Pope and his clergy be not on our side, we need not greatly to care. And the true affection of true religion is proved by continuance and vehemency, which was of singular force at that time, principally when the Jews were in greatest misery.

8. *Why should.* I do not doubt but that he proved that both by reason, and also by testimonies of Scripture, which he taught concerning the resurrection and the heavenly life. But for good causes doth he call back those unto whom he speaketh unto the power of God, lest they judge thereof according to their own weak capacity. For nothing can more hardly sink into men's brains, than that men's bodies shall be restored when as they be once consumed.[1] Therefore, seeing it is a mystery far surpassing man's wit, let the faithful remember how far the infinite power of God doth reach, and not what they themselves comprehend; as the same Paul teacheth in the third chapter to the Philippians, (Philip. iii. 21.) For when he hath said that our vile bodies shall be made like to the glorious body of Christ, he addeth immediately, " according to the mighty working whereby he is able to subdue all things to himself." But men are for the most part injurious[2] to God, who will not have his arm to reach any farther than their understanding and reason can reach; so that so much as in them lieth they would desire to restrain the greatness of his works (which surpasseth heaven and earth) unto their straits.[3] But, on the other side, Paul commandeth us to consider what God is able to do, that being lifted up above the world, we may learn to conceive the faith of the resurrection, not according to the weak capacity of our mind, but according to his omnipotency.

9. *And I verily thought that I ought to do many things against the name of Jesus of Nazareth.*

[1] " Ubi in nihilum redacta fuerint," after being reduced to nothing
[2] " Maligni . . . et injurii," malignant and injurious.   [3] " Ad suas angustias," to their narrow capacity.

10. *Which thing I also did at Jerusalem; and I shut up many of the saints in prison, having received power from the high priests; and when they were put to death, I gave sentence.*

11. *And punishing them oftentimes throughout all synagogues, I enforced them to blaspheme; and being yet more mad upon them, I did persecute them even into strange cities.*

12. *And as I went to Damascus for this intent, with authority and commission from the high priests,*

13. *At mid-day, O king, I saw in the way a light from heaven, passing the brightness of the sun, shine round about me and those which journeyed with me.*

14. *And when we were all fallen to the earth, I heard a voice speaking unto me, and saying in the Hebrew tongue, Saul, Saul, why persecutest thou me? it is hard for thee to kick against the pricks.*

15. *And I said, Who art thou, Lord? But he said unto me, I am Jesus whom thou persecutest.*

16. *But rise, and stand up upon thy feet: for to this end did I appear unto thee, that I may make thee a minister and witness both of those things which thou hast seen, and also of those things wherein I will appear unto thee;*

17. *Delivering thee from the people, and from the Gentiles, unto whom now I send thee,*

18. *That thou mayest open their eyes, that they may be converted from darkness to light, and from the power of Satan unto God, that they may receive forgiveness of sins, and an inheritance among those who are sanctified by the faith which is in me.*

9. **And I truly.** If Paul had not spoken more things than those which Luke hath hitherto recited, his speech had not hanged well together.[1] Whence we prove that which was said before, that after that he had spoken of the covenant of God, he intreated of the grace and office of Christ, as the matter required. And he repeateth the history of his conversion for this cause, not only that he may remove from himself all suspicion of lightness, but that he may

---

[1] " Abrupta esset," would have been abrupt.

testify that God had called him, and that he was even enforced by a commandment coming from heaven. For, seeing that he was, contrary to his expectation, suddenly made a sheep of a wolf, such a violent change is of no small importance to purchase credit to his doctrine.

Therefore, he amplifieth that his heat and vehement desire which he had to punish[1] the members of Christ, and also that stubbornness whereunto he was wholly given over. If he had been nousled [brought] up in the faith of Christ from his youth, or if he had been taught by some man, he should have embraced it willingly and without resistance, he himself should have been sure of his calling, but it should not have been so well known to others. But now, seeing that being inflamed with obstinate and immoderate fury, being moved with no occasion, neither persuaded by mortal man, he changeth his mind, it appeareth that he was tamed and brought under by the hand of God.

Therefore, this contrariety is of great weight,[2] in that he saith that he was so puffed up with pride, that he thought he should get the victory of Christ, whereby he teacheth that he was nothing less than made[3] a disciple of Christ through his own industry. The name of Jesus of Nazareth is taken in this place for the whole profession of the gospel, which Paul sought to extinguish, by making war ignorantly against God, as we may see.[4]

10. *Which thing I did.* He proveth by his very facts with what force of zeal he was carried away to strive against Christ, until greater force did pull him back, and made him go the quite contrary way. Furthermore, his adversaries were witnesses of this his vehemency, so that it was most certain that he was suddenly changed; and undoubtedly the priests would never have put him in any such office, unless he had behaved himself courageously in exercising cruelty;

---

[1] " Nocendi," to persecute.   [2] " Magnum ergo pondus habet ista antithesis," there is a great force, therefore, in the antithesis.   [3] " Nihil minus .quam factum," that he was by no means made.   [4] " Hoc modo," in this way

and it was meet that he should be very courageous who should satisfy their fury. This is also to be noted, that Paul was not ashamed to confess how sore he had offended against God, so that that might turn to the glory of Christ. It was to him undoubtedly reproachful, to have been carried away with blind zeal, so that he enforced those to blaspheme which did desire to serve God; to have troubled the good and simple diversely; to have given sentence of the shedding of innocent blood; finally, to have lifted up his horns even unto heaven. until he was thrown down. But he doth not spare his own estimation, but doth willingly utter his own shame, that the mercy of God may the more plainly appear thereby.

Wherefore, there could no sinister suspicion rest in his speech, seeing that (without having any respect of himself) he saith, that he did utterly offend[1] in those things whereby he got the praise of all the people. Therefore, he condemneth his very zeal of madness, which others did honour.

Whereby it appeareth how filthy the ambition of those men is, who are ashamed simply to confess, if they have offended through ignorance or error. For although they do not altogether excuse the same, yet they go about to lessen or paint these things, for which they ought humbly with sorrow and tears to crave pardon. But though Paul might have retained the fame of a courageous man, yet he confesseth he was a madman. For the participle which Luke useth importeth thus much, that he compelled many to blaspheme. By this we know that there was great corruption even in the very first fruits of believers, seeing that having first professed themselves to be disciples of Christ, and being afterwards discouraged with fear or stripes, they did not only deny him, but also spake evil of his blessed name. Though the very denial itself containeth an horrible blasphemy.

13. *At mid-day, O king.* The narration tendeth to this

[1] " Ultro sibi in crimen imputat," voluntarily charges upon himself as criminal.

end, that king Agrippa may understand that it was no vain visure or ghost, neither was it any such trance as brought him into some madness, so that he was destitute of judgment.[1] For though he fell to the earth for fear, yet he heareth a plain voice; he asketh who it was that spake; he understandeth the answer which was made, which are signs that he was not beside himself. Hereupon it followeth that he did not rashly change his mind, but did godlily and holily obey the heavenly oracle, lest he should of set purpose proceed to strive against God.

16. *But rise.* Christ did throw down Paul that he might humble him; now he lifteth him up, and biddeth him be of good courage. And even we are daily thrown down by his voice to this end, that we may be taught to be modest; but look whom he throweth down, he doth raise the same again gently. And this is no small consolation, when Christ saith that he appeared to him not as a revenger to plague him[2] for his madness, for those stripes which he had unjustly and cruelly given, for his bloody sentences, or for that trouble wherewith he had troubled the saints, for his wicked resisting of the gospel, but as a merciful Lord, intending to use his industry, and to call him to an honourable ministry. For he made him a witness of those things which he saw, and which he should afterward see. This vision was worthy to be recorded, by which he learned that Christ reigneth in heaven, that he might no longer proudly contemn him, but acknowledge that he is the Son of God, and the promised Redeemer; he had other revelations afterward, as he saith in the Second Epistle to the Corinthians, and 12th chapter, (2 Cor. xii. 1.)

17. *Delivering thee.* He is armed in this place against all fear, which was prepared for him; and also he is prepared to bear the cross; notwithstanding, seeing he addeth imme-

---

[1] " Quæ mentis sanitatem vel judicium illi eriperet," as deprived him of his sober senses, or the power of judging. [2] " Qui pœnam exigat," to punish him

diately that Paul should come to lighten the blind, to reconcile those to God which were estranged from him, and to restore salvation to those which were lost; it is a marvel why he doth not also promise that they shall on the other side receive him joyfully, who shall by means of him receive such and so great benefits. But the unthankfulness of the world is noted out unto us in this place, because the ministers of eternal salvation are far otherwise rewarded, as frantic men do rail upon their physicians. And Paul is admonished, that whithersoever he shall come, a great part of those to whom he shall study to do good shall hate him, and seek his overthrow. And he saith plainly, that he is appointed to be a witness both to Jews and Gentiles, lest that turn to his reproach, because he made the gospel common to both alike. For the Jews had conceived such deadly hatred against him for this cause, because it grieved them that the Gentiles should be made their fellows. And though they made a show that this did proceed of zeal, because they would not have the covenant which God made with the posterity of Abraham profaned, by being translated unto strangers, yet mere ambition did prick them forward, because they alone would be excellent, all other being underlings. But in the person of one man, all godly teachers are encouraged to do their duty, that they be not hindered or kept back with the malice of men from offering the grace of God unto miserable men, though they be unworthy.

18. *That thou mayest open their eyes.* Paul, in taking to himself that which is proper to God, doth seem to exalt himself too high. For we know that it is the Holy Ghost alone which doth lighten the eyes. We know that Christ is the only Redeemer which doth deliver us from the tyranny of Satan. We know that it is God alone who, having put away our sins, doth adopt us unto the inheritance of the saints. But this is a common thing, that God doth translate unto his ministers that honour which is due to himself alone, not that he may take any thing from himself, but that he may commend that mighty working of his Spirit which he doth show forth in them. For he doth not send them to

work, that they may be dead instruments, or, as it were, stage-players; but that he may work mightily by their hand. But it dependeth upon the secret power of his Spirit that their preaching is effectual, who worketh all things in all men, and which only giveth the increase.

Therefore, teachers are sent, not to utter their words in vain in the air, or to beat the ears only with a vain sound, but to bring lively light to the blind, to fashion again men's hearts unto the righteousness of God, and to ratify the grace of salvation which is gotten by the death of Christ. But they do none of all these, save only inasmuch as God worketh by them, that their labour may not be in vain, that all the praise may be his, as the effect cometh from him.

And, therefore, we must note, that so often as the Scripture doth extol the external ministry so honourably, we must not separate it from the Spirit, which quickeneth the same even as the soul doth the body. For it teacheth in other places how little man's industry can do of itself. For they must plant and water, but it is God alone which giveth the increase, (1 Cor. xi. 6.) But because many are hindered by their own ignorance and malice, that they cannot reap such fruit of the gospel as they ought, we must note this description, which setteth before our eyes briefly and plentifully that incomparable treasure. Therefore, this is the drift of the gospel, that being delivered from blindness of mind, we may be made partakers of the heavenly light; that being delivered from the thraldom of Satan, we may be turned to God; that having free forgiveness of sins, we may be made partakers of the inheritance among the saints. Those which will rightly profit in the gospel must direct all their senses to this end; for what good shall the continual preaching thereof do us, if we know not the true use thereof? Also, the way and means to attain to salvation is described to us, all men boast that they be desirous of salvation, but few consider how God will save them.

Therefore, this place, wherein the means is prettily comprehended, is, as it were, a key to open the gate of heaven. Furthermore, we must know that all mankind is naturally deprived of those good things which Christ saith we have by believing the gospel; so that it followeth that all are blind, because they be lightened by faith; that all are the bond-slaves of Satan, because they are set free by faith from his tyranny; that all men are the enemies of God, and subject to eternal death, because they receive remission of sins by faith. So that nothing is more miserable than we, if we be without Christ, and without his faith, whereby it appeareth how little, yea, that nothing is left for the free will of men's merits. As touching every part, this lightening is referred unto the knowledge of God, because all our quickness of sight is mere vanity and thick darkness, until he appear unto us by his truth. That reacheth farther which followeth afterward: To be turned from darkness to light; for that is when we are renewed in the spirit of our mind.

Therefore, in my judgment, this member, and that which followeth, express both one thing, to be turned from the power of Satan unto God. For that renewing which Paul declareth more largely in the second chapter to the Ephesians, (Ephes. ii. 10, and iv. 23,) is expressed in divers forms of speech. Remission of sins followeth next, whereby God doth freely reconcile us to himself, so that we need not doubt but that God will be favourable and merciful to us. At length, the furnishing and filling of all things is put in the last place; to wit, the inheritance of eternal life. Some do read it falsely in one text, among those who are sanctified by faith, because this word is extended unto the whole period. Therefore, the meaning thereof is, that by faith we come unto the possession of all those good things which are offered by the gospel. And faith is properly directed unto Christ, because all the parts of our salvation are included in him. Neither doth the gospel command us to seek the same any where else save only in him.

19. *Whereupon, O king Agrippa, I was not disobedient to the heavenly vision:*
20. *But I preached first to those which are at Damascus, and at Jerusalem, and through every region of Judea, and then to*

the Gentiles, that they should repent, and be turned unto God, doing works which become those which repent.

21. For this cause the Jews, having caught me in the temple, went about to kill me.

22. Therefore, seeing I have obtained help of God, *I* stand until this present day, testifying both to small and great, saying none other things than those which the prophets and Moses said should come to pass:

23. Whether Christ should suffer, whether he should be the first that should rise from the dead, to show light to the people, and to the Gentiles.

19. He declareth now briefly to what end he rehearsed the history of his conversion; to wit, that Agrippa and the rest might understand that he had God for his author of all those things which the Jews condemned of sacrilege and apostacy. He speaketh to Agrippa by name, because he knew that Festus and the Romans knew not what an heavenly vision meant. Now, it appeareth that there is nothing in the very sum of his doctrine which dissenteth from the law and the prophets; whereby the oracle doth win greater credit, whereby Paul was commanded to teach nothing but that which was agreeable to the Scripture. Conversion, or turning unto God, is joined with repentance, not as some peculiar thing, but that we may know what it is to repent. Like as, also, on the contrary, the corruption of men and their frowardness[1] is nothing else but an estranging from God. And because repentance is an inward thing, and placed in the affection of the heart, Paul requireth, in the second place, such works as may make the same known, according to that exhortation of John the Baptist: "Bring forth fruits meet for repentance," (Matth. iii. 8.) Now, forasmuch as the gospel calleth all those which are Christ's unto repentance, it followeth that all men are naturally corrupt, and that they have need to be changed. In like sort, this place teacheth that these men do unskilfully pervert the gospel which separate the grace of Christ from repentance.

[1] "Pravitas," depravity.

21. *They went about to kill me.* He complaineth in this place of the iniquity of his adversaries, that it may thereby appear that their cause and conscience were both evil.[1] For if Paul had offended they might have gone to law with him; and even there should they have stand [stood] in better state, seeing they did far pass him both in favour and authority. Therefore, their madness doth testify that they are destitute of reason. Whereas Paul saith that he was saved by the help of God, it maketh for the confirmation of his doctrine. For how is it that he reacheth out his hand to help him, save only because he acknowledged his minister, and because he will defend the cause which he alloweth, [approveth?] Moreover, this ought to have encouraged him to go forward so much the more boldly in his office, in that he was thus holpen by God. For it had been a point of an unthankful man to withdraw himself from him which had holpen him. By which example we be taught, that so often as we be delivered from danger, the Lord doth not therefore prolong our days that we may afterward live idly, but that we may do our duty cheerfully, and be ready to die every hour to his glory, who hath reserved us to himself. And yet Paul did not forget how much he was indebted to the chief captain; but in this place he commendeth the help of God, that he may show that it became him to spend all the rest of his course in his service by whom he was delivered, though that came to pass, and were done through the industry and by the hand of man.

Testifying both to small and great. We have said elsewhere that it is more to testify than to teach, as if there were some solemn contestation made between God and men, that the gospel may have his [its] majesty. And he saith that he is a witness both to great and small, that king Agrippa may perceive that this doth appertain even to him; and that when the gospel is offered even to every simple man, that doth no whit hinder but that it may ascend even unto the throne of princes. For Christ doth gather all

---

[1] " Malam causam ipsos agere mala conscientia," that they pleaded a bad cause with a bad conscience.

men into his bosom with one and the same embracing, that those who lay before in the dunghill, and are now extolled unto so great honour, may rejoice in his free goodness; and that those who are placed in high degree of honour may willingly humble themselves, and not grudge to have some of the base and contemptible multitude for their brethren, that they may be made the children of God. So in the first chapter to the Romans, he saith that he is indebted both to the fools and to the wise, lest the Romans should be kept back with the confidence which they might repose in their wisdom from submitting themselves to his doctrine. By this let us learn that it is not in the teacher's will to make choice of his hearers, and that they do no less injury to God than defraud men of their right, whosoever they be which restrain their labour unto great men, whom God doth join with those which are small. It were too cold to restrain this unto ages.[1] Wherefore, I do not doubt but that Paul taketh away the exception which used to be between the noble and ignoble, because he was neither afraid of the dignity of the one, neither did he loathe the baseness of the other, but did show himself a faithful teacher to both alike.

Saying no other thing. First, this is worth the noting, that Paul, to the end he may bring in fit and substantial witnesses of his doctrine, doth not take the same from among men, but he citeth Moses and the prophets, to whom the Lord had granted undoubted authority. And surely this is one principle to be observed, when we will teach soundly, to utter nothing but that which did proceed out of the mouth of God. Secondly, this is worth the noting, that these were the principal points of the disputation which Luke doth now touch; that this was the proper office of Christ, by his death to make satisfaction for the sins of the world, by his resurrection to purchase righteousness and life for men; and that the fruit of his death and resurrection is common both to Jews and Gentiles. But forasmuch as there is no manifest and (as they say) literal

---

[1] " Ad ætates hoc 1estringere," to confine this to periods of time.

testimony extant in the law concerning the death and resurrection of Christ, undoubtedly they had some doctrine delivered by hand from the fathers, out of which they did learn to refer all figures unto Christ. And as the prophets, which did prophesy more plainly of Christ, had their doctrine from that fountain, so they made the men of their time believe that they delivered unto them no new thing, or which did dissent from Moses. And now Paul did either not finish his apology, or else he gathered more evident testimonies of all those things wherein he professed Moses and the prophets to be his authors.

The first of those which. There were some other whose resurrection went before Christ's in time; namely, if we admit that the saints of whom the Evangelists speak (Matth. xxvii. 52) did come out of their graves before Christ, which may likewise be said of the taking up of Enoch and Elias, (Gen. v. 24; 2 Kings ii. 11.) But he calleth him in this place the *first;* as in another place the first fruits of those which rise again, (1 Cor. xv. 23.) Therefore, this word doth rather note out the cause than the order of time, because, when Christ did rise again, he became the conqueror of death and Lord of life, that he might reign for ever, and make those who are his partakers of [his own] blessed immortality. Under this word light, he comprehendeth whatsoever doth pertain unto perfect felicity, as by darkness is meant death and all manner of misery. And I do not doubt but that Paul alluded unto the sayings of the prophets, "The people which walked in darkness saw great light," (Isaiah ix. 2.) And again, "Behold, darkness shall cover the earth, and a mist the people: but the Lord shall be seen upon thee," (Isaiah lx. 2.) Again, "Behold, those which are in darkness shall see light," (Isaiah xlii. 16.) Again, "I have made thee a light of the Gentiles," (Isaiah xlix. 6.) And it appeareth by many oracles that the light of life should come out of Judea, and should be spread abroad among the Gentiles.

24. *And as Paul answered for himself, Festus saith with a loud*

voice, *Paul, thou art beside thyself; much learning doth make thee mad.*

25. *And Paul said, I am not mad, most noble Festus; but speak forth the words of truth and sobriety.*
26. *For the king knoweth of these things, before whom I also speak freely: for I think that none of these things are hidden from him; for this was not done in a corner.*
27. *King Agrippa, believest thou the prophets? I know that thou believest.*
28. *And Agrippa said unto Paul, Thou briefly persuadest me to become a Christian.*
29. *And Paul saith, Would to God that not only thou, but also all which hear me this day, were both almost, and altogether such as I am, except these bonds.*
30. *And when he had thus spoken, the king arose, and the governor, and Bernice, and those which sat with them.*
31. *And when they were gone apart, they talked together between themselves, saying, This man doth nothing worthy of death or bonds.*
32. *Then Agrippa said to Festus, This man might have been loosed, if he had not appealed unto Cæsar.*

24. *Festus said with a loud voice.* This outcry which Festus doth make doth show how much the truth of God prevaileth with the reprobate; to wit, though it be never so plain and evident, yet is it trodden under foot by their pride. For though those things which Paul had alleged out of the law and prophets had nothing in them which was any thing like to madness, but were grounded in good reason, yet he doth attribute the same to madness, not because he seeth any absurdity, but because he refuseth those things which he doth not understand. Nothing was more foolish or more unsavoury than the superstitions of the Gentiles, so that their high priests were for good causes ashamed to utter their mysteries, whose folly was more than ridiculous.

Festus doth grant that there was learning packed[1] in

---

[1] " Recᵔnditam eruditionem," recondite erudition.

Paul's speech; nevertheless, because the gospel is hidden from the unbelievers, whose minds Satan hath blinded, (2 Cor. iv. 3,) he thinketh that he is a brain-sick fellow which handleth matters intricately. So that though he cannot mock and openly contemn him, yet he is so far from being moved or inwardly touched, that he counteth him a man which is frenzy [frenzied] and of mad curiosity. And this is the cause that he cannot away to mark what he saith, lest he make him mad also; as many at this day fly from the word of God, lest they drown themselves in a labyrinth. And they think that we be mad because we move questions concerning hidden matters, and so become troublesome both to ourselves and also to others. Wherefore, being admonished by this example, let us beg of God that he will show us the light of his doctrine, and that he will therewithal give us a taste thereof, lest through obscurity and hardness it become unsavoury, and at length proud loathsomeness break out into blasphemy.

25. *I am not mad.* Paul is not angry, neither doth he sharply reprehend Festus for his blasphemous speech; yea, he speaketh unto him with great submission.[1] For it was no place for reprehension, and it became him to pardon the ignorance of the man, seeing he did not set himself face to face against God. Also, he had respect unto his person, [office.] For though he were unworthy of honour, yet was he in authority. And yet for all that he doth not therefore give place to his blasphemy, but he defendeth the glory of the word of God. Whereby we do also see, that not caring for himself, he did only take thought for his doctrine. For he doth not vaunt of his wit;[2] he doth not labour in defence of his wisdom; but he is content with this defence alone, that he teacheth nothing but that which is true and sober.

Furthermore, [the] truth is set against[3] all manner [of] fal-

---

[1] "Honorifice eum compellat," addresses him in terms of honour
[2] "Acumen," acuteness
[3] "Opponitur," is opposed to.

lacies and fraud : sobriety against all manner [of] frivolous speculations and thorny subtilties, which are only seeds of contention. Paul doth, indeed, refute Festus' error; yet we may gather by this, which is the best manner of teaching, to wit, that which is not only clean from all fallacies and deceit, but also doth not make the minds of men drunk with vain questions, and doth not nourish foolish curiosity, nor an intemperate desire to know more than is meet, but is moderate and good for sound edification.

26. *For the king knoweth of these things.* He turneth himself unto Agrippa, in whom there was more hope. And, first, he saith that he knew the history of the things; but he calleth him straightway back to the law and the prophets. For it was to small end for him to know the thing which was done, unless he did know that those things which had been spoken before of Christ were fulfilled in the person of Jesus which was crucified. And whereas Paul doth not doubt of Agrippa's faith, he doth it not so much to praise him, as that he may put the Scripture out of all question, lest he be enforced to stand upon the very principles. Therefore, his meaning is, that the Scripture is of sufficient credit of itself, so that it is not lawful for a man that is a Jew to diminish any jot of the authority thereof. And yet Paul doth not flatter him ; for though he did not reverence the Scripture as became a godly man, yet he had this rudiment from his childhood, that he was persuaded that nothing is contained therein besides the oracles of God. As the common sort of men, though they do not greatly care for the word of God, yet they acknowledge and confess generally and confusedly that it is the word of God, so that they are letted with some reverence either to reject or to despise the same.

28. *And Agrippa said unto Paul.* The apostle prevailed thus far at least, that he wrung out of king Agrippa a confession, though it were not voluntary, as those use to yield who can no longer resist the truth, or, at least, to show some

token of assent. Agrippa's meaning is, that he will not willingly become a Christian; yea, that he will not be one at all; and yet that he is not able to gainsay, but that he is drawn after a sort against his will. Whereby it appeareth how great the pride of man's nature is until it be brought under to obey by the Spirit of God.

Interpreters expound this εν ολιγω diversely. Valla thought that it ought to be translated thus, Thou dost almost make me a Christian. Erasmus doth translate it *a little*. The old interpreter dealeth more plainly[1] *in a little*; because, translating it word for word, he left it to the readers to judge at their pleasure. And surely it may be fitly referred unto the time, as if Agrippa had said, Thou wilt make me a Christian straightway, or in one moment. If any man object that Paul's answer doth not agree thereto, we may quickly answer; for seeing the speech was doubtful, Paul doth fitly apply that unto the thing which was spoken of the time. Therefore, seeing Agrippa did mean that he was almost made a Christian in a small time, Paul addeth that he doth desire that as well he as his companions might rise from small beginnings, and profit more and more; and yet I do not mislike that that εν ολιγω doth signify as much as almost. This answer doth testify with what zeal, to spread abroad the glory of Christ, this holy man's breast was inflamed, when as he doth patiently suffer those bonds wherewith the governor had bound him, and doth desire that he might escape the deadly snares of Satan, and to have both him and also his partners to be partakers with him of the same grace, being in the mean season content with his troublesome and reproachful condition. We must note that he doth not wish it simply, but from God, as it is he which draweth us unto his Son; because, unless he teach us inwardly by his Spirit, the outward doctrine shall always wax cold.

Except these bonds. It is certain that Paul's bonds were not so hard, ne [nor] yet did they cause him such sorrow, wherein he did oftentimes rejoice, and which he doth men-

[1] " Simplicius," more simply.

tion for honour's sake, as being the badge of his embassage, (Gal. vi. 17;) but he hath respect to those to whom he wisheth faith without trouble or cross. For those who did not as yet believe in Christ were far from that affection to be ready to strive for the gospel. And surely it behoveth all the godly to have this gentleness and meekness, that they patiently bear their own cross, and that they wish well to others, and study so much as in them lieth to ease them of all trouble, and that they do in no case envy their quietness and mirth. This courtesy[1] is far contrary to the bitterness of those who take comfort in wishing that other men were in their misery.

31. *They spake together.* In that Paul is acquitted by the judgment of them all, it turned to the great renown of the gospel. And when Festus agreeth to the rest he condemneth himself, seeing he had brought Paul into such straits through his unjust dealing, by bringing him in danger of his life under colour of changing the place. And though it seemeth that the appeal did hinder[2] the holy man, yet because this was the only way to escape death, he is content, and doth not seek to get out of that snare; not only because the matter was not even now safe and sound,[3] but because he was admonished in the vision that he was also called by God to Rome, (Acts xxiii. 11.)

CHAPTER XXVII.

1. *And after that it was decreed that we should sail into Italy, they delivered both Paul and also certain other prisoners to a centurion named Julius, of the band of Augustus.*
2. *And we entered into a ship of Adramyttium, purposing to*

---

[1] "Humanitas et moderatio," humanity and moderation. [2] "Damnosa esse," was injurious to. [3] "Res jam non erat integra," matters were no longer entire.

sail by the coasts of Asia, and we launched forth, having
Aristarchus of Macedonia, a Thessalonian, with us
3. And the next day we arrived at Sidon, and Julius did courteously intreat Paul, and suffered him to go to his friends,
that they might refresh him.
4. And when we were gone thence, we sailed hard by Cyprus,
because the winds were contrary.
5. And when we had sailed on the sea which is over against
Cilicia and Pamphylia, we came to Myra, a city of Lycia.
6. And when the centurion had found there a ship of Alexandria
sailing into Italy, he put us in it.
7. And when we had sailed slowly many days, and were scarce
come over against Cnidus, because the wind did let us, we
sailed hard by Crete, beside Salmone;
8. And with much ado we sailed beyond it, and came to a certain
place which is called The fair havens, near unto which was
the city of Lasea.

1. Luke setteth down Paul's voyage by sea most of all to this end, that we may know that he was brought to Rome wonderfully by the hand of God; and that the glory of God did many ways appear excellent in his doings and sayings even in the very journey, which did more establish his apostleship. He is delivered to be carried with other prisoners; but the Lord doth afterward put great differ- ence between him and the evil-doers, who were in bonds as well as he. Yea, moreover, we shall see how the captain doth loose him, and let him be at liberty, when the rest lie bound. I know not what band that was which Luke calleth the band of Augustus, unless, peradventure, it be that which was commonly called the prætor's [1] band, before the monarchy of the Cæsars. And Luke setteth down in plain words, that they were put in a ship of Adramyttium; because they should sail by the coast of Asia. For Adra- myttium is a city of Æolia. I cannot tell out of what haven they launched. Because they could not sail with a straight course to Sidon, unless the maps do greatly deceive me, we may well guess that they were brought thither, either

---

[1] "Prætoria," the Prætorian

because they could find a ship no where else, or else because they were to take the other prisoners, of whom mention is made, out of that region.

2. *And there continued with us.* Luke seemeth so to commend one man's constancy, that he nippeth the rest. For there were more which did accompany him to Jerusalem; whereof we see two only which remained with him. But because it may be that the rest were letted with some just causes, or that Paul refused to have them to minister unto him, I will say nothing either way. Neither is it an unmeet thing to say[1] that Luke had some special reason for which he doth commend this man above the rest, albeit he was but one of many. Surely, it is likely that he was a rich man, seeing he was able to bear the charges whereat he was by the space of three years, having left his house. For we heard before (Acts xvii. 11) that many of the chief families in Thessalonica did receive Christ, and Luke saith, for honour's sake, that Aristarchus and Secundus came with Paul into Asia, (Acts xx. 4.) Therefore, let it suffice us to hold that which is certain and good to be known, that there is set before us an example of holy patience, because Aristarchus is not wearied with any trouble, but doth willingly take part with Paul in his trouble,[2] and after that he had been in prison with him two years, he doth now cross the seas, that he may likewise minister to him at Rome, not without the reproachings of many, besides the loss of his goods at home, and so great charges.

3. *He suffered him to go to.* Paul might have hid himself[3] in a large city, which joined to the sea; but he was bound with the oracle, that he could not withdraw himself from the calling of God. Again, because the centurion had so courteously entertained him, that he suffered him to go to

[1] " Nec vero absurdum est," and there is no absurdity in supposing.
[2] " Sponte eandem cum Paulo fortunam subeat," spontaneously shares in Paul's fortunes. [3] " Latebras nancisci poterat," might have found a place of concealment.

his friends, that they might dress and refresh him, whom he might have left in the stinking ship,[1] he ought not nor could he provide for his own life, with the other man's danger, without filthy treachery.[2] Neither must we in any case suffer those who have courteously intreated us to be deceived by their courtesy through our fault. Let the readers fet [seek] the voyage whereof Luke speaketh out of those which describe places and countries;[3] only I say thus much, that all that which is said tendeth to this end, that we may know that their sailing was dangerous and tempestuous, after that they were once gone out of the haven of Sidon, until they came near to Melita; and that afterward the mariners did strive long time with contrary winds, until a cruel storm[4] arose, whose end was shipwreck, as we shall see.

> 9. And when much time was spent, and when sailing was now jeopardous, because all the time of fasting was now passed, Paul admonished them,
> 10. Saying unto them, Sirs, I see that this voyage will be with hurt and great loss, not only of the burthen and of the ship, but also of our souls, [lives.]
> 11. But the centurion believed rather the governor and the master of the ship, than those things which were spoken of Paul.
> 12. And because the haven was unfit to winter in, many took counsel to depart thence, if by any means they might come to Phenice, and there winter. That is a haven of Candia, and lieth toward the south-west and by west, and north-west and by west.
> 13. And when the south wind blew softly, supposing to obtain their purpose, when they had loosed nearer, they sailed beyond Candia.
> 14. But not long after there arose over against it a stormy wind, which is called Euroclydon.
> 15. And when the ship was caught, and could not resist the wind, we let her go, and were carried away.

[1] " Navis pædore," the stench of the ship. [2] "Turpi perfidia," base perfidy. [3] " Ex geographis," out of geographers. [4] " Sævior procella,' a fiercer storm.

16. *And when we were carried into a certain isle called Candia,* [Clauda,] *we could scarce get the boat:*
17. *Which they took up, and used helps, undergirding the ship; and, fearing lest they should fall into syrtes,* [quicksands,] *they strake sail, and so were carried.*
18. *And when we were tossed with an exceeding tempest, on the morrow they lightened the ship;*
19. *And the third day we cast out with our own hands the tackling of the ship.*
20. *Furthermore, when neither sun nor stars appeared now many days, and no small tempest lay upon us, all hope that we should be saved was then taken away.*

9. *When sailing was now jeopardous.* He doth not only mean that the winds were contrary then, but also that the time of the year was not then commodious, which he expresseth more plainly afterward, when he saith that the fast was passed; for I think that this word was added by way of exposition, to note the end of harvest. Neither do I pass for that, that that solemn time of fasting, whereof Luke speaketh, was strange to the centurion and the rest of the mariners; for he noteth out the times of the year according to the custom of the Jews. Furthermore, we need not doubt but that it was the harvest [autumnal] fast. Though I am not of their mind who think that it was one of the four fasts which the Jews did appoint after the carrying away into Babylon. For Luke would not have put down simply, without adding any distinction, the third fast, which was in the seventh month, seeing it was not more famous than the rest, being commanded to be kept because of the death of Godolia, and because of the destruction of the rest of the people. Again, I cannot tell whether that custom were retained by the people after their return. It is more likely that he meaneth the feast of the atonement, wherein the Lord commanded them to humble their souls seven days. And they began the tenth day of the seventh month; whereto partly September and partly October doth now agree, (Lev. xvi. 29.) Therefore, seeing they were now entered into October, it is said, not

without cause, that sailing was jeopardous at that time. But and if you refer it unto hunger, (as some do,) I do not see what sense can be gathered thence; for they had as yet store of wheat in the ship, so that they needed not to be hunger starved. And why should he say that the time of the voluntary fast was passed? Moreover, it shall hereafter appear by the text, that they were, therefore, exhorted by Paul to stay because winter was at hand, whose sharpness [severity] useth to shut up the seas. For though he were assured that God would govern the ship, yet he would not tempt him rashly by making too great haste.

11. *But the centurion.* The centurion is not reproved because he hearkened rather to the master and governor of the ship than to Paul. For what should he have done? For though he did well like[1] Paul's counsel in other matters, yet he knew that he was unskilful in sailing. Therefore he suffered himself to be governed by those which were expert, which was a point of a wise and modest man. Yea, very necessity did almost compel him to do this; for the haven was not commodious to winter in. Neither did the governor give counsel to commit the ship to the main sea, but to thrust into the next haven, which was almost in view. So that, with taking a little pains, they might commodiously pass the winter. Luke reciteth this not in vain; but that we may know that Paul was from the beginning furnished with the sense of the Spirit, so that he did better see what things were profitable than did the masters. We know not whether he were taught by oracles, or whether he gave this counsel through secret inspiration. This is certain, that it served afterward to his commendation. Furthermore, in that he saith that they sailed beyond the coast of Candia, until they were caught and carried away; our friend Beza doth justly reprove the error of interpreters in this word ασσον, who make of an adverb the name of a city.

---

[1] "Plurimum deferret," he had very great deference for

15. *When the ship was caught.* Luke saith that that fell out here, which useth to fall out in extreme danger; namely, they suffered themselves to be carried of the winds. Seeing they were first gone some space, and the mariners thought that all things fell out as they would have it, undoubtedly they did deride Paul's admonition; as rash men use commonly to wax proud if fortune favour them. Being now caught, they are grievously punished for their boldness; yea, when they drew near to an haven,[1] they were no less afraid lest they should break the ship, than they were before of overturning the same. Luke doth diligently note all these things, out of which we may gather, that the storm was so vehement and fierce, and that it continued still at one stay, that they were still in danger of death. Also he declareth, that they did courageously use all remedies which might save them from suffering shipwreck, and that they spared not the merchandise and tackling; whence we gather that they were enforced, with a lively feeling of danger, to do what they were able. And Luke addeth, that when they had essayed all things, they despaired of their safety. And surely the very darkness of heaven was as it were a grave. Neither need we doubt but that the Lord meant by this means to commend and make more notable the grace of their deliverance which ensued shortly after. Nevertheless, he suffered his servant to labour with the rest, until he thought he should die. For he did not appear unto him by his angel, before it might seem that he was past hope of recovery. Wherefore his body was not only tossed amidst many storms, but his soul was also shaken with violent tentations. Notwithstanding the end doth show, that he stood upright by faith, so that he did not faint. Luke speaketh nothing of his prayers; but because he himself saith afterward that the angel of God, whom he served, appeared to him, it is likely that when others did curse both heaven and earth, he made his prayers to God, and so was quiet, and did patiently

---

[1] " Insulam," island.

tarry the Lord's leisure. And whereas he saith that all hope of safety was taken away, it must not be referred unto his sense, but only unto the means which men could use;[1] as if he should say, that things were so far out of order, that there was no safety to be looked for at men's hands.

21. *But after long abstinence Paul stood in the midst and said, Sirs, ye should have hearkened to me, and not have loosed from Candia, neither have brought upon us this injury and loss.*
22. *And now I exhort you that ye be of good courage: for there shall be no loss of any man's life, but only of the ship.*
23. *For there stood by me this night the angel of God, whose I am, and whom I worship,*
24. *And he said to me, Fear not, Paul; thou must be brought before Cæsar: and, behold, God hath given thee all those which sail with thee.*
25. *Wherefore be of good courage, sirs: for I believe God that it shall be so, as it hath been told me.*
26. *But we must fall into a certain island.*
27. *And when the fourteenth night was come, as we sailed in the Adriatic Sea, about midnight the mariners supposed that some country appeared to them.*
28. *And when they had sounded, they found it twenty fathoms: and when they were gone a little farther, they sounded again, and they found it fifteen fathoms.*
29. *And fearing lest they should have fallen into some rough places, having cast four anchors out of the stern, they wished for day.*
30. *And when the mariners sought to fly out of the ship, when they had let down the boat into the sea, under a colour as if they would have cast anchors out of the foreship,*
31. *Paul said to the centurion and the soldiers, Unless these abide in the ship, you cannot be saved.*
32. *Then the soldiers cut off the ropes of the boat, and they suffered it to fall away.*

---

[1] " Ad humana media,' to human means.

21. *After long abstinence.* Though Luke doth not plainly express how the mariners and soldiers behaved themselves, yet he doth plainly distinguish Paul from them, declaring that he stood in the midst of them that he might comfort their faint hearts; for no man is fit to exhort but he who is himself an example of constancy and fortitude. Furthermore, Paul deferred this exhortation until they were all even at the last cast. We may easily gather out of the common custom of the infidels, that they raged and made much ado at the first. A moderate and soft voice could never have been heard amongst those cries and tumults. Now, after they be weary with working and howling, they sit still all in a damp, and Paul beginneth to speak to them. Therefore, it was meet that they should languish like men half dead, until they were somewhat quiet, and could hear a man which would give them good counsel.

Notwithstanding, Paul seemeth to deal unseasonably, when as he objecteth to them foolishness, because they would not do after his counsel when all was well, seeing that they knew that he was inexpert in sailing, as he himself also knew how unskilful and ignorant he was.

But if we consider what an hard matter it is to bring men unto soundness of mind, this reprehension was very profitable. Paul's authority should have been nothing worth, neither should it have moved them any whit, unless they should know this, that it had not gone well with them because they had despised him before. Chiding is indeed cruel, and bringeth no comfort; but if it be tempered with some remedy, it is now a part of the medicine. So, after that Paul had made the mariners attentive, and had taught by the very event that they ought to believe him, he exhorteth them to be of good courage, and promiseth them safety. And this is a token of no small boldness, when he saith that they ought to have obeyed him. Therefore, he testifieth by these words, that he spake nothing unadvisedly; but did command them to do that which God had prescribed. For though we do not read that he had some especial revelation then given him, yet he himself knew that the Spirit did secretly govern him, so that he might without fear take upon him to give counsel, seeing he had the Spirit of God to be his guide. Whereby that doth better appear which I touched of late, that Paul in speaking thus doth awake the mariners, that they may more attentively hear what he will say. Otherwise, it had been a ridiculous thing for a man which was in danger of drowning, to promise safety to those who were partakers with him in like calamity.

23. *For there stood by me.* Lest he might be accused of rashness, for promising so fully that they should be all safe, he bringeth in God for his author and witness. Neither is it to be doubted but that he was fully persuaded that it was a true vision, so that he did not fear Satan's jugglings. For because that father of lies doth oftentimes deceive men under a colour of revelations, God did never appear to his servants, either by himself or by his angels, but he put them out of doubt by showing them some plain and evident tokens; and, secondly, did furnish them with the spirit of discretion, that they might not be deceived. But Paul doth extol the name of his God in plain words among profane men, not only that they may learn that the true God is worshipped in Judea, but also that Paul himself doth worship him. They all knew why he was put in prison. Now, seeing angels come down unto him from heaven, they may easily gather that his cause is approved of God. Therefore, there is in these words a secret commendation of the gospel. Nevertheless, we see how Paul triumpheth in his bonds, when he is the minister of safety to so many men, and the interpreter of God.

24. *Fear not, Paul.* He is very desirous to bring to pass that they may give God alone the praise for their deliverance, lest these superstitious men do falsely translate it unto their idols; and by this means he inviteth them unto the true faith. But by this it appeareth how great the men's wickedness is, in that they shut their ears against sound and wholesome counsel, and do forthwith forget the grace of

God, though it were familiarly known to them. Yea, (that which worse is,) they do not see nor perceive it when it is present before their eyes. But, howsoever, the more part was unthankful, yet this oracle was not revealed without fruit; yea, this was good, that those might be made without excuse who did flatter themselves too much in their deceit. And, seeing it was said that he must be presented before Cæsar, it tended to this end, that his confession might the more strengthen the godly, when as they should know that he came forth from God as a witness to confirm and avouch the doctrine of the gospel, and that he was appointed and saved to that end.

Hath given thee all the souls. Luke seemeth to give us to understand by these words, that Paul prayed not only for himself, but also for the rest, that God would save them all from drowning.[1] And, surely, it is not likely, that, seeing he saw the danger common to them all, he was so careful for his own life, that he cared not for the rest whom he saw in like danger. Notwithstanding, it may be that the Lord did of his own accord prevent his prayers. Neither is it any new thing, that his blessing should reach even unto the unworthy, who are joined to the faithful with any society. So he would have saved Sodom, if there had been ten good men found there.

Here ariseth a question, how far the integrity of the saints doth profit the wicked? First, we must remove the superstition of the Papists, who, when they hear that God is good to the bad, for the good's sake, dream that they be mediators, who obtain salvation for the world through their merits. And they be twice fools in that, that they apply these titles of the living unto the dead; and think that God will be favourable to them for no other cause, save only because he beholdeth them, and therefore they make them their patrons. I omit that, that by extolling men's merits they darken the free goodness of God. Now, that we may answer the question propounded, we must briefly note this,

---

[1] " E naufragio," from shipwreck.

that forasmuch as the good are mixed with the bad, as well prosperity as adversity doth happen as well to the one as to the other; and yet it falleth out sometimes that when the Lord doth spare his, he beareth also with the wicked for a time together with them. Again, that there be many causes for which God doth good to the wicked and reprobate for the faithful's sake. " He blessed the house of Potiphar for Joseph's sake," (Gen. xxxix. 5,) that he might move him to handle this holy man gently. He declared his good-will toward Paul in saving many men, that he might bear witness of his godliness, that the majesty of the gospel might thereby appear more plainly. But we must note this, that whatsoever benefits God bestoweth upon the wicked, they turn at length to their destruction; as, on the other side, punishments are profitable for the godly, which they suffer together with the reprobate.

In the mean season, this is a singular pledge of God's love toward us, in that he maketh certain drops of his goodness distil from us unto others.

25. *For I believe God.* Paul telleth them again whence he had such boldness, that he affirmeth that though they be amidst infinite gulfs of the sea, yet shall they all come safe to the haven, namely, because God had promised it should be so; in which words the nature of faith is expressed, when there is a mutual relation made between it and the Word of God, that it may strengthen men's minds against the assaults of temptations. And he doth not only exhort the mariners, by his own example, to believe, but doth, as it were, take upon him the office of a promiser,[1] that he may win credit to the oracle. That which followeth immediately touching the isle is a latter sign, whereby it may more plainly appear after the end of the matter, that this their sailing was not uncertain, otherwise it had been to no end for the mariners to know how they should escape. Therefore, we see how God doth give that safety which he promised, a mark

---

[1] " Sponsoris," sponsor or cautioner.

that it may not seem to come by chance. Notwithstanding, we must note, that God kept them still in some doubt, partly that he may exercise the faith of his servant, partly that they may all know that Paul learned that of the Holy Ghost, which he could not as yet comprehend by man's reason.[1] Notwithstanding, Luke teacheth in the text itself, that he was not believed for all this. For, seeing the mariners thought that there began some country[2] to appear unto them, it did not agree with the promise made touching their arriving in an isle. Therefore, we see how that they were scarce enforced, even by experience, to think that he spake the truth.

30. *And as the mariners sought.* The grace of the Holy Spirit appeareth in Paul, even in this point also, in that he did wisely admonish that the mariners should not be suffered to fly. For why doth not rather the centurion, or some other of the company, smell out their fraud, save only that Paul may be the minister of their deliverance, even unto the end? But it is a marvel that he saith, that the rest could not be saved unless the mariners should remain in the ship; as if it were in their power to make the promise of God of none effect. I answer, that Paul doth not dispute, in this place, precisely of the power of God, that he may separate the same from his will and from means; and surely God doth not, therefore, commend his power to the faithful, that they may give themselves to sluggishness and carelessness, contemning means, or rashly cast away themselves when there is some certain way to escape. God did promise Hezekiah that the city should be delivered, (Isaiah xxxvii. 6, and 35.) If he had set open the gates to the enemy, would not Isaiah straightway have cried, Thou destroyest both thyself and the city? And yet for all this it doth not follow that the hand of God is tied to means or helps; but when God appointeth

---

[1] " Quod humano sensu nondum comprehendi poterat," which could not yet be comprehended by human sense.   [2] " Aliquam regionem mediterraneam," some mainland

this or that means to bring any thing to pass, he holdeth all men's senses, that they may not pass the bounds which he hath appointed.

33. *And when the day began to appear, Paul exhorted them all to take meat, saying, This is the fourteenth day that ye have tarried and continued fasting, receiving nothing at all.*
34. *Wherefore I exhort you to take meat: for this no doubt is for your health; because there shall not one hair fall from the head of any of you.*
35. *And when he had thus spoken, he took bread, and gave thanks to God in the sight of them all; and when he had broken it, he began to eat.*
36. *Then were they all refreshed in their minds, and they also took meat.*
37. *And all the souls which were in the ship were two hundred threescore and sixteen.*
38. *And when they had eaten enough, they did lighten the ship, casting out the wheat into the sea.*
39. *And when it was day, they knew not the land; but they spied a certain haven having a bank, into the which they minded to thrust the ship.*
40. *And when they had taken up the anchors, they committed themselves to the sea, also, having loosed the rudder bands, and hoised up the mainsail to the wind, they drew toward the shore.*
41. *But when they were fallen into a place where two seas met, they thrust in the ship, and the fore part did stick fast, and moved not; but the hinder part brake through the violence of the waves.*
42. *Furthermore, the soldiers' counsel was to kill the prisoners, lest any, after he swam out, should escape.*
43. *But the centurion, being desirous to save Paul, kept them from their purpose, and commanded that those which could swim should cast themselves first into the sea, and should escape to land*
44. *And the other, some on boards, and some on broken pieces of the ship; and so it came to pass, that they all escaped safe to land.*

33. *And when the day began.* Whatsoever the mariners think, Paul's faith doth not quail;[1] but he leaneth stedfastly to the promise which was made to him. For he doth not only exhort them to take meat, as did he who, in extreme despair, uttered these words, Dine, soldiers, we shall sup in hell;[2] but continuing stedfast in his prophecy, he willeth them to be of good courage. The force of faith doth therein show itself, when as it armeth us unto patience, and doth valiantly bear off and beat back those assaults wherewith Satan goeth about to shake it. But whereas he saith, that they continued fasting for the space of fourteen days, it may seem absurd and false. There may some one man be found which can abide to fast long, but it is scarce credible of so great a multitude. We may easily answer, That their unwonted abstinence from meat is improperly called fasting; because they had never filled their belly during all that time; because those who are in sorrow and heaviness do almost loathe meat. And because despair was the cause of this their loathing of meat, he affirmeth again that they shall live, so they be of good courage. For a faithful minister of the word must not only bring abroad the promises, but also counsel men to follow God whithersoever he calleth them; and that they be not slothful and sluggish. Furthermore, the meaning of the words is this, God hath determined to save you, this confidence ought to animate you, and to make you merry,[3] that you be not negligent in your own business.

35. *He took bread.* That he may the better encourage them, by his own example, he taketh bread and eateth. Luke saith that he gave thanks, not only according to his daily custom, but because that served greatly to testify his boldness and good confidence. It is not to be doubted but that Paul himself did that when he took meat, which he

---

[1] "Vacillat," waver.
[2] "Apud inferos," with the dead.
[3] "Alacres," alert, active

commandeth other men; but now he doth not only testify his thankfulness, neither doth he only desire of God that he will sanctify the meat which he is about to eat; but he calleth upon God without fear, who is the author of his life, that those poor wretches, which were drenched in sorrow, might conceive some good hope. And he prevailed thus far, at least, that they gathered so much courage to them as to take meat, who had, through fear, forgotten to care for their life.

37. *All the souls.* The number of the men is recited, first, that it may more plainly appear that none of the multitude did perish. For Luke doth not show how many men did swim to the shore, but how many men were then in the ship. Secondly, that the miracle may be made more evident and also famous; for, in man's judgment, it is a thing impossible that two hundred threescore and sixteen men should escape to land, having suffered shipwreck, without loss of any man's life. For it is likely that few had any skill in swimming except the mariners. And though they were somewhat refreshed with the meat which they had eaten, yet they were brought so low with sorrows and wearisomeness, that it is a marvel that they were so nimble as that they could move their arms. And now we must consider what a stir they kept; whereas it is seldom seen that twenty or thirty men do so swim in danger, but one of them doth hinder or drown another. Therefore, God did plainly stretch forth his hand out of heaven, seeing all those came to shore safe and sound which had cast themselves into the sea.

38. *And when they had eaten enough.* This circumstance doth show that they were at length moved with Paul's words. It was not yet light, that they could know whether there were any haven near. And yet they cast out into the sea the wheat which remained, that they might lighten the ship. They would not have done this unless Paul's

authority had prevailed more with them now than before. But as all unbelievers are unstable, that persuasion did quickly vanish out of their minds.

41. *They thrust in the ship.* And then it might seem that both God had mocked Paul, and that he, with trifling, had brought his partners in a vain hope;[1] but God did forthwith put away that error by giving them prosperous success. It was meet that when the ship was broken, they should be so discouraged, and that their souls should so melt, that despair might increase the glory of the miracle. For God useth to moderate and govern his works so, that he maketh some show of difficulty by reason of many lets [hindrances] which fall out. By this means he sharpeneth our senses unto greater attentiveness, that we may at length learn that, though all the world strive against him, yet will he have the victory. This is the reason why he had lieffer [rather] draw Paul and his companions to the shore after that the ship was lost,[2] than bring the ship whole to land.

42. *The counsel of the soldiers.* This was too horrible unthankfulness. Though the soldiers might thank Paul twice or thrice for their lives, yet are they minded to kill him, for whose sake they ought to have spared the rest. He had saved them even as an angel of God; he had given them wholesome counsel; he had refreshed them in the same day when they were past hope; and now they stick not to seek to destroy him, by whom they were so often and so many ways delivered. Wherefore, if it so fall out that we be ill rewarded for our good deeds, there is no cause why the unthankfulness of men should trouble us, which is a disease too common. But they are not only unthankful to Paul, who was the minister of their life, but also their filthy misbelief and forgetfulness of the goodness of God doth betray itself. They had of late received that oracle,

---

[1] " Socios naufragii vana spe lactasse," had deluded his companions in shipwreck with a vain hope. [2] " Fracta," wrecked.

that their souls were given to Paul; and now seeing they will be saved after he is dead, what other thing go they about but to resist God, that they may save themselves from death contrary to his will? Therefore, they have now forgotten that grace whereof they tasted against their will in extreme despair, neither doth it taste any longer,[1] after that they see the haven nigh at hand. But it behoveth us to consider the wonderful counsel of God, as well in saving Paul as in fulfilling his promise; when as he bringeth those men to land, who did what they could to make his promise of none effect. Thus doth his goodness oftentimes strive with the wickedness of men. Yet he doth so pity the wicked, that, deferring their punishment until so fit opportunity, he doth not quite discharge them; yea, the longer he tarrieth, the more grievously he punisheth, and so by that means he maketh amends for his long tarrying.

CHAPTER XXVIII.

1. *And when they were escaped, they knew that the isle was called Melita.*
2. *And the barbarians showed us no little kindness; for they kindled a fire and received us all, because of the present shower, and because of the cold.*
3. *And when Paul had gathered a bundle of sticks, and had laid them on the fire, a viper came out of the heat, and leaped on his hand.*
4. *Now, when the barbarians saw the beast hang upon his hand, they said among themselves, This man surely is a murderer, whom, though he hath escaped the sea, vengeance doth not suffer to live.*
5. *But he shook off the viper into the fire, and suffered no harm.*
6. *But they thought that it would come to pass, that he would*

---

[1] " Nec amplius quicquam sapit," nor hath it any longer any relish.

swell and fall down dead suddenly. And as they waited long, and saw no harm come to him, changing their mind, they said he was a god.

1. That doleful spectacle is described in the beginning of the chapter, when so many men being wet, and also all berayed with the foam and filth of the sea, and stiff with cold, did with much ado crawl to the shore; for that was all one as if they had been cast up by the sea to die some other death. After that, Luke declareth that they were courteously entertained of the barbarians, that they kindled a fire that they might dry their clothes, and refresh their joints, which were stiff with cold, and at length that they were saved[1] from the shower. Therefore, in that Paul commendeth these duties, he showeth his thankfulness; and so great liberality toward strangers is for good causes advanced, whereof there be rare examples in the world. And though common nature doth wring out of the barbarous Gentiles some affection of mercy in so great necessity; yet undoubtedly it was God which caused the men of Melita to handle these men so courteously, that his promise might be sure and certain, which might seem imperfect if the shipwreck had caused the loss of any man's life.

A viper coming out of the heat. The very event did prove that Paul was a true and undoubted prophet of God. Now, that God may make him famous as well by land as by sea, he sealeth the former miracles[2] with a new miracle; and so he ratifieth his apostleship among the men of Melita. And though there were not many which did profit thereby, yet the majesty of the gospel did shine even among the unbelievers; also this did greatly confirm the oracles to the mariners, which they had not sufficiently reverenced. Neither did the viper come out of the sticks by chance; but the Lord did direct her by his secret counsel to bite Paul, because he saw it would turn to the glory of his gospel.

4. *So soon as the barbarians saw.* This judgment was

[1] " Protectos," protected.   [2] " Oracula," predictions.

common in all ages, that those who were grievously punished had grievously offended. Neither was this persuasion conceived of nothing; but it came rather from a true feeling ot godliness. For God, to the end he might make the world ithout excuse, would have this deeply rooted in the minds of all men, that calamity and adversity, and chiefly notable destruction, were testimonies and signs of his wrath and just vengeance against sins. Therefore, so often as we call to mind any notable calamity, we do also remember that God is sore offended, seeing he punisheth so sharply. Neither did ungodliness ever get the upper hand so far, but that all men did still retain this principle, that God, to the end he may show himself to be the Judge of the world, doth notably punish the wicked. But here crept in an error almost always, because they condemned all those of wickedness[1] whom they saw roughly handled. Though God doth always punish men's sins with adversity, yet doth he not punish every man according to his deserts in this life; and sometimes the punishments of the godly are not so much punishments as trials of their faith and exercises of godliness.

Therefore, those men are deceived, who make this a general rule to judge every man according to his prosperity or adversity. This was the state of the controversy between Job and his friends, (Job iv. 7;) they did affirm that that man was a reprobate, and hated of God, whom God did punish; and he did allege, on the other side, that the godly are sometimes humbled with the cross. Wherefore, lest we be deceived in this point, we must beware of two things. The former is, that we give not rash and blind judgment of things unknown,[2] according to the event alone, for because God doth punish the good as well as the bad; yea, it falleth out oftentimes that he spareth the reprobate, and doth sharply punish those who are his; if we will judge aright, we must begin at another thing than at punishments, to wit, that we inquire after the life and deeds. If any adulterer, if

[1] " Sine exceptione," without exception, omitted. [2] " De hominibus ignotis," of persons unknown.

any blasphemous person, if any perjured man or murderer, if any filthy person, if any cozener, if any bloody beast be punished, God doth point out his judgment as it were with his finger. If we see no wickedness, nothing is better than to suspend our judgment concerning punishment.

The other caution is, that we wait for the end. For so soon as God beginneth to strike, we do not by and by see his drift and purpose; but the unlike end doth at length declare, that those differ far before God who seem in men's eyes both alike in the likelihood of punishment. If any man object that it is not in vain so often repeated in the law, that all private and public miseries are the scourges of God, I grant indeed that that is true; but yet I deny that it doth keep God from sparing whom he will for a time, though they be of all men the worst, and from punishing those more sharply whose fault is mean.[1] Nevertheless, it is not our duty to make that perpetual which falleth out oftentimes. We see now wherein the men of Melita were deceived, to wit, because having not scanned Paul's life, they judge him to be a wicked man, only because the viper doth bite him; secondly, because they stay not the end, but give judgment rashly. Nevertheless, we must note that these are detestable monsters, who go about to pluck out of their hearts all feelings of God's judgment, which is ingrafted in us all naturally, and which is also found in the barbarians and savage men. Whereas they think that Paul is rather guilty of murder than of any other offence, they follow this reason, because murder hath always been most detestable.

Vengeance doth not suffer. They gather that he is a wicked man, because vengeance doth persecute him though he have escaped the sea. And they feigned that the revenging goddess did sit by the seat of Jupiter, which they commonly called Δικη; grossly, I grant, as men ignorant of pure religion, and yet not without some tolerable signification, as if they had painted out God to be Judge of the world. But

---

[1] "Mediocris," trivial.

by these words the wrath of God is distinguished from fortune, and so the judgment of God is avouched against all blind chances. For the men of Melita take it to be a sign of the heavenly vengeance, in that though Paul be saved, yet can he not be safe.

5. *Shaking off the viper.* The shaking off of the viper is a token of a quiet mind. For we see how greatly fear doth trouble and weaken men; and yet you must not think that Paul was altogether void of fear. For faith doth not make us blockish, as brain-sick men do imagine, when they be out of danger.[1] But though faith doth not quite take away the feeling of evils, yet it doth temperate the same, lest the godly be more afraid than is meet; that they may always be bold and have a good hope. So though Paul understand that the viper was a noisome beast, yet did he trust to the promise which was made to him, and did not so fear her plaguy[2] biting, that it did trouble him; because he was even ready to die if need had been.

6. *Changing their minds, they said.* This so wonderful and sudden a change ought to have inwardly touched the men of Melita, and to have moved them to give the glory to the mercy of God, as they did before to vengeance. But as man's reason is always carried amiss unto extremities, they make Paul at a sudden a god, whom they took before to be a wicked murderer. But if he could not choose but be the one, it had been better for him to be counted a murderer than a god. And surely Paul would rather have wished to be condemned, not only of one crime, but also to have sustained all shame,[3] and to have been thrust down into the deep pit of hell,[4] than to take to himself the glory of God, which thing those knew full well who had heard him preach amidst the storms. Notwithstanding, it may be, that, being

---

[1] " In umbra et extra teli jacturam," in the shade, and out of bowshot.
[2] " Pestiferum," pestiferous, deadly   [3] " Omni infamiæ genere," every kind of infamy.   [4] " Ad inferos," to the dead.

taught afterward, they did confess that God was the author of the miracle.

Furthermore, let us learn by this history, with patient and quiet minds, to wait for the prosperous event of things,[1] which seem at the first to tend toward the robbing of God of his honour. Which of us would not have been terrified with this spectacle which did arm the wicked to slander with all manner of slanderous speeches the glory of the gospel? Yet we see how God did in good time prevent this inconvenience; therefore, let us not doubt but that after he hath suffered his to be darkened with clouds of slanders, he will send remedy in his good time, and will turn their darkness into light. In the mean season, let us remember that we must beware of the judgment of the flesh. And because men do always forget themselves, let us beg of God the Spirit of moderation, that he may keep us always in the right mean. Furthermore, let us learn by this how ready the world is to fall to superstition. Yea, this wickedness is in a manner born with us, to be desirous to adorn creatures with that which we take from God.

Wherefore, no marvel if new errors have come abroad[2] in all ages, seeing every one of us is, even from his mother's womb, expert in inventing idols. But lest men excuse themselves therewithal, this history doth witness that this is the fountain of superstitions, because men are unthankful to God, and do give his glory to some other.

> 7. And in those places were the possessions of the chief man of the isle, whose name was Publius; who received us, and lodged us courteously.
> 8. And so it was, that the father of Publius lay sick of the fever and bloody flux; to whom Paul entered in, and when he had prayed, and had laid his hands upon him, he healed him.
> 9. Therefore, when he had done thus, the rest also, which had infirmities in the isle, came, and were healed:

---

[1] "Tristium rerum," of gloomy affairs   [2] "Subinde," ever and anon.

10. *Who did also give us great honour ; and when we departed, they laded us with things necessary.*
11. *And after three months we sailed in a ship of Alexandria, which had wintered in the isle, whose badge was Castor and Pollux.*
12. *And when we came to Syracuse, we stayed there three days.*
13. *And from thence we fetched a compass, and came to Rhegium : and after one day when the south wind blew, we came the next day to Puteoli :*
14. *Where we found brethren, and were desired to stay with them seven days : and so we came to Rome.*

7. *And in those places.* Because this name, Publius, is a Roman name, I suspect that this man, of whom mention is made, was rather a citizen of Rome than born in the isle. For the Grecians and other strangers were not wont to borrow their names of the Latins unless they were men of small reputation. And it may be that some of the noble men of Rome came then to see his possessions, and is called the chief man of the isle, not because he dwelt there, but because no man could compare with him in wealth and possessions. And it is scarce probable that all the whole multitude of Grecians was lodged there three days. I do rather think, that, when he entertained the centurion, he did also honour Paul and his companions, because, being admonished by the miracle, he did believe that he was a man beloved of God. Notwithstanding, howsoever it be, his hospitality was not unrewarded. For shortly after the Lord restored his father to health by the hand of Paul, who was indeed sick of a dangerous disease. And by this means he meant to testify how greatly that courtesy, which is showed to men in misery and to strangers, doth please him. Although those who are holpen be unmindful and unthankful for that benefit which they have received, or they be not able to recompense those who have done good to them, yet God himself will abundantly restore to men whatsoever they have bestowed at his commandment; and he hath sometimes appointed, to those which be merciful and given

to hospitality, some of his servants, which bring with them a blessing. This was now great honour, in that Publius did lodge Christ in the person of Paul. Notwithstanding, this was added as an overplus, in that Paul came furnished with the gift of healing, that he might not only recompense his courtesy, but also give more than he had received.

Also, we know not whether he learned the first principles of faith, as miracles do for the most part win the rude and unbelievers unto faith,[1] Luke mentioneth the kind of disease that he may the better set forth the grace of God. For seeing it is an hard matter to cure a bloody flux,[2] especially when the ague is joined therewith, the old man was cured thus suddenly only by the laying on of hands and prayer, not without the manifest power of God.

8. *And had laid his hands upon him.* Paul declareth by prayer that he himself is not the author of the miracle, but only the minister, lest God be defrauded of his glory. He confirmeth this self-same thing by the external sign. For, as we saw before, in other places, the laying on of hands was nothing else but a solemn rite of offering and presenting. Wherefore, in that Paul doth offer the man to God with his own hands, he professed that he did humbly crave his life of him. By which example, not only those who have excellent gifts of the Spirit given them are admonished to beware, lest by extolling themselves they darken the glory of God, but also we are all taught in general that we must so thank the ministers of the grace of God that the glory remain to him alone. It is said, indeed, that Paul healed the man which had the bloody flux; but it is plainly expressed by the circumstances which are added, that it was God which bestowed this benefit, making him the minister thereof. Whereas Luke saith afterwards, that others which were sick in the isle were cured, he doth not extend it unto all; but his meaning is, that the power of God, which ap-

---

[1] " Ad docilitatem," to docility. [2] " Nam quam difficilis et lenta sit dysenteriæ curatio," for since the cure of dysentery is slow and difficult

peared evidently enough, was proved by many testimonies, that the apostleship of Paul might be thereby ratified. Neither need we doubt but that Paul sought as well to cure their souls as their bodies. Yet Luke doth not declare what good he did, save only that the barbarians gave him and his fellows victual and necessary things when they loosed from the haven. In the mean season, we must note, that though Paul might have withdrawn himself, and have escaped many ways, yet was the will of God to him instead of voluntary fetters, because he was often cited by the heavenly oracle to appear before the judgment-seat of Nero to bear witness of Christ. Again, he knew that if he should run away, he could no longer have preached the gospel, but should have lurked in some corner during his whole life.

11. *In a ship of Alexandria.* By these words, Luke giveth us to understand, that the former ship was either drowned, or else so rent and beaten, that it served for no use afterward; whereby the greatness of the shipwreck doth the better appear. And he setteth down expressly that the badge of the ship of Alexandria, wherein they were carried to Rome, was Castor and Pollux, that we may know that Paul had not liberty granted to sail with such as were like to himself; but was enforced to enter into a ship which was dedicated to two idols. The old poets did feign that Castor and Pollux came of Jupiter and Leda; for which cause they are called in Greek διοσκουροι; which word Luke useth in this place, as if you should say, Jupiter's sons. Again, they said[1] that they are the sign in the zodiac called Gemini. There was also another superstition among the mariners, that those fine exhalations which appear in tempests are the very same. Therefore, in times past, they were thought to be gods of the seas, and were therefore called upon as at this day, Nicholas and Clement, and such like. Yea, as in Popery, they retain the old er-

---

[1] " Fabulati," they fabled

rors, changing the names only; so at this day they worship these exhalations under the name of Saint Hermes, or Saint Ermus. And because if one exhalation appear alone, it is a doleful token; but if two together, (as Pliny writeth,) then they foreshow a prosperous course. To the end the mariners of Alexandria might have both Castor and Pollux to favour them, they had both for the badge of their ship. Therefore, as touching them, the ship was polluted with wicked sacrilege; but because Paul did not make choice thereof, of his own accord, he is not polluted thereby.

And surely seeing an idol is nothing, it cannot infect the creatures of God, but that the faithful may use them purely and lawfully. And we must needs think thus, that all those blots wherewith Satan doth go about to stain the creatures of God through his juggling, are washed away by no other means but by a good and pure conscience, whereas the wicked and ungodly do defile those things which are of themselves pure, though they do but touch them. Finally, Paul was no more defiled by entering into this ship, than when he did behold the altars at Athens; because, being void of all superstition, he knew that all the rites of the Gentiles were mere illusions. Again, the men could not think that he did agree to that profane error; for if he had been to do any worship to Castor and Pollux, though it had been only for fashion's sake, he would rather have died a thousand deaths than once have yielded.

Therefore, because he needed not to fear any offence, he entereth the ship without any more ado; and undoubtedly he did this heavily, and with inward sorrow; because he saw the honour which is due to God alone given to vain inventions. Therefore, this ought to be numbered among his exercises, in that he had those to be his guides, who thought that they were governed of idols, and had committed their ship to their tuition.

12. *When we were come to Syracuse.* Luke prosecuteth the residue of the course of their sailing, that they arrived

first in Sicilia. And after that they set a compass[1] by reason of the tempest and raging of the sea, and sailed over into Italy. And as that haven whereof Luke speaketh in this place is the most famous haven of all Sicilia, so is it farther from the coast of Italy than is that of Messina, over against which is Rhegium, whereof he maketh mention. And it is in the country of the Brutians, as is Puteoli, a city of Campania. But forasmuch as the brethren kept Paul at Puteoli seven days, by this we gather how favourably and gently the centurion handled Paul. Neither do I doubt but that the holy man would have made him a faithful promise that he would always return in due time. But he was persuaded of his uprightness, so that he was not afraid that he would deceive him. And now we gather out of this place, that the seed of the gospel was then sown abroad, seeing there was some body of the Church even at Puteoli.

15. *And when the brethren had heard of us from thence, they came out to meet us at Appii Forum, and at The three Taverns; whom when Paul saw, he gave thanks to God, and waxed bold.*
16. *And when we were come to Rome, the centurion delivered the prisoners to the chief captain of the host; but Paul was suffered to dwell alone with a soldier which kept him.*
17. *And after three days Paul called together the chief of the Jews; and when they were come, he said to them, Men and brethren, though I have done nothing against the people, or ordinances of the elders, yet was I delivered a prisoner from Jerusalem into the hands of the Romans.*
18. *Which, when they had examined me, they would have let me go, because there was no cause of death in me.*
19. *But when the Jews spake contrary, I was enforced to appeal to Cæsar: not as if I have anything to accuse my nation of.*
20. *For this cause, therefore, have I sent for you, that I might see you, and speak to you; for the hope of Israel am I bound with this chain.*

---

[1] " Oblique . . . trajecerint," they made an indirect passage.

15. *When the brethren heard.* God did comfort Paul by the coming of the brethren who came forth to meet him, that he might the more joyfully make haste to defend the gospel. And the zeal and godly care of the brethren appeareth therein, in that they inquire for Paul's coming, and go out to meet him. For it was at that time not only an odious thing to profess the Christian faith, but it might also bring them in hazard of their life. Neither did a few men only put themselves in private danger, because the envy redounded to the whole Church. But nothing is more dear to them than their duty wherein they could not be negligent, unless they would be counted sluggish and unthankful. It had been a cruel fact to neglect so great an apostle of Jesus Christ, especially seeing he laboured for the common salvation.

And now forasmuch as he had written to them before, and had of his own accord offered his service to them, it had been an unseemly thing not to repay to him brotherly good-will and courtesy. Therefore, the brethren did, by this their dutifulness, testify their godliness toward Christ; and Paul's desire was more inflamed, because he saw fruit prepared for his constancy. For though he were endued with invincible strength,[1] so that he did not depend upon man's help; yet God, who useth to strengthen his by means of men, did minister to him new strength by this means. Though he were afterward forsaken when he was in prison, as he complaineth in a certain place, (2 Tim. iv. 16,) yet he did not despair; but did fight no less valiantly and manfully under Christ's banner, than if he had been guarded with a great army. But the remembrance of this meeting did serve even then to encourage him, seeing he did consider with himself that there were many godly brethren at Rome, but they were weak, and that he was sent to strengthen them. And there is no cause why we should marvel that Paul was emboldened at this present when he saw the brethren, because he did hope that the confession

---

[1] "Fortitudine." fortitude.

of his faith would yield no small fruit. For so often as God showeth to his servants any fruit of their labour, he doth, as it were, prick them forward with a goad, that they may proceed more courageously in their work.

16. *The centurion delivered the prisoners.* Luke doth signify that Paul had more liberty granted him than the rest; for his condition and estate was peculiar. For he was suffered to dwell in an house by himself, having one keeper with him, whereas the rest were shut up in the common prison. For the general captain [1] knew by Festus' report that Paul was guiltless; and the centurion, as it is likely, did faithfully rehearse such things as might serve to bring him into favour. Notwithstanding, let us know that God did govern [2] from heaven the bonds of his servant; not only that he might ease him of his trouble, but that the faithful might have freer access unto him. For he would not have the treasure of his faith shut up in prison, but he would have it laid open, that it might enrich many far and wide. And yet Paul was not so at liberty, but that he did always carry a chain. Luke calleth the general captain στρατοπεδαρχης, who was appointed over the army which kept the city, as histories make mention.[3]

17. *And after three days.* Paul's humanity [4] was wonderful, in that, though he had suffered such cruel injuries of his nation, he studied, notwithstanding, to appease the Jews which are at Rome, and he excuseth himself to them, lest they hate his cause, because they hear that the priests do hate him. He might well have excused himself before men, if he passed over these Jews and turned himself to the Gentiles. For though he had continually, in divers places, essayed to bring them to Christ, yet they were more and more nettled and moved;[5] and yet he had omitted

---

[1] " Præfectus," the præfect   [2] " Moderatum," temper
[3] " Præfectum prætorio cujus illud officium fuisse ex historiis satis notum est," præfect of the prætorium, to whom it is well known from history that office belonged   [4] " Mansuetudo, ' meekness
[5] " Exacerbati," exasperated

nothing, neither in Asia, nor in Greece, neither at Jerusalem, which might mitigate their fury. Therefore, all men would have justly pardoned him, if he had let those alone whom he had so often tried [experienced] to be of desperate pride.[1] But because he knew that his Master was given of his Father to be the minister of the Jews, to fulfil the promises whereby God had adopted to himself the seed of Abraham to be his people; he looketh unto the calling of God, and is never weary. He saw that he must remain at Rome, seeing he had liberty granted to teach, he would not that they should be deprived of the fruit of his labour. Secondly, he would not have them moved through hatred of his cause to trouble the Church; because a small occasion might have caused great destruction. Therefore, Paul meant to beware, lest, according to their wonted madness, they should set all on fire.[2]

I have done nothing against the people. These two things might have made the Jews hate him; either because he should have done hurt to the commonwealth of his nation, as some runagates did increase their bondage, which was too cruel, through their treachery; or because he should have done somewhat against the worship of God; for though the Jews were grown out of kind,[3] and religion was depraved and corrupted among them with many errors, yet the very name of the law and the worship of the temple were greatly reverenced. Furthermore, Paul denieth not but that he did freely omit those ceremonies whereto the Jews were superstitiously tied; yet he cleareth himself of the crime of revolting whereof he might be suspected. Therefore, understand those ordinances of the fathers, whereby the children of Abraham, and the disciples of Moses ought, according to their faith, to have been distinguished from the rest of the Gentiles. And surely in that he did cleave so holily to Christ, who is the soul and perfection of the law, he is so far from impairing the or-

---

[1] "Pervicaciæ," obstinacy and petulance
[2] "Pessimi incendii faces essent," they should be torches to kindle a very bad fire
[3] "Degeneres," degenerate.

dinances of the fathers, that none did better observe the same.

19. *I was enforced to appeal.* This appeal was full of hatred and envy for this cause, because the authority and liberty of the Jewish nation did seem to be sore opprest, who could have been content to have lived with their own laws. Secondly, because his defence was joined with infamy and loss of all the people. Therefore he answereth this objection also, because he was enforced with the stubbornness of his enemies to fly to this fortress, [asylum.] For he is excused by necessity, because he had no other way to escape death. And after that he had excused that which was done already, he promiseth that he will so handle his matter hereafter,[1] that he will not labour against the Jews.

20. *For the hope of Israel.* We must understand much more under these words than Luke expresseth; as we gather out of the answer, where the Jews speak of the sect; to wit, repeating his speech, which Luke omitteth. Therefore Paul intreated of Christ, that it might plainly appear that neither the law nor the temple did profit the Jews anything without him; because the covenant of adoption is grounded in him, and the promise of salvation is in him confirmed. Neither did they doubt but that the restoring of the kingdom did depend upon the coming of the Messias; and even at that time their misery and decay did increase the hope and desire of him. Wherefore Paul saith, for good causes, that he is bound for the hope of Israel. Whereby we be also taught, that no man doth hope aright, but he which looketh unto Christ and his spiritual kingdom; for when he placeth the hope of the godly in Christ, he excludeth all other hopes.

21. *But they said unto him, We neither received letters from*

---

[1] " Ita causam suam acturum," will so plead his cause.

Judea touching thee, neither did any of the brethren come and show us or speak any evil of thee.

22. But we will hear of thee what thou thinkest; for as concerning that sect, we know that it is spoken against everywhere.

23. And when they had appointed him a day, many came to him to his lodging; to whom he expounded and testified the kingdom of God, and persuaded them of Jesus out of the law of Moses, and out of the prophets, from morning till night.

24. And certain believed those things which were spoken, but certain believed not.

21. *Neither by letters.* The priests and scribes did not hold their peace, because they were become more gentle towards Paul, or to the end they might spare him; that proceeded rather of contempt, or else of despair, because they neither knew how to oppress him when he was so far from them, and his carrying into Italy was[1] to them instead of a grave. For they did lord it no less carelessly than proudly, so that nobody did trouble them at home. Furthermore, though the Jews come not altogether rightly prepared to hear, yet they show some desire to learn, when as they do not refuse to hear the defence of his doctrine, which is spoken against everywhere. For many do stop the way before themselves with this prejudice, because they cannot abide to hear that which is refused by common judgment, but subscribe to the opinion of other men to the condemning of doctrine which they know not. Nevertheless, this is not without fault (as I said) that they object gainsaying to cause hatred, or to procure evil suspicion; as if it had not been said before by Isaiah, that God should be a stone of offence to all the people. It is uncertain, whether upon the day appointed Paul disputed all the day, or they reasoned one with another; save only, because we may guess, by the circumstance of time, that Paul did not continue speaking still.[2] For he could scarce have framed a speech which could have continued from morning to night. Wherefore I

---

[1] "Videri poterat," might seem.   [2] "Uno tenore," without stopping.

do not doubt, but that after the apostle had briefly expounded the sum of the gospel, he granted liberty to the hearers to propound questions,[1] and did make answer to the questions which were objected to him.

But we must note the state of the disputation, which Luke saith is double. For Paul taught first, after what sort the kingdom of God was amongst them, and principally what manner [of] chief felicity and glory that was which was promised to them, which the prophets do so highly extol. For seeing that many of them did dream of a frail estate of the kingdom of God in the world, and did place the same falsely in idleness, pleasure, and in plenty of present good things, it was necessary that it should be rightly defined, that they might know that the kingdom of God is spiritual, whose beginning is newness of life, and the end thereof blessed immortality and the heavenly glory. Secondly, Paul exhorted them to receive Christ, the author of the promised felicity.

And, again, this second point had two members, for it could not be handled profitably and soundly unless he did expound the office of the promised Redeemer; secondly, unless he did show that he is already given, and that the Son of Mary is he in whom the fathers hoped. It was indeed a common maxim among the Jews, that the Messias should come and restore all things into perfect order.

But Paul laboured another point, which was not so well known; that the Messias was promised, who should, with the sacrifice of his death, make satisfaction for the sins of the world; who should reconcile God to men; who should purchase eternal righteousness; who should fashion men after the image of God, being regenerate with his Spirit; who should, finally, make his faithful servants heirs with him of eternal life; and that all those things were fulfilled in the person of Jesus Christ crucified. He could not intreat of those things; but he must needs call back the Jews from

---

[1] ' Vicissim,' in their turn.

their gross and earthly inventions into heaven, and also take away the stumbling-block of the cross, seeing he taught that there was no other way or means whereby we are reconciled with God.

And let us note, that (as Luke doth testify) Paul took all that which he spake of Christ out of the law and prophets. For true religion differeth from all feigned religions, because the word of God alone is the rule thereof. Also the Church of God differeth from all profane sects in this, because it heareth him speak alone, and is governed by his commandment. And now by this we see the agreement that is between the Old and the New Testaments to establish the faith of Christ; secondly, that double profit of the Scripture which the same Paul commendeth in another place, to wit, that it is sufficient as well to instruct those which are willing to learn, as to refute the stubbornness of those which set themselves against the truth, (2 Tim. iii. 16; Titus i. 9.) Therefore, let those who desire to be wise with sobriety, and to teach others well, appoint themselves these bounds, that they utter nothing but out of the pure fountain of the word. The philosophers deal otherwise, who contend only with reasons, because they have no sound authority, whom the Papists imitate too much, who set apart the oracles of God, and lean only to the inventions of man's brain, that is, to mere folly.

24. *Some believed.* Luke declareth that this was at length the success of the disputation, that they did not all profit[1] in the same doctrine. We know that the apostle was endued with such grace of the Spirit, that he ought to have moved stones; and yet he could not, after long disputing and testifying, win all men unto Christ. Wherefore, let us not marvel, if the unbelief of many do at this day resist the plain doctrine of the gospel, and if many remain obstinate, to whom the truth of Christ is no less made manifest than the sun at noon-day. Moreover, those return from Paul blind

---

[1] "Pariter," equally

and blockish, who came unto him willingly, as if they had been desirous to learn. If there were such stubbornness in voluntary hearers, what marvel is it if those refuse Christ with a malicious[1] mind, who swell with pride and malice, [bitterness,] and do openly fly and hate the light?

> 25. *And when they could not agree, they departed, after that Paul had spoken one word, Well spake the Holy Ghost by Esaias to our fathers,*
> 26. *Saying, Go to this people, and say, Ye shall hear with your ears, and not understand; and seeing ye shall see, and not perceive;*
> 27. *For the heart of this people is waxed gross, and their ears are dull with hearing, and with their eyes they have winked, lest at any time they see with their eyes, and hear with their ears, and understand with their heart, and they be converted, and I heal them.*
> 28. *Be it known therefore unto you, that this salvation of God is sent to the Gentiles, and they shall hear it.*
> 29. *And when he had said these things, the Jews went out from him, and had great reasoning among themselves.*
> 30. *And Paul remained two years full in a thing he had hired for himself,[2] and he received all those which came in unto him,*
> 31. *Preaching the kingdom of God, and teaching those things which concern the Lord Jesus, with all boldness, and no man did let* [hinder] *him.*

25. *And when they could not.* The malice and frowardness of the unfaithful is the cause of this, that Christ, who is our peace, and the only bond of holy unity, is an occasion of dissension, and doth cause those to go together by the ears who were friends before. For, behold, when the Jews come together to hear Paul, they think all one thing, and speak all one thing; they do all profess that they embrace the law of Moses. So soon as they hear the doctrine of reconciliation, there ariseth dissension among them, so that they are divided.[3] And yet for all this we must not think that the

---

[1] " Amarulento," bitter.   [2] " In suo conducto," in his hired room.
[3] " In diversas partes," into different parties.

preaching of the gospel is the cause of discord; but that privy displeasure, which lurked before in their malicious minds, doth then break out; and as the brightness of the sun doth not colour things otherwise than they were, but doth plainly show the difference, which was none so long as it was dark. Therefore, seeing God doth illuminate his elect peculiarly, and faith is not common to all men, let us remember that it cannot be but that, so soon as Christ cometh abroad, there will be a division among men. But then let us call to mind that which Simon foretold of him, that he shall be a sign which shall be spoken against, that the thoughts of many hearts may be disclosed, (Luke ii. 34, 35;) and that unbelief which striveth against God is the mother of dissension.

After that Paul. At the first he went about to allure them meekly and gently; now, so soon as he espieth their obstinacy, he inveigheth sharply, and doth severely denounce the judgment of God. For the rebellious must be handled thus, whose pride cannot be tamed with plain doctrine. The same order must we keep; we must gently govern those who are apt to be taught and gentle, but we must cite the stubborn unto God's judgment-seat. Whereas he bringeth in rather the Holy Ghost speaking than the prophet, it maketh to the credit of the oracle. For seeing God requireth that he alone be heard, doctrine cannot otherwise be of authority, than if we know that it did proceed from him, and that it did not issue out of man's brain. Again, he declareth therewithal that the stubbornness of one age only is not there noted, but that the oracle of the Spirit is extended unto the time to come.

26. *Go to this people.* This is a notable place, because it is cited six times in the New Testament, (Matth. xiii. 14; John xii. 40; Rom. xi. 8; Mark iv. 12; Luke viii. 10;) but because it is brought in elsewhere to another end, we must mark for what purpose Paul applieth it unto the present cause; namely, he meant with this, as with a mallet, to beat in pieces the hardness and frowardness of the wicked, and

to encourage the faithful, who were as yet weak and tender, lest the unbelief of others should trouble them.

Therefore, the sum is, that that was fulfilled which was foretold by the prophet, and that, therefore, there is no cause why the reprobate should flatter themselves, or that the faithful should be terrified, as it were, with some new unwonted thing. And though it be certain that this blindness whereof the prophet spake began in his time, yet John showeth that it did properly appertain unto the kingdom of Christ. Therefore, Paul doth fitly apply it unto that contempt of the gospel which he saw; as if he should have said, This is the very same thing which the Holy Ghost foretold in times past by the mouth of Isaiah. And though this place be diversely applied not only by the Evangelists, but also by Paul himself, the show of contrariety is easily put away and answered. Matthew, Mark, and Luke, say that this prophecy was fulfilled when Christ spake by parables unto the people, and did not reveal to them the mysteries of the kingdom of heaven. For then the unfaithful heard the voice of God with their outward ears, but they did not profit thereby. John saith in a sense not much unlike to this, that the Jews were not brought to believe, no, not with many miracles, (John xii. 37,) so that this same prophecy of the prophet was fulfilled.

Therefore, these four agree in this, that it came to pass by the just judgment of God, that the reprobate in hearing should not hear, and in seeing should not see. Now, Paul calleth to mind that which the prophet did testify concerning the Jews, lest any man wonder at their blindness. Furthermore, in the Epistle to the Romans, (Rom. xi. 5, 7,) he mounteth higher, showing that this is the cause of blindness, because God doth give the light of faith only to the remnant whom he hath chosen freely. And surely it is certain that because the reprobate reject the doctrine of salvation, this cometh to pass through their own malice, and that therefore they themselves are to be blamed. But this next cause doth not let but that the secret election of God may distinguish between men; that those may believe who are ordained to life, and that the other may remain blockish. I will not stand long about the words of the prophet, because I have expounded the same elsewhere. Neither did Paul curiously recite the words which are in the prophet; but did rather apply his words unto his purpose. Therefore, he imputeth that making blind, which the prophet attributeth to the secret judgment of God, to their malice. For the prophet is commanded to stop the eyes of his hearers; and Paul in this place accuseth the unbelieving of his time, because they shut their own eyes. Though he setteth down both things distinctly, that God is the author of their blindness, and that yet, notwithstanding, they shut their own eyes, and become blind of their own accord; as these two things do very well agree together, as we said elsewhere.

In the last, remember where it is said, Lest they see with their eyes, or hear with their ears, or understand with their heart; God showeth how clear his doctrine is, to wit, that it is sufficient to lighten all the senses, unless men do maliciously darken themselves; as Paul also teacheth in another place, that his gospel is plain, so that none can be blind in the light thereof, save those who are ordained to destruction, whose eyes Satan hath blinded, (2 Cor. iv. 3.)

Lest they be converted, and I heal them. By this we gather that the Word of God is not set before all men that they may return to soundness of mind; but that the external voice soundeth in the ears of many, without the effectual working of the Spirit, only that they may be made inexcusable. And here the pride of flesh doth rashly murmur against God; as we see many object, that men are called in vain, yea, absurdly, unless it be in their power to obey; though we see no reason why God appeareth to the blind, and speaketh to the deaf; yet his will alone, which is the rule of all righteousness, ought to be to us instead of a thousand reasons.

In the conclusion, we must note the wholesome effect of the Word of God; namely, the conversion of men, which is not only the beginning of health, but also a certain resurrection from death to life.

28. *Therefore be it.* Lest the Jews may afterward accuse him of revolting, because he forsaketh the holy stock of Abraham, and goeth to the profane Gentiles; he denounceth that which the prophets did so often testify, that the salvation whereof they were the proper, at least the principal[1] heirs, should be translated unto strangers. Notwithstanding, whereas he saith that salvation was sent to the Gentiles, he meaneth, in the second place, to wit, after that the Jews had rejected it, as we have said before more at large, (Acts xiii. 46.) Therefore, the sense is, that there is no cause why the Jews should complain if the Gentiles be admitted into the void possession after that they have forsaken it. Neither doth he make faith common to all the Gentiles in general, when he saith that they shall hear. For he had full well tried, that even many of the Gentiles did wickedly resist God, but he setteth so many of the Gentiles as believed against the unbelieving Jews, that he may provoke them unto jealousy; as it is in the Song of Moses, (Deut. xxxii. 21.) In the mean season, he signifieth that the doctrine which they refuse shall profit others.

29. *Having much reasoning.* No doubt, the wicked were more nettled because he cited the prophecy against them; for they are so far from waxing meek when they are reproved, that they are more inflamed with fury. This is the reason why they reasoned[2] when they were gone out from Paul, because the more part would not be quiet. But seeing there was such disputing, it appeareth that some did so embrace those things which Paul had spoken, that they doubted not to defend and stoutly to avouch that which they believed. But it is in vain for any man to object thereupon, that the gospel of Christ is the seed of contention, which cometh undoubtedly from man's pride and way-

---

[1] " Primarii," primary.   [2] " Disceptaverunt," disputed.

wardness; and assuredly, if we will have peace with God, we must strive against[1] those which contemn him.

30. *He received all.* The apostle showed an excellent example of constancy, in that he offered himself so willingly to all those which were desirous to hear him. Surely he was not ignorant what great hatred he did purchase; and that this was his best way, if by holding his peace he might appease the hatred of his adversaries. For a man being desirous to provide for himself alone would not have done thus; but because he remembered that he was no less the servant of Christ, and a preacher of the gospel, when he was in prison, than if he had been at liberty, he thought it was not lawful for him to withdraw himself from any which was ready to learn, lest he should foreslow [neglect] the occasion which was offered him by God, and therefore he did more regard the holy calling of God than his own life. And that we may know that he did incur danger willingly, Luke doth shortly after expressly commend his boldness, as if he should say, that setting all fear aside, he did faithfully obey the commandment of God, neither was he terrified with any danger,[2] but did proceed to take pains with whomsoever he met.

Preaching the kingdom of God. He doth not separate the kingdom of God, and those things which belong to Christ, as diverse things, but doth rather add the second thing by way of exposition, that we may know that the kingdom of God is grounded and contained in the knowledge of the redemption purchased by Christ. Therefore, Paul taught that men are strangers[3] and foreigners from the kingdom of God, until having their sins done away they be reconciled to God, and be renewed into holiness of life by the Spirit; and that the kingdom of God is then erected, and doth then flourish among them, when Christ the Mediator doth join them to the Father, having both their sins freely for-

---

[1] "Bellare necesse est," we must of necessity war with difficultatibus," by any difficulties. [3] "Exules," exiles. [2] "Ullis

given them, and being also regenerate unto righteousness, that beginning the heavenly life upon earth, they may always have a longing desire to come to heaven, where they shall fully and perfectly enjoy glory. Also, Luke setteth forth a singular benefit of God, in that Paul had so great liberty granted him. For that came not to pass through the winking and dissimulation of those who could hinder it, seeing they did detest religion, but because the Lord did shut their eyes. Wherefore, it is not without cause that Paul himself doth boast that the Word of God was not bound with his bonds, (2 Tim. ii. 9.)

THE END OF THE LATTER PART OF THE COMMENTARIES
UPON THE ACTS OF THE APOSTLES.

ALL GLORY TO GOD.

INDEX

TO

COMMENTARY

UPON

THE ACTS OF THE APOSTLES.

INDEX.

THE REFERENCES ARE TO THE CHAPTERS AND VERSES.

ABRAHAM, the father of the faithful, vii. 3.
blessed in the seed of, what, iii 25.
prevented by the grace and goodness of God, vii. 2.
why God called the God of, vii. 32.
his children of two sorts, iii. 25; vii 52, xiii. 16, 33; xxvi. 7
fanatical allegory as to, xiii. 33.
his obedience worthy of singular commendation, vii. 3; x. 14.
his patience, vii 5.
Abstinence, unwonted fasting designated by, xxvii. 33.
Abuse of miracles, iii. 9.
of tongues, x. 46.
Acceptance of persons condemned, x 34.
Accusation, sharp and open, not always to be condemned, xxiii. 3.
Adoption, circumcision a token and pledge of, vii 8.
the end of our, x. 43.
Adramyttium, a city of Æolia, xxvii. 2.

Advocate, Christ is our, ii. 21.
Affections, natural, not of themselves corrupt, viii. 2; xx. 37.
Afflictions from God, x. 38; xi. 28.
of sin, xxviii 4.
common to the godly as well as the wicked, xxiii. 8; xxvii. 24; xxviii. 4.
for Christ's sake glorious, v. 41, 42; xvi. 22.
cannot hurt the elect, vii 30.
to be suffered with patience, xiv. 22.
profit of, xi 19; xiv. 22; xvi. 22, 29; xviii. 2, 41.
of the faithful various, xiv. 21.
of the faithful honourable, xvi. 22.
of the faithful, also the afflictions of Christ, xxii. 7.
After, the word, used for *moreover*, or *besides*, v. 36.
Agabus, in what sense called a prophet, xi 27.
took girdle of St Paul, xvii. 18.
Agrippa, Herod, the elder, xii. 1.
son of Agrippa the elder, xxv. 13.

Alexander, an apostate, xix. 33.
Allegory of the burning bush, vii. 30.
   fanatical, as to Abraham's children, xiii. 33.
Alms precious to God, v. 5.
Ambition, a great vice, v. 1.
   very hurtful to the Church, viii. 14.
   always envious and malicious, xi 23
   of Papists, xvi 19.
   the mother of dissension, xxiii. 9.
   the mother of all heresies, xx. 30.
Anabaptists refuted, ii. 35, 45.
   error of, concerning infant baptism, viii. 37; xi. 17.
   doting of, as to a community of goods, iv. 34; v. 4
   doting of, as to the children of Abraham, iii. 25.
   illusions of, vii 31.
Ananias, Paul's teacher, ix 6, 10.
   why the vision appeared to, ix. 10.
   who commanded Paul to be smitten, whether he was the high priest, xxiii. 2; xxiv. 1.
   and Sapphira, the grievous sin of, v. 5.
Angel, whether every man has his, xii. 15.
   who appeared to Moses was Christ, vii 30.
Angels and devils, fanatical opinion as to, xxiii. 8.
   called "men," x. 30.
   messengers and witnesses in publishing the law, vii. 53.
   ministers of the faithful, v. 19; xii 11, 15.
Anger, how holy, xiii 10; xiv. 14; xvii. 16.
Anointing of Christ, x. 38.
Antichrist, his bondslaves, xii 3.

Antichrist, the miracles of, false, ii 22.
Antioch, an excellent ornament of, xi 26
   Christians first so called at, ib.
   faith of the men of, xi. 27.
Antiquity, how far we must lean to, xiv. 16, 30; xxiv. 14.
Antonia, a tower built by Herod, iv. 1.
Apollonias, or Asson, a city of Troas, xx. 13.
Apollos, the successor of Paul at Corinth, xviii 24.
Apostle, how Barnabas an, xiv. 14.
Apostles, witnesses of Christ, i. 8; x. 39.
   ministers, not authors of miracles, iii. 46; xvi. 18; xix. 11; xxviii. 8.
   directed by the Spirit, iii. 5; ix. 34; xiv 9
   spake with strange tongues, ii. 4.
   why they went fearfully forward in preaching the gospel, viii. 1.
   had wives, i 14
   brought in no new religion, iii. 13; v 30
   why did not preach the gospel immediately after Christ's resurrection and ascension, i. 4.
   why began to preach the gospel at Jerusalem, i 4.
   authority of the, vi. 2
   constancy of the, v. 12, 36, 42; viii. 2
   modesty of the, v. 12; xix. 30; xxi. 18
   office of the, xi 22; xv. 4.
   erroneous opinion of, concerning the kingdom of Christ, i. 6.
   the power of, xiii 11.
   certain calling of, i. 2.
   sincere zeal of, iv. 25, 33.

Apostles, difference between and Pastors, i. 23; xiv 23
difference between and Elders, xiv. 23.
had no certain place of abode, ix. 32.
name of, used in a large sense, xiv. 14
accused of sedition, v. 28.
their mode of quoting Scripture, xv 16.
appointed after Christ's resurrection, i. 4
why had the gift of tongues, ii. 2.
miserable bondage of the Jews in the time of, xvi 3.
Aquila, Paul's host, xviii 2
Aratus, quotation from, xvii 28.
Aretas, governor of Damascus, ix. 23.
Aristarchus, the companion of Paul, xxvii 2.
Aristotle, authority of, among the Sorbonnists, xvii 28.
quoted, i 3.
Arrogance of the Jews, xiii 42; xxii 22; of Papists, vii. 1; of the Pope, xiii. 3; xv. 16, xxii i
Ascension of Christ the conclusion of the gospel history, i. 2.
Ashdod, also called Azotus, viii. 40.
Assaron, the name of a city, ix. 32.
Assemblies of the faithful in time of persecution, xii. 12.
Assos, a city of Troas, called also Apollonia, xx. 13.
Astrology, judicial, condemned, xix. 19.
Astronomy, study of advantageous, vii 22
Athens, St Paul there, xvii. 18.
Augustine attacked by the Pelagians, xv. 10.
his complaint of the multiplicity of traditions, xvi. 4
quoted, i. 11; ii. 1; vii. 56; viii. 1, 24; x. 4; xiii. 33; xvi. 4; xxiii. 5
Auricular confession of the Papists, xix. 19.
Author of Life, Christ the only, ii. 24.
Authority of Christ, how great, iii. 23.
of the word of God, viii. 25; xiii. 51; xx. 23; xxviii. 25.
Avoiding offences, x. 28; xiii. 27; xv. 1; xviii. 18, xx. 3, 33, 34; xxii 27; xxviii. 17, 18.
Azotus or Ashdod, viii. 40.

BAD men, in this world, mingled with the good, vi. 1, 5; viii. 13; xiii. 40; xv. 12, 24; xvii. 32; xx. 30; xxvii. 24.
Band of Augustus, xxvii. 1.
how many soldiers in a, x. 1.
Baptism, the word used improperly, i 5.
sometimes referred to the gifts of the Spirit, xix. 5.
of the Spirit committed to Christ, i. 15.
titles of, i 5
the end of, viii. 37.
the form of, x. 48.
the form of, whether observed by Peter, ii. 38.
the force of, on what depends, ii. 38; xi. 16; xxii. 16.
of John put for his whole ministry, x. 37; xviii 25.
comparison between that of John and Christ, i. 5.
difference between John's and ours, xix. 4.
the rite of in ancient times, viii. 38.
a pertinent of spiritual grace, x. 47.
a pertinent of faith, viii. 37.
grounded in Christ, viii. 37.
a seal wherewith the promise of grace is confirmed, ii. 38.
Christ the end of, x. 48.

Baptism, its dignity, how defaced by Papists, x. 47.
a token of newness of life, viii. 36.
a token of repentance, ii 38
not to be denied to infants, ii. 39, viii. 37; x 47.
Barnabas, how an apostle, xiv. 14
a minister of the Gentiles, xiv. 13.
his simplicity, xi. 24, 25.
his zeal, xiv. 14; xv 28.
discord between Paul and, xv. 37.
Beasts, unclean, law as to, abrogated, x. 13
Benefits of God, the end of, vii. 7.
Bernice, sister of Agrippa the younger, xxv. 13.
Bishops and elders, x. 28.
how ridiculous the Popish are, iv. 11; xx 28
Popish, the tyranny of, xv 30.
Blasphemy of the Jews, xiii. 45; xviii. 6.
of Papists against baptism, viii. 16
and against the Scriptures, xvii 2, 11, 28; xviii. 18.
Blastus won with gifts, xii. 20.
Blessed in the seed of Abraham, what, iii 25.
Blessing of the priest, iii. 26.
Christ the only fountain and author of, iii. 26.
Blindness of the Jews, xvii. 3, 4; xxviii. 26.
of Papists, xxiii. 12.
Blood, eating of, forbidden in times past, xv. 19.
Boasting, proud, of the Jews, vii. 9.
of the Pope, iv. 11, 19; v. 28, 29.
Body of Christ not infinite, i. 11.
of Christ now in heaven, i. 11, vii. 56.
of Christ, the Church so styled, i. 18.

Body, resurrection of the, a work of divine power, xxvi. 8.
Bondslaves of Antichrist, xii. 3.
Breaking of bread, used for Lord's Supper, ii. 42, xx. 7.
Brethren, denote the faithful converted to God, xiv. 2.
Brutus, what vision seen by, xvi. 10.
Budæus quoted, i. 1.
Burning bush, allegory of the, vii. 30.
Burying, what gained by, ix. 37.
why to be respected, viii. 2.

CAIAPHAS had two names, iv 5
Calling upon God, his principal worship, ii. 21.
diligence to be used in our, i. 8; vii. 3; xx. 23, xxvii. 3, xxviii. 17, 30.
of the apostles certain, i. 2.
of pastors certain, xvi. 5.
common, of the faithful depicted in Christ, xiii. 22.
Candace, general name for the Queens of Ethiopia, viii 27
Castor and Pollux, fabulous account of, xxviii 4.
Celestial Hierarchy, the Books of, improperly attributed to Dionysius the Areopagite, xvii. 34.
Ceremonial Law, abrogated by the coming of Christ, viii. 27.
Ceremonies abrogated by the coming of Christ, vi. 14; viii. 27; xiii. 38; xv. 9, 16; xvi. 3; xxi. 10.
multiplicity of in Popery, xvi 3.
weakness of, xiii. 38.
use of, xiii. 38; xv. 9; xvii 25.
free before the Gospel, xvi. 3; xviii. 18.
Certainty of faith, i. 4.
Chaldea comprehended under the name of Mesopotamia, vii. 2.
Children of Abraham of two sorts, iii. 25; vii. 52; xiii. 16, 33; xxvi 7

INDEX. 439

Children, doting of Anabaptists as to, iii. 25.
of God, who, xvii. 28.
Christ, why called Jesus of Nazareth, x. 38.
the angel who appeared to Moses, vii. 30.
what to bear the name of, ix. 15.
the only author of life, ii 24.
the Head of the Church, ii. 25, 36.
the perpetual Guardian of the Church, ix 5.
the only Master and Teacher of the Church, iii. 21; vii. 37, ix. 36, x 24, xiii 47; xv. 2; xx 30.
the Lord, ii. 36.
the guide of his people, v. 31.
the son of David, ii 30; xiii. 23.
the Son of God, ii. 22; viii. 37, ix. 20; xiii 33; xvi. 31.
the end and consummation of the law, xx 30; vii. 37, 52, xiii. 38; xxviii 17.
the only fountain and author of blessing, iii 26.
the fountain of salvation, iv 12.
the foundation of the Church, iv. 11.
the only foundation of faith and repentance, ii. 38.
truly man, vii. 30
the restorer of the Church, ii. 17; xv 16.
the image of the invisible God, x. 4.
the Judge of the world, i 2; iii. 20; x. 42; xvii. 31.
why called Just, vii. 52, xxii. 24
the Mediator, ii. 21, 33, vii. 30, x. 4, 36, 43; xiii. 38; xx. 21; xxvi. 6; xxvii 24, xxviii. 31
the true Messiah, iv 10
why called a Nazarite, x. 38.
participation with God only by, vii. 30

Christ our peace, xxviii. 25.
the pledge and substance of eternal life, ix. 37.
the first fruits of the resurrection, xxvi. 23.
the chief of all the prophets, iii 22.
the eternal King, ii. 35; x. 38.
the end of baptism, x. 48.
a priest, x. 38.
the proper object of faith, iii. 16, xvi. 31; xx. 21; xxvi. 18.
a sign which is spoken against, xxviii. 25.
the Saviour of his people, v 31.
the blessed " seed," iii. 25.
the Sun of righteousness, ii 7; ix. 13, xiii. 8, xvii. 2, xviii. 2
alone must be heard, ix 6.
crucified in the eighteenth year of the reign of Tiberius, iv. 5.
appointed first for the Jews, iii. 26
for what end sent into the world, x 36.
how without corruption, ii 29
not extinguished by death, viii. 33.
must be invoked by the godly, ix. 14, 21.
how slain by the Jews, ii. 23.
not idle in heaven, i. 11.
suffered according to the will of God, iii. 18
promised to David peculiarly, ii 30.
must be sought by faith, i. 11.
is eternal God, ii. 33; vii. 30, 59; ix 3, 14; xx. 28.
is our Advocate, ii. 21.
the immaculate Lamb, viii. 32.
the soul of the law, vii. 38, xxviii. 17.
the earnest of our election, xiii. 48.
the author of miracles, xvi 18.

440 INDEX.

Christ must be sought in heaven, i. 11.
is above Moses, vii. 36.
why appeared so often to his Apostles after his resurrection, i. 3.
was anointed, x. 38.
went to Jerusalem on the feast days, iii. 1.
baptized with the Spirit, i 5.
compared to a sheep, viii. 32.
why did not show himself openly to all men, x. 41.
did indeed depart out of this world, i 2.
how governed by the Spirit, i 2
to what end he rose again, x 37.
how he standeth or sitteth at the right hand of God, vii. 56.
lived in private till he was thirty years of age, i. 1 ; ii. 1
danger of denying, iii 17, v. 40, xxvi 10.
how great his authority, iii 23.
his body not infinite, i 11.
how his body is in heaven, i. 11, vii 56.
his sayings not all written down, xx 35.
his ascension the conclusion of the gospel history, i 2.
baptism grounded in, viii. 37.
baptism of the Spirit committed to, i. 15.
ceremonies abrogated by the coming of, vi. 14 ; viii. 27 ; xiii. 38 ; xv 9, 16 ; xxi. 10.
erroneous opinion of the Apostles as to the kingdom of, i. 6.
afflictions for his sake glorious, v. 41, 42, xvi. 22.
how great the dignity of, x. 38 ; xvii. 31.

Christ, the knowledge of his doctrine, how necessary, i. 1.
the sum of the doctrine of, i. 3.
the glory of, wonderful, viii. 33.
his glory to be held in high esteem, xi. 25 ; xxvi 10
the grace of reacheth unto all degrees, xvii. 11.
the grace of must not be separated from his presence, xxvi 19.
how gently he dealeth with his people, x 41.
his innocence, xiii 28.
his majesty, ii. 34, ix. 3 ; xiii. 25
tendency of the miracles of, x. 38.
the death of, ignominious, v. 30.
the death of foretold, viii. 32.
his death voluntary, viii 37.
the office of, i 1, 5, ii 33, iii. 25 ; x. 43, xiii. 38 ; xvii. 3 ; xxvi. 22.
the kingdom of, shadowed by figures, xxi 7 ; eternal, ii. 35 ; viii 33 ; xiii 34 ; spiritual, xvii. 7 ; xviii. 18 ; xix. 8 ; xxviii. 22 ; never quiet in this world, iv. 25 ; nature of, i 6 ; ornament of, xxi. 9 ; perfection of deferred, iii. 21 ; misunderstood by his Apostles, i 6 ; the resurrection of is true, xiii. 30, 33 ; is a principal point of the Gospel, i. 21 ; is as it were the consummation of the Gospel, iv. 33 ; the knowledge of very necessary, i. 3, the use of, xiii. 34 ; a work of Divine power, xxvi 8 ; he was the first fruits of, xxvi. 33
the sacrifice of, voluntary, viii. 32.
triumph of, in death, viii. 33

Christ, power of the voice of, ix. 40.
difference between and his Apostles, iii 13.
comparison between and John Baptist, i 5.
difference between and Pastors or Ministers of the Word, i. 5; vii. 36, xi. 16.
all things subject to, vii. 59; ix. 5. See God.
Christianity cannot be without doctrine, ix 36.
the true rule of, i 1.
the sum of, i 3, ii. 38; viii. 32.
Christians sometimes called Disciples, ix. 36, xiv. 23; xviii. 22, xxi. 4.
who are true, xiv. 23; xviii. 22
how far ought to flee persecution, xi. 20
Chrysostom quoted, viii. 33, 36; xviii 3.
Church, there has always been a, xxiii. 6.
majesty of the, v. 15.
warfare not yet come, iii. 21.
how to be restored, i 17.
four marks of the, i 42
the peace of not of long continuance, xi 31; xii. 1.
perpetuity of, avouched, viii. 33
punishment awaiting the persecutors of the, i 20; ix. 5.
why continued so long in error, xiv. 16.
may err in the election of ministers, vi 5.
always in need of some reformation, vi. 1.
assaulted on every side for divers causes. xii. 3.
edifying of, hard and laborious, xviii. 11.
condition of, stable in the manifestation of Christ, ii. 17.

Church, state of the, vii. 30.
true and right ordering of the, xv. 16.
Christ the perpetual governor of, x 42.
is the body of Christ, i. 18.
as the house of God, ix 31.
compared to a building, iv. 11.
the temple of God, ix 31.
gathered from Jews and Gentiles, xv. 16.
generally composed of the ordinary ranks of life, ix. 43.
how precious to God, xx. 28.
ought not to be without discipline, iii. 1.
cannot be without an ordinary ministry, xiv. 23.
God the deliverer of his, vii. 7.
how increased, i. 15; ii. 41; iv. 32, v 14, vi. 1, 7; ix. 32; xi 19; xiii. 49; xvi. 5, 16; xvii. 12; xix 1, 20.
state of, among the Jews in the Apostles' times, ii. 7.
of Jerusalem, its state in the time of Paul, xxiii 2
ambition very hurtful to the, viii. 14.
Christ the Head of, ii 25, 36; x 42
Christ the perpetual Keeper of, ix. 5.
Christ the only Master and Teacher of, iii. 21; vii. 37; ix 36; x 24; xiii. 47; xv. 2, xx. 30.
Christ the foundation of, iv. 11.
Churches, principal, tend to keep other Churches in order, xv. 36.
unity of, how profitable and necessary, viii. 14.
Cicero quoted, ix. 25; xvii 21.
Circumcision, in what sense called "the Eternal Covenant," xv. 9.

Circumcision, a token and pledge of free adoption, vii. 8.
Citizens, privileges of Roman, xxii. 25.
Common, the term used to denote that which is profane, x 14.
people, inconstancy of, xvi. 22, xxi. 30.
Community of goods, doting of Anabaptists as to, iv. 34, v. 4.
how so among the faithful, ii. 45, iv 33, 34; v. 4
Complaint of Gregory Nanzianzen as to Councils, xv. 2
Concord, brotherly, commended, i. 14, iv 32.
Confession, auricular, of the Papists, xix. 19.
external, of faith necessary, viii. 36
Confirmation of faith necessary, viii. 25; xvii. 11.
Conscience has two parts, xxiv. 16.
security of, necessary, x. 20.
evil, examples of, v. 2; vi. 12.
evil, effects of, vii. 26.
of the faithful, to be ruled by the Word of God only, xvi. 4.
how Papists presume to bind, xv. 28.
Consent of the wicked in oppressing the Gospel, xxiii. 6.
Consolation of the faithful, iii. 20; iv. 18, v. 17, 41; vii. 55, 59, viii 2, ix. 5, 37; xii. 3, 23, xiv. 21; xxii. 7.
Conspiracy to kill Paul, xxiii. 12.
Constancy of the Apostles, v. 12, 36, 42; viii. 2.
of Pastors, iv. 20, vii. 54; ix. 16; xviii. 9; xix. 29. See Paul, Peter, &c.
Contention to be avoided, xxiii 9, 10.
Contradictions, apparent, of Scripture, how to be reconciled. See Scriptures

Conversion is in the hand of God, xiv 1.
of St Paul, viii. 3.
Corinth, a sumptuous and populous city, xviii 1.
how long Paul preached at, xviii. 11.
Apollos Paul's successor at, xviii 24.
Cornelius, the centurion, x. 1, 2.
brought into the faith of Christ after a heavenly manner, x. 3.
was one of the faithful before Peter was sent unto him, x. 4.
wherein he offended in kneeling to Peter, x. 25.
his willing obedience, x. 7.
Council, lawful pattern of a, xv. 12
of Laodicea, decree of, as to the election of Pastors, xiv. 23.
Councils, what the authority of, xv. 2, 28.
complaint of Gregory Nanzianzen as to, xv 2.
abortive trust of Papists in, ib.
Counsels, doubtful, unhappy result of, v. 4.
of God to be sought in his Word, xx. 26.
Courtesy a virtue, xxiii. 19.
of St Paul, xx. 13; xxi. 26.
of St Peter, iv. 43.
Covenant of God cannot be void, xvii 4
Covetousness of Papists, i. 6.
of Pastors condemned, xx. 33.
Creation, why world created in six days, xii. 10.
Credulity, excessive, to be avoided, xxi 17.
Cripple healed by St Peter, iii. 7.
by St Paul, xiv 10.
Crispus, the ruler of the Synagogue, xviii. 7.

Crucifixion of Christ, in eighteenth year of Tiberius, iv. 5.
Curiosity natural to man, i. 7.
  the sources of, i. 8
  ought to be avoided, i 7, 22 ; x. 41, xvii. 21, 30, xix. 19.

DAMASCUS, Aretas governor of, ix. 23.
David a figure of Christ, i. 18 ; iv. 11, 25, xiii. 22, 33.
  the son of, Christ, ii. 30 ; xiii. 23.
  Christ promised to, ii 30
  his temporal kingdom, ii. 35.
Day, great, of the Lord, ii. 18.
  of the Lord to whom joyful, iii. 20.
  of judgment, iii 20.
  Sabbath, xix. 12
Days, how anciently divided, ii. 14 ; iii 1 ; x. 3 ; xii 14.
  world, why created in six, xii. 10.
Deacons, to what end ordained, vi. 1, 3.
  how to be chosen, vi 3
  subject to the elders, xi. 30.
  murmuring against the, vi. 3.
  kind of, in Popery, vi 2
  why the Apostles laid their hands on, vi. 6. See Elders.
Dead, how far we may lament the, viii 2.
  prayers for, vain, xv 10.
  bodies of the, why washed, ix. 37.
  burial of, why to be respected, viii 2.
  what gained by, ix. 37.
Death, fear of, even saints subject to, ix. 13.
  of Christ ignominious, v. 30.
  of Christ foretold, viii. 32.
  of Christ voluntary, viii. 37.
  holy example of in Stephen, vii 59

Death, Christ not destroyed by, viii. 33.
  triumphs of Christ in, ib.
  the sorrows of, ii 24.
  Eutychus raised from, vii. 59 ; xx 10.
  quiet, of the faithful, vii 59.
  of the faithful precious to God, xii. 2, 3.
Decree of the Council of Laodicea, xiv. 23.
Decrees of God, immutability of, ii 23
  of the Apostles, xvi. 4
Demas, viii 13.
Demetrius, the silversmith, xix. 23.
Demosthenes quoted, xii. 20.
Denial of Christ dangerous, iii. 17 ; v. 40 ; xxvi. 10.
Devil, the father of lies, xvi. 16. See Satan.
Devils, the term used for lesser gods and angels, xvii. 18.
  fanatical opinion as to, xxiii 8.
  forced to yield to the majesty of the Gospel, viii. 7.
Diana, the image of, x. 35.
Diligence in our calling, i. 8 ; viii. 3 ; xx 23, xxvii 3 ; xxviii. 17, 30.
  of Pastors, vi 4.
Dionysius, the Areopagite, xvii. 34.
Diospolis, or Lydda, ix. 32.
Disciples, the term used for Christians in general, ix. 36 ; xiv. 23 ; xviii. 22 ; xxi 4.
  the office of, xxi. 3.
Discipline necessary in the Church, iii. 1.
Discord, its cause, xxiii. 9.
  between Paul and Barnabas, xv. 37
  the pernicious consequences of, xv. 1.
Dispersion of the Jews, advantage of, xvii. 4.
Disputation, true method of, xvii. 2

Dissension, ambition the mother of, xxiii. 9.
Divines, Popish, overthrown by the mere voice of the Martyrs, vi 9.
Doctors, Evangelists between them and Apostles, xxi. 8
Doctrine as it were the soul of the Church, ii 42.
   no true Christianity without, ix. 36.
   without zeal unprofitable, xviii. 25.
   how handled by the Jews in Paul's time, xiii 15.
   of the Gospel no new doctrine, in 21.
   sound, the authority and immortality of, vii 38.
   of Christ, the sum of, i 3
   of the Apostles, the sum of, viii 25.
   knowledge of, how necessary, i. 1.
   no Christianity without, ix 36.
   external, rejected by fanatics, xvi 14.
Donatists, x 15
Dorcas, also called Tabitha, ix. 36
   why raised from the dead, ib
Dreams and visions, difference between, xviii. 9
Drunkenness a gross vice, ii. 14.
Drusilla, xxiv. 25.
Dust, shaking off from the feet, what meant by, xiii 51.
Duty and function of Pastors. See Pastors.

East, prevalence of licentiousness in the, xv 19.
Eating of blood forbidden in times past, ib
Ecclesiastical meetings profitable, iii. 1, v. 12.
Edify, we must study to, x. 24; xi. 24, 25; xiii. 15; xv. 28, xvi. 5, xx 20.
Edifying of the Church, difficulty of, xviii. 11
   wherein it consisteth, xx. 21.
Egypt, lamentable state of the fathers in, vii. 6.
Egyptians, the idolatry of the, v. 41
Elders, difference between and Apostles, xiv 23.
   Deacons inferior to, xi. 30.
   and Bishops, x 28.
   who, in the Apostles' time, xi. 30; xx 16 See Deacons.
Elect, afflictions cannot hurt the, vii 30
   alone truly believe, xiii 48; xvi 14, xxviii. 25, 26.
   and reprobate, difference between, iii. 20; v. 11; ix. 5, 6, 29, xii 13, xiv. 22; xvi. 16, 30, 33; xvii 32.
Election the cause of all good things, xiii. 17
   free, of God, xvi 5.
   goeth before faith, xiii. 48.
   Christ the earnest of, xiii 48.
   a double, of the children of Abraham, xiii 33
   free, whence the denial of it, xx. 26.
   a vessel of, put for an excellent minister, ix. 15.
   of ministers, the Church may err in the, vi. 5.
   decree of Council of Laodicea as to this, xiv. 23.
   faith dependent on, xiii. 48.
Eloquence, the gift of God, xxiv. 1.
   how far useful, xviii. 24.
Encratites, x 15.
Eneas, the faith of, ix 37.
Ennius quoted, ix 37.
Envy condemned, xi. 23, 24.
Ephesians, Synagogue of, entertains Paul courteously, xix. 9.
Ephesus, books burnt at, xix. 19.

INDEX. 445

Epicureans, dotings of, xvii. 18.
   make semblance of faith, viii. 15.
   difference between and Sadducees, xxiii. 8
Error in supposing the baptism of Christ and of John to be different, i. 5.
   how Papists to be convicted of, xiv. 15.
   of the Jews as to Messiah's kingdom, i. 8.
   stubbornness the companion of, xi. 2.
Errors once conceived not easily plucked out of men's minds, x. 45.
   old, retained in Popery, with a change of name, xxviii. 11.
Essenes, the sect of the, xxvi 4.
Ethiopian Queens, Candace a general term for, viii 27.
Eunice, xvi. 3.
Eunuch, Ethiopian, the faith of the, viii 37.
   the modesty of the, viii. 31.
Eunuchs, noblemen sometimes so called, viii. 27.
Eusebius quoted, xii. 17, xv 13.
Eutyches, a heretic, xxx. 28
Eutychus raised from death, vii. 59, xx. 10.
Evangelists stand between Apostles and Doctors, xxi 8.
Events, foreknowledge of, how far permitted, i. 7.
   to be left to God, ib.
Evil, God not the author of, ii. 23.
Example of a holy death in Stephen, vii. 59
Exhortations, the necessity of, xi. 23; xiv. 20; xix 8
Exorcists, Popish, xix. 13.
External rites, severity in to be avoided, viii. 38.
   shows, world addicted to, vi. 14.

FAITH, Christ the proper object of, iii. 16, xvii. 31; xx 21, xxvi. 18.
   true nature of, x. 43; xi. 21, xvi 31, 33.
   put for the Word of God and profession of the Gospel, vi. 7.
   the gift of God, xv. 5, xvi. 14.
   cometh by hearing, viii 6.
   the soul of the Church, xxiii. 6.
   the only foundation of godliness, xxiv. 14; xxv. 19.
   makes us wholly subject to Christ, x. 33.
   of the fathers (Jews) always founded on Christ alone, xv. 11.
   grounded in the Word of God, xiii. 9
   alone doth justify, xiii. 39.
   dependent on election, xiii. 48.
   leaneth on the resurrection of Christ, i 3.
   purifies the heart, xv 9.
   must not be separated from the knowledge of Christ, x. 4.
   of the men of Antioch, xi. 17.
   entangled, of Papists, xvi. 31.
   the certainty of, i 4
   confirmation of, necessary, viii. 25; xvii. 11.
   external confession of, necessary, viii 36, x 1.
   the fruit of, viii 39.
   the foundation of, xxiv. 14.
   increase of, viii. 37; x. 48.
   righteousness of, xiii 38.
   nature of, xxvii. 25.
   obedience of, x. 20.
   office of, xv 9.
   trial of, vii 5; x. 40.
   external profession of, necessary, viii. 27; x i.
   security of, i. 14.
   the force and efficacy of, iii. 16; x. 43; xiii. 39.

INDEX.

Faith, distinction between and repentance, xvii. 18.
difference between true faith and Gentile superstition, xvii. 18.
Christ must be sought by, i. 11.
leads to self-denial, viii. 18.
of the Ethiopian eunuch, viii. 37.
Christ the only foundation of, ii. 38.
baptism a pertinent of, viii. 37.
promises of God to be embraced by, vii. 5.
Faithful, the, must always be ready to give account of life and doctrine, xi. 3.
Abraham, the father of the, vii. 3.
how made partakers of Christ's flesh and blood, i 11.
precious in God's sight, xx. 28.
confirmation necessary to, xiv. 30, xv. 36; xvi. 5; xviii. 9; xx. 32; xxviii. 15.
death not the extinction of the, viii. 31.
make daily progress, v. 11; x. 48; xiv. 23; xvi. 5; xvii. 11; xx. 32
are daily reconciled to God, xiii. 38.
not regenerate at once, in all respects, x. 45.
their afflictions various, xiv. 21.
their afflictions honourable, xvi. 22.
their afflictions are also the afflictions of Christ, xxii. 7.
souls of the, immediately pass into glory, vii. 59.
assemblies of, in time of persecution, xii. 12.
the state of, in this world, iv 21; vii 6, 30; v. 17; xxiv. 8; xii. 3; xiii. 27; xiv. 23; xvii. 6; xviii. 7; xxviii. 4.
Faithful, consciences of, to be ruled by the Word only, xvi. 4.
exposed to slander, xvii. 6; xxv. 7.
designated by the name of disciples, vi. 2.
all the, are priests, ii. 17; iii. 2.
content with Christ alone, xxviii 20.
made partakers of divine gifts, by hope, i. 4.
the constancy of the, xx. 37.
households of, how to be ordered, xvi. 15.
the felicity of the, xiv 22.
the strength of, in Christ only, vii 55.
the joy of, ii 25, 29, 46, v. 41; viii. 8, 39; xi 23; xiii. 48, 52; xvi 33; xx. 24.
the glory of, v. 41.
the warfare of the, iv. 23; v. 17, ix 16; xii. 1; xiv. 22; xxviii. 29.
the quiet death of the, vii. 59.
the death of, precious in the sight of God, xii. 2, 3.
the patience of the, xxvi. 29; xxvii. 2.
the perfection of, wherein consisteth, xx 37.
purity of, on what depends, xv. 9.
the security of, whence it comes, xviii. 10.
the simplicity of, v. 22.
the hope of, in Christ alone, xxviii. 20
the fear of, xiv. 5.
the triumph of, xv. 22.
the victory of, iv. 21.
common calling of, depicted in Christ, xiii. 22.

Faithful, profit of, always annexed to the glory of God, ix. 41.
zeal of the, xiv. 14; xvii 16.
we must do good, especially to the, xi. 29.
angels the ministers of the, v. 19.
Families, how to be conducted, x. 2, 7, xvi 15
Fanatics, their error concerning angels and devils, xxiii. 8.
their allegory concerning the children of Abraham, xiii. 33.
under colour of the Spirit reject external doctrine, xvi. 14.
their error concerning the soul, x 41.
erroneous spirit of, x 44.
refuted, viii. 2.
Fasting, the term used for unwonted abstinence, xxvii. 33.
a help to prayer, xiii. 3.
the use of, xiv. 23.
Fathers, what and how far to be imitated, iii 13.
whether partakers of the promises, xiii. 12.
of the Jews, slain by their own brethren, vii. 9.
lamentable state of the, in Egypt, vii. 6.
the faith of, always founded in Christ, xv. 11.
difference between the and believers under the New Testament, ii. 17, 33; xiii. 32; xv. 11.
how God revealed himself to, ii. 17.
Favour and mercy of God to his people, ii. 30, v. 19; ix. 31, 39; x. 4, 30, 45; xiii. 18, 20; xiv. 17; xv. 10; xvii. 24; xviii. 9, 10; xxii. 19.
Fear, every kind of, not to be condemned, ix. 17.

Fear, excessive, inconsistent with pure and free preaching of the Gospel, xviii. 19.
of God, in the faithful, v. 11.
how necessary, xvi. 2, 35; xiii. 16, 41.
of death, even saints subject to, ix. 13; xiii. 13.
how far allowable, v. 11; x. 24.
Feast days, Christ went to Jerusalem on the, iii. 1.
Felix, his character, xxiv. 25, 26.
moved by Paul's preaching, xxiv. 26.
Festus, his character, xxv. 9.
Figures used to shadow forth the kingdom of Christ, xxi. 7.
Flesh and blood of Christ, how far faithful partakers of, i 11.
Folly, universal prevalence of, xvi. 22.
Force and efficacy of the Word of God, iii. 6; v 5, 33; viii. 6, 13; ix. 22; xix. 6; xxiv. 26.
Foreknowledge of events, how far permitted, i. 7.
must be left to God, i. 7.
of God, how to be considered, ii 23; xvii 26.
Fortitude, invincible, of pastors, xv. 2.
Fountain of salvation, Christ the, iv. 12.
Free will of man destroyed, xxii. 14; xxvi. 18.
Fulfilled, *to be*, the term used for *to come*, ii. 1.
Function and duties of pastors. See Pastors.

GALLIO, xviii. 17.
Gamaliel, v. 34.
his character, v. 34.
was Paul's master, xxii. 3.
his counsel, how far allowable, v. 34, 36.

Garments, custom of rending, xiv. 14.
Gaza, also called Haza, viii 26.
Gentile, denoted by the word " Greek," xvi. 3.
Gentiles, how in times past admitted to the service of God, x. 12.
passages relating to the calling of, i. 8 ; ii. 9, 23 ; iii. 25 ; viii. 25 , x. 12, 44 ; xi 1 ; xiii. 33, 46 , xiv. 27 ; xv. 7, 13 ; xviii. 6 ; xxviii 28.
God, the author of the calling of the, xv. 13
Barnabas, a minister of the, xiv. 13.
why the Jews did not keep company with, x. 28 ; xi. 3.
superstition of, difference between and true faith, xv. 9 ; xvii 18.
Gentleness of Christ, x 41
Girdle of St Paul, taken by Agabus, xvii 18.
Glory to be given to God alone, xxvi 21.
souls of the faithful immediately pass into, vii 59.
of Christ wonderful, viii 33.
of Christ, how highly to be esteemed, xi 25 ; xxvi. 10.
of God, profit of the faithful always annexed to, ix 41.
God alone the author of salvation, xvi 9.
the author of the calling of the Gentiles, xv. 13.
the natural goodness of, xiv 17.
the knower and searcher of the hearts, i 24, 26 , v. 9 ; xv. 8 ; xvi. 24.
the Creator of heaven and earth, iv. 24 ; xiv 15 ; xvii 24.
the guide of his people, xix 21.
the Judge of the whole world, v. 8 ; vii. 7 ; x. 15; xxviii. 4.

God is incomprehensible, iii. 13 ; vii 32.
the deliverer of his Church, vii. 7.
the Father of Christ, xxii. 14.
always like himself, xvii. 26.
why called the God of Abraham, Isaac, and Jacob, vii. 32.
alone must be heard in Christ, ix.
alone must be invoked, xii. 5.
must be sought in heaven, vii. 17.
how he dealeth with the godly, xii. 6 , xix 21.
why he created the world in six days, xii. 10.
why sometimes delays to help, xxiii. 11.
has a peculiar care of his people, ii 25 , iv. 21 ; v. 19 ; vii. 34 ; viii. 33 , ix 5, 89 , xii. 2, 7 ; xiv. 23, xiv 27 ; xvi 26 ; xx. 1, 9 ; xxi. 31, 34 ; xxiii. 16 ; xxv. 1 ; xxviii. 16
knows the heart, viii 23.
why he did swear, ii 30.
often gives the godly more than they desire, xii. 15
how he revealed himself to the Fathers, ii. 17.
uses preventing grace, iii 3.
why delays the punishment of the wicked, xxvii. 24.
why he would have only a few miracles wrought, and that for a short time, xiv. 11.
how uses the instrumentality of the wicked, iv. 28 ; xiii. 21, 27 ; xvii. 26 ; xxiii. 23, 27.
free love of, xiii 17 ; xxvii 24.
secrets of, not to be pryed into, xiv 16 , xvi 5 ; xvii. 30.
the end of his benefits, vii 7.
how great the goodness of, to

INDEX.

his people, ii. 25, 28; iii. 3; vii 38, xi 3, xii 15; xvii. 27.

God graciously strives with the wickedness of men, xxvii 42.

the knowledge of, how necessary, viii 39

the counsel of, to be sought in his Word, xx 26

the lawful worship of, xiv 15

the worship of, always spiritual, vii 44, xv 9, xvii. 25.

decrees of, immutable, ii 23.

use of the gifts of, ii 22.

election of, free, xvi 5.

the election of, the cause of all good things, xiii 18, xxii. 14

covenant of, cannot be void, xvii. 4

glory of, what account we ought to make of, iv 30, viii. 20, ix 45, xxviii 6

the grace of, never tied to ceremonies, vii 7

the grace of, not tied to the sacraments, xxii 16

the grace of, the first cause of our salvation, ii 47

the grace of, free, xvi 5.

the grace of, necessary for all men, x. 43

the preventing grace of, v 31; vii 2, x 4, 5, 35; xiii 5, xiii 48, xxii 14.

the favour and mercy of, to his people, ii 30; v 19; ix. 31, 39, x. 4, 30, 45, xiii. 18, 20, xiv 17, xv 10, xvii 24, xviii 9, 10; xxii. 19.

calling upon, his principal worship, ii 21

calling upon, always necessary, vii 59.

the infinite mercy of, ix 3.

the mercy of, necessary for all men, x. 43

God, the nature of, i. 26; iv. 29; viii 14, xiii 21.

the works of, never without fruit, ii 12

patience of, towards the people of Israel, vii 36.

power of, how to be considered, xx. 32.

power of, not to be separated from his counsel, xv. 10.

power of, in Christ's resurrection, i 30

power of, how great, iv. 24; ix 1, 40, xii. 7, xxvi. 8.

foreknowledge of, how to be considered, ii 23; xvii. 26.

the presence of, fearful, ix. 3; x. 4.

sanctifies the place, vii. 33.

sense of the presence of, the best stay of the godly, ii 25.

the promises of, peculiarly given to the Jews, ii 39.

the promises of, to be embraced by faith, vii 5.

the promises of, in Christ, xiii. 32, 34

the Providence of, how to be weighed, iv 28

how reverently and modestly it is to be considered, xvii. 30

denial of, whence it proceeds, xx 26.

Providence of, passages relating to the, i 18, 26; ii. 23; iv 21, 24, v. 7; vii 17; viii. 4, 32; x 10, xii. 2, 20, xiii 21, 27, 37; xiv. 17, xvi 5, 17, 26, 28; xviii 24; xix 2; xxi. 31, 33, xxiii 16, 23, xxv. 22; xxviii 3.

kingdom of, wherein it consists, i 3; xxviii 31.

how the kingdom of, erected within us, viii. 5

the kingdom of, spiritual, xvii.

18 ; xviii. 18 ; xix. 8 ; xxviii 22.

God, fear of, in the faithful, v. 11.
fear of, how necessary, xiii. 16, 41 ; xvi. 2, 35.
Word of, why compared to a sword, ii. 37.
double mode in which it increases, vi 7.
how the godly stand in awe of it, x. 4.
why it is set before the reprobate, xxviii. 27.
the authority of the Word of, viii. 25 ; xiii. 51 ; xx. 23, xxviii. 25.
the majesty of the Word of, xii 52.
plainness of the Word of, ii. 27.
force and efficacy of the Word of, iii 6 ; v. 5, 33 , viii. 6, 13 ; ix. 22 ; xix. 6 ; xxiv. 26
manifold use of the Word of, xiv. 20.
we must neither add to, nor take away from, the Word of, xxvi 22.
how far the reprobate profit by the truth of, xxvi 24.
calling of, is free, xvi 5.
calling of, what account we must make of, xvii. 1.
calling of, we must follow, xx. 23 ; xxiii. 12.
the will of, the chief law of equity, xiv 16.
the will of, must be preferred to all things, xxi. 2, 13, 14.
the will of, must be sought in the law, ii. 23.
the will of, sufficient for the godly, xxviii 27.
the voice of, how terrible it shall be to the wicked, v. 3.
the lawful way to worship, viii. 28.

God, difference between, and all creatures, xvii. 28.
difference between, and men, x. 33 ; xi 16 ; xv 8.
difference between, and idols, vii. 2.
difference between, and the world, v. 41.
we must obey, without delay, xv. 4 , xvi. 20, 23, 29.
all praise and glory must be given to, xiv. 26 , xxvi. 21 ; xxviii. 8.
man's duty to seek, xvii. 27.
what it is to tempt, v. 9 ; xv. 20.
must not be worshipped with human traditions, xv. 29 ; xvi. 4.
the unity of, xiv. 15.
is no respecter of persons, i. 26 ; x. 34 ; xvi. 22 ; xxii. 1.
has the power of life and death, vii 55.
is not the author of evil, ii. 23.
is alone the author of miracles, xiv. 3 , xix 11 , xxviii 8.
the eternal Christ is, ii. 33 ; vii. 30, 59 , ix. 3, 14 ; xx. 28. See Christ.

Godliness, none without right instruction, xviii. 22.
faith, the foundation of, xxiv. 14 ; xxv. 19.
why the great majority devoid of, xiv. 15.

Godly, the peace of the, ii. 25.
the scarcity of the, ii. 15, 46.
how necessary patience is to the, vii. 5, 6 , viii. 32, 33 ; ix. 16 , xiv. 5, 22.
as well as wicked, afflictions common to, xxiii. 8 ; xxvii. 4 ; xxviii. 4.
how God dealeth with the, xii. 6 ; xix. 21.
life, must study to lead a, xx. 21

Good men mixed with the bad, vi.
1, 5; viii. 13; xiii 40, xv.
12, 24; xvii 32, xx. 30,
xxvii. 24.
man, character of a, xi. 24.
works. See Works
Goodness of God, ii 25, 28; iii 3;
vii 38, xi 3, xii 15, xiv.
7; xvii 27.
Goods, how common among the
faithful, ii. 45; iv. 33, 34;
v. 4.
Gospel arose out of small beginnings, viii. 26.
propagation of the, ib.
why preached, xvii. 30.
why set before the reprobate,
xxiv. 25.
the certainty of the, iii. 24
the authority of the, xvii. 30;
xix. 17.
a commendation of the, iii 22,
23, 24.
the state of the, vi 8; vii. 54;
xiii 27; xvii. 6.
free profession of, a singular
gift of God, iv 31.
confirmation of the, iii 21.
contempt of the, will be severely punished, iii. 20, 22;
iv. 26; xiii. 41, 51, xix. 16
dignity and excellency of the,
ix. 5.
doctrine of, slandered, vi 14
doctrine of, not new, iii. 21;
xx 43, xiii. 17, 32.
titles of the, v 20.
glory of the, accompanied with
divers truths, vi 8.
the end and scope of the, i. 3;
xi 18; xx. 8.
the majesty of the, xxvi. 22.
likened to leaven, xiii. 49.
how the cause of trouble. xiv. 4
why called "the kingdom of
God," xx. 25.
why called "the word of
grace," xiv. 13.

Gospel is the word of salvation,
xiii. 20.
is the word of life, v. 20.
was appointed for the Jews,
iii. 25.
is not preached to us unadvisedly, ii. 2.
established by miracles, xiv.
3.
the parts of the, xx. 21; xxiii.
8.
the preaching of, of great importance, x. 21.
the preaching of, most acceptable to God, vi. 2; xxiv. 25.
the preaching of, the cause of
salvation, xi. 3.
the preaching of, very effectual,
x. 44.
the preaching of, strongly urged, x. 42.
the sweetness of the, xiii 26.
the sum of the, i 1; v. 32;
viii. 34, x. 43.
the force of the, xix. 9.
why all do not believe the,
xiii. 48.
grace put for the faith of, xiii.
43.
profession of faith put for, vi. 7.
why preached fearfully by the
Apostles, viii 1.
why not preached immediately
after Christ's resurrection
and ascension, i 4.
why preached first at Jerusalem, i. 4
before the, the use of ceremonies, free, xvi 3; xvii 18
not freely and purely preached
where fear excessive, xviii.
19.
Grace, put for the faith of the gospel, xiii. 43
put for the power of the Spirit,
xiv 26.
put for calling into the hope of
salvation, xiii. 43.

Grace of the Spirit not tied to signs, x 47
    spiritual baptism a pertinent of, viii. 37.
    the promise of, confirmed by baptism, ii 38
    and goodness of God, Abraham prevented by, vii 2
    of Christ reacheth unto all degrees, xvii 11.
    of Christ not to be separated from his presence, xxvi 19.
Greek, the term put for Gentile, xvi 3
Greeks, put for the dispersed Jews, ix 29
Gregory Nanzianzen, the complaint of, xv. 2
Guardian of the Church, Christ the perpetual, ix 5
Guide, Christ the, of his people, v. 31
Guilt, dreadful, of the Jews, ii 36, iii 13; iv. 10; vii. 52

HAND, put for power, ii 33, v 31, xi 21.
    put for principality, vii 36.
Hands, why the Apostles laid, on the Deacons, vi. 6 See Laying on
Haza, another name for Gaza, viii 26
Head of the Church, Christ the, ii. 25, 36, x 42
Hearing is the beginning of faith, viii 6.
Heart, put for the mind, xvi. 14.
    put for the will, iv 32
    of man in the hand of God, ix. 6, xvi 14; xxiii 19, 23; xxv 1, xxviii 1
    the whole, for a sincere heart, viii 37.
    God knows the, viii 23.
    singleness of, how acceptable to God, v. 1.
    purified by faith, xv. 9.

Heaven, diversely taken, i 11.
    and earth, God the Creator of, iv 24, xiv. 15
    God must be sought in, vii. 7
Heavens, how Stephen saw them open, vii 56.
    the opening of, what meant by, x 11.
Hebraisms, abundance of, in Luke, ii 3
Help, why God sometimes delays to give, xiii 11
Heresy, ambition the mother of all, xx 30
    originally not taken in a bad sense, xxiv 14
Heretics, how to be confuted, ix 22.
Herod, how moved to persecute the Church, xii 3
    tower of Antonia built by, iv. 5.
    the blindness of, xii 19
Hierarchy, Popish, how ridiculous, xx 28
    celestial, the books of improperly attributed to Dionysius the Areopagite, xvii. 34
Hierome See Jerome
High Priest, whether Ananias were the, xxiii 2, xxiv. 1.
Hirelings, noted, viii 39
History, Gospel, Christ's ascension the conclusion of, i 2
Holy Ghost promised of the Father, i 4
    appointed peculiarly for the Church, ii 18.
    why poured out on the Apostles at Pentecost, ii 1.
    sometimes designated by the word "tongues," ii 3.
    not given to profane despisers, ii. 18
    the author of miracles, ix. 34
    is God, v. 4, xiii 2
    personality of, xiii 2
Hope, the nature of, i. 4.
    the faithful made partakers of divine gifts by, ib.

Horace quoted, xvii 21.
House of God, the Church, ix. 31.
Human merit. See Merit
   nature prone to vanity, xvi 11.
   traditions, God not to be worshipped by, xv 29 ; xvi. 4
Humanity to our brethren, xxi 13.
   necessary in a magistrate, xxiii 19.
   commendation of, ii 27, ix. 5, 6 ; x 23, 48, xii. 23 ; xxviii 7.
   of Christ See Christ.
   of Peter, ix 43
Humility of St Paul, xx 19.
Hypocrisy natural to men, viii 23.
   of the Jews, vii 53, 57.
   the blindness of, vi 11, ix 23.
   to be detested, v 1, 3, 8.
Hypocrites, the ambition of, vii 57.
   the cruel disposition of, ix 29
   not easily discerned, viii 13
   how to be treated, vii. 53, viii. 20, 23
   the feigned modesty of, xiv 14.
   the manner of, iv 1, v 4, 21, vii 1, xiii. 50, xiv. 14; xxiii 4
   the careless security of, xxiv. 2
   the furious bloody zeal of, iv. 7 ; v. 17, vi 11 ; ix 29, xvii 5, xix. 23, 27, xxiii. 12

IDOLATRY, the blindness of, xiii 6
   of the Egyptians, v 41.
   hypocrisy of, xvii 17.
   whence it came, vii 40.
   tendency to propagate itself, v. 42
Idols, difference between God and, vii 2
Ignorance, how far excusable, iii. 17, xiv. 17 ; xvii 30.
Image of the invisible God, Christ the, x. 4

Image of Diana, ix. 35.
Images, use of among the Gentiles, xvii 29.
   and pictures of the Papists, vii. 43
Immaculate Lamb, Christ styled the, viii 32.
Immutability of the divine decrees, ii. 23
Impiety of the Israelites, vii. 36
Imposition of hands, a temporary ceremony, viii. 18.
   a solemn sign of consecration, vi 6.
   what meant by in times past, ix. 17, xiii 3 ; xix. 6 ; xxviii. 8.
Impudence of the Pope, xxiii. 25
Incomprehensibility of God, iii. 13 ; viii. 32.
Inconstancy a common vice, xvi. 22.
   of the common people, ib. ; xxi. 30
Increase of faith, viii 37, x 48.
Incredulity, the profane tendency of, x 28.
Infant baptism, error of the Anabaptists, viii. 37 ; xi. 17
Infants, baptism must not be denied to, ii 39, viii 37, x. 47.
Infinite mercy of God, ix 3.
Innocency of Christ, xiii 28.
   of Pastors, xxv 10
   of St Paul, xxiv. 23 ; xxv. 10 ; xxvi 4.
Instrumentality of the wicked, how God uses, iv 28.
Invocation of dead Saints overthrown, iii. 12
   to be made to God alone, xii. 5.
Irony, iv. 9, xxiii 5.
Isaac, why God called the God of, vii 32.
Israelites, impiety of, vii. 36.
   patience of God towards, vii. 36
Italians, the pride of, x. 1.

JACOB, how God called the God of, vii. 32.
Jailor, the conversion of the, xvi. 33
James, the brother of John, slain, xii 2.
 the son of Alpheus, xii. 17, xiii 15.
Jason assaulted, xvii 5
Jehovah, meaning of the term, xvii. 28
 doting of the Jews as to the term, iii 6
Jerome quoted, i 12, vii. 14; xv. 10, 13; xvii. 23, xix 6
Jerusalem, why Gospel first preached at, i. 4.
 visited by Christ on feast days, i 5
 state of the Church of in St Paul's time, xxiii 2.
Jesus of Nazareth, Christ why called, x. 38.
Jews were the first begotten in the Church, i 8, ii. 39; iii. 26; x. 12, xiii. 26, xvi. 3, xx. 21, xxviii 28.
 their crucifixion of Christ, ii. 23, 36, iv 10
 why did not keep company with the Gentiles, x 28; xi. 3
 the arrogance of, xiii 42; xxii 22.
 the blasphemy of, xiii. 45; xviii. 6.
 the blindness of, xvii 3, 4; xxviii. 26.
 dreadful guilt of, ii. 36; iii. 13; iv 10; vii 52.
 advantages of their dispersion, xvii. 4.
 a double election of the, xiii. 33.
 their proud boasting, vii. 9.
 mixture of ignorance and hypocrisy in, iii. 17.
 their monstrous unbelief, xiii 27.

Jews, their unthankfulness, ii. 36; vii 26; xiii 46.
 hypocrisy of, vii. 53, 57.
 the language of corrupted, xxii 2
 the fathers of, did murder their brethren, vii 9
 the stubbornness of, vii. 51.
 were corrupters of Scripture, xvii. 3.
 provincial, inveterate enemies of the Gospel, vi 9.
 graciously adopted by God, x. 15
 the privileges of, xiii. 46
 the rejection of, ib
 their religion corrupt in the Apostles' time, xiii 6.
 their religion condemned by Roman edicts, viii. 27, x. 2; xvi 20.
 their religion everywhere hated, xvi. 13
 three sects of, xxiii. 6.
 the blind zeal of, iii. 17; xxiii. 6.
 equality of and Gentiles, xvii. 29.
 difference between and Gentiles, ii 39.
 their miserable bondage in the Apostles' time, xvi. 3.
 state of the Church among the, ii 7.
 doctrine how handled by, in Paul's time, xiii. 15.
John Baptist, the office of, i. 5; x. 37; xiii 24, xix 3.
 comparison between and Christ, i 5.
 comparison between his baptism and ours, xix. 4.
John Mark leaveth Paul and Barnabas, xiii. 13.
 the sin of, xv. 37.
Jonathas the High Priest, why slain, xxiv. 2.
Josephus quoted, iv. 15; v. 36,

viii 5; xi. 28; xii. 1, 21; xv. 13, xxi 37; xxiii. 2; xxiv. 2, 5; xxv. 13.

Journey, Sabbath day's, i. 12.

Joy of the faithful, ii. 25, 29, 46, v 41; viii 8, 39; xi. 23; xiii 48, 52; xvi 33; xx 24.
  of Pastors, xi. 23.

Judas, a raiser of sedition, v 36.

Judge, of quick and dead, Christ the, i. 2, iii. 20, x. 42; xvii 31.
  God the, of the whole world, v. 8, vii. 7, x. 15; xxviii. 4.

Judges, put for rulers and governors, xiii. 20
  raised up by God, v. 30

Judgment, the great day of, ii. 18; iii 20.
  divine, how necessary to proclaim, iii. 20, xvii. 37
  rash, condemned, x. 15; xxviii. 4.

Judicial astrology, condemned, xix. 19.

Just, why Christ called, vii. 52; xxii. 24.

Justice, put for honesty and innocence before men, x 35.

Justification by faith only, xiii. 39. See Faith.

Justify, used for *deliver* and *acquit*, xiii. 38

Justin, his fable as to Moses, v. 2.

KING, Christ the eternal, ii 35; x. 38.

Kingdom of God, put for the doctrine of the Gospel, xx 25.
  of Christ, error of the Apostles as to, i. 6.
  how small its beginnings, xvi. 11
  shadowed by figures, xxi. 7.
  of God, spiritual, xvii 7; xviii. 18; xix. 8; xxviii. 22.
  wherein it consists, i. 3; xxviii. 31

Kingdom of God, how erected in us, viii. 5.

Knowledge of God, how necessary, viii. 39.

LABOUR of pastors, not in vain, xi. 21

Lamb, immaculate, Christ the, viii. 32.

Language of the Jews corrupted, xxii. 2.

Laodicea, decree of the Council of, xiv. 23.

Law, ceremonial, abrogated by the coming of Christ, viii 27.
  angels messengers and witnesses in publishing, vii. 53.
  Christ the end and consummation of, vii. 37, 52, xiii 38; xx 30, xxviii. 17.
  the will of God must be sought in, ii 23.
  as to unclean beasts abrogated, x. 13.
  man cannot possibly fulfil the, xv. 10.
  how counted a yoke, xv 10.
  the rule of a good life, x. 35.
  how regarded as a living speech, vii. 38.
  word sometimes used improperly, i 5
  the authority of the, vii. 53.
  the sole end of, xv. 11.
  the office of, xv. 1, 10.
  the perpetuity of grounded in Christ, xv. 9.
  difference between and the Gospel, xvii. 2.
  Christ the soul of the, vii. 38; xxviii. 17.
  of Porcius, xvi. 37; xxii. 25.
  of Sempronius, xvi. 37; xxii. 25.
  whether the faithful may go to, before an unbelieving judge, xxv 11

Laying on of hands, a temporary ceremony, viii 18.
    a solemn sign of consecration, vi 6.
    what meant by, in times past, ix. 17; xiii. 3, xix. 6; xxviii 8
    wait for Paul, ix 23
Leaven, the Gospel likened to, xiii. 49
Legion, how many soldiers in, x. 1.
Liberality, what pleasing to God, iv 32.
    must be voluntary, xi 29.
    commended, x 25, xx 25.
Libertines, Synagogue of, name whence derived, vi 9
Life, Christ the author of, ii 24.
    and death, the power of in God, vii 55
    and doctrine, the faithful must be ready to give an account of, xi. 3.
    of pastors should be dear to the godly, xii 5
    eternal, Christ the pledge and substance of, ix 37.
    the way to order aright, x 2.
    wherein the integrity of consisteth, x. 35
    present, the abuse of, xvii 27.
    newness of, necessary, iii 26
    must study to lead a godly, xx 21.
    and death, bond of appointed for men, xiii 37
    how we are said to save or contemn, xx. 24, xxiii 27.
Lord. See Christ
Lord's day. See Sabbath.
    Supper, denoted by breaking of bread, ii. 42; xx. 7.
Lot, diversely taken, i. 26
Lots, how far lawful to cast, i 26.
Love commended, iv. 32, v 12.
    degrees of, xi 29.
    free, of God, xiii. 17; xxviii. 24.

Lucianists make semblance of faith, viii 13
Luke, abundance of Hebraisms in, ii 3
Lydda, also called Diospolis, ix. 32
Lydia, the first fruits of the Church at Philippi, xvi. 13.

MACEDONIUS, a heretic, xv. 2.
Magical effects ascribed by Papists to the Sacraments, viii. 13; x 47, xxii. 16
Magistrate, the office of, xvi 15, 22, xviii. 12.
    humanity necessary in a, xxiii. 19.
    how far obedience is due to, v. 29, xxiii 25.
Magistrates, the unfaithfulness of certain, xi 17.
Mahommedans imagine a new God, xxii 14.
Majesty of Christ, ii. 34; ix 3; xiii 25
    of the Word of God, xii 52.
Malice, obstinate, of Popish priests, iv 13
Man, to what end born, xvii. 26.
    what able to do of himself, ix. 15.
    accursed without Christ, iii. 25, 26.
    how great his blindness, xvii. 27.
    his conversion in the hand of God, xiv 1.
    his heart in the hand of God, ix 6, xvi 14, xxiii. 19, 23, xxv. 1; xxviii. 1.
    the unthankfulness of, xvii 26.
    his merit overthrown, vii. 35; x 4; xii 17, 39, 48; xv. 9, xxvi 18.
    his nature prone to vanity, xiv 11.
    his careless security, xvii. 32.

Man, his recklessness how great, ii. 12.
things sometimes attributed to, which proper to God only, vii 30, 36, xiii. 47; xvi. 9, xxvi 18
Christ truly, vii 30
Manichees, their error as to the soul, xvii 28.
Manifold use of the Word of God, xiv. 20.
Man's duty to seek God, xvii 28.
Mark, John, leaves Paul and Barnabas, xiii. 13.
the sin of, xv. 37.
Martyrs, who are true, xxi. 34.
must be comforted, xxiv 23.
constancy and courage of, in time of Calvin, vi. 9; xix. 34.
difference between, and evildoers, vii. 58.
Popish divines refuted by the voice of, vi 9.
Mass, the stage play of the Papists, vii 22
attempt to colour, xiii 2.
horrible sacrilege of, xvi. 3.
Matthias divinely appointed an Apostle, i 23
Means not to be neglected, xxvii. 30
Mediator, Christ the, ii 21, 33; vii. 30; x 4, 36, 43; xiii. 38, xx 21, xxvi 6; xxvii. 24, xxviii 31. See Christ.
Meekness of the faithful, xxvi. 29. See Christ
Melita, error of the men of as to Paul, xxviii 4.
inconstancy of the men of, xxviii 6.
Men, four kinds of, xiii 50
Mercury, the fabled interpreter of the gods, xiv. 11
Mercy of God infinite, ix. 3.
necessary for all men, x 43
Merit, human, overthrown, vii 35; x. 4, xiii. 17, 39, 48, xv. 9; xxvi 18.
Mesopotamia comprehends Chaldea, vii 2.
Messiah, Christ the true, iv. 10.
Jewish error as to the kingdom of, i 8. See Christ
Ministers, how to be chosen in the Church, vi. 2.
Church may err in the election of, vi. 5. See Ministry. Pastors
Ministry of the Word necessary in the Church, xiv. 23.
laborious nature of the, vi 2
commended, i 2; ii 2, 4, 7; viii. 31, ix 6, x. 5, 36, 44, xi 3, xv. 28, xvi. 9, 14, xvii 30, xxii. 10; xxvi 18.
Miracles, why called signs and wonders, ii 22, xix. 11.
why only few wrought, and for a short time, xiv. 11
ought never to be separated from the Word of God, v. 12, xiv 3
what efficacy in themselves, iii 9
who profit by, ii 5.
whether sufficient as a proof, ii 22
use and end of, iii. 6, 13; iv 10, v 15, viii. 6; ix. 32, 34, 42; x. 38; xiv. 3; xv. 11, 13; xxviii. 7.
abuse of, iii. 9.
Christ the author of, xvi. 18
the Gospel established by, xiv. 3.
tendency of Christ's, x. 38.
of Antichrist false, ii 22.
Apostles only the ministers, not the authors of, iii 46; xvi 18; xix 11; xxviii. 8.
performed by the Spirit, ix. 34.
Popish, effect and abuse of, iii. 9, v 15; xiv. 3

Mockers of the Word of God, ii. 12
Moderation, pretence of, xvii. 6; xx 20.
Modesty commended, ix. 5, 6, xii. 18.
feigned, of hypocrites, xiv. 14
of the Apostles, v. 12; ix. 3; xix. 30; xxi. 18
of the Ethiopian Eunuch, viii. 31.
of Moses, vii. 22.
Monks, the arrogance and pride of, xv. 5
the impudence of, ii. 45.
followers of Judaism, ix. 37.
Montanus, a heretic, vii 24.
Moon turned into blood, ii. 18
Moses, the minister of deliverance, vii. 24.
in what sense called a redeemer, vii 36.
subject to Christ, vii 36
the modesty of, vii. 22.
Jesus, the angel who appeared to, vii. 30.
fable of Justin in reference to, v. 2.
Mouth, to open, what meant by in Scripture, viii. 34, x. 34.
of the Lord, we must always ask at the, xxii. 10.
Multitude, we must not always cleave to, xiv. 16, xix. 27
Murder, its heinous nature, xxviii. 4.

Name, put for authority, iv 7
put for the cause or means, iv. 12.
put for rule and power, iii. 6.
put for the profession of the Gospel, ix. 24
of Christ, what it is to bear, ix. 15.
of Jesus of Nazareth, for the whole profession of the Gospel, xxvi. 9

Natural affections not of themselves corrupt, viii. 2; xx. 37.
Nature of God, i. 26; iv. 29; viii 14; xiii. 21.
Natures, two in Christ, xx. 28
Nazareth, Christ why called Jesus of, x. 38.
Nazarites, the sect of, xxiv. 5.
Nero, his cruelty, xii 8.
Nestorius, a heretic, xx. 28.
Newness of life necessary, iii. 26.
baptism a token of, viii. 36.
Nicholas, the Deacon, the author of a wicked sect, vi. 5.
Nicodemites, how they colour their dissimulation, xxi. 26.
Noblemen sometimes called Eunuchs, viii 27.
Note, an universal is not always taken universally, viii. 1; ix. 35; x 2.
Nuns chosen, in imitation of the Vestal Virgins, xiv. 15.

Obedience, the fruit of, viii. 27.
trial of, viii 26
how far due to magistrates, v. 29; xxiii. 25.
unhesitating, due to God, xv. 4, xvi. 20, 23, 29.
Abraham's, worthy of singular commendation, vii. 3; x. 14.
of St Peter, xii. 9.
of faith, x. 20.
Occasion, we must not leave any to the wicked, vi. 14.
Offences must be avoided, x. 28, xiii. 27, xv. 1, xviii. 18; xx 3, 33, 34; xxii. 27; xxviii. 17, 19.
Office of Christ, i. 1, 5; ii. 33; iii. 25; x. 43; xiii. 38; xvii. 3; xxvi. 22.
of faith, xv. 9.
One, taken for first, xx 7.
Opportunity to be embraced, iii. 1, x. 48; xiii. 40; xx 16,

INDEX. 459

xxi 4 ; xxii. 27 ; xxviii 17, 19

PAPHOS, the city of, xiii 6.
Papists, the vain titles of, vii. 2
  the vain and proud boasting of, iii. 13 ; vii. 2, 52.
  the gross ignorance of, i 7 ; xiii. 39 , xvii. 34
  their usage of the worshippers of God, xxiii. 4
  the false miracles of, v. 15.
  effects of their false miracles, iii. 9.
  the prejudice of, xvi 21.
  their fancied preparatives overthrown, xxii 14.
  the relics of, under what colour they boast of, vi. 15; xix 11.
  vain satisfactions of, x. 43 ; xiii 38.
  folly of the, xvi. 14.
  stupidity of, xxiii 12.
  the superstitions of, how they crept in, xiv 11.
  the anointing (extreme unction) of, xix 6.
  furious and bloody zeal of, v. 17 , vi. 11 ; ix 23 , xi. 16, xvi. 19 ; xviii. 25.
  images and pictures of, vii 4, 3.
  the stage-play mass of, vii. 22.
  mode in which they colour the mass, xiii. 2
  addicted to external shows, vi 14
  the vows of, whence derived, xviii 18.
  invent to themselves a new God, xxii. 14.
  defend every thing ancient, xxiv. 14.
  under what colour they cloak their idolatry, xiv. 15.
  include Christ in the bread and wine, vii. 49.
  under what colour presume to bind consciences, xv 28.

Papists, give the power of God to the saints, iii. 12.
  their trust in abortive Councils, xv. 2
  the dignity of baptism, how defaced by, x 47.
  cannot teach the doctrine of repentance, iii 19.
  almost confine repentance to external rites, ii 38.
  the entangled faith of, xvi 31.
  attribute more to philosophers than to the Scriptures, xxviii 23.
  attribute a magical force to the sacraments, viii 13 ; x. 47 ; xxii 16.
  under what colour boast of their relics, v. 15.
  ambition of, xvi 19.
  arrogance of, vii. 1.
  covetousness of, i 6.
  boldness of, xvii 34.
  blasphemy of against baptism, viii 16.
  blindness of, xxiii 12.
  blaspheme the Scriptures, xvii. 2, 11, 28 ; xviii 18.
  how to be convicted of error, xiv 15
  are corrupters of true doctrine, ii 42 , vi 11 , xiii. 15.
  refuse to be reformed, iv. 1.
  are without excuse, xvii 29.
  how ridiculous they are, ix 17.
  abuse miracles, xiv 3.
  tie the grace of Christ to their magical inventions, xxii 16
  tie the grace of the Spirit to signs, x. 4, 7.
  how colour their changing or abrogating the institutions of Christ, ii. 38.
  attempt of, to prove a self-authority in the Church, xv. 28.
  their error as to Peter's supremacy, i. 3, 16
  disparage the grace of God, ix. 5

Papists, endless inventions to obtain salvation, iv. 12
the auricular confession of, xix 19.
Pastor is also a bishop, xx 28.
in what respect may fly in persecutions, viii 1.
Pastors are master-builders, iv 11
ministers of life, xi 3.
in what sense are priests, xiii 2.
who should be appointed, i 24.
must be honoured, xvi 9
exposed to slander, vi 14, vii 26, xvi 20, xvii 6; xviii 12; xix 23, xxi 17; xxv 17.
must not choose their hearers, xxvi 22.
must be constant in prayer, vi 4
ambition of, hurtful to the Church, xx 30
ambition of, corrupts the purity of the Gospel, ib
covetousness in, condemned, xx 33
authority of, vi 3
how their sermons must be tempered, iii 17
state of, xiv 19, xv 2
constancy of, iv 20, vii 54; ix 16; xviii 9, xix 29.
the lawful mode of appointing, xiv 23
the people must be allowed to choose their, xxiv. 23.
decree of council of Laodicea as to election of, ib
the joy of, xi 23.
sloth of, how pernicious, xv. 36
innocence of, xxv. 10.
labour of, not in vain, xi 21.
invincible fortitude of, xv. 2.
warfare of, xix 23.
difficult office of, xiv. 23.
function and duty of, ii 40; ii 13, 39, iv. 11, 20; v. 8, 32; vi. 2, 8; viii. 17, 25; ix. 22, 26; x. 43; xi 1, 17; xiii 15, xiv 14, 20, xv. 28; xvi 9, xvii 5, 10, 18, 31, 32; xviii 6, 9, 19, xx. 18, 20, 24, 26, xxi 13, 37; xxii 18, xxiii. 17, xxvi. 17, 22.
Pastors, patience of, ix 16
true trial of, xx 19
wisdom of, xviii. 4, xx 26.
diligence of, vi 4
pride of, how hurtful to the Church, xv. 22
timidity of, how hurtful to the Church, xviii 9
vehemency of, not to be condemned, ix 31, xiii 10.
vigilance of, xx 28, 29.
life of, should be dear to the godly, xii 5
certainty of the calling of, xvi. 5
what zeal ought to be in, xiii. 10, 51, xiv 14
difference between and Apostles, i 23, xiv. 23.
how far we must obey, iv. 19; v 29
difference between and Christ, i 5, vii 36, xi. 16 See Ministry
Patience, how necessary in the godly, vii. 5, 6, viii. 32, 33, ix 16, xiv 5, 22
of God toward the Israelites, vii 36
of St Paul, ix 26; xvi. 23, xvii 1.
afflictions to be suffered with, xiv 22.
Abraham's, vii 5.
of Pastors, ix 16.
Paul, the invincible constancy of, xiii 46, xiv 13, 14, 19, 20; xvii. 2, 10, 30, xviii. 18; xix 30, xxi. 1, 10, 12, xxiv 25, xxvii. 21; xxviii 30.

Paul, how fruitful the conversion of, ix 20
conversion of, was famous, viii. 3.
the sum of the doctrine of, xx. 21
courtesy of, xx. 13 ; xxi 26.
humility of, xx 19.
innocence of, xxiv. 23 , xxv. 10 ; xxvi 4
integrity of, xxviii 14
just anger of, xiii 10 , xvii 16.
warfare of, xvii 5 , xviii 11
modesty of, xix 30 , xxi 18.
patience of, ix. 26 , xvi 23 ; xvii 1
preaching of, how effectual, xvii 11, 32, 34 ; xviii 9, 10.
the appeal of, to Cæsar, xxviii 19
the wisdom of, xvi 37 , xviii. 4 , xx 24, 25.
cruelty of, before his conversion, ix. 2.
his life, how precious to the faithful, xx 3 , xxiv. 23.
his calling certain, xiv 27.
zeal of, ix. 22 , xiii 40 , xiv 14 , xv 28 , xvii 16 , xxvi 28
the Apostle and teacher of the Gentiles, xiii. 1, 46
had two names, xiii. 10
no common minister of Christ, ix 15
a prophet, xxviii 3
a witness as well to Jews as Gentiles, xxvi 17
was stoned, xiv. 19
how desirous of peace, xvi 4
why he circumcised Timothy, xvi 3
the girdle of, which Agabus took, xvii 18
dispute at Athens with the Jews, ib.
sum of his preaching, ix 20
healeth a cripple, xiv. 10.

Paul, Ananias his teacher, ix 6, 10.
succeeded by Apollos at Corinth, xviii 24
entertained by Aquila, xviii. 2.
conspiracy against, xxiii 12
how long he preached at Corinth, xviii 11.
Peace, put for reconciliation between God and man, x 36
what sort of, we must keep, xv. 1 , xxiii 6.
of the Church not of long continuance, ix 31 , xii 1.
of the godly, ii 25
Christ our, xxviii 25
Pelagians, Augustine attacked by, xv. 10.
Pelagius, a heretic, x. 34
Pentecost, Holy Ghost poured out on the day of, ii 1.
People, common, inconstancy of, xvi 22 , xxi 30
God, the guide of his, xix. 21.
God's peculiar care of, ii 25.
often get more than they desire, xii 15.
the, must not be excluded from the affairs of the Church, xxii 22
Perfection of the faithful, wherein consists, xx 37.
Perpetuity of the Church, viii 33
of the Law grounded in Christ, xv 9
Persecution raised by Herod, xii 1.
how far it is lawful to flee, xi 20
Tertullian's opinion on this point, viii 1.
it helps the course of the Gospel, viii 1
the benefit derived from, xi 19.
we must not yield to, viii. 4.
assemblies of the faithful during, xii 12.
Persecutors, severe punishment awaits, i 20 , ix. 5.

Perseverance, the gift of God, v. 31.
  in prayer, i 4; x. 2.
  in Christian doctrine, iv. 30; vii 3; xi 23; xiv. 22; xv. 36; xx. 19; xxvii. 7.
Persius quoted, xvii. 25.
Person, put for the external state or appearance, x. 30.
Personality of the Holy Spirit, xiii 2.
Persons, respect of, condemned, x. 34.
  God not a respecter of, i. 26; xxvi 21; xxviii. 8.
Peter, his fabled disputation with Simon Magus, viii 24.
  why called Simon, xv. 13.
  what pre-eminence had he among the Apostles, i. 3, 16; viii. 19, ix. 32.
  constancy of, iv. 8, 11
  courtesy of, iv 43.
  modesty of, xi. 3.
  obedience of, xii. 9.
  whence the Papists derive the supremacy of, i. 13, 16; ix. 32
  the wisdom of, iv 8.
  heals the cripple, iii. 7.
  wherein Cornelius offended in giving honour to, x 25.
  whether the form of baptism was observed by, ii. 38.
  humanity of, ix. 43.
Pharisees, whence their name, xxiii. 6
  the great pride of, xv 5.
Philip, the Deacon, vi. 5; viii 5.
  the Evangelist, xxi 8.
  the constancy of, viii. 21.
  the boldness of, viii 40.
Philippi, Church at, from small beginnings, xvi 14.
  Lydia, the first fruits of the Church at, xvi. 13.
Philosophers, the doctrine of, xvii 18.

Philosophers, why they called man a microcosm, xvii 27.
Place, the, sanctified by the presence of God, vii. 33.
Plainness of the word of God, ii. 27.
Plato quoted, xiii 37, xvii. 18.
Plays, the licentious, of the Pope, iii. 6.
Pliny quoted, vii 2; viii. 27; xvii. 1; xx. 13; xxviii 11.
Plural number put for the singular, xiii. 14.
Pollux and Castor, fable as to, xxviii 11.
Pomponius Mela, error of, viii. 26.
Poor, to whom the care of should be committed, vi 2.
  we should care for, ix. 34.
Pope, the minister of Satan, v. 28.
  error as to alleged supremacy of St Peter, i. 3, 16; viii. 19.
  union of wicked sects in the, x. 15.
  the arrogance of, xiii. 3; xv. 16; xxii. 1.
  the vain boasting of, iv. 11, 19; v 28, 29
  impudence of, xxiii. 25.
  yoke of, the faithful must shake off, xxiii. 25.
  wicked law of, touching the choice of meats, x. 15.
  licentious plays of the, iii. 6.
  showy titles of, xvi 16.
  great tyranny of, ix. 32, x. 15, xi 3; xiv 15; xv. 16, 28, 30, xix. 19; xxii. 1.
  Popery, hierarchy of, how ridiculous, iv. 11; xx. 28.
  what kind of Deacons in, vi. 2
  old errors in, with a change of name, xxviii. 11.
  multiplicity of ceremonies in, xvi 3.
Popish bishops, how ridiculous, iv. 11; xx. 28.
  the tyranny of, xv 30.

Popish exorcists, xix. 13.
   false miracles, effects of, and abuse of real, iii. 9; v. 15; xiv. 3.
Power of God, how to be considered, xx. 32.
   not to be separated from his counsel, xv. 10
   manifested in Christ's resurrection, i 30.
   of God, how great, iv. 24; ix. 1, 40, xii 7; xxvi. 8.
   of life and death belongs to God, vii 55.
   what, granted to the Apostles, xiii. 11.
   devoid of the power of God, how deadly, iv. 17.
Praise and glory, all must be given to God, xiv. 26, xxvi. 21, xxviii 8.
Prayer, the true rule of, iv. 24; xvi. 13.
   must be without ceasing, xii. 5, 6.
   for the increase of doctrine, xx. 36.
   for persecuted Christians, xii. 5
   must flow from faith, viii 22.
   for the dead is vain, xv 10.
   must be offered to Christ, ix. 14, 21.
   perseverance in, i. 4; x. 2
   fasting a help to, xiii. 3.
Preaching of the Gospel not unadvised, ii 2.
   of St Paul, how effectual, xvii. 11, 32, 34; xviii. 9, 10.
   great importance of, x. 21.
   most acceptable to God, vi. 2; xxiv. 25.
   efficacy of, x. 44.
   strongly urged, x. 42.
Preparatives, fancied, of sophisters, overthrown, xxii. 14.
   fancied, of Papists, overthrown, xxii. 4.

Presence of God fearful, ix. 3; x. 4.
   sanctifies the place, vii 33.
   divine, a sense of, the best stay of the godly, ii. 25.
Pride naturally in all men, ix. 5.
   hateful to God, xii. 26.
   wars against God, xii 23.
   of pastors, how hurtful to the Church, xv. 22.
Priest, under the law, a figure of Christ, iii 26
   Christ, a, x. 38.
Priesthood of Christ, x. 38
   the Christian, xiii 2.
Priests, Popish, are Simonists, viii. 21.
   covetousness of, xiv. 13.
   evil conscience of, iv. 13.
   impudence of, ib.
   obstinate malice of, ib.
   tyranny of, iv. 9.
   preposterous zeal of, iv. 1.
   ridiculous shaving of, xviii. 18.
   all the faithful are Priests unto God, ii. 17, iii 2.
Princes, the office of, xvi. 15.
   how far we must obey, xvii. 7; xxiii. 25.
Privileges of the Jews, xiii. 46.
   of Roman citizens, xxii. 25
Profane, denoted by what is common, x. 14.
   despisers, Holy Spirit not given to, ii. 18.
Profession, free, of the Gospel, a singular gift of God, iv 31
Promises of God given peculiarly to the Jews, ii 39.
   to be embraced by faith, vii. 5.
   in Christ, xiii. 32, 34.
   whether the fathers partakers of, xiii. 12.
Proof, whether miracles a sufficient, ii. 22.
Propagation of the Gospel, viii. 26.
Prophecies, all gathered into one volume, vii. 42; xiii. 40; xv. 15.

Prophecy, put for rare and singular gift of understanding, ii. 17.
how great the force of, xxiv 26.
why ceased after the return from captivity, iii 22
Prophet, the word taken diversely, xii. 27
how said to be raised by God, iii. 26, v. 30
Prophets, Christ the chief of all the, iii 22
the term, used for excellent interpreters of Scripture, xiii. 1.
false, ape the true, xxi. 11.
customs of false, ib.
their vehemency, xiii 10
used to denote those endued with knowledge of divine mysteries, xv 32
all testified of Christ, iii 21.
wrote their doctrine out of the law, xxvi 22
the custom of, xxi. 11
the consent of, xv 15
the use of the doctrine of, xv 6.
the office of, i 7, vii 52
why they have ceased in the Church, xxi 9.
for the most part confirmed by miracles, xxi 11.
Proselytes, the modesty of, xiii. 42.
Prosperity, regard to be had to, xiii 37.
Proverbs, certain, i 45, 53, ii 25; vi 1, 2, 4; vii. 1, 54, ix 5, xiii 41; xiv 22; xv 21; xvi 3, 16, xviii 1, 9
Providence of God, how to be pondered, iv 28.
is reverently and modestly to be considered, xvii 30
passages relating to, i 18, 26, ii 23, iv 21, 24; v 7, vii. 17; viii 4, 32; x. 10, xii 2, 20; xiii 21, 27, 37, xiv. 17; xvi 5, 17, 26, 28; xviii. 24, xix. 2, xxi. 31, 33; xxiii. 16, 23; xxv 22; xxviii. 3.
Publius, his hospitality, xxviii. 7.
Python, fable of the Poets as to, xvi. 16.

QUESTIONS, divers, with their answers, i 5, 21, 23, ii. 17, 18, 22; iii 1, 5, 17, 20, 22, 25; iv 27, v 32; vi. 5; vii 2, 30, 32, 33, 38, 49, 56, 58, 60, viii 1, 13, 16, 24; ix. 25, 39, x 4, 12, 24, 25, 30, 35, 41, xi 1, 29, xii. 5, xiii 22, 34, 37, xiv 9; xv 2, 9, 10, 16, 19, xvi 3, 6, 13, 16, 22, 27; xvii 23, 27, xviii 10, xix 2, 5, xx 20, xxi 4, xxii 16, 19, xxiii 25, 28, xxiv 6; xxvii 4, 20
frivolous, must be avoided, xx 21
Quick and dead, Christ the Judge of, i 2, iii 20, x. 42; xvii 41
Quiet and calm death of the faithful, vii 59.

RASHNESS to be guarded against, xvi 35.
Rationale of divine offices, vii 22.
Real presence, Popish doctrine of, in the sacramental elements, vii 49.
Recklessness of man by nature, ii. 12
Reconciliation between God and man, x 36
Redemption still in course of accomplishment, iii 21.
the end of, vii. 7.
Reformation of the Church always needed, vi. 1
Regeneration, an effect of faith, x. 43
the beginning of the kingdom of God, i 3

INDEX.

Rejection of the Jews, xiii. 46.
Relics, under what colour Papists boast of, vi. 15; xix. 11.
Religion, true, rarely found, ii 12.
what true is, vii. 59; xiv. 15; xvii. 4.
what the invention of man, xvii. 16.
no new brought in by the Apostles, iii. 13; v. 30.
Jewish, was corrupt in the Apostles' time, xiii 6.
condemned by Roman edicts, viii. 27; x. 2; xvi. 20.
Popish, its tendency, xx. 30.
difference between true and false, xxviii. 23.
Remission of sins must be preached to all, viii 22; xiii. 38.
Repentance, its true nature, ii. 37, 38; v. 31, xvi. 19.
the gift of God, v. 31.
must not be separated from faith, xi. 18.
distinction between and faith, xviii. 18.
must always be preached in the Church, ii. 38; iii. 26.
how cold, as preached under Popery, iii. 19.
the beginning of, ii. 37; v. 31.
not properly taught by Papists, iii. 19
confined by Papists to external rites, ii. 38.
the signs of, viii. 34.
difference between and faith, xx. 21.
baptism a token of, ii. 38.
Christ the only foundation of, ii. 38.
Reprobate and elect, difference between, iii. 20; v. 11, ix. 5, 6, 29; xii. 13; xiv. 22; xvi. 16, 30, 33; xvii 32.
Reprobates, how to be treated, v 33; vii. 54

Reprobates, why the Gospel preached to, xxiv. 25.
how far they profit by the Word of God, v. 33; vii. 54; xxvi. 24.
Respect of persons condemned, x. 34.
Respecter of persons, God not a, i. 26; x. 34; xxii. 1; xxvi. 22; xxvii. 7.
Resurrection, why Christ appeared so often to the Apostles after the, i. 3.
of the body, a work of divine power, xxvi. 8.
Christ the first fruits of, xxvi. 23.
of Christ true, xiii. 30.
a principal point of the Gospel, i. 21.
as it were the accomplishing of the Gospel, iv 33.
knowledge of very necessary, i. 3.
use of, xiii. 34.
Revelation, a new, not to be looked for, x. 5.
Rich, the, ought to minister to the poor, xi. 29.
Right hand, used for the hand of power, ii. 33; v. 31; xi 21.
Righteousness of faith, xiii. 38.
Christ, the Sun of, ii. 7; ix. 13; xiii 8; xvii. 2; xviii. 2.
Rites, external, severity in to be avoided, viii 38.
Roman rulers, the conduct of, vii. 58.
proud boasting of, xi. 26.
citizens, the privileges of, xxii. 25.

SABBATH, why appointed, xiii. 14; xix. 12.
day's journey, i. 12.
Greeks and Romans, it was capital for them to observe, xvi. 13.

Sabellius, a heretic, xiii. 2.
Sacraments, their offices not instantly apparent, viii. 13.
  must not be separated from the Word of God, vii. 8 ; x. 37; xiii. 24.
  profanation of in Popery, x. 37.
  the force of, viii 13.
  the true use of, xviii. 25 ; xxii. 16.
  Papists ascribe a magical power to, viii. 13 ; x 47 ; xxii 16.
Sacrifice, the abuse of, xiv. 11.
  Mass, not a, xiii 2.
  of Christ, voluntary, viii. 32.
Sacrilege, horrible, of the Mass, xvi. 3.
Sadducees, great authority of, among the Jews, iv. 1, 33 ; v 17.
  their zeal, v. 17
  the errors of, xxiii. 8.
  difference between them and the Epicureans, xxiii 8.
Saints, dead, must not be invoked, iii. 12 ; xiii. 37 ; xxvii. 24.
  example of, how far we should imitate, iii. 13.
  how far their righteousness profits the wicked, xxvii. 24.
  Papists give the power of God to, iii 12.
  invocation of overthrown, iii. 12.
Salvation sure in calling upon the name of God, ii. 21.
  the matter of our, x 37.
  a brief definition of, xvi. 31.
  endless inventions of Papists to obtain, iv. 12.
  God alone the author of, xvi. 9.
  Christ the fountain of, iv. 12.
Samaria, also called Sebaste, viii 5.
Sapphira and Ananias, grievous sin of, v. 8.
Satan, an utter enemy to the truth, iv. 1 ; vi 8 ; xix. 23.

Satan termed God's executioner, i 38 ; xii. 23.
  apes the power of God, vii. 5 ; xxiii. 11.
  the craft of, ii. 23 ; iii 9 ; v. 1, 21, vi. 1, 14, 37, vii. 30, 31; viii. 11 ; ix 10 ; xi. 12 ; xiii. 6, 8 ; xiv. 11 ; xvi. 10, 16, xix. 16 ; xxi. 17 ; xxiii 6, xxvii. 23.
  the wickedness of, xvii. 13.
  the impostures of, how they differ from the miracles of God, ii. 22.
  how great the power of in stirring up adversaries, vii. 54, viii. 1, 6, 11 ; ix. 23 ; xii. 19 ; xiii. 45 ; xvi. 22 ; xvii. 7, 13 ; xviii. 9 ; xix. 16, 23, 29 ; xxi. 31 ; xxiii 2, 12 ; xxv. 5.
  slain with the sword of the Word, ix. 22.
  cannot hurt, whenever he will, iv 4
  is subject to God's providence, xiii. 27.
  the father of lies, xvi 16.
  the Pope styled the minister of, v. 28
Satisfactions, Popish, the vanity of, x 43 ; xiii 38.
Saul, see Paul
Saviour, Christ the, of his people, v. 31. See Christ.
Sayings of Christ not all written, xx. 35.
Scoffers at the Word of God, ii. 12.
Scriptures, how great the authority of, i. 16 ; xxiv. 14.
  how profitable the reading of, viii. 28, 34 ; xiii. 27 ; xvii. 11.
  the division of, xxiv. 14.
  apparent contradictions of, reconciled, iv. 7, 15, vii. 2, viii 32 ; x. 14 ; xiii. 2, 29, 33, xiv. 17 ; xv. 19 ; xvi.

1, 4, 18; xvii 24; xviii. 25;
xx. 22; xxi 4; xxii. 9.
Scriptures, manifold advantages of,
xiv 20; xvii. 2; xviii. 28,
xx. 20; xxvii. 23.
regular order not always observed in, vii 2.
speak of God after the manner of men, x. 10, 14.
how they speak of the Sacraments, xi. 16
how to be read, viii. 28.
held in little estimation by the Papists, xxviii. 23
mode in which quoted by the Apostles, xv. 16.
difference between Old and New Testaments, ii. 17; xxviii. 23 See Word.
Searcher of hearts, God the, i. 24, 26, v 9; xv 8; xvi. 24.
Secrets of God not to be pryed into, xiv. 16; xvi 5, xvii. 30.
Sects, three, among the Jews, xxiii. 6.
in Popery, how produced, xxiii. 6.
Security of the faithful, whence, xviii 10.
Sedition, to be avoided, v. 21.
the Apostles unjustly accused of, v. 28.
Seducers, to be avoided, xv. 24
Seed, Christ the blessed, iii. 25.
Seeking God, the duty of, xvii. 27.
Self-denial enjoined, vii 3; xiv. 16, xx. 28.
the result of true faith, viii. 18.
Semblances of virtue, difficulty of maintaining, xx. 19.
Sergius, his prudence, xiii. 6.
Sermons of pastors, how to be tempered, iii. 17
Servetus, his heresies, xv. 11; xx. 28.
Severity in external rites to be avoided, viii. 38.

Shaking off the dust from the feet, what meant by, xiii. 51.
Shaving, ridiculous, of Popish priests, xviii. 18
Sheep, Christ compared to a, viii. 32.
Signs and wonders, why miracles so termed, ii 22, xix. 11.
grace of the Spirit not tied to, x 47.
must not be separated from the Word of God, vii. 8.
a miracle the effect of, viii. 17.
of repentance, viii. 34.
Silas, or Silvanus, an ambassador to the Gentiles, xv. 22.
Simon, the tanner, Peter's host, ix. 43.
Simon Magus, whether he did truly repent, viii 24.
a sacrilegious person, viii. 21.
the ambition of, viii. 18.
the faith of, viii. 13.
the hypocrisy of, viii. 18.
the impiety of, viii 20.
Peter's fabled disputation with, viii. 24.
Simonists, the Papists are, viii. 2.
Simony, what the Papists call, viii. 21.
Simplicity of heart, what, ii. 46.
of the faithful, ii. 22.
Sin cannot be the work of God, ii. 23.
voluntary, does not always bring despair, iii. 17.
confession of, necessary, xix. 19.
remission of, part of the Gospel, v. 31.
remission of, must be always preached, xxiii. 8.
remission of, grounded in Christ, ii. 38; x. 43.
no forgiveness of, without the Church, ii. 47.
followeth repentance, iii. 19.
Singleness of heart, acceptable to God, vi. 1.

Sinners, how we must awaken, iii. 20; xvii. 31.
Slackness, how great men's is, x. 17.
Slander, the faithful exposed to, xvii. 6; xxv. 7.
Sloth must be shaken off, i. 14; ii. 18; iii. 20; viii. 26, 36; ix. 15, 31; x. 2, 7, 17, xii. 5; xiii. 38; xiv. 22; xvi. 5; xvii. 11, 16, 30, 31; xx. 28, 29, 36; xxvii. 30.
of Pastors, how pernicious, xv. 36.
Sobriety to be cultivated, x 30.
of mind commended, i. 7; xvii. 30.
Soldiers, how many in a band, x. 1.
may serve God, x. 7.
Solitude, a great help to prayer, x. 10.
Solomon's porch, iii. 11.
Sorbonnists, the authority of Aristotle among, xvii. 28.
Sosthenes, Paul's companion, xviii. 17.
Soul, taken for the life, ii. 27.
taken for the will, iv. 32.
of man, an essential spirit, vii. 59.
lives after death, vii. 32, 50, 60; xxiii. 8.
fanatical opinion as to, ix. 41.
error of the Manichees as to, xvii. 28.
Souls of the faithful immediately pass into glory, vii. 59.
Speech put for thing, x. 36.
Spirit put for the gifts of the Spirit, v. 32; vi. 5; viii. 16; xix. 2.
the guide and governor of the faithful, xx. 22.
of discretion, necessary for the godly, xvii. 11.
of wisdom and strength, also necessary, iv. 8.
erring, of fanatics, x. 44.

Spirit, gifts of, bestowed even on the unworthy, viii. 21.
grace of not tied to signs, x 47.
grace of, no gift more excellent than, ii. 17.
who they are that resist, vii. 51.
the Apostles directed by, iii. 5; ix. 34; xiv. 9.
the baptism of, committed to Christ, i. 15.
use of the gifts of, cometh from God himself, x. 4.
gifts of, sometimes denoted by baptism, xix. 5.
pretext of, abused by fanatics, xix. 14. See Holy Ghost.
Stephen accused of blasphemy, vi. 14.
full of the Spirit and faith, vi. 5, 8.
stoned to death, violently and tumultuously, vii. 58.
the courage of, vi. 15; vii. 56.
the love of, vii. 59, 60.
wonderful constancy of, vii. 60.
faith of, vii. 59.
his holy example in death, ib.
modesty of, vii. 2.
how he saw the heavens opened, viii. 56.
Stoics, the doting of, xvii. 18
Strength of the faithful in Christ alone, vii. 59.
Stubbornness a companion of error, xi. 2.
of the Jews, vii. 51.
Suetonius quoted, xi. 28.
Sum of Christianity, i. 3; ii. 38; viii. 32.
Sun, how turned into darkness, ii. 18.
Superiors, how far obedience due to, iv. 19; v. 29.
Superstition, self-contradictory, xvii. 24.
proneness of the world to, xxviii. 6.
the blindness of, xvii. 22.
the cruelty of, ix. 29.

Superstition, whence derived, vii. 3, 4; xiv. 11; xxviii. 6.
Gentile, difference between, and true faith, xvii. 18
Supper, Lord's, denoted by breaking of bread, ii. 22; xx. 7.
Supremacy of Peter, error as to, i. 3, 16; viii. 19.
Swear, why God did, ii. 30.
Synagogue of the Libertines, whence the name, vi. 9.
    of the Ephesians, entertains Paul courteously, xix. 9.
    in divers places of Jerusalem, xxiv. 12.
Synods, holy, why assembled from the beginning, xv. 2.
    form and order of assembling, xv. 6.

TABERNACLE of David, restored by Christ, i. 6, 15.
Tabitha, otherwise called Dorcas, why raised from the dead, ix. 36.
    the commendation of, ib.
Tatian's heretics, x. 15.
Teachableness the gift of God, ix. 5; x. 10; xvi. 5, 14.
    how necessary, ii 37; viii. 6, 31; xvii. 17.
Teacher of the Church, Christ the only, iii. 21; vii. 37; ix. 36; x. 24.
Teachers, what kind of, the Papists have, xx 20.
Teaching, the true way of, ii. 38; iii 29; x. 43; xx. 26; xxvi 22, 25.
Tempest during Paul's voyage, xxvii. 18.
Temple, the captain of, iv. 1; v. 21, 34.
    of God, the Church, ix. 31.
    how far lawful to worship in, xxiv. 11.
Tempting God, what meant by, v. 9; xv. 20.

Terror sent by God, iv. 5; v. 24.
Tertullian, his opinion as to flight in persecution, viii. 1.
Tertullus, a lying rhetorician, xxiv. 2.
Testament, difference between the Old and New, ii. 17; xxviii. 23.
Theudas, v. 36.
Thyatira, where situated, xvi. 14.
Tiberius, Christ crucified in the eighteenth year of the reign of, iv. 5.
Timidity of pastors, how hurtful to the Church, xviii. 9.
Timothy, why circumcised by Paul, xvi 3.
Titles of the Gospel, v. 20.
    showy of the Pope, xvi. 16.
Titus, why not circumcised, xvi. 3.
Tongues, abuse of, x 46.
    the Apostles spoke with, ii. 4.
    why given to the Apostles, ii. 2.
    sometimes used to denote the Holy Ghost, ii. 3.
Traditions, human, God not to be worshipped by, xv. 29; xvi. 4.
Transubstantiation of the Papists, vii. 49.
Trial of faith, vii 5; x. 40.
    of pastors, xx. 19.
Triumph of the faithful, xv. 22.
    of Christ in death, viii. 33.
Troas, Asson, or Apollonia, a city of, xx. 13.
Trouble, the Gospel how the cause of, xiv. 4.
Truth, how highly to be esteemed, xv. 37.
    the firmness and certainty of, xiii. 27.
    hatred which it causes, ix. 23.
    how great the force of, ix. 22; xv. 22; xix. 9.
    of God, how far the reprobate profit by, xxvi. 24.

Tumults maliciously imputed to the Gospel, xvii. 6.
Turks, because of their victories, deride the Gospel, xxv. 19.
Tyrannus, the school of, xix. 9.
Tyranny, atrocious, of the Pope, ix. 32; x. 15; xi 3, xiv. 15; xv. 16, 28, 30; xix. 19; xxii. 1.
Tyrants afraid of change, xii 1.
spiritual, their arrogance, v. 28.
Tyre and Sidon, xii. 20.

UNBELIEF, the punishment of, viii. 11.
monstrous of the Jews, xiii. 27
Unbelievers polluted, x. 28.
Unclean beasts, law as to, abrogated, x 13.
Unction, extreme, of the Papists, xix 6.
Understanding of spiritual things a peculiar gift of God, xvi 4.
Unity of Churches, how profitable and necessary, viii. 14.
of God, xiv 5.
Unthankfulness must be avoided, x. 41.
of man, xvii. 26
of the Israelites, vii. 36, 40.
of the Jews, ii. 36; vii 26, xiii. 46.
of the world, xxvi 17.
Use, the parent of wisdom, vi. 2.
manifold, of the Word of God, xiv. 20.
and abuse of miracles. See Miracles.

VANITY, man naturally prone to, xiv. 11.
Vehemency of pastors, if to be condemned, ix. 31; xiii. 10
Vengeance belongs to God, vii 7; xvi. 37; xxiii. 3.
Vestal Virgins, nuns imitators of, xiv. 15.
Victory of the faithful, iv. 21.

Vigilance of pastors, xx. 28, 29.
Virgil quoted, xvi. 35; xvii. 28.
Virtue, difficulty of maintaining semblances of, xx. 19.
Virtues, signs and wonders put for miracles, ii. 22; iv. 30.
Vision seen by St Paul, xvi. 9; xviii. 9; xxii. 18; xxvii 23.
seen by St Peter, x. 3, 12
what, seen by Brutus, xvi. 10.
why appeared to Ananias, ix. 10
Visions, use of, ix 10.
difference between and dreams, xviii. 9.
Voice of God, how terrible it shall be to the wicked, v 3.
of Christ, its power, ix. 40.
Voluntary sacrifice of Christ, viii. 32.
liberality pleasing to God, iv. 32, xi. 29.
commended, x. 25, xx. 25.
Vows of Papists, whence derived, xviii 18
Voyage of St Paul, tempest during, xxvii. 18.

WALLS, why the scaling of forbidden, ix 25.
Warfare of the Church, iii. 21
of the faithful, iv 23; v. 17; ix. 26; xii 1; xiv. 22; xxviii. 29.
of pastors, xix. 23.
of St Paul, xvii. 5; xviii 11.
Washing the dead, ix. 37.
Way put for *sect*, xix. 25.
Ways of the Lord, xiii 10.
of men, xiv. 16.
Whoredom, its prevalence, xv. 19.
accursed in the sight of God, ib.
Wicked, the malice of, xiii. 27.
the fear of, xvi. 38.
the manner of, ix. 23.
hatred of, against the truth, ix. 23.

Wicked, obstinacy of, v. 21.
  instrumentality of, how God uses, iv. 28.
  rage of, inflamed by the Gospel, xiii 45.
  diligence of, in oppressing the truth, iv 1.
  the pride of, the godly must despise, xiii 48, 52.
  the fears of, xxiii. 12
  the zeal of, xvii 5.
  how to be dealt with, iv. 11 ; v. 33 , vii 54 , viii 20, 23 ; xiii. 10, 40 ; xviii. 6 ; xix. 9, xxiii 3 ; xxiv. 26 ; xxviii 25.
  join hand in hand to oppress the Gospel, xxiii. 6.
  though against their will, confirm the Gospel, iv. 21.
  always invent causes to sin, xvi 19.
  are not able to hurt as much as they would, ii 43 ; iii 18 ; iv. 1, 4, 21, 28 ; xii 2 ; xviii. 10 ; xxv. 1.
  how obey God, ii 23.
  return always to their natural disposition, xxiv. 27.
  are easily seduced by Satan, ii 22.
  establish the Providence of God, xvii. 26.
  sometimes fear men, v. 21.
  the afflictions of, xiv 22.
  the blindness of, v 17 ; ix 23.
  the evil conscience of, v. 13, 17.
  the vain counsels of, iv 5, 25, 27 ; ix. 23 ; xxiii 16.
  the end of, i. 20 ; viii. 20.
  frail and vain felicity of, xii 20.
  the destruction of the, ix. 5 ; xii. 20.
  the judgment of, to be despised, xvi 1.
  lust of, must be bridled, xvi. 37.
  the children of the devil, xiii. 10.

Wicked, the bond-slaves of Satan, xiii. 51.
  the ministers of Satan, xxi. 11.
  how abominable in the sight of God, xiii. 9.
  must sometimes be set together by the ears, xxiii. 6.
  always wax worse and worse, viii. 1 ; ix. 6 , xii 19 , xiii. 45; xix. 9; xxvi. 24, xxviii. 29.
  must not be allowed to govern in the Church, iv. 17.
  are without excuse, ii. 23 ; xviii. 6 ; xxiv. 25 ; xxviii. 27.
  punishment of, why delayed, xxvii 24.
  how God strives with, xxvii. 42.
Will of God the chief law of equity, xiv 16.
  must be preferred to all things, xxi. 2, 13, 14.
  must be sought in the law, ii. 23.
  sufficient for the godly, xxviii. 27.
  of man, its freedom destroyed, xxii 14 , xxvi. 18.
Wisdom of pastors, xviii. 4 ; xx. 26.
  of St Paul, xvi. 37 ; xviii. 4 ; xx. 24, 25.
  of St Peter, iv. 8.
Wives, the Apostles had, i. 14.
Women must not be kept from the Word, xviii. 26.
Wonders, signs and, why miracles so termed, ii. 22 , xix. 11.
Word put for thing, v. 32 ; x. 36.
  majesty of, whence derived, x. 33.
  how the godly stand in awe of, x. 4.
  why set before the reprobate, xxviii 27.

Word, authority of, viii. 25; xiii. 51; xx. 23; xxviii. 25.
plainness of the, ii. 27.
force and efficacy of, iii. 6; v. 5, 33, viii. 6, 13; ix. 22; xix. 6; xxiv. 26.
manifold use of, xiv. 20.
we must neither add to nor take from the, xxvi. 22.
ministry of, necessary in the Church, xiv. 23.
of salvation, the Gospel is, xiii. 20.
of life, the Gospel is, v. 20.
of God, faith put for, vi. 7.
difference between Old and New Testaments, ii. 17; xxviii. 23. See Scripture.

Works, good, not the cause of salvation, x. 35.
do not purchase God's favour, x. 35.
commended, ix. 36; xxiii. 8.
the reward of, x. 4.

World must be subject to the preaching of the Gospel, i. 2.
contempt of the, xiii. 1.
creation of, how to be considered, iv. 24.
addicted to external shows, vi. 14.
unthankfulness of, xxvi. 17.
wickedness of, how great, xiv. 19.
difference between and God, v. 41.
created by God, xiv. 15, 17.
why created in six days, xii. 10.
how prone to superstition, xxviii. 6.
governed by the counsel of God, xvii 26, 28.
Christ the Judge of, i. 2; iii. 20; x. 42; xvii. 31.

Worship, how far lawful to worship in the Temple, xxiv. 11.
civil, must be distinguished from religious, x. 25, 54.
bastardly and corrupt, must be distinguished from good and sincere, vii. 44.
what acceptable to God, vii. 42.
lawful mode of, viii. 28.
Popish worship of saints, iii. 12.
not by human traditions, xv. 29; xvi. 4.

Yoke, the Law why counted a, xv. 10.
of the Pope must be shaken off by the faithful, xxiii. 25.

Zeal, the sincere, of the Apostles, iv. 25, 33.
of the faithful, xiv. 14.
what kind of should be in Pastors, xiii. 10, 51; xiv. 14.
without doctrine unprofitable, xviii. 25.
of the Sadducees, v. 17.
the furious, of hypocrites, iv. 7; v. 17; vi. 11; ix. 29; xvii. 5; xix. 23, 27; xxiii. 12.
rash, v. 17.
blind, of the Jews, iii. 17; xxiii. 6.
bloody and furious, of the Papists, v. 17; vi. 11; ix. 23; xi. 16; xvi. 19; xviii. 25.
of St Paul, ix. 22; xiii. 40; xiv. 14; xv. 28 xvii. 16; xxvi. 28.

THE END.